CliffsNotes®

PSAT/NMSQT®

CRAM PLAN™

CliffsNotes®

PSAT/NMSQT®

CRAM PLAN™

Jane R. Burstein and Carolyn C. Wheater

Houghton Mifflin Harcourt
Boston • New York

About the Authors

Jane Burstein taught English at Herricks High School in New Hyde Park, New York, for 36 years. She has been an ACT and SAT tutor for 30 years, an instructor at Hofstra University, and a reader for AP exams. She is the author of several other review books including those for the ACT, GMAT, GRE, and ASVAB.

Carolyn Wheater taught middle school and upper school mathematics at the Nightingale-Bamford School in New York City for 25 years and taught math and computer technology for more than 40 years to students from preschool through college. She writes extensively on standardized test mathematics. She resides in Hawthorne, New Jersey.

Acknowledgments

Jane would like to thank her family, her editor Christina Stambaugh and all the others at HMH, and the students it has been her pleasure to teach through the years at Herricks and Hofstra.

Carolyn would like to thank the students and colleagues who taught her so much about teaching and learning math, and all the folks at HMH, especially Christina Stambaugh, Lynn Northrup, and Mary Jane Sterling, whose work helps her improve.

Editorial

Executive Editor: Greg Tubach
Senior Editor: Christina Stambaugh
Copy Editor: Lynn Northrup
Production Editor: Jennifer Freilach
Technical Editors: Barbara Swovelin, Mary Jane Sterling, and Tom Page
Proofreader: Susan Moritz

CliffsNotes® PSAT/NMSQT® Cram Plan™

Library of Congress Control Number: 2018932978
ISBN: 978-0-544-97427-2 (pbk)

Printed in the United States of America
DOC 10 9 8 7 6 5 4 3 2 1

Note: If you purchased this book without a cover, you should be aware that this book is stolen property. It was reported as "unsold and destroyed" to the publisher, and neither the author nor the publisher has received any payment for this "stripped book."

For information about permission to reproduce selections from this book, write to trade.permissions@hmhco.com or to Permissions, Houghton Mifflin Harcourt Publishing Company, 3 Park Avenue, 19th Floor, New York, New York 10016.

www.hmhco.com

Table of Contents

Introduction xi
   About the Test xi
   Using a Graphing Calculator xi
   About This Book xii
   General Test-Taking Strategies xii

I. Two-Month Cram Plan 1

II. One-Month Cram Plan 5

III. One-Week Cram Plan 9

IV. Diagnostic Test 11
   Answer Sheet 13
   Section 1: Reading Test 15
   Section 2: Writing and Language Test 24
   Section 3: Math Test—No Calculator 29
   Section 4: Math Test—Calculator 34
   Answer Key 41
      Section 1: Reading Test 41
      Section 2: Writing and Language Test 41
      Section 3: Math Test—No Calculator 41
      Section 4: Math Test—Calculator 41
   Answer Explanations 42
      Section 1: Reading Test 42
      Section 2: Writing and Language Test 44
      Section 3: Math Test—No Calculator 46
      Section 4: Math Test—Calculator 48
   Scoring the Diagnostic Test 52

V. Evidence-Based Reading and Writing: The Reading Test 53
   A. Overview 53
   B. Content 54
      1. U.S. and World Literature 54
      2. Analysis in History/Social Studies 54
      3. Science 54
   C. Focus Skills 54
      1. Words in Context 55
      2. Command of Evidence 58
         a. Skills: Comprehend, Find the Main Idea, and Determine the Primary Purpose 58
         b. Skills: Make Inferences, Locate Evidence, and Find Relationships 60
         c. Skills: Synthesize and Extend Reasoning 62
         d. Skills: Understand Structure and Evaluate Persuasiveness 64

3. Analysis of Data in Graphics 66
4. Disciplinary Literacy 68
    a. Literature 68
    b. History/Social Studies 70
    c. Science 71
D. Additional Practice 74
  Answer Explanations 81

VI. Evidence-Based Reading and Writing: The Writing and Language Test 85
A. The Format of the Writing and Language Test 85
B. Specific Skills Tested on the Writing and Language Test 85
1. Conventions of Punctuation 85
    a. Apostrophes 85
    b. Commas 87
    c. Colons 91
    d. Semicolons 93
    e. Dashes 94
    f. Parentheses 95
    g. Question Marks and Exclamation Marks 96
2. Conventions of Usage in Standard Written English 97
    a. Pronoun Use 97
    b. Agreement 101
    c. Comparisons 104
    d. Verb Use 107
    e. Modification 110
    f. Parallelism 112
    g. Sentence Structure 113
3. Rhetoric 115
    a. Style 115
    b. Writing Strategy 116
    c. Organization 117
    d. Redundancy 119
    e. Idioms 120
    f. Diction and Vocabulary 121
    g. Quantitative Literacy 122
C. Additional Practice 124
  Answer Explanations 127

VII. Tier 2 Vocabulary 129

VIII. The Heart of Algebra 137
A. Linear Expressions and Functions 137
  Practice 138
  Answers 139
B. Linear Equations in One Variable 139
  Practice 140
  Answers 141

C. Linear Inequalities in One Variable 142
   Practice 142
   Answers 143
D. Graphs of Linear Equations and Inequalities in Two Variables. 144
   Practice 145
   Answers 146
E. Systems of Linear Equations in Two Variables 147
   Substitution Method 148
   Elimination Method 148
   Practice 148
   Answers 150
F. Systems of Linear Inequalities in Two Variables 151
   Practice 151
   Answers 154

IX. Problem Solving and Data Analysis 157
A. Ratios and Rates 157
   Practice 157
   Answers 158
B. Proportions and Percents. 159
   Practice 160
   Answers 161
C. Measurement and Unit Conversions. 162
   Practice 162
   Answers 163
D. Scatterplots and a Line or Curve of Best Fit 164
   Practice 165
   Answers 168
E. Linear and Exponential Growth 169
   Practice 170
   Answers 172
F. Two-Way Tables and Probability. 172
   Practice 173
   Answers 175
G. Statistics 176
   Practice 176
   Answers 178

X. Passport to Advanced Math. 179
A. Equivalent Expressions and Isolating Variables 179
   Practice 179
   Answers. 180
B. Compositions of Functions and Transformations. 181
   Practice 185
   Answers 187
C. Solving Quadratic Equations 188
   Practice 189
   Answers. 190

D. Systems of Equations Consisting of One Linear and One Non-Linear Equation 191
    Practice 192
    Answers 194
E. Arithmetic Operations on Polynomials 196
    Practice 197
    Answers 198
F. Zeros and Factors of Polynomials 199
    Practice 200
    Answers 201
G. Arithmetic Operations on Rational Expressions 202
    Practice 203
    Answers 205
H. Rational Exponents and Radicals 206
    Practice 207
    Answers 208
I. Rational and Radical Equations 209
    Practice 210
    Answers 211

XI. Additional Topics in Math **215**
A. Volume, Area, and Perimeter 215
    Practice 215
    Answers 217
B. Pythagorean Theorem 217
    Practice 218
    Answers 220
C. Congruence and Similarity 220
    Practice 222
    Answers 223
D. Trigonometric Ratios 224
    Practice 226
    Answers 228
E. Geometry of the Circle 228
    Practice 229
    Answers 231
F. Radians, Degrees, and Arc Lengths 233
    Practice 234
    Answers 236
G. Circles in the Coordinate Plane 237
    Practice 237
    Answers 239
H. Complex Numbers 240
    Practice 241
    Answers 242

XII. Full-Length Practice Test with Answer Explanations 245

Answer Sheet...245
Section 1: Reading Test 247
Section 2: Writing and Language Test 259
Section 3: Math Test – No Calculator 268
Section 4: Math Test – Calculator...274
Answer Key...288
   Section 1: The Reading Test 288
   Section 2: The Writing and Language Test.................................288
   Section 3: Math Test – No Calculator 289
   Section 4: Math Test – Calculator.......................................289
Answer Explanations 290
   Section 1: The Reading Test 290
   Section 2: The Writing and Language Test.................................294
   Section 3: Math Test – No Calculator 298
   Section 4: Math Test – Calculator.......................................300
Scoring the Full-Length Practice Test...306

Appendix: Using a Graphing Calculator 309

A. Evaluate a Numerical Expression 309
B. Evaluate Trigonometric Ratios and Functions 311
C. Perform Arithmetic with Complex Numbers...................................313
D. Solve an Equation Using Zeros (x-intercepts) 315
E. Solve an Equation or Inequality Using Intersecting Graphs 317
F. Solve a System of Equations Using Intersecting Graphs......................319
G. Find Statistical Measures of Center 321
H. Create a Plot of Data Points and Find an Equation to Fit Them 322

Introduction

The PSAT/NMSQT and the PSAT 10 are the first steps in getting ready to take the SAT or other standardized tests. Your performance on these tests will be helpful to you as you begin the college planning process because they measure your achievement in areas considered essential to academic success. By taking the PSAT, you can get feedback on your strengths and weaknesses in those areas critical for doing well in college. In addition, the PSAT/NMSQT is the start of the selection process for National Merit Scholarship Semi-Finalists and Commended Scholars. You can also use your scores to see how you compare to other students who will be applying to college with you. Whether you are a tenth grader taking the PSAT 10 or an eleventh grader taking the PSAT/NMSQT and preparing for the SAT or ACT, this book will help you get ready to do your best. All you need is a study plan, one that's simple, organized, and doable—in other words, one you'll be able to stick to as you embark on the path to PSAT success.

About the Test

The PSAT is comprised of four sections: one evidence-based reading section, one evidence-based writing and language section, and two mathematics sections. The whole test takes 2 hours and 45 minutes. Here is a sample test format.

Section	Subject	Type of Questions	Time Allotted
1	Reading	47 evidence-based critical reading multiple-choice questions	60 minutes
2	Writing and Language	44 evidence-based writing and language multiple-choice questions	35 minutes
3	Math (No calculator)	13 multiple-choice questions 4 student-produced response questions (grid-ins)	25 minutes
4	Math (Calculator)	27 multiple-choice questions 4 student-produced response questions (grid-ins)	45 minutes

Using a Graphing Calculator

The PSAT Math Test is divided into two sections:

- No Calculator: 25 minutes, 17 questions
- Calculator: 45 minutes, 31 questions

While most questions on the math portion of the PSAT can be solved without a calculator, using a calculator, particularly a graphing calculator, can help solve a problem more quickly and prevent careless errors. If you do not own a graphing calculator, there is no reason to buy one for the PSAT, but if you have one and feel comfortable using it, it can be helpful. The appendix of this book explains how to use the TI-84 graphing calculator, one of the most versatile and easy-to-use calculators permitted for use on the PSAT Math Test, to solve common problems. In chapters 8–11 in this book, every question that can be solved with the help of a graphing calculator is indicated by a calculator icon. Go to https://collegereadiness .collegeboard.org/psat-nmsqt-psat-10/taking-the-tests/test-day-checklist/approved-calculators for the latest information on which calculators are permitted on the PSAT.

About This Book

The first step in getting ready for the PSAT is to determine exactly how much time you have and then follow the appropriate plan: the two-month plan, the one-month plan, or the one-week plan. Each plan has a schedule along with the approximate time you'll need to allot to each task. In addition, each subject-review chapter gives you strategies for that part of the test. Included in each subject-review chapter are practice exercises to assist you in the areas in which you're weakest and to help you continue to maximize your strengths.

Once you determine which cram plan to follow, the next step is to take the Diagnostic Test. For the math tests, the answer key and answer explanations will guide you to the specific chapters that cover the topics in which you need the most help.

General Test-Taking Strategies

- Become familiar with the format of the test. If you know what to expect, you will be less nervous and more confident on the day of the test.

- Use this book to familiarize yourself with the directions for each section of the test. Knowing the directions for each section ahead of time will save you precious minutes on the day of the test.

- Work at a steady pace. You do not have the time to get bogged down on any one question. If you are having difficulty with a question, take your best educated guess and move on. The Diagnostic Test and the Practice Test will help you learn to pace yourself properly.

- Read each question very carefully, and be sure you know exactly what it asks. Many questions require you to note very specific details. Watch for **signal words** like *most, seldom, highest,* and *lowest.*

- Always read all the answer choices carefully, and use the process of elimination to narrow down the answer choices.

- Answer every question: There is no guessing penalty on the PSAT. Use the answer choices to help you when you are unsure. On any multiple-choice question, the answer is always right in front of you.

- For the math sections, all figures are drawn to scale unless otherwise stated. (This means that you can often use the given figure to make an educated guess on the length of a line segment or the measure of an angle.)

- Make sure you completely fill in the corresponding circle on your answer sheet. Check yourself every five questions.

- Bring everything you will need with you on the day of the test: sharpened no. 2 pencils with good erasers, approved calculator, and tissues. It is a good idea to bring your own watch (smart watches are not allowed); you cannot be sure you will have a visible clock in the testing room. Cell phones are prohibited. You'll also need your admission ticket and a valid school- or government-issued photo ID.

I. Two-Month Cram Plan

Two-Month Cram Plan			
	The Math Test	**The Reading Test**	**The Writing and Language Test**
8 weeks before the test	**Study Time:** 2 hours ❏ Take the **Diagnostic Test** and review the answer explanations. ❏ Based on the questions you missed, identify difficult topics and their corresponding chapters. These chapters are your targeted chapters.		
7 weeks before the test	**Study Time:** 1½ hours ❏ **Heart of Algebra:** Chapter VIII 　❏ Read sections A–C. 　❏ Do practice questions 1, 3, and 5 in each section. ❏ **Problem Solving and Data Analysis:** Chapter IX 　❏ Read sections A–D. 　❏ Do practice questions 1, 3, and 5 in each section.	**Study Time:** 1½ hours ❏ **Reading:** Chapter V 　❏ Read sections A–C.1. 　❏ Do the practice questions in each section. ❏ **Tier 2 Vocabulary:** Chapter VII 　❏ Read *aberration–credulous*. 　❏ Highlight unfamiliar words; divide them into 5 equal groups, and study 1 group each night. 　❏ Review all 5 groups for 2 nights.	**Study Time:** 1 hour ❏ **Writing and Language:** Chapter VI 　❏ Read sections A–B.1.a–c. 　❏ Do half the practice questions in each section. 　❏ For targeted areas, do all the practice questions.
6 weeks before the test	**Study Time:** 1½ hours ❏ **Passport to Advanced Math:** Chapter X 　❏ Read sections A–D. 　❏ Do practice questions 1, 3, and 5 in each section. ❏ **Additional Topics in Math:** Chapter XI 　❏ Read sections A–D. 　❏ Do practice questions 1, 3, and 5 in each section.	**Study Time:** 1½ hours ❏ **Reading:** Chapter V 　❏ Read sections C.2.a–b. 　❏ Do the practice questions in each section. ❏ **Tier 2 Vocabulary:** Chapter VII 　❏ Read *curtail–hypocrisy*. 　❏ Highlight unfamiliar words; divide them into 5 equal groups, and study 1 group each night. 　❏ Review all 5 groups for 2 nights.	**Study Time:** 1 hour ❏ **Writing and Language:** Chapter VI 　❏ Read sections B.1.d–g. 　❏ Do half the practice questions in each section. 　❏ For targeted areas, do all the practice questions.
5 weeks before the test	**Study Time:** 1½ hours ❏ **Heart of Algebra:** Chapter VIII 　❏ Read sections D–F. 　❏ Do practice questions 1, 3, and 5 in each section. ❏ **Problem Solving and Data Analysis:** Chapter IX 　❏ Read sections E–G. 　❏ Do practice questions 1, 3, and 5 in each section.	**Study Time:** 1½ hours ❏ **Reading:** Chapter V 　❏ Read sections C.2.c–d. 　❏ Do the practice questions in each section. ❏ **Tier 2 Vocabulary:** Chapter VII 　❏ Read *iconoclasm–misnomer*. 　❏ Highlight unfamiliar words; divide them into 5 equal groups, and study 1 group each night. 　❏ Review all 5 groups for 2 nights.	**Study Time:** 1 hour ❏ **Writing and Language:** Chapter VI 　❏ Read sections B.2.a–c. 　❏ Do half the practice questions in each section. 　❏ For targeted areas, do all the practice questions.

continued

	The Math Test	The Reading Test	The Writing and Language Test

4 weeks before the test	**Study Time:** 2 hours
	 ❑ **Passport to Advanced Math:** Chapter X
	  ❑ Read sections E–G.
	  ❑ Do practice questions 1, 3, and 5 in each section.
	 ❑ **Additional Topics in Math:** Chapter XI
	  ❑ Read sections E–G.
	  ❑ Do practice questions 1, 3, and 5 in each section.
	 ❑ **Using a Graphing Calculator:** Appendix
	  ❑ Read sections A–D.
		Study Time: 1½ hours
		 ❑ **Reading:** Chapter V
		  ❑ Read sections C.3–4.a.
		  ❑ Do the practice questions in each section.
		 ❑ **Tier 2 Vocabulary:** Chapter VII
		  ❑ Review all the highlighted words from *aberration* to *misnomer*.
			Study Time: 1 hour
			 ❑ **Writing and Language:** Chapter VI
			  ❑ Read sections B.2.d–g.
			  ❑ Do half the practice questions in each section.
			  ❑ For targeted areas, do all the practice questions.

3 weeks before the test	**Study Time:** 2 hours
	 ❑ **Passport to Advanced Math:** Chapter X
	  ❑ Read sections H–I.
	  ❑ Do practice questions 1, 3, and 5 in each section.
	 ❑ **Additional Topics in Math:** Chapter XI
	  ❑ Read section H.
	  ❑ Do practice questions 1, 3, and 5 in each section.
	 ❑ **Using a Graphing Calculator:** Appendix
	  ❑ Read sections E–H.
		Study Time: 1½ hours
		 ❑ **Reading:** Chapter V
		  ❑ Read sections C.4.b–c.
		  ❑ Do the practice questions in each section.
		  ❑ Do additional practice questions 1–8 at the end of the chapter.
		 ❑ **Tier 2 Vocabulary:** Chapter VII
		  ❑ Read *modicum–quandary*.
		  ❑ Highlight unfamiliar words; divide them into 5 equal groups, and study 1 group each night.
		  ❑ Review all 5 groups for 2 nights.
			Study Time: 1 hour
			 ❑ **Writing and Language:** Chapter VI
			  ❑ Read section B.3.
			  ❑ Do half the practice questions in each section.
			  ❑ For targeted areas, do all the practice questions.

2 weeks before the test	**Study Time:** 3 hours ❑ Take the **Practice Test** and review the answer explanations. ❑ Based on your errors on the Practice Test, identify difficult topics and their corresponding chapters. These chapters are your targeted areas.		

	Study Time: 1½ hours
	 ❑ **Heart of Algebra:** Chapter VIII
	  ❑ Re-read sections A–F.
	  ❑ Do practice questions 2, 4, and 6 in each section.
		Study Time: 1 hour
		 ❑ **Reading:** Chapter V
		  ❑ Review targeted sections and re-read practice questions.
		  ❑ Do additional practice questions 9–15 at the end of the chapter.
		 ❑ **Tier 2 Vocabulary:** Chapter VII
		  ❑ Read *quibble–zealous*.
		  ❑ Highlight unfamiliar words; divide them into 5 equal groups, and study 1 group each night.
		  ❑ Review all 5 groups for 2 nights.
			Study Time: 1 hour
			 ❑ **Writing and Language:** Chapter VI
			  ❑ Based on results of the Practice Test, begin to review all targeted areas.
			  ❑ Do practice questions 1–10 at the end of the chapter.

	The Math Test	The Reading Test	The Writing and Language Test
7 days before the test	**Study Time:** 1½ hours ❏ **Problem Solving and Data Analysis:** Chapter IX ❏ Re-read sections A–F. ❏ Do practice questions 2, 4, and 6 in each section.	**Study Time:** 1 hour ❏ **Reading:** Chapter V ❏ Review targeted sections and re-read practice questions. ❏ Do additional practice questions 16–25 at the end of the chapter. ❏ **Tier 2 Vocabulary:** Chapter VII ❏ Divide all highlighted words into 5 equal groups, and study the first group of words.	**Study Time:** 1 hour ❏ **Writing and Language:** Chapter VI ❏ Divide targeted areas into 4 sections. For first targeted area, do all remaining practice questions.
6 days before the test	**Study Time:** 1½ hours ❏ **Passport to Advanced Math:** Chapter IX ❏ Re-read sections A–G. ❏ Do practice questions 2, 4, and 6 in each section.	**Study Time:** 1 hour ❏ **Reading:** Chapter V ❏ Continue to review sections that present problems. ❏ **Tier 2 Vocabulary:** Chapter VII ❏ Study the second group of highlighted words.	**Study Time:** 1 hour ❏ **Writing and Language:** Chapter VI ❏ For second targeted area, do all remaining practice questions.
5 days before the test	**Study Time:** 2 hours ❏ **Additional Topics in Math:** Chapter X ❏ Re-read sections A–I. ❏ Do practice questions 2, 4, and 6 in each section.	**Study Time:** 1 hour ❏ **Reading:** Chapter V ❏ For sections that still present problems, review and re-read practice questions. ❏ **Tier 2 Vocabulary:** Chapter VII ❏ Study the third group of highlighted words.	**Study Time:** 1 hour ❏ **Writing and Language:** Chapter VI ❏ For third targeted area, do all remaining practice questions.
4 days before the test	**Study Time:** 1 hour ❏ **Additional Topics in Math:** Chapter XI ❏ Re-read sections A–H. ❏ Do practice questions 2, 4, and 6 in each section.	**Study Time:** 1 hour ❏ **Reading:** Chapter V ❏ Continue to review all sections. ❏ **Tier 2 Vocabulary:** Chapter VII ❏ Study the fourth group of highlighted words.	**Study Time:** 1 hour ❏ **Writing and Language:** Chapter VI ❏ For fourth targeted area, do all remaining practice questions.
3 days before the test	**Study Time:** 1 hour ❏ Focus on your target sections. ❏ Re-read the section. ❏ Cover the solutions of any worked practice questions and try to solve them. ❏ Re-do any questions you did not solve correctly on the first try.	**Study Time:** 1 hour ❏ **Reading:** Chapter V ❏ Continue to review all sections. ❏ **Tier 2 Vocabulary:** Chapter VII ❏ Study the last group of highlighted words.	**Study Time:** 1 hour ❏ **Writing and Language:** Chapter VI ❏ Look over answers to targeted questions in Chapter VI and review any issues that are still problematic.

continued

	The Math Test	The Reading Test	The Writing and Language Test

2 days before the test	**Study Time:** 1 hour
	❑ Focus on your target sections.
	  ❑ Re-read the section.
	  ❑ Cover the solutions of any worked practice questions and try to solve them.
	  ❑ Re-do any questions you did not solve correctly on the first try.
		Study Time: 1 hour
		❑ Re-read the general strategies for each section of Chapter V.
		❑ **Tier 2 Vocabulary:** Chapter VII
		  ❑ Review all highlighted words.
			Study Time: 1 hour
			❑ **Writing and Language:** Chapter VI
			  ❑ Look over answers to targeted questions in Chapter VI and review any issues that are still problematic.

Night before the test	❑ Relax! You're well prepared for the test. Have confidence in your ability to do well. ❑ Exercise. It helps to relieve stress, improve sleep quality, and boost brain performance. ❑ Get a good night's sleep. Try to unplug from electronic devices at least 30 minutes before bedtime, and remove any distractions that might wake you during the night.		

Morning of the test	**Reminders:**
	❑ Eat a well-balanced, nutritious breakfast.
	❑ Take the following items with you on test day:
	  ❑ Your admission ticket and photo ID
	  ❑ Several no. 2 pencils and erasers
	  ❑ A calculator with fresh batteries
	  ❑ A watch
	❑ Try to go outside for a few minutes and walk around before the test to relieve stress.
	❑ **Most important:** Stay calm and confident during the test. Take deep, slow breaths and think positive thoughts if you feel at all nervous. You can do it!		

II. One-Month Cram Plan

One-Month Cram Plan			
	The Math Test	**The Reading Test**	**The Writing and Language Test**
4 weeks before the test	**Study Time:** 2 hours ❏ Take the **Diagnostic Test** and review the answer explanations. ❏ Based on the questions you missed, identify difficult topics and their corresponding chapters. These chapters are your targeted chapters.		

	Study Time: 2½ hours
	❏ **Heart of Algebra:** Chapter VIII
	  ❏ Read the chapter.
	  ❏ Do practice questions 1, 3, and 5 in each section.
	❏ **Problem Solving and Data Analysis:** Chapter IX
	  ❏ Read the chapter.
	  ❏ Do practice questions 1, 3, and 5 in each section.
		Study Time: 1½ hours
		❏ **Reading:** Chapter V
		  ❏ Read sections A–C.2.a.
		  ❏ Do the practice questions in each section.
		❏ **Tier 2 Vocabulary:** Chapter VII
		  ❏ Read *aberration–duplicity*.
		  ❏ Highlight unfamiliar words; divide them into 5 equal groups, and study 1 group each night.
		  ❏ Review all 5 groups for 2 nights.
			Study Time: 1 hour
			❏ **Writing and Language:** Chapter VI
			  ❏ Read sections A–B.1.a–g.
			  ❏ Do half the practice questions in each section.
			  ❏ For targeted areas, do all the practice questions.

3 weeks before the test	**Study Time:** 2½ hours
	❏ **Passport to Advanced Math:** Chapter X
	  ❏ Read sections A–E.
	  ❏ Do practice questions 1, 3, and 5 in sections A–E.
	❏ **Additional Topics in Math:** Chapter XI
	  ❏ Read sections A–E.
	  ❏ Do practice questions 1, 3, and 5 in sections A–E.
	❏ **Using a Graphing Calculator:** Appendix
	  ❏ Read sections A–D.
		Study Time: 1½ hours
		❏ **Reading:** Chapter V
		  ❏ Read sections C.2.b–d and C.3.
		  ❏ Do the practice questions in each section.
		  ❏ Do additional practice questions 1–8 at the end of the chapter.
		❏ **Tier 2 Vocabulary:** Chapter VII
		  ❏ Read *ebullient–nefarious*.
		  ❏ Highlight unfamiliar words; divide them into 5 equal groups, and study 1 group each night.
		  ❏ Review all 5 groups for 2 nights.
			Study Time: 1 hour
			❏ **Writing and Language:** Chapter VI
			  ❏ Read sections B.2.a–g.
			  ❏ Do half the practice questions in each section.
			  ❏ For targeted areas, do all the practice questions.

continued

	The Math Test	The Reading Test	The Writing and Language Test

2 weeks before the test	**Study Time:** 2½ hours
	 ❑ **Passport to Advanced Math:** Chapter X
	    ❑ Read sections F–I.
	    ❑ Do practice questions 1, 3, and 5 in sections F–I.
	 ❑ **Additional Topics in Math:** Chapter XI
	    ❑ Read sections F–H.
	    ❑ Do practice questions 1, 3, and 5 in sections F–H.
	 ❑ **Using a Graphing Calculator:** Appendix
	    ❑ Read sections E–H.
		Study Time: 1½ hours
		 ❑ **Reading:** Chapter V
		    ❑ Read sections C.4.a–c.
		    ❑ Do the practice questions in each section.
		    ❑ Do additional practice questions 9–15 at the end of the chapter.
		 ❑ **Tier 2 Vocabulary:** Chapter VII
		    ❑ Read *negligent–zealous*.
		    ❑ Highlight unfamiliar words; divide them into 5 equal groups, and study 1 group each night.
		    ❑ Review all 5 groups for 2 nights.
			Study Time: 2 hours
			 ❑ **Writing and Language:** Chapter VI
			    ❑ Read sections B.3.a–g.
			    ❑ Do half the practice questions in each section.
			    ❑ For targeted areas, do all the practice questions.

7 days before the test	**Study Time:** 3 hours ❑ Take the **Practice Test** and review the answer explanations. ❑ Based on your errors on the Practice Test, identify difficult topics and their corresponding chapters. These chapters are your targeted areas.		

6 days before the test	**Study Time:** 1 hour
	 ❑ **Heart of Algebra:** Chapter VIII
	    ❑ Review targeted areas.
	    ❑ Do practice questions 2, 4, and 6 in each section.
		Study Time: 1 hour
		 ❑ **Reading:** Chapter V
		    ❑ Review sections A–C.2.a.
		    ❑ Do additional practice questions 16–25 at the end of the chapter.
		 ❑ **Tier 2 Vocabulary:** Chapter VII
		    ❑ Divide all highlighted words into 4 equal groups, and study the first group of words.
			Study Time: 1 hour
			 ❑ **Writing and Language:** Chapter VI
			    ❑ Based on results of the Practice Test, begin to review all targeted areas.
			    ❑ Do practice questions 1–10 at the end of the chapter.

5 days before the test	**Study Time:** 1 hour
	 ❑ **Problem Solving and Data Analysis:** Chapter IX
	    ❑ Review targeted areas.
	    ❑ Do practice questions 2, 4, and 6 in each section.
		Study Time: 1 hour
		 ❑ **Reading:** Chapter V
		    ❑ Review sections C.2.b–d and C.3.
		 ❑ **Tier 2 Vocabulary:** Chapter VII
		    ❑ Study the second group of highlighted words.
			Study Time: 1 hour
			 ❑ **Writing and Language:** Chapter VI
			    ❑ Based on results of the Practice Test, continue to review all targeted areas.

4 days before the test	**Study Time:** 1 hour
	 ❑ **Passport to Advanced Math:** Chapter X
	    ❑ Review targeted areas.
	    ❑ Do practice questions 2, 4, and 6 in each section.
		Study Time: 1 hour
		 ❑ **Reading:** Chapter V
		    ❑ Review sections C.4.a–c.
		 ❑ **Tier 2 Vocabulary:** Chapter VII
		    ❑ Study the third group of highlighted words.
			Study Time: ½ hour
			 ❑ **Writing and Language:** Chapter VI
			    ❑ Based on results of the Practice Test, continue to review all targeted areas.

	The Math Test	The Reading Test	The Writing and Language Test

3 days before the test	**Study Time:** 1 hour
	❏ **Additional Topics in Math:** Chapter XI
	   ❏ Review targeted areas.
	   ❏ Do practice questions 2, 4, and 6 in each section.
		Study Time: 1 hour
		❏ **Reading:** Chapter V
		   ❏ Review any sections that were targeted in the Practice Test.
		❏ **Tier 2 Vocabulary:** Chapter VII
		   ❏ Study the last group of highlighted words.
			Study Time: ½ hour
			❏ **Writing and Language:** Chapter VI
			   ❏ Based on results of the Practice Test, continue to review all targeted areas,

2 days before the test	**Study Time:** 1½ hours
	❏ Focus on your target sections.
	   ❏ Re-read the sections.
	   ❏ Cover the solutions of any worked practice questions and try to solve them.
	   ❏ Re-do any questions you did not solve correctly on the first try.
		Study Time: 1 hour
		❏ **Reading:** Chapter V
		   ❏ Continue to review any sections that were targeted in the Practice Test.
		❏ **Tier 2 Vocabulary:** Chapter VII
		   ❏ Review all highlighted words.
			Study Time: ½ hour
			❏ **Writing and Language:** Chapter VI
			   ❏ Based on results of the Practice Test, continue to review all targeted areas.

Night before the test	❏ Relax! You're well prepared for the test. Have confidence in your ability to do well. ❏ Exercise. It helps to relieve stress, improve sleep quality, and boost brain performance. ❏ Get a good night's sleep. Try to unplug from electronic devices at least 30 minutes before bedtime, and remove any distractions that might wake you during the night.		

Morning of the test	**Reminders:**
	❏ Eat a well-balanced, nutritious breakfast.
	❏ Take the following items with you on test day:
	   ❏ Your admission ticket and photo ID
	   ❏ Several no. 2 pencils and erasers
	   ❏ A calculator with fresh batteries
	   ❏ A watch
	❏ Try to go outside for a few minutes and walk around before the test to relieve stress.
	❏ **Most important:** Stay calm and confident during the test. Take deep slow breaths and think positive thoughts if you feel at all nervous. You can do it!		

III. One-Week Cram Plan

One-Week Cram Plan		
	The Math Test	**The Reading Test**	**The Writing and Language Test**
7 days before the test	**Study Time:** 2 hours ❑ Take the **Diagnostic Test** and review the answer explanations. ❑ Based on the questions you missed, identify difficult topics and their corresponding chapters. These chapters are your targeted chapters.		

6 days before the test	**Study Time:** 2 hours
	❑ **Heart of Algebra:** Chapter VIII
	  ❑ Read the chapter.
	  ❑ Do the practice questions in each section.
		Study Time: 2 hours
		❑ **Reading:** Chapter V
		  ❑ Read sections A–C.2.
		  ❑ Do the practice questions in each section.
		❑ **Tier 2 Vocabulary:** Chapter VII
		  ❑ Read *aberration–duplicity*.
		  ❑ Highlight unfamiliar words and study them.
			Study Time: 2 hours
			❑ **Writing and Language:** Chapter VI
			  ❑ Read sections A–B.1.a–g.
			  ❑ Do half the practice questions in each section.
			  ❑ For targeted areas, do all the practice questions.

5 days before the test	**Study Time:** 2 hours
	❑ **Problem Solving and Data Analysis:** Chapter IX
	  ❑ Read the chapter.
	  ❑ Do the practice questions in each section.
		Study Time: 2 hours
		❑ **Reading:** Chapter V
		  ❑ Read section C.3.
		  ❑ Do the practice questions in this section.
		❑ **Tier 2 Vocabulary:** Chapter VII
		  ❑ Read *ebullient–hypocrisy*.
		  ❑ Highlight unfamiliar words and study them.
			Study Time: 1 hour
			❑ **Writing and Language:** Chapter VI
			  ❑ Read sections B.2.a–c.
			  ❑ Do half the practice questions in each section.
			  ❑ For targeted areas, do all the practice questions.

4 days before the test	**Study Time:** 2½ hours
	❑ **Passport to Advanced Math:** Chapter X
	  ❑ Read the chapter.
	  ❑ Do the practice questions in each section.
		Study Time: 2 hours
		❑ **Reading:** Chapter V
		  ❑ Read section C.4.
		  ❑ Do the practice questions in this section.
		❑ **Tier 2 Vocabulary:** Chapter VII
		  ❑ Read *iconoclasm–punitive*.
		  ❑ Highlight unfamiliar words and study them.
			Study Time: 1½ hours
			❑ **Writing and Language:** Chapter VI
			  ❑ Read sections B.2.d–g.
			  ❑ Do half the practice questions in each section.
			  ❑ For targeted areas, do all the practice questions.

3 days before the test	**Study Time:** 2½ hours
	❑ **Additional Topics in Math:** Chapter XI
	  ❑ Read the chapter.
	  ❑ Do the practice questions in each section.
		Study Time: 2 hours
		❑ **Reading:** Chapter V
		  ❑ Do additional practice questions 1–25 at the end of the chapter.
		❑ **Tier 2 Vocabulary:** Chapter VII
		  ❑ Read *quandary–zealous*.
		  ❑ Highlight unfamiliar words and study them.
			Study Time: 1 hour
			❑ **Writing and Language:** Chapter VI
			  ❑ Read section B.3.
			  ❑ Do half the practice questions in the section.
			  ❑ For targeted areas, do all the practice questions.

continued

	The Math Test	The Reading Test	The Writing and Language Test
2 days before the test	**Study Time:** 3 hours ❑ Take the **Practice Test** and review the answer explanations. ❑ Based on your errors on the Practice Test, identify difficult topics and their corresponding chapters. These chapters are your targeted areas.		
1 day before the test	**Study Time:** 1½ hours ❑ Focus on your target sections. ❑ Re-read the sections. ❑ Cover the solutions of any worked examples and try to solve them. ❑ Re-do any questions you did not solve correctly on the first try.	**Study Time:** 1 hour ❑ **Reading:** Chapter V ❑ Review targeted sections and re-read practice questions. ❑ **Tier 2 Vocabulary:** Chapter VII ❑ Review all highlighted words.	**Study Time:** 1 hour ❑ **Writing and Language:** Chapter VI ❑ Based on results of the Practice Test, continue to review sections that still need attention. ❑ Do practice questions 1–10 at the end of the chapter.
Morning of the test	**Reminders:** ❑ Eat a well-balanced, nutritious breakfast. ❑ Take the following items with you on test day: ❑ Your admission ticket and photo ID ❑ Several no. 2 pencils and erasers ❑ A calculator with fresh batteries ❑ A watch ❑ Try to go outside for a few minutes and walk around before the test to relieve stress. ❑ **Most important:** Stay calm and confident during the test. Take deep slow breaths and think positive thoughts if you feel at all nervous. You can do it!		

IV. Diagnostic Test

This Diagnostic Test is half the length of a full-length PSAT Test. The Diagnostic Test has four sections designed to predict your performance on the SAT Test : Reading Test, Writing and Language Test, Math Test—No Calculator, and Math Test—Calculator.

When you take the Diagnostic Test, try to simulate test conditions by avoiding interruptions and distractions and following the time allotments carefully. Each question is numbered. Choose the best answer for each question and fill in the corresponding circle on the answer sheet provided. If you finish a section before the allotted time runs out, don't go back to an earlier section or ahead to the next section.

You will need 1 hour and 24 minutes to complete the Diagnostic Test.

Reading Test	24 questions	30 minutes
Writing and Language Test	22 questions	18 minutes
Math Test—No Calculator	9 questions	13 minutes
Math Test—Calculator	15 questions	23 minutes

Answer Sheet

Section 1: Reading Test

1 (A) (B) (C) (D)
2 (A) (B) (C) (D)
3 (A) (B) (C) (D)
4 (A) (B) (C) (D)
5 (A) (B) (C) (D)

6 (A) (B) (C) (D)
7 (A) (B) (C) (D)
8 (A) (B) (C) (D)
9 (A) (B) (C) (D)
10 (A) (B) (C) (D)

11 (A) (B) (C) (D)
12 (A) (B) (C) (D)
13 (A) (B) (C) (D)
14 (A) (B) (C) (D)
15 (A) (B) (C) (D)

16 (A) (B) (C) (D)
17 (A) (B) (C) (D)
18 (A) (B) (C) (D)
19 (A) (B) (C) (D)
20 (A) (B) (C) (D)

21 (A) (B) (C) (D)
22 (A) (B) (C) (D)
23 (A) (B) (C) (D)
24 (A) (B) (C) (D)

Section 2: Writing and Language Test

1 (A) (B) (C) (D)
2 (A) (B) (C) (D)
3 (A) (B) (C) (D)
4 (A) (B) (C) (D)
5 (A) (B) (C) (D)

6 (A) (B) (C) (D)
7 (A) (B) (C) (D)
8 (A) (B) (C) (D)
9 (A) (B) (C) (D)
10 (A) (B) (C) (D)

11 (A) (B) (C) (D)
12 (A) (B) (C) (D)
13 (A) (B) (C) (D)
14 (A) (B) (C) (D)
15 (A) (B) (C) (D)

16 (A) (B) (C) (D)
17 (A) (B) (C) (D)
18 (A) (B) (C) (D)
19 (A) (B) (C) (D)
20 (A) (B) (C) (D)

21 (A) (B) (C) (D)
22 (A) (B) (C) (D)

Section 3: Math Test—No Calculator

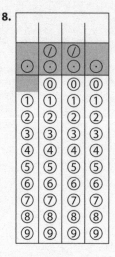

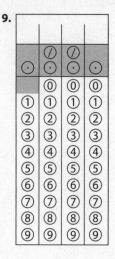

Section 4: Math Test—Calculator

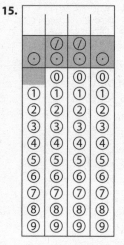

Section 1: Reading Test

24 questions

30 minutes

Directions: Read the following passages and answer the questions based on the information in the passages and any accompanying graphs or charts.

Questions 1–8 are based on the following passages.

Passage 1 is an excerpt adapted from the novel *Kidnapped* by Robert Louis Stevenson (1886). The novel, set in the 18th century, is narrated by David, a young Scot wrongfully sold to a ship captain by his unscrupulous uncle. Passage 2 is adapted from *The War of 1812: Stoking the Fires: The Impressment of Seaman Charles Davis by the U.S. Navy* by John P. Deeben (archives.gov).

Passage 1

Here I lay for the space of many days a close prisoner, and not only got my health again, but came to know my companions. They were a rough lot indeed, as sailors mostly are: being
(5) men rooted out of all the kindly parts of life, and condemned to toss together on the rough seas, with masters no less cruel. There were some among them that had sailed with the pirates and seen things it would be a shame
(10) even to speak of; some were men that had run from the king's ships, and went with a halter round their necks, of which they made no secret; and all, as the saying goes, were "at a word and a blow" with their best friends. Yet I
(15) had not been many days shut up with them before I began to be ashamed of my first judgment, when I had drawn away from them at the Ferry pier, as though they had been unclean beasts. No class of man is altogether bad, but
(20) each has its own faults and virtues; and these shipmates of mine were no exception to the rule. Rough they were, sure enough; and bad, I suppose; but they had many virtues. They were

kind when it occurred to them, simple even
(25) beyond the simplicity of a country lad like me, and had some glimmerings of honesty.

There was one man, of maybe forty, that would sit on my berthside for hours and tell me of his wife and child. He was a fisher that
(30) had lost his boat, and thus been driven to the deep-sea voyaging. Well, it is years ago now: but I have never forgotten him. ... Indeed, many of these poor fellows (as the event proved) were upon their last cruise; the deep
(35) seas and cannibal fish received them; and it is a thankless business to speak ill of the dead.

Among other good deeds that they did, they returned my money, which had been shared among them; and though it was about
(40) a third short, I was very glad to get it, and hoped great good from it in the land I was going to. The ship was bound for the Carolinas; and you must not suppose that I was going to that place merely as an exile. The trade was
(45) even then much depressed; since that, and with the rebellion of the colonies and the formation of the United States, it has, of course, come to an end; but in those days of my youth, white men were still sold into slavery on the planta-
(50) tions, and that was the destiny to which my wicked uncle had condemned me. ...

I did my best in the small time allowed me to make some thing like a man, or rather I should say something like a boy, of the poor creature,
(55) Ransome [the cabin-boy]. But his mind was scarce truly human. He could remember nothing of the time before he came to sea; only that his father had made clocks, and had a starling in the

GO ON TO THE NEXT PAGE

(60) parlour, which could whistle "The North Countrie;" all else had been blotted out in these years of hardship and cruelties. He had a strange notion of the dry land, picked up from sailor's stories: that it was a place where lads were put to
(65) some kind of slavery called a trade, and where apprentices were continually lashed and clapped into foul prisons. In a town, he thought every second person a decoy, and every third house a place in which seamen would be drugged and murdered. To be sure, I would tell him how
(70) kindly I had myself been used upon that dry land he was so much afraid of, and how well fed and carefully taught both by my friends and my parents: and if he had been recently hurt, he would weep bitterly and swear to run away; but
(75) if he was in his usual crackbrain humour, or (still more) if he had had a glass of spirits in the roundhouse, he would deride the notion.

Passage 2

On the night of November 12, 1811, the 36-gun British frigate HMS *Havannah* lay
(80) anchored at Spithead, a sheltered strait near the naval harbors of Portsmouth and Gosport in Hampshire, England. Spithead served as one of the principal bases for the Royal Navy along the English Channel, and the *Havannah,*
(85) as a member of the Channel Fleet, regularly patrolled the area, watching for French vessels from Brest or Le Havre attempting to infiltrate coastal waters.

In the darkness, the deck watch suddenly
(90) heard splashing sounds and spotted a figure in the water swimming frantically toward them. Dropping a longboat from the gunwales, crewmen pulled aboard what they initially thought was an American deserter from the nearby
(95) frigate USS *Constitution,* which had recently put into Spithead for a courtesy call or to take on supplies. Instead, the drenched man identified himself as Irish seaman Charles Davis; he claimed to have just escaped from forced servi-
(100) tude in the United States Navy.

Davis subsequently recounted his ordeal to Capt. Robert Hall of the HMS *Royal William,* who communicated the incident to Adm. Sir Roger Curtis, commander-in-chief of the
(105) naval station at Portsmouth. In his report, Hall reiterated the pivotal assertion that Davis "never was in America before…he has been detained by the commanding officer of the *Constitution.*" It appeared to be a clear case of
(110) foreign impressment; however, there is little evidence to suggest anything further came of the incident in diplomatic circles, even though procedures were in place at that time to lodge a formal complaint with the United States
(115) government. (Since 1796, an American agent had been stationed in London to investigate impressment issues and secure the release of American victims.) But for the fact that a copy of Hall's report eventually found its way into
(120) the general records of the U.S. State Department—along with a few other documents about impressed seamen of British origin—the ordeal of Charles Davis might have faded into history.

(125) The impressment or forcible seizure of American seamen by the British Royal Navy in the late 18th and early 19th centuries has traditionally been viewed as a primary cause of the War of 1812. Americans at that time
(130) regarded impressment as a deliberate and dastardly act perpetrated by a foreign power against innocent men. Although modern scholars now question the true extent and impact of the practice as a precursor to war—
(135) between 1789 and 1815, the British impressed fewer than 10,000 Americans out of a total population of 3.9 to 7.2 million—impressment nonetheless stoked popular outrage, provoking Congress into legislative action and
(140) raising diplomatic tensions with Britain. The experience of Charles Davis, however, illuminates a lesser known aspect about American culpability in the whole impressment issue. To a certain extent (and apparently not widely
(145) admitted by American officials), the United States reciprocated impressment against the British, seizing unsuspecting seamen to serve aboard American warships.

1. Which choice best summarizes Passage 1?

   A. A young man is taken prisoner and constantly subjected to horrific punishment.

   B. After an unforeseen imprisonment, a young man is able to find redeeming qualities in his captors.

   C. An elderly man reflects on the hardships and cruelties inflicted on him in his youth by pirates.

   D. A journey begins that fulfills the expectations of a young boy who sets out to make his fortune at sea.

2. What does the narrator suggest about how he ultimately came to view the sailors with whom he lived at sea?

   A. To a man, they were uncouth beasts.

   B. They remained an alien crew to him, unknown and unknowable.

   C. With the passage of time, they changed and were characterized mostly by their good deeds.

   D. Like most groups of people, they represented both good and evil facets of human nature.

3. Which choice provides the best evidence for the answer to the previous question?

   A. Lines 3–7 ("They were…less cruel.")

   B. Lines 7–11 ("There were…king's ships")

   C. Lines 19–22 ("No class…the rule.")

   D. Lines 32–36 ("Indeed…dead.")

4. The narrator believes he is destined to

   A. be thrown overboard and eaten by fish.

   B. be exiled in the Carolinas.

   C. be a sailor for the rest of his life.

   D. be sold as a slave.

5. On line 70, the word "used" most nearly means

   A. employed.

   B. consumed.

   C. treated.

   D. operated.

6. According to the author of Passage 2, current thinking is that the role of impressment in the 1812 conflict between the United States and Britain was

   A. direct and causative.

   B. possibly questionable.

   C. of little or no significance.

   D. outrageous and cruel.

7. Which of the following best represents the relationship between the two passages?

   A. Passage 1 is a fictional account of the actual events described in Passage 2.

   B. Passage 2 describes the historical context for the plot of Passage 1, which is based on those historical events.

   C. Passage 1 portrays an imagined adventure that has parallels in the nonfiction account of Passage 2.

   D. The hero of Passage 1 is based on the real-life journeys of Charles Davis, the historical character featured in Passage 2.

8. Both passages provide evidence that the author of Passage 1 and the author of Passage 2 would agree with which of the following statements?

   A. One of the major causes of the 1812 conflict between the United States and Britain was the impressment of sailors.

   B. Not all members of a ship's crew are onboard voluntarily.

   C. In order to run a tight ship, the captain must be harsh and dictatorial.

   D. Maritime laws (laws on the sea) are substantially different from domestic laws.

GO ON TO THE NEXT PAGE

Questions 9–17 are based on the following passage.

This passage is adapted from the Genomic Science Program of the Department of Energy (www.energy.gov).

The global carbon cycle plays a central role in regulating atmospheric carbon dioxide levels and Earth's climate, but knowledge of the bio-logical processes operating at the most founda-
(5) tional level of the carbon cycle remains limited. These processes are intimately linked to higher-scale biogeochemical processes and form key linkages between global carbon, nitrogen, and water cycles. Even minor changes in the rate
(10) and magnitude of biological carbon cycling can have immense impacts on whether ecosys-tems will capture, store, or release carbon. Developing a more sophisticated and quantita-tive understanding of molecular scale processes
(15) that drive the carbon cycle represents a major challenge, but this understanding is critical for predicting impacts of global climate change.

The carbon cycle is heavily dependent on microbial communities that decompose or
(20) transform organic material in the environ-ment. Massive amounts of organic carbon currently are stored in ecosystems (e.g., the soils of forests, grasslands, and permafrosts), and microbes are known to play key roles in
(25) determining the longevity and stability of this carbon and whether or not it is released into the atmosphere as carbon dioxide or methane, both greenhouse gases, under any given set of environmental variables. However, large
(30) uncertainties remain regarding the nature and magnitude of carbon cycle processes per-formed by environmental microbes; critical knowledge gaps in this area have proven diffi-cult to address given the limited understand-
(35) ing of key groups of organisms and significant technical difficulties in characterizing micro-bial community functional processes in soil environments. Microbially mediated processes are only minimally represented in most higher-
(40) scale carbon cycle models, a factor contribut-ing to uncertainties and limiting predictive capabilities.

Consequently, there is a critical need to advance understanding of the systems biology
(45) properties of microbes performing key carbon cycle processes and develop new approaches to link the structural and functional characteriza-tion of microbial communities with quantita-tive measurements of carbon cycle processes.
(50) Understanding and predicting processes of the global carbon cycle require bold new research approaches aimed at linking global-scale climate phenomena; biogeochemical processes of ecosystems; and functional activ-
(55) ities encoded in the genomes of microbes, plants, and biological communities. This goal presents a formidable challenge, but emerging systems biology research approaches provide new opportunities to bridge the knowledge
(60) gap between molecular- and global-scale phe-nomena. Systems-level research emphasizes studies on the underlying principles of intact, complex systems and facilitates scaling of concepts and data across multiple levels of
(65) biological organization. Applying this approach to the global carbon cycle will require multifaceted but highly integrated research that incorporates experimentation on model organisms and systems, collection
(70) of observational data on communities and ecosystems, and mechanistic modeling of pro-cesses ranging from metabolic to global scales.

9. The first paragraph serves mainly to

   A. explain the importance of a gap in understanding.
   B. note a common misinterpretation of a process.
   C. describe a counterintuitive phenomenon.
   D. present a recent study and summarize its findings.

10. As used in line 15, the word "drive" most nearly means

    A. operate.
    B. restrain.
    C. power.
    D. absorb.

11. According to the author, understanding molecular scale processes of the carbon cycle is important because

    A. it will allow scientists to control the linkages between global carbon, nitrogen, and water cycles.
    B. the study of such processes will give scientists the ability to regulate atmospheric carbon dioxide.
    C. it changes the rate and magnitude of biological carbon cycling.
    D. it will allow researchers to foresee the effects of global climate change.

12. Which choice provides the best evidence for the answer to the previous question?

    A. Lines 6–9 ("These processes…water cycles.")
    B. Lines 13–17 ("Developing…change.")
    C. Lines 29–38 ("However… environments.")
    D. Lines 50–53 ("Understanding… phenomena")

13. In line 44, the word "advance" most nearly means

    A. proceed.
    B. improve.
    C. suggest.
    D. lend.

14. Based on the information in the passage, which of the following best describes the function of the microbial communities?

    A. To link and release
    B. To capture and store
    C. To bridge and facilitate
    D. To decompose and transform

15. Based on the information in the passage, scientists are most unsure of

    A. the importance of the global carbon cycle in regulating the levels of carbon dioxide in the atmosphere.
    B. the intrinsic qualities and enormity of carbon cycle processes that environmental microbes perform.
    C. the links between the elements that comprise the carbon cycle.
    D. which aspects of the carbon cycle to emphasize in systems-level research.

16. Which choice provides the best evidence for the answer to the previous question?

    A. Lines 1–5 ("The global…limited.")
    B. Lines 9–12 ("Even…carbon.")
    C. Lines 29–32 ("However…microbes…")
    D. Lines 61–65 ("Systems-level… organization.")

17. It can be inferred that the author believes some knowledge of the global carbon cycle is "difficult to address" (lines 33–34) because

    A. scientists lack the sophisticated equipment required to conduct the research.
    B. scientists are more focused on the genome of microbes.
    C. researchers have incomplete understanding of some of the organisms and their functions.
    D. the research done so far is multifaceted and integrated.

Questions 18–24 are based on the following passage and supplementary material.

The following passage is adapted from United States Department of Labor (bis.gov) "Self-employment in the United States" by Steven F. Hipple and Laurel A. Hammond and from the U.S. Small Business Association website (sba.gov).

GO ON TO THE NEXT PAGE

Starting your own business can be an exciting and rewarding experience. It can offer numerous advantages such as being your own boss, setting your own schedule and making a living doing (5) something you enjoy. Becoming a successful entrepreneur requires thorough planning, creativity, and hard work, but it can certainly be lucrative. In fact, what do Apple Computer, Hershey's, Mary Kay Cosmetics, and the Ford Motor (10) Company have in common? These well-known corporations all started out as home-based businesses. Indeed, more than half of all U.S. businesses are based out of an owner's home.

Since the late 1940s, data on self-employment (15) have been collected regularly as part of the Current Population Survey (CPS), a monthly sample survey of about 60,000 households that provides employment and unemployment data for the nation's civilian noninstitutional popula- (20) tion ages 16 and older. Since 1967, the official Bureau of Labor Statistics estimates of self-employment have included only the unincorporated self-employed (those who work for themselves in an unincorporated business).

(25) Although it is possible to identify the incorporated self-employed (people who work for themselves in corporate entities) separately, they are counted as wage and salary workers in the official statistics because, legally, they are employees of (30) their own business. This Spotlight on Statistics examines recent trends in self-employment by various demographic and socioeconomic characteristics, including both the unincorporated and the incorporated self-employed, as well as data on (35) paid employees who work for the self-employed.

Self-employment continues to be an important source of jobs in the United States. In 2015, 15 million people, or 10.1 percent of total U.S. employment, were self-employed, including (40) those who had incorporated their businesses and those who had not. Of all the self-employed, 9.5 million, or about 6 in 10, were unincorporated; the remaining 5.5 million were incorporated. People who are self-employed typically (45) incorporate their businesses in order to receive traditional benefits of the corporate structure, including limited liability, tax considerations,

and enhanced opportunity to raise capital through the sale of stocks and bonds.

(50) The self-employment rate—the proportion of total employment made up of self-employed workers—has trended down over the past two decades. In 1994, the self-employment rate was 12.1 percent; by 2015, the rate had (55) declined to 10.1 percent. From 1994 to 2015, the unincorporated self-employment rate fell from 8.7 percent to 6.4 percent.

The long-term decline in unincorporated self-employment partially reflects an overall (60) decrease in agricultural employment, where a large share of workers are self-employed. At the same time, there has been decline in the agricultural self-employment rate, which might be due to a decrease in the number of small farms and (65) the emergence of large farming operations.

The decline in the unincorporated self-employment rate might also reflect a general increase in the likelihood of businesses to incorporate. From 1994 to 1999, the share of (70) total employment made up of the incorporated self-employed ranged from 3.2 percent to 3.5 percent. Over the 2000–2008 period, the incorporated self-employment rate rose from 3.3 percent to 4.0 percent. The rate then edged (75) down to 3.7 percent in 2010 and remained at that level over the 2011–2015 period.

The self-employment rate for older workers continued to be higher in 2015 than that for younger workers. The unincorporated self- (80) employment rate among workers aged 65 years and older was the highest (15.5 percent) of any age group; in contrast, the rates were much lower for their counterparts aged 16 to 24 (1.9 percent). A possible reason is that younger workers rarely (85) have accumulated the capital and the managerial skills required to start a business, whereas many older workers may be able to acquire these resources through their own efforts or through access to credit. For all age groups, incorporated (90) self-employment rates were lower than unincorporated rates; however, incorporated self-employment rates also rose with age.

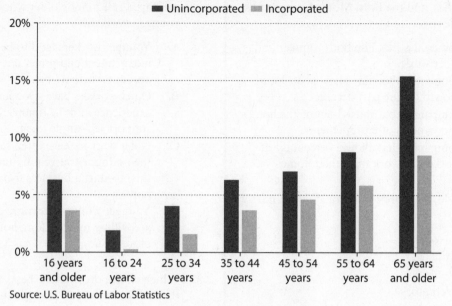

Figure 1
Self-Employment Rates by Age, Annual Averages, 2015

Source: U.S. Bureau of Labor Statistics

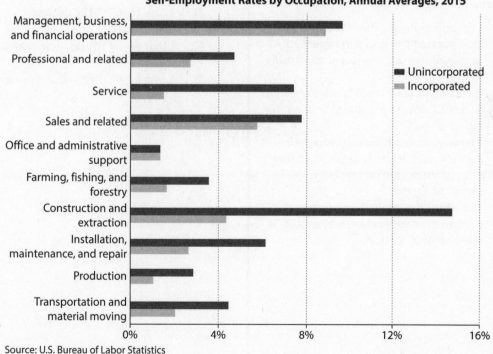

Figure 2
Self-Employment Rates by Occupation, Annual Averages, 2015

Source: U.S. Bureau of Labor Statistics

GO ON TO THE NEXT PAGE

18. The author mentions such companies as Apple Computer, Hershey's, Mary Kay Cosmetics, and the Ford Motor Company as examples of

    A. companies that hire both younger and older workers.
    B. companies that have shown continued growth for the past decade.
    C. companies that started out of the homes and garages of entrepreneurs.
    D. companies that allow a percentage of workers to work from their homes.

19. In line 46, the word "traditional" most nearly means

    A. customary.
    B. outdated.
    C. ritualistic.
    D. celebratory.

20. Which of the following is true based on the information in the passage?

    A. The self-employment rate for incorporated and unincorporated self-employed workers has increased steadily since the year 2000.
    B. As the number of small family farms decreases, fewer agricultural workers are self-employed.
    C. The average salary for self-employed agricultural workers is higher than that of agricultural workers on large, corporate farms.
    D. The education level of corporately employed workers is higher than that of self-employed workers.

21. According to the passage, which of the following accounts for the higher self-employed rate among older workers versus younger workers?

    A. Younger workers tend to be more independent and prefer not to be accountable to a boss.
    B. Older workers have stronger executive experience and the financial resources to support self-employment.
    C. Older workers have often retired from their administrative jobs and have the time to start a business from their homes.
    D. Younger workers are more energetic and are willing to work long hours to make more money.

22. Which choice presents the best evidence for the answer to the previous question?

    A. Lines 50–53 ("The self-employment rate...two decades.")
    B. Lines 66–69 ("The decline...incorporate.")
    C. Lines 84–89 ("A possible reason...credit.")
    D. Lines 89–92 ("For all age groups...with age.")

23. Which statement from the passage is best supported by the data in Figure 1?

   A. Lines 36–37 ("Self-employment…United States.")
   B. Lines 44–49 ("People…bonds.")
   C. Lines 61–65 ("At the same time… operations.")
   D. Lines 77–79 ("The self-employment… workers.")

24. Which of the following is true according to the data in Figure 2?

   A. In every industry listed in Figure 2, the number of unincorporated workers is greater than the number of incorporated workers.
   B. Of all the industries included in the data, the greatest numbers of unincorporated workers are employed in the construction and extraction industry.
   C. More workers in the production industry are incorporated than are unincorporated.
   D. Of all the industries included in the data, the difference between the number of unincorporated workers versus the number of incorporated is greatest in the service industry.

IF YOU FINISH BEFORE TIME IS CALLED, CHECK YOUR WORK ON THIS SECTION ONLY. DO NOT WORK ON ANY OTHER SECTION IN THE TEST.

Section 2: Writing and Language Test

22 questions

18 minutes

Directions: The Writing and Language Test consists of a series of passages accompanied by a number of questions. As you answer the questions, think about how the passage may be revised to improve the expression of ideas, the grammatical constructions including mechanics and usage, the sentence structure, and the punctuation. Some passages will be accompanied by a chart or a graph to which you will refer as you answer the questions.

Some questions will ask you to consider an underlined portion; some will ask you to look at a specific location in the passage; and some will ask you about the passage as a whole.

Read each passage before you begin to answer the questions; then, look for the most effective and grammatically correct answer to each question. Many questions offer the option of NO CHANGE. If you think the most effective choice is to leave the underlined portion as it is, choose NO CHANGE.

How to Investigate a Flying Saucer

[1]

Southbound on a ☐1 lone, desert highway, police officer, Lonnie Zamora was in pursuit of a speeding car outside the town of Socorro, New Mexico, when ☐2 he heard a loud roar! Seconds later, he saw a large flame rise from the ground and pierce the sky above a remote patch of desert southwest of the highway. Fearing a nearby dynamite shack ☐3 might have exploded, Zamora let the speeding car go, turned right, and drove down a bumpy gravel road that ran alongside the shack.

[2]

Zamora's cruiser clunked along the rocky road until he came upon a steep hill. Rising from behind ☐4 the hill, a smokeless fire that glowed in a funnel of blue and orange tinted flames. The hill obscured the origin of the flames, so Zamora attempted to drive up it. His ☐5 cruisers tires slipped and swayed on the loose gravel, but after three attempts, Zamora finally made it to the top.

[3]

A shiny object, the size of a sedan, sparkled in the late afternoon sunshine about 150 to 200 yards from where Zamora was perched on the hilltop. ☐6 However, he thought it was a car overturned in an arroyo (a dry creek bed), but when he drove closer, it appeared to be aluminum in color, not chrome, and oval-shaped like a football. ☐7

[4]

Zamora drove toward the object, along the hill's crest, for about 50 feet and then stopped the car. He radioed back to the sheriff's office that he would be busy checking on a wreck "down in the arroyo," and then he descended on foot down the hill toward the object.

[5]

Roooaaarrr! Zamora was startled again by a very loud rumble, not exactly like a blast but also not steady like a jet engine. ☐8 They started at a low frequency, with the pitch slowly rising. The flame appeared to be coming from the underside of the object, glowing light blue on top and orange at the bottom.

Zamora panicked, afraid the object was about to blow.

[6]

Zamora sprinted to his car, hit his leg on the fender, and crashed to the ground. He got up, ran another 25 feet or so, and when he looked back again, he saw the object begin 9 to rise. It rose to the level of the car, then higher, about 20 to 25 feet in the air. Zamora ran another 50 feet from his car, just over the edge of the hill, and ducked. Kneeling as close to the ground as he could, he covered his face with his arms for protection. Suddenly, the roar stopped. In the uneasy silence, Zamora lifted his head and looked. The object 10 speed away from him, toward the southwest, appearing to go in a straight line at about 10 to 15 feet off the ground. It cleared the 8-foot-tall dynamite shack by about 3 feet and then continued in a southwesterly direction, until it went over the high desert mountains and disappeared…

[7]

He ran to take cover but turned back to look at the object as he fled. He noticed a red symbol on the side, shaped like a point that was about 2 inches high and 2 inches wide. The object was smooth, a shiny white aluminum, with no visible windows or doors. There appeared to be two metal legs, slanted outward, supporting it. 11

[8]

Hector Quintanilla, the last chief officer of the U.S. Air Force's famous UFO investigation program, Project BLUE BOOK, was in charge of the Zamora case. His team was convinced that Zamora was telling the truth, and despite an extremely thorough investigation, they were unable to locate the object or its origins. In an article for *Studies in Intelligence* called "The Investigation of UFOs," Quintanilla says that the Zamora sighting is "the best-documented case on record." It remains unsolved.

1. **A.** NO CHANGE
   B. lone desert highway, police officer, Lonnie Zamora
   C. lone desert highway, police officer Lonnie Zamora
   D. lone, desert highway, police officer, Lonnie Zamora,

2. Which of the following choices best emphasizes the effect of the noise on Zamora?
   A. NO CHANGE
   B. he was startled by
   C. he listened to
   D. he heeded

3. **A.** NO CHANGE
   B. has been exploded
   C. have exploded
   D. are exploding

4. **A.** NO CHANGE
   B. the hill was a smokeless fire
   C. the hill and a smokeless fire
   D. the hill with a smokeless fire

5. **A.** NO CHANGE
   B. cruisers tire's
   C. cruisers' tires'
   D. cruiser's tires

6. **A.** NO CHANGE
   B. Nevertheless,
   C. Driving closer,
   D. At first glance,

GO ON TO THE NEXT PAGE

7. At this point, the writer is considering adding the following true statement:

   > An arroyo is a small steep-sided watercourse or gulch with a nearly flat floor, usually dry except after heavy rains.

   Should the writer make this addition here?

   A. Yes, because it adds information that the reader needs to understand the central focus of the essay.
   B. Yes, because it adds an essential description that is missing from the paragraph.
   C. No, because it adds more information than is necessary to the paragraph.
   D. No, because *arroyo* is a Spanish word that will confuse the reader.

8. A. NO CHANGE
   B. These
   C. It
   D. Some

9. A. NO CHANGE
   B. to raise
   C. raising
   D. a rise

10. A. NO CHANGE
    B. speeding away
    C. sped away
    D. sped toward

11. For the sake of logic and cohesion, the best placement for Paragraph 7 is

    A. where it is now.
    B. after Paragraph 4.
    C. before Paragraph 6.
    D. after Paragraph 8.

Colony Collapse Disorder: Perfect Storm for Beekeepers

During the winter of 2006 to 2007, [12] some people in the United States became alarmed that honeybee colonies were dying in large numbers, with reported losses of 30 to 90 percent in some beekeeping operations. While many of the colonies lost during this time period exhibited symptoms consistent with those typically observed when under attack by parasitic [13] mites. As many as 50 percent of all colonies were reportedly lost, demonstrating symptoms inconsistent with mite damage, or any other known causes of death. This suggested that increased stress or a new, unidentified agent could potentially be responsible. This unexplained cause of death has been given the name "Colony Collapse Disorder," or CCD. Subsequent investigations suggested that these outbreaks of unexplained colony collapse [14] has been occurring for at least two years.

Symptoms of CCD include: (i) sudden loss of the colony's adult bee population with very few bees found near the dead colonies; (ii) several frames with healthy, capped brood with low levels of parasitic [15] mites, indicating that colonies were relatively strong shortly before the loss of adult bees and that the losses cannot be attributed to a recent infestation of mites; (iii) food reserves that have not been robbed, despite active colonies in the same area, suggesting avoidance of the dead colony by other bees; (iv) minimal evidence of wax moth or small hive beetle damage; and (v) a laying queen often present with a small cluster of newly emerged attendants. [16]

Many [17] effected beekeepers indicated that their colonies were under some form of stress at least two months before the first incidence of CCD. Stresses could include poor nutrition (due to apiary overcrowding, pollination of crops with low nutritional value, or pollen or nectar dearth), limited or contaminated water supplies, exposure to pesticides, or high levels of varroa mites. [18] Therefore, case studies of beekeeping operations suggested the possible involvement of a pathogen or toxin in CCD. Some beekeepers losing colonies to CCD placed the abandoned "dead out" hive boxes on top of boxes containing strong colonies. [19] These also then suffered CCD.

[20] There have been some recent changes. At the end of 2006, the honeybee genome was fully sequenced, permitting the creation of new molecular approaches in honeybee genomics and molecular physiology. Using these tools, scientists can identify which genes are being turned on and off in bees, in effect allowing the bees themselves to show how they are being impacted, and helping scientists identify the most likely causal factors underlying CCD.

These analyses **[21]** that have the potential to reveal how the bees are responding to potential pathogens, environmental toxins, or other stressors. Likewise, new approaches (e.g., a new generation of sensors) for the detection of new or re-emerging pathogens or for the sensitive detection of environmental chemicals may help in unraveling the underlying causes of CCD and other problems in the health of honeybees and other pollinators. **[22]**

U.S. Honey-Producing Colonies

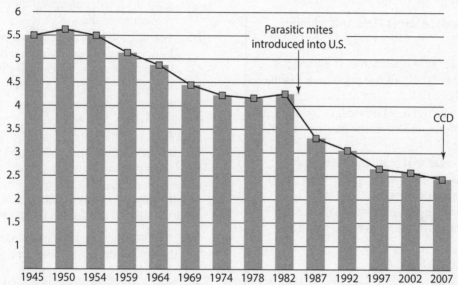

Data source: U.S. Department of Agriculture's (USDA) National Agricultural Statistics Service (Nass) NB. Data collected for producers with five or more colonies. Honey-producing colonies are the maximum number of colonies from which honey was taken during the year. It is possible to take honey from colonies that did not survive the entire year.

12. Which of the following choices is the most specific and relevant to the central focus of the paragraph?

   A. NO CHANGE
   B. animal activists
   C. beekeepers
   D. doctors

13. Which choice most effectively combines the sentences at the underlined portion?

   A. mites; and many
   B. mites, as many
   C. mites, which can be as many
   D. mites—those are as many

GO ON TO THE NEXT PAGE

14. **A.** NO CHANGE
    B. has occurred
    C. occurred
    D. have been occurring

15. **A.** NO CHANGE
    B. mites, which are indicating
    C. mites who are indicating
    D. mites; they are indicating

16. At this point, the writer is considering adding the following sentence:

    > Bees have an incredibly developed set of senses to aid in their daily routines.

    Should the writer make this addition here?

    A. Yes, because it reinforces the passage's main point about bee populations being hardy.
    B. Yes, because it acknowledges a common counterargument to the passage's central claim.
    C. No, because it blurs the paragraph's focus by introducing a new and undeveloped point.
    D. No, because it undermines the passage's claim about the vulnerability of bees.

17. **A.** NO CHANGE
    B. affected
    C. affective
    D. effective

18. **A.** NO CHANGE
    B. Yet,
    C. Alternatively,
    D. Delete the underlined word and capitalize "case."

19. **A.** NO CHANGE
    B. These are the ones who also
    C. These strong colonies also
    D. Also, these

20. Which choice is the best introductory sentence for the paragraph?

    A. NO CHANGE
    B. Clearly, scientists can now identify genes in bees, which has led to improvements in identifying causal factors of CCD in honeybees.
    C. Furthermore, recent studies show that the health of honeybees has a far-reaching impact on agriculture and economics in the U.S.
    D. Fortuitously, new information on honeybees and new technical approaches are available to help determine the underlying causes of CCD in honeybees.

21. **A.** NO CHANGE
    B. have the potential
    C. potentially have
    D. are a potential

22. Which choice offers an accurate interpretation of the data in the graph?

    A. In 2007, there were twice as many honey-producing colonies as there were in 1945.
    B. The biggest drop in honey-producing colonies occurred immediately before the parasite was introduced into the U.S.
    C. The years immediately preceding the introduction of the parasite in the U.S. saw a slight rise in the number of honey-producing colonies.
    D. In no year after the introduction of the parasite into the U.S. did honey-producing colonies decline in number.

IF YOU FINISH BEFORE TIME IS CALLED, CHECK YOUR WORK ON THIS SECTION ONLY. DO NOT WORK ON ANY OTHER SECTION IN THE TEST.

Section 3: Math Test—No Calculator

9 questions

13 minutes

Turn to Section 3 of your answer sheet to answer the questions in this section.

For **questions 1–7,** solve each problem, choose the best answer from the choices provided, and fill in the corresponding circle on your answer sheet. For **questions 8–9,** please refer to the directions before question 8 on how to enter your answers in the grid.

1. The use of a calculator **is not permitted.**
2. All variables and expressions used represent real numbers unless otherwise indicated.
3. Figures provided in this test are drawn to scale unless otherwise indicated.
4. All figures lie in a plane unless otherwise indicated.
5. Unless otherwise indicated, the domain of a given function f is the set of all real numbers x for which $f(x)$ is a real number.

Reference

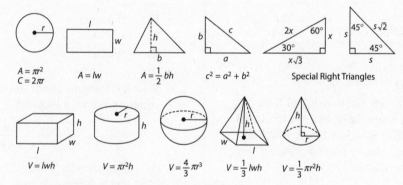

$A = \pi r^2$
$C = 2\pi r$

$A = lw$

$A = \frac{1}{2} bh$

$c^2 = a^2 + b^2$

Special Right Triangles

$V = lwh$

$V = \pi r^2 h$

$V = \frac{4}{3} \pi r^3$

$V = \frac{1}{3} lwh$

$V = \frac{1}{3} \pi r^2 h$

The number of degrees of arc in a circle is 360.

The number of radians of arc in a circle is 2π.

The sum of the measures in degrees of the angles of a triangle is 180.

GO ON TO THE NEXT PAGE

1. Kier needs to purchase supplies for his cabinet-making business. He will order hinges at \$2.89 each and handles at \$6.57 each. Which of these equations represents the total cost, T, of an order of handles, x, and 100 hinges?

   A. $T = 289 + 6.57x$
   B. $T = 657 + 2.89x$
   C. $T = 100(6.57 + 2.89x)$
   D. $T = 289(100 + 6.57x)$

2. When a division is performed, the dividend, D, the divisor, p, the quotient, q, and the remainder, r, are related by the formula $D = pq + r$. Which of these is a formula for the quotient, q, in terms of D, p, and r?

   A. $q = D - r - p$
   B. $q = \dfrac{D - r}{p}$
   C. $q = pD + r$
   D. $D = pq + r$
   $q = \dfrac{D}{p} - r$

3. A student was advised to drink at least 48 ounces of water daily, but not to exceed 100 ounces. If 8 ounces = 1 cup, which of these describes the student's optimal water intake, W, in cups, in 7 days?

   A. $6 \le W \le 87.5$
   B. $42 \le W \le 100$
   C. $336 \le W \le 700$
   D. $42 \le W \le 87.5$

4. The average of $6x^2 - 7x + 2$ and $8 - 3x + 2x^2$ is

   A. $8x^2 - 10x + 10$
   B. $7x^2 - 5x + 2$
   C. $4x^2 - 5x + 5$
   D. $9x^2 - 5x$

5. If the system below is solved correctly, what is the value of $x + y$?

   $$8x + 15y = 109$$
   $$-3x + 4y = 65$$

   A. 18
   B. 5
   C. 4
   D. −5

6. If the linear inequality $2x - 10 < -5y$ is graphed in the xy-plane, which of these points is not in the solution set?

   A. $(1, -7)$
   B. $(9, 0)$
   C. $(-7, 1)$
   D. $(-3, 0)$

7. Which statement about the solution(s) of the equation below is correct?

   $$\frac{x}{x-2} - \frac{3}{x+5} = \frac{5}{x^2 + 3x - 10}$$

   A. The equation has two solutions: $x = 2$ and $x = -5$.
   B. The equation has one solution: $x = 3$.
   C. The equation has one solution: $x = -1$.
   D. The equation has no solution.

Directions for Student-Produced Response Questions (grid-ins): Questions 8–9 require you to solve the problem and enter your answer by carefully marking the circles on the special grid. Examples of the appropriate way to mark the grid follow.

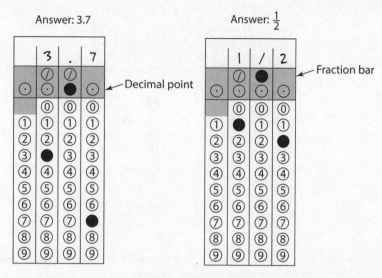

Answer: 3.7 — Decimal point

Answer: $\frac{1}{2}$ — Fraction bar

Do not grid in mixed numbers in the form of mixed numbers. Always change mixed numbers to improper fractions or decimals.

Answer: $1\frac{1}{2}$

or

GO ON TO THE NEXT PAGE

Space permitting, answers may start in any column. Each grid-in answer below is correct.

Answer: 123

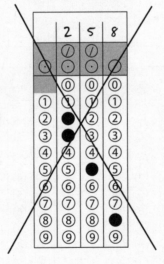

Note: Circles must be filled in correctly to receive credit. Mark only one circle in each column. No credit will be given if more than one circle in a column is marked. Example:

Answer: 258 (no credit)

Always enter the most accurate decimal value that the grid will accommodate. For example, an answer such as .8888… can be gridded as .888 or .889. Gridding this value as .8, .88, or .89 is considered inaccurate and, therefore, not acceptable. The acceptable grid-ins of $\frac{8}{9}$ are:

Answer: $\frac{8}{9}$

Be sure to write your answers in the boxes at the tops of the circles before doing your gridding. Although writing out the answers above the columns is not required, it is very important to ensure accuracy. Even though some problems may have more than one correct answer, grid only one answer. Grid-in questions contain no negative answers.

8. If the equation $2x^2 - 6x + 3 = 14x - 15$ is solved correctly, what is one possible solution?

9. A trapezoid has a height of 7 centimeters and an area of 32 square centimeters. If one base is increased by 5 centimeters and the height is doubled, what is the area of the new trapezoid, in square centimeters?

IF YOU FINISH BEFORE TIME IS CALLED, CHECK YOUR WORK ON THIS SECTION ONLY. DO NOT WORK ON ANY OTHER SECTION IN THE TEST.

Section 4: Math Test—Calculator

15 questions

23 minutes

Turn to Section 4 of your answer sheet to answer the questions in this section.

For **questions 1–13,** solve each problem, choose the best answer from the choices provided, and fill in the corresponding circle on your answer sheet. For **questions 14–15,** please refer to the directions before question 14 on how to enter your answers in the grid.

1. The use of a calculator **is permitted.**
2. All variables and expressions used represent real numbers unless otherwise indicated.
3. Figures provided in this test are drawn to scale unless otherwise indicated.
4. All figures lie in a plane unless otherwise indicated.
5. Unless otherwise indicated, the domain of a given function f is the set of all real numbers x for which $f(x)$ is a real number.

Reference

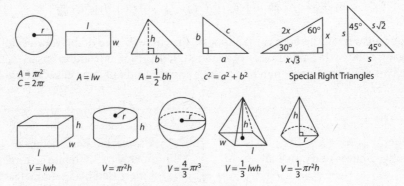

$A = \pi r^2$
$C = 2\pi r$

$A = lw$

$A = \frac{1}{2}bh$

$c^2 = a^2 + b^2$

Special Right Triangles

$V = lwh$

$V = \pi r^2 h$

$V = \frac{4}{3}\pi r^3$

$V = \frac{1}{3}lwh$

$V = \frac{1}{3}\pi r^2 h$

The number of degrees of arc in a circle is 360.

The number of radians of arc in a circle is 2π.

The sum of the measures in degrees of the angles of a triangle is 180.

Questions 1–2 refer to the following information.

The scatterplot below shows the relationship between the number of oranges on a tree and the average weight, in pounds, of a fruit on that tree.

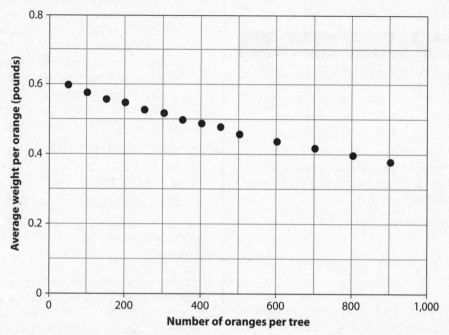

1. Based on the information provided in the scatterplot, estimate the average weight, in pounds, of oranges from a tree with 750 oranges.

   A. 0.5
   B. 0.45
   C. 0.4
   D. 0.35

2. Based on the information provided in the scatterplot, which of the following is NOT true?

   A. As the number of oranges on the tree increases, the average weight of a fruit from the tree decreases.
   B. The oranges harvested in this orchard have a weight range of approximately 0.23 pounds.
   C. The median number of oranges per tree is approximately 375.
   D. The line of best fit will have a positive slope.

3. Which of the following is equivalent to

   $$-7(2x+3)+5(9-x)+\frac{4x-6}{-2}?$$

   A. $-21x + 21$
   B. $-21x + 27$
   C. $-21x - 10$
   D. $-16x + 7$

4. If $f(x) = (2x - 1)^2$ and $g(x) = \frac{1}{2}(x+1)$, which of the following is the correct equation for the function $f(g(x))$?

   A. $f(g(x)) = x$
   B. $f(g(x)) = x^2$
   C. $f(g(x)) = (x + 1)^2$
   D. $f(g(x)) = \frac{1}{2}(2x)^2$

GO ON TO THE NEXT PAGE

35

Questions 5 and 6 refer to the following information.

The table below shows the breakdown of the U.S. House of Representatives by gender and party in 2017, according to the government website.

House of Representatives			
	Democrat	Republican	Total
Men	126	217	343
Women	67	22	89
Total	193	239	432

5. To the nearest whole percent, what percentage of the membership of the House are Republican women?

    A.   5%
    B.   9%
    C.   16%
    D.   21%

6. If a Representative is chosen at random from the House membership, what is the probability that person is a male Democrat?

    A.   56%
    B.   50%
    C.   45%
    D.   29%

7. If the system of equations below is graphed in the xy-plane, which of the following is true?

$$1 - y = 2x$$
$$y + 3 = x^2 - 2x$$

    A.   The graphs intersect at two points.
    B.   The graphs intersect at one point.
    C.   The graphs do not intersect.
    D.   The graphs share more than two points.

8. The Hassan family has budgeted to spend at least $300 but not more than $400 for a new washer and at least $250 but not more than $350 for a new dryer. A local store is offering a 15% discount on washer and dryer sets, which allows the family to consider appliances that are a bit higher priced, knowing the discount will reduce their expense. If W represents the price of the washer and D represents the price of the dryer, which of these inequalities best describes the Hassans' shopping plan?

    A. $250 \le W + D \le 400$
    B. $0.15(250) \le W + D \le 0.15(400)$
    C. $550 \le W + D \le 750$
    D. $550 \le 0.85(W + D) \le 750$

Questions 9 and 10 refer to the following information.

The table below contains selected information about bird species in three national parks. For each of the categories listed (Owls, Hummingbirds, etc.), the chart shows the number of distinct species in that group that have been identified in each of the three national parks: Glacier National Park, Montana; Everglades National Park, Florida; and Yosemite National Park, California.

Bird Species in National Parks			
	Glacier	Everglades	Yosemite
Owls	12	6	8
Pigeons, Doves	4	8	2
Swans, Geese, Ducks	32	34	6
Hummingbirds	6	3	6
Vultures, Hawks, Eagles, Falcons	19	23	14
Woodpeckers	11	9	12
TOTAL	84	83	48

9. What is the average number of species of hummingbirds for the three parks?

   A. 6
   B. 5
   C. 4
   D. 3

10. Suppose a new table were created that showed each category (owls, hummingbirds, woodpeckers, etc.) as a percentage of the total number of species in that park. For example, woodpeckers are 12 of 48, or 25% of the species in Yosemite National Park. The percentage for Owls in Everglades National Park is closest to the percentage for which category in Glacier National Park?

   A. Pigeons and Doves
   B. Woodpeckers
   C. Hummingbirds
   D. Owls

11. If the equation $ax + 2y = 4$ is graphed in the xy-plane, the line passes through the point $(-4, 8)$. What is the value of a?

   A. −5
   B. −3
   C. 3
   D. 5

12. The chart below shows the value of Ms. Bergstrom's retirement account at the end of each month for a 5-month period. Which of these is the best description of the growth of her account?

Month	1	2	3	4	5
Savings	$3,642.00	$3,678.42	$3,715.20	$3,752.36	$3,789.88

   A. A linear relationship, increasing approximately $35 per month
   B. A linear relationship, increasing approximately $40 per month
   C. An exponential relationship, increasing approximately 1% per month.
   D. An exponential relationship, increasing approximately 101% per month.

13. Indira wants to put a brace on her back gate that will stretch from corner to diagonally opposite corner. If the gate is a rectangle 50 inches high and 36 inches wide, what is the shortest board, in feet, that Indira can purchase to use for the brace?

   A. 5
   B. 6
   C. 10
   D. 62

GO ON TO THE NEXT PAGE

Directions for Student-Produced Response Questions (grid-ins): Questions 14–15 require you to solve the problem and enter your answer by carefully marking the circles on the special grid. Examples of the appropriate way to mark the grid follow.

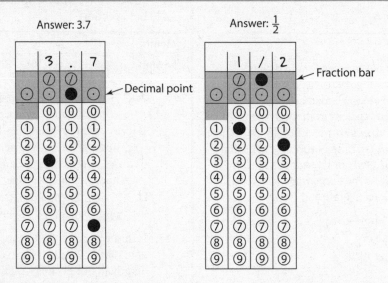

Do not grid in mixed numbers in the form of mixed numbers. Always change mixed numbers to improper fractions or decimals.

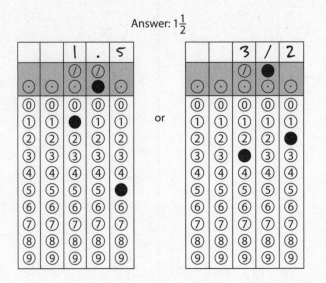

Space permitting, answers may start in any column. Each grid-in answer below is correct.

Answer: 123

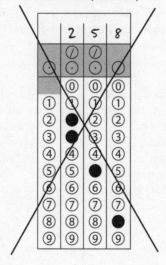

Note: Circles must be filled in correctly to receive credit. Mark only one circle in each column. No credit will be given if more than one circle in a column is marked. Example:

Answer: 258 (no credit)

GO ON TO THE NEXT PAGE

Always enter the most accurate decimal value that the grid will accommodate. For example, an answer such as .8888… can be gridded as .888 or .889. Gridding this value as .8, .88, or .89 is considered inaccurate and, therefore, not acceptable. The acceptable grid-ins of $\frac{8}{9}$ are:

Answer: $\frac{8}{9}$

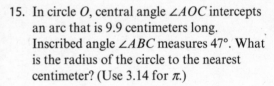

Be sure to write your answers in the boxes at the tops of the circles before doing your gridding. Although writing out the answers above the columns is not required, it is very important to ensure accuracy. Even though some problems may have more than one correct answer, grid only one answer. Grid-in questions contain no negative answers.

---

 14. The Hubble Space Telescope orbits the earth at a distance of 547 kilometers, and completes one orbit in 95 minutes. Assume the orbit is roughly circular and that the radius of the earth is 6,371 kilometers. To the nearest thousand kilometers, how far does the Hubble Telescope travel in a day? (Use 3.14 for π.)

15. In circle O, central angle $\angle AOC$ intercepts an arc that is 9.9 centimeters long. Inscribed angle $\angle ABC$ measures 47°. What is the radius of the circle to the nearest centimeter? (Use 3.14 for π.)

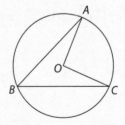

IF YOU FINISH BEFORE TIME IS CALLED, CHECK YOUR WORK ON THIS SECTION ONLY. DO NOT WORK ON ANY OTHER SECTION IN THE TEST.

Answer Key

Section 1: Reading Test

1. B	7. C	13. B	19. A
2. D	8. B	14. D	20. B
3. C	9. A	15. B	21. B
4. D	10. C	16. C	22. C
5. C	11. D	17. C	23. D
6. B	12. B	18. C	24. B

Section 2: Writing and Language Test

1. C	7. C	13. B	19. C
2. B	8. C	14. D	20. D
3. A	9. A	15. A	21. B
4. B	10. C	16. C	22. C
5. D	11. C	17. B	
6. D	12. C	18. D	

Section 3: Math Test—No Calculator

1. A (HA)	6. B (HA)
2. B (PAM)	7. C (PAM)
3. D (HA)	8. 1 or 9 (PAM)
4. C (PAM)	9. 99 (ATM)
5. C (HA)	

(HA) – The Heart of Algebra

(PSDA) – Problem Solving and Data Analysis

(PAM) – Passport to Advanced Math

(ATM) – Additional Topics in Math

Section 4: Math Test—Calculator

1. C (PSDA)	9. B (PSDA)
2. D (PSDA)	10. C (PSDA)
3. B (HA)	11. C (HA)
4. B (PAM)	12. C (PSDA)
5. A (PSDA)	13. B (ATM)
6. D (PSDA)	14. 652 through 659 (HA)
7. A (PAM)	15. 6 (ATM)
8. D (HA)	

(HA) – The Heart of Algebra

(PSDA) – Problem Solving and Data Analysis

(PAM) – Passport to Advanced Math

(ATM) – Additional Topics in Math

Answer Explanations

Section 1: Reading Test

1. **B.** Passage 1 describes the kidnapping of a young man who is at first appalled by his rough treatment. Eventually, however, he comes to see that there is both good and bad in his captors. making Choice B correct. Choice A is incorrect because he isn't constantly subjected to horrific punishments. Choice C is incorrect because the narrator isn't reflecting on only hardships and cruelties. Choice D is incorrect because the young man is kidnapped; he doesn't set out to make a life at sea.

2. **D.** The narrator indicates he came to see his kidnappers as having the faults and virtues found in most human beings, Choice D. He doesn't say that to a man, they were "uncouth beasts," so Choice A is incorrect. They don't remain unknown and unknowable (Choice B). While he did change his opinion of them, they weren't characterized mostly by their good deeds (Choice C).

3. **C.** Lines 19–22, Choice C, provide the best evidence for the answer to the previous question: *No class of man is altogether bad, but each has its own faults and virtues; and these shipmates of mine were no exception to the rule.* The other lines don't provide the necessary evidence.

4. **D.** In lines 48–51, the narrator states, *but in those days of my youth, white men were still sold into slavery on the plantations, and that was the destiny to which my wicked uncle had condemned me*, making Choice D correct. He doesn't expect to be thrown overboard and eaten by fish (Choice A); he does say that some other sailors were received by the sea and eaten by cannibal fish. He does say the ship was bound for the Carolinas (Choice B), but then he says, *you must not suppose that I was going to that place merely as an exile.* There is no indication in the passage that he plans to be a sailor for the rest of his life (Choice C).

5. **C.** In line 70, the context suggests the word *used* most nearly means "treated," Choice C. He says, *I would tell him how kindly I had myself been used upon that dry land…* Although the other choices can mean "used" in different contexts, none fits this context.

6. **B.** The author of Passage 2 states that while in the late-18th and early-19th centuries impressment was often regarded as a primary cause of the War of 1812, modern scholars now *question the true extent and impact of the practice as a precursor to war*, Choice B. He doesn't say it was direct and causative (Choice A), of little or no significance (Choice C), or outrageous and cruel (Choice D).

7. **C.** Passage 1 is a fictional account of a kidnapping; Passage 2 is a nonfictional account of impressment (essentially kidnapping men and forcing them to serve as crew aboard ships), Choice C. Choice A is incorrect because the two passages don't describe the same event. Choice B is incorrect because the events of Passage 1 take place in the 18th century, while the events of Passage 2 take place in the 19th century (see the introductory notes); thus, Passage 1 can't be based on historical events that haven't taken place. Choice D is incorrect because there is no evidence to suggest the hero of Passage 1 is based on Charles Davis.

8. **B.** Both passages deal with men who are captured and taken aboard ship, Choice B: Passage 1 describes the adventures of a young man who is kidnapped, and Passage 2 describes impressment during the War of 1812. Choice A is incorrect because Passage 1 doesn't mention the War of 1812 (since it is set a hundred years earlier). Passage 2 doesn't indicate any characteristics of the captain, so Choice C is incorrect. Neither passage mentions maritime law, so Choice D is incorrect.

9. **A.** The first paragraph discusses the limited nature of important knowledge about the biological processes of the carbon cycle, Choice A. It doesn't note a common misinterpretation of the process (Choice B), describe a counterintuitive phenomenon (Choice C), or present a recent study and a summary of its findings (Choice D).

10. **C.** The context in lines 14–15 (*...molecular scale processes that drive the carbon cycle...*) suggests the word *drive* most nearly means "power," Choice C, as the processes provide the power to drive the carbon cycle. Choice A is close in meaning, but the word *operate* suggests some kind of manipulation is involved rather than providing the power. Choice B is incorrect because it is opposite in meaning to what the context suggests. Choice D is incorrect because it is illogical for the processes to absorb the carbon cycle.

11. **D.** The passage explains that there is a critical need to understand the process to develop new approaches to climate changes, making Choice D correct. Choice A is incorrect because scientists can understand the linkages, but not control them. This knowledge won't allow scientists to regulate atmospheric carbon dioxide, so Choice B is incorrect. Choice C is incorrect because understanding the processes won't change the rate and magnitude of carbon cycling.

12. **B.** Lines 13–17, Choice B, provide the best evidence for the answer to the previous question: *Developing a more sophisticated and quantitative understanding of molecular scale processes that drive the carbon cycle represents a major challenge, but this understanding is critical for predicting impacts of global climate change.* The other choices don't provide evidence to support the answer to the previous question.

13. **B.** In line 44, the word *advance* most nearly means "improve," Choice B. In this context (*Consequently, there is a critical need to advance understanding of the systems biology properties of microbes...*), the writer clearly means better, improved understanding is needed. The other choices don't make sense in the context of this sentence.

14. **D.** According to the passage, *The carbon cycle is heavily dependent on microbial communities that decompose or transform organic material in the environment* (lines 18–21), making Choice D correct. The microbial communities don't link and release (Choice A), capture and store (Choice B), or bridge and facilitate (Choice C).

15. **B.** According to the passage, *large uncertainties remain regarding the nature and magnitude of carbon cycle processes performed by environmental microbes* (lines 29–32), making Choice B correct. Scientists know how important the carbon cycle is to regulating the levels of carbon dioxide in the atmosphere, so Choice A is incorrect. The passage doesn't say scientists are uncertain about the elements that comprise the cycle, so Choice C is incorrect. Lines 61–65 discuss the emphases of systems-level research, so Choice D is incorrect.

16. **C.** Lines 29–32, Choice C, provide the best evidence for the answer to the previous question: *However, large uncertainties remain regarding the nature and magnitude of carbon cycle processes performed by environmental microbes....* These lines indicate that scientists aren't sure about the intrinsic qualities ("the nature") and the enormity ("magnitude") of the carbon cycle processes. The other choices don't provide evidence to answer the previous question.

17. **C.** It can be inferred that addressing the global carbon cycle is difficult because researchers have incomplete understanding of some of the organisms and their functions, Choice C. The author emphasizes the need to deepen our understanding of certain biological processes of microbial communities. The passage doesn't indicate that scientists lack the necessary equipment (Choice A) or that they are more focused on the genome of microbes (Choice B). The research may be multifaceted and integrated (Choice D), but the author doesn't imply that this is causing difficulty.

18. **C.** The author mentions these companies as examples of successful companies that were started by entrepreneurs in homes and garages, Choice C. While they may hire both younger and older workers (Choice A), have shown continual growth (Choice B), and allow a percentage of workers to work from their homes (Choice D), these aren't the reasons that the author mentions them.

19. **A.** In this context, *traditional* most nearly means "customary," Choice A. There is no suggestion in the context that the benefits are outdated (Choice B), ritualistic (Choice C), or celebratory (Choice D).

20. **B.** The passage indicates that the decline in agricultural workers is most likely due to the decrease in the number of small farms, Choice B. Choice A is incorrect because the self-employment rate has declined. Choice C is incorrect because nothing in the passage refers to the average salary for agricultural workers. Choice D is incorrect because nothing in the passage compares the educational level of workers.

21. **B.** The passage indicates that the self-employment rates for older workers may be higher than for younger workers because older people have accumulated more money and more managerial skills during their careers, Choice B. While Choices A, C, and D may be true, there is no evidence in this passage to support these assertions.

22. **C.** Lines 84–89, Choice C, provide evidence for the answer to the previous question: *A possible reason is that younger workers rarely have accumulated the capital and the managerial skills required to start a business, whereas many older workers may be able to acquire these resources through their own efforts or through access to credit.* The other lines don't provide evidence to support the answer to the previous question.

23. **D.** The data in Figure 1 support lines 77–79, Choice D: *The self-employment rate for older workers continued to be higher in 2015 than that for younger workers.* Choices A and C are incorrect because the data are only given for the year 2015, so no conclusions about trends can be drawn. Choice B is incorrect because the data do not address the reasons for incorporating a business.

24. **B.** According to the data in Figure 2, the greatest number of unincorporated workers are employed in the construction and extraction industry, Choice B. Choice A is inaccurate based on the data; the percentages of unincorporated and incorporated workers are the same for office and administrative support. Choice C is the opposite of what is represented in the graph. Choice D is inaccurate; the difference is greatest in construction and extraction.

Section 2: Writing and Language Test

1. **C.** Choice C is correct because no comma is needed between *lone* and *desert* (remember the "and rule" with coordinate adjectives) and no comma is needed between *officer* and *Lonnie Zamora* because the name is essential to the meaning of the sentence. Choices A, B, and D contain unnecessary commas.

2. **B.** Choice B is correct because *startled* reveals the effect of the noise on Zamora. Choice A (*he heard*), Choice C (*he listened to*), and Choice D (*he heeded*) simply indicate Zamora heard the noise but don't describe the effect the noise had on him.

3. **A.** No change is needed; the singular subject *shack* needs the singular form of the verb. The verb *might have exploded* is needed because the action is in the past, but the police officer isn't sure of what happened. Choice B is incorrect because it doesn't use the verb *might* to indicate uncertainty. Choice C is incorrect because it uses the plural form of the verb and omits conditional *might*. Choice D is incorrect because it uses present tense plural verb *are exploding*.

4. **B.** Choice B is correct because it adds the necessary verb *was* to the sentence. Choices A, C, and D are sentence fragments because they don't have verbs for the subject *fire*.

5. **D.** Choice D is correct because it uses an apostrophe with the word *cruiser's*. Choice A is incorrect because it omits the apostrophe. Choice B incorrectly uses an apostrophe with *tire's*. Choice C misplaces the apostrophe (*cruisers'*) and incorrectly uses an unnecessary apostrophe (*tires'*).

6. **D.** Choice D correctly uses the phrase *At first glance* to indicate the transition between Zamora's seeing an object and his trying to make an identification of the object. Choices A and B illogically use transitional words of contrast, *however* and *nevertheless*. Choice C is repetitious because the sentence contains the words "…when he drove closer…"

7. **C.** The writer should not add the sentence because the arroyo is identified earlier in the paragraph (*a dry creek bed*) and that's all the information the reader needs. Choices A and B are incorrect because the reader doesn't need the information to understand the central focus of the essay, and the information isn't an essential description. Choice D is incorrect because the fact that *arroyo* is a Spanish word is irrelevant.

8. **C.** Choice C is correct because the pronoun *It* is needed to refer to the singular antecedent *rumble*. Choices A, B, and D are incorrect because they are all plural pronouns.

9. **A.** No change is needed: The infinitive form of the verb (*to rise*) is needed after the verb *begin*. Choice B incorrectly uses a transitive verb (*to raise*) that takes an object. Choice C incorrectly uses the progressive form of the verb *raising*. Choice D incorrectly changes the verb to a noun (*a rise*).

10. **C.** Choice C correctly uses the past tense verb phrase *sped away*. Choice A incorrectly uses the plural form of the verb *speed*. Choice B incorrectly uses the form of the verb *speeding*, which would require the helping verb *was* to make sense. Choice D changes the meaning of the sentence.

11. **C.** The best placement for Paragraph 7 is before Paragraph 6. The logic of the essay suggests that Officer Zamora ran to take cover after *he panicked, afraid the object was about to blow* (the end of Paragraph 5). Moving Paragraph 7 after Paragraph 4 (Choice B), after Paragraph 8 (Choice D), or leaving it where it is (Choice A) doesn't make logical chronological sense.

12. **C.** Choice C, *beekeepers*, is the most specific and relevant choice for the context. Choice A is much too general and vague. Choice B isn't relevant to the focus of the passage. Choice D is off-topic; *doctors* have nothing to do with the passage.

13. **B.** Choice B is the most effective way to combine the sentences. Choice A is incorrect; the first clause in the sentence is a subordinate clause, so the semicolon is the wrong punctuation mark, and the use of the word *and* to begin the second clause is illogical in this sentence (*and many as* doesn't make sense). Choice C is incorrect because the use of *which* makes the second clause a subordinate clause; you then have two subordinate clauses and no main clause. Choice D incorrectly uses the dash to join the clauses and *those are as many as* doesn't make sense in the sentence.

14. **D.** The correct verb form is Choice D; the plural form *have* agrees with the plural subject *outbreaks*. Choices A and B are incorrect because they use the singular form of the verb *has*. Choice C incorrectly uses the simple past tense *occurred* rather than the present perfect progressive, which is needed because the action is ongoing; it took place *for at least two years*.

15. **A.** No change is needed. Choices B, C, and D add unnecessary words.

16. **C.** The writer should not add the sentence because it blurs the paragraph's focus by introducing a new and undeveloped point—the bees' set of senses isn't relevant to the focus on CCD. The sentence doesn't reinforce the passage's main point (Choice A), acknowledge a counterargument (Choice B), or undermine the passage's claim about the vulnerability of bees (Choice D).

17. **B.** Choice B, the adjective *affected*, is the correct word to modify *beekeepers*, indicating they are influenced or touched by an external factor (in this case, ailing bee colonies). Choice A, *effected*, is the past tense of the verb *to effect*, which means to cause to happen or to bring about. Choice C, *affective*, is a psychological term that means relating to moods, feelings, and attitudes. Choice D, *effective*, is an adjective that means successful in producing a desired result.

18. **D.** Choice D is the best choice here because it fits the logic of the relationship between the two sentences. There is no reason to use a transitional word meaning as a result (Choice A, *Therefore*), nor is there any reason to use a word of contrast (Choice B, *Yet,* and Choice C, *Alternatively*) to begin the next sentence.

19. **C.** Choice C is the best choice because it corrects the vague pronoun *These* in Choice A. It's vague because it could refer to *boxes* or to the *colonies*. Choices B and D don't correct the vague pronoun error.

20. **D.** Choice D is the best introductory sentence for the paragraph because it begins with the transitional adverb *Fortuitously*, which indicates the positive outlook elaborated on in the rest of the paragraph. In addition, it indicates that the paragraph will give details about *new information* and *new technical approaches*. Choice A is too vague and unfocused. Choice B incorrectly suggests the whole paragraph will be about genes, which is actually only one detail in the paragraph. Choice C incorrectly suggests the paragraph will develop the impact of the health of honeybees on agriculture and the economy.

21. **B.** Choice B is the best choice because it corrects the sentence fragment (Choice A) by removing the pronoun *that*. Choice C incorrectly changes the meaning of the sentence. Choice D is illogical; it doesn't make sense to say *These analyses are a potential to reveal…*

22. **C.** The data in the graph support the assertion that there was a slight rise in the number of honey-producing colonies in the years immediately preceding the introduction of the parasite into the U.S. Choice A is an inaccurate interpretation of the data (2.4 in 2007 is not twice as much as 5.5 in 1945). Choice B is incorrect because the biggest drop occurred after the introduction of the parasite. Choice D is contradicted by the data in the graph: Honey-producing colonies declined in every year after the introduction of the parasite.

Section 3: Math Test—No Calculator

1. **A.** The cost of x handles and y hinges can be represented as $2.89y + $6.57x$, but only the value of y is given. Kier ordered 100 hinges. So the total is $T = 2.89(100) + 6.57x = 289 + 6.57x$. (*The Heart of Algebra*)

2. **B.** To isolate q, first subtract r from both sides, and then divide by p. $D = pq + r$ becomes $D - r = pq$, and then $\frac{D - r}{p} = q$. (*Passport to Advanced Math*)

3. **D.** The student's daily consumption of water is between 48 and 100 ounces. Over 7 days, it is between $7(48)$ and $7(100)$ ounces. That situation can be described by $336 \le W \le 700$, but the question asks for cups, so divide each number of ounces by 8. $\frac{336}{8} \le W \le \frac{700}{8}$ becomes $42 \le W \le 87.5$. (*The Heart of Algebra*)

4. **C.** To find the average, first add the polynomials.

$$\left(6x^2 - 7x + 2\right) + \left(8 - 3x + 2x^2\right) = \left(6x^2 + 2x^2\right) + \left(-7x - 3x\right) + \left(2 + 8\right)$$
$$= 8x^2 - 10x + 10$$

Then divide the total by 2: $\dfrac{8x^2 - 10x + 10}{2} = \dfrac{\cancel{2}\left(4x^2 - 5x + 5\right)}{\cancel{2}} = 4x^2 - 5x + 5$. (*Passport to Advanced Math*)

5. **C.** Multiply the first equation by 3 and the second by 8, then add to eliminate the *x*-terms.

$\begin{array}{l} 3(8x + 15y) = 3(109) \\ 8(-3x + 4y) = 8(65) \end{array}$ becomes $\begin{array}{l} 24x + 45y = 327 \\ -24x + 32y = 520 \end{array}$, and adding produces $77y = 847$. Divide by 77 to find

y: $y = \dfrac{847}{77} = \dfrac{7(121)}{7(11)} = \dfrac{\cancel{7}\,\cancel{(11)}(11)}{\cancel{7}\,\cancel{(11)}} = 11$. Substitute 11 for y in the second equation: $-3x + 4(11) = 65$,

and solve $-3x + 44 = 65$ to get $-3x = 21$ and $x = -7$. Therefore, $x + y = -7 + 11 = 4$. (*The Heart of Algebra*)

6. **B.** A sketch may help.

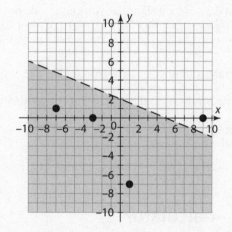

If you want to test answer choices, remember you'll be looking for the point that is NOT a solution of the inequality. Choice A gives you $2(1) - 10 < -5(-7)$ or $-8 < 35$, which is true, and therefore, not the point you're looking for. Choice B gives you $2(9) - 10 < -5(0)$ or $8 < 0$, which is not true. Therefore, Choice B is not part of the solution. (*The Heart of Algebra*)

7. **C.** Begin by factoring the denominator on the right side of the equation: $\dfrac{x}{x-2} - \dfrac{3}{x+5} = \dfrac{5}{(x-2)(x+5)}$.

Multiply through by the common denominator, $(x-2)(x+5)$, to clear fractions, and then solve.

$$(x-2)(x+5)\left(\dfrac{x}{x-2} - \dfrac{3}{x+5}\right) = (x-2)(x+5)\left(\dfrac{5}{(x-2)(x+5)}\right)$$

$$(x-2)(x+5)\dfrac{x}{x-2} - (x-2)(x+5)\dfrac{3}{x+5} = 5$$

$$x(x+5) - 3(x-2) = 5$$

$$x^2 + 5x - 3x + 6 = 5$$

$$x^2 + 2x + 1 = 0$$

$$(x+1)(x+1) = 0$$

$$x = -1$$

The equation has one solution: $x = -1$. (*Passport to Advanced Math*)

8. **1 or 9** Bring all terms to one side, equal to 0: $2x^2 - 6x + 3 = 14x - 15$ becomes $2x^2 - 20x + 18 = 0$. Notice that all the coefficients are even, a sign that you can divide both sides of the equation by 2 to get $x^2 - 10x + 9 = 0$. Factoring gives $(x - 1)(x - 9) = 0$. Setting each factor equal to zero and solving gives $x = 1$ or $x = 9$. (*Passport to Advanced Math*)

9. **99** The area of the original trapezoid is $A_{\text{original}} = \dfrac{1}{2}(b_1 + b_2)h = \dfrac{1}{2}(b_1 + b_2) \cdot 7 = \dfrac{7}{2}b_1 + \dfrac{7}{2}b_2$. If one of the bases is increased by 5 and the height is doubled from 7 to 14 centimeters, the new area is

$A_{\text{new}} = \dfrac{1}{2}(b_1 + b_2 + 5)(2h) = \dfrac{1}{2}(b_1 + b_2 + 5) \cdot 14 = 7b_1 + 7b_2 + 35$. This is equal to

$2\left(\dfrac{7}{2}b_1 + \dfrac{7}{2}b_2\right) + 35 = 2A_{\text{original}} + 35 = 2(32) + 35 = 64 + 35 = 99$. (*Additional Topics in Math*)

Section 4: Math Test—Calculator

1. **C.** The pattern of the plot is a slow decline in the average weight of fruit as the number of oranges per tree increases. The point representing 700 oranges per tree is slightly above 0.4 pounds per orange, and the point for 800 oranges per tree is at or just below 0.4 pounds. Therefore, the best estimate for 750 oranges per tree among the answer choices is 0.4. (*Problem Solving and Data Analysis*)

2. **D.** Although the rate of decrease is very slow, the plot does show that the average weight of fruit does decrease as the number of oranges on the tree increases, so Choice A is a true statement. The range of the weight of the oranges is from slightly below 0.4 (perhaps 0.37) to about 0.6; $0.6 - 0.37 = 0.23$, so the estimate of the range in Choice B is reasonable. The median, or middle value, for number of oranges per tree is between the 7th and 8th values, which are 350 and 400, so the estimate of 375 in Choice C is appropriate. Choice D, however, actually contradicts Choice A. The trend is a decreasing relationship, which would produce a negative slope, not a positive slope. Choice D is not true. (*Problem Solving and Data Analysis*)

3. **B.** Simplify $-7(2x+3)+5(9-x)+\dfrac{4x-6}{-2}$ by first distributing to remove parentheses:

$-7(2x+3)+5(9-x)+\dfrac{4x-6}{-2}=-14x-21+45-5x+\dfrac{4x-6}{-2}$. Combine like terms, and perform the

division: $-14x-21+45-5x+\dfrac{4x-6}{-2}=(-14x-5x)+45-21+\dfrac{4x}{-2}-\dfrac{6}{-2}=-19x+24-2x+3=-21x+27$.
(*The Heart of Algebra*)

4. **B.** If $f(x)=(2x-1)^2$ and $g(x)=\dfrac{1}{2}(x+1)$, you can form $f(g(x))$ by replacing x in the definition of $f(x)$

with the definition of $g(x)$: $f(x)=(2x-1)^2=\left(2\left(\dfrac{1}{2}(x+1)\right)-1\right)^2=(x+1-1)^2=x^2$. (*Passport to Advanced*

Math)

5. **A.** There are 22 Republican women out of 432 members of the House: $\dfrac{22}{432}=\dfrac{11}{216}\approx0.05$. Therefore,

approximately 5% of the House members are Republican women. (*Problem Solving and Data Analysis*)

6. **D.** The probability of an event is the number of "successes" divided by the total number of outcomes. You are choosing from a pool of 432 members, and there are 126 male Democrats who would count as

"successes": $\dfrac{126}{432}=\dfrac{63}{216}=\dfrac{21}{72}=\dfrac{7}{24}\approx0.29$. Therefore, there is a 29% chance of randomly choosing a

male Democrat. (*Problem Solving and Data Analysis*)

7. **A.**

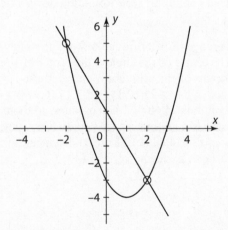

Sketching the graphs may be sufficient to see there are two points of intersection, but you can also check by solving algebraically. Use $1-y=2x$ or $1-2x=y$ to substitute into $y+3=x^2-2x$ to get $1-2x+3=x^2-2x$ or $0=x^2-4$, and solve to get $x=\pm2$. This question does not require that you find the corresponding y-coordinates, but if you wish to, substitute each x-coordinate into $1-y=2x$. When $x=2$, $1-y=2(2)$, and $y=-3$. When $x=-2$, $1-y=2(-2)$ and $y=5$. (*Passport to Advanced Math*)

8. **D.** The washer budget is $300 \leq W \leq 400$ and the dryer budget is $250 \leq D \leq 350$. The budget for the two purchases would basically be $300 + 250 \leq W + D \leq 400 + 350$, or $550 \leq W + D \leq 750$. The possibility of the 15% discount, however, means that the family will only pay $100 - 15 = 85\%$ of $W + D$. Therefore, the budget is $550 \leq 0.85(W + D) \leq 750$. (*The Heart of Algebra*)

9. **B.** The average number of hummingbird species for the three parks can be found by adding the number of species of hummingbirds in the three parks and dividing by 3: $(6 + 3 + 6) \div 3 = 15 \div 3 = 5$. There is an average of 5 species of hummingbirds. (*Problem Solving and Data Analysis*)

10. **C.** To express numbers as a percentage of all species in a park, you'll need to reference the total number of species listed for each park in the bottom row of the table. The total for Glacier National Park is 84; Everglades is 83; and Yosemite is 48. For owls in Everglades National Park, the percentage is $\frac{6}{83} \approx 0.07$, or 7%. The percentages for Glacier National Park are approximately: Pigeons and Doves, 5%; Woodpeckers, 13%; Hummingbirds, 7%; and Owls, 14%. The percentage for hummingbirds is most similar. (*Problem Solving and Data Analysis*)

11. **C.** If $ax + 2y = 4$ and, when graphed, passes through point $(-4, 8)$, that ordered pair is a solution of the equation. Replace x with -4 and y with 8 and solve for a. $a(-4) + 2(8) = 4$ becomes $-4a + 16 = 4$ or $-4a = -12$. Divide by -4 to get $a = 3$. (*The Heart of Algebra*)

12. **C.** The change in the savings amount is relatively small, so Choice D, which would more than double the amount each month, can reasonably be eliminated. Neither of the increases proposed in choices A and B is consistent for the 5 months. The best answer choice is C, an exponential relationship increasing approximately 1% per month. (*Problem Solving and Data Analysis*)

13. **B.** Use the Pythagorean theorem with $a = 50$ inches and $b = 36$ inches to get the length of the brace in inches, or convert to feet first for smaller numbers. $(50)^2 + (36)^2 = 2{,}500 + 1{,}296 = 3{,}796 = c^2$, so $c = \sqrt{3{,}796} \approx 61.61$ inches. That's about 5.1 feet. Rounding down would make the board too short, so 6 feet will be needed. (*Additional Topics in Math*)

14. **652 through 659** Values in the range of 652 through 659 are acceptable. The Hubble Space Telescope is in a roughly circular orbit. The center of the circle is the center of the earth, and the radius is the radius of the earth plus the height of the orbit above the earth, so $r = 6{,}371 + 547 = 6{,}918$ kilometers. Each orbit will cover a distance of $2\pi r = 2\pi(6{,}918) \approx 2(3.14)(6{,}918) \approx 43{,}445.04$ kilometers. Each orbit takes 95 minutes, and a day contains $24(60) = 1{,}440$ minutes, so there are $1{,}440 \div 95 \approx 15.16$ orbits. 15 orbits $\times$ 43,445 kilometers $\approx 651{,}675$ kilometers. (If you do not round before multiplying, this could be as large as $15.16 \times 43.445.04 \approx 658{,}626.8064$.) The total distance traveled is between 652 thousand and 659 thousand kilometers. (*The Heart of Algebra*)

15. **6** Arc length is a fraction of the circumference, $C = 2\pi r$. The denominator of the fraction is 360°, the full circle, and the numerator is the measurement in degrees of the central angle. That measurement is not given directly, but the inscribed angle intercepts the same arc. The measure of the inscribed angle is half the measure of the arc, and therefore, half the measure of the central angle. The inscribed angle measures 47°, so the central angle for that same arc is 94°. The arc length, 9.9 centimeters, is equal to $\dfrac{94}{360} \cdot 2\pi r$. Solve for r:

$$\frac{94}{360} \cdot 2\pi r = 9.9$$

$$\frac{47\pi}{90} r = 9.9$$

$$r = \frac{(9.9)(90)}{(47\pi)} = \frac{891}{(47\pi)} \approx 6.04$$

Therefore, the radius to the nearest centimeter is 6. (*Additional Topics in Math*)

Scoring the Diagnostic Test

To calculate your score on the Diagnostic Test, add up the total number of questions you answered correctly for each section of the test:

The Reading Test   Number correct: _____

The Writing and Language Test   Number correct: _____

The Math Tests (total number correct on both math sections) Number correct: _____

For your Reading and Writing score, look up the raw score for each section and find the converted score. Add the two converted scores (Reading Test + Writing and Language Test). Then, multiply that number times 10. That is your Reading and Writing score.

For your Math score, using the total number correct on Section 3 and Section 4, look up the raw score, and find the converted score. That is your Math score.

Raw Score (# of correct answers)	Converted Reading Test Score	Converted Writing and Language Test Score	Converted Math Test Score
24	38		760
23	37		750
22	36	38	740
21	36	37	730
20	35	36	720
19	34	35	690
18	33	33	670
17	31	31	640
16	30	30	620
15	28	29	600
14	27	28	580
13	26	27	570
12	25	26	540
11	24	25	520
10	23	24	500
9	22	22	480
8	20	21	460
7	19	19	430
6	18	17	400
5	17	16	370
4	16	15	340
3	14	13	290
2	12	12	240
1	10	10	210
0	8	8	160

V. Evidence-Based Reading and Writing: The Reading Test

A. Overview

How well do you read challenging material in different content areas? The Reading Test on the PSAT consists of 47 questions designed to assess your reading, reasoning, and comprehension skills. You have 60 minutes to complete the 47 questions. You're presented with a series of passages, ranging in content and complexity, followed by a set of questions. To answer the questions, you must refer to what the passages state **explicitly** and draw conclusions from information that is presented **implicitly**. On paired passages, you must understand each writer's point of view as well as the connections and dissimilarities. Some of the passages will be accompanied by informational graphics (charts, graphs, diagrams) to which you refer when you're answering specific questions.

Guessing strategy: There is no penalty for incorrect answers on the PSAT. This means that you should answer every question on the test. First, eliminate answer choices that appear to be irrelevant or incorrect; then, take an educated guess. If you have no idea, just fill in a circle on your answer sheet.

Here are some general strategies for successfully completing the reading passages:

- **Always read actively.** Focus on what the author is trying to tell you. Think as you read—don't allow your mind to drift. Have a mental dialogue with the text. Sometimes it's helpful to visualize and see the passage unfold in front of your eyes like a movie or to annotate (mark up the passage and take brief notes) as you read.

- **Always read any introductory material given before the passage or passages carefully.** These notes may give you important literary, historical, or scientific background.

- **If you're confused by a sentence or a paragraph, don't reread.** The sentence or paragraph may become clearer as you read, or there may not be any questions about that part of the passage. If you have to reread, do so as you answer the questions.

- **Psych yourself up and try to be interested in the passage.** Link the passage in your mind to a familiar topic. This strategy will help you stay focused. You may also want to underline key points in the passage, star them, or jot down a note or two. Just don't get so involved with underlining that you slow down and lose the sense of the passage.

- **Don't allow your personal feelings or your own knowledge about the topic to influence your answers.** Always go back to what is stated in or implied by the text to support your answer.

- **Always read *all* the answer choices before you select an answer.** Use the process of elimination as you read the answer choices. If you are sure an answer choice is wrong, cross out the letter of the choice. If you think it could be right, leave it alone. When you have read all the answer choices, look again only at the ones that are not crossed out, and evaluate their accuracy. Don't be fooled by an answer choice that makes a correct statement but does not answer the specific question. A statement may be true based on the information in the passage, but it may still be the wrong answer because it doesn't answer the question you're being asked.

- **Be on the lookout for EXCEPT questions.** For EXCEPT questions, three of the answer choices will be true. In these questions, you're looking for the answer choice that is false. Circle the word *EXCEPT* in your test booklet so you won't look for answer choices that are true.

■ **Pay particular attention to the ends of the answer choices.** Many of the answer choices start out right, but then the last word or phrase is incorrect. These are set up to trick you if you're rushing through the answer choices.

B. Content

The PSAT is designed to measure how well you read material in different content areas. In your high school classes, you read a wide range of content areas that comprise most secondary school curricula. The passages on the Reading Test are designed to evaluate your ability to understand and respond to the different reading requirements of different fields of study. The questions on each passage are crafted to reflect the varying subject-specific approaches to literacy that you're expected to demonstrate on the test. In other words, you don't read a chapter in a novel the same way that you read an analysis of a scientific experiment. You focus on a distinct set of reading techniques as you switch from subject to subject. On each test, at least one or two of the passages are accompanied by graphically represented data that you must interpret as you answer the related questions.

1. U.S. and World Literature

These passages are taken from previously published works of fiction or literary criticism. The questions address your understanding of such important literary elements as theme, characterization, and tone.

2. Analysis in History/Social Studies

These passages are drawn from important documents in U.S. history or those that are considered part of the "Great Global Conversation," documents that consider such topics as freedom and human rights. The passages cover political developments, global issues, environmental issues, and critical moments in history, and may be accompanied by graphically represented data.

3. Science

These passages are drawn from selections in science writing. The questions address your ability to understand an experiment, to analyze research findings, to compare/contrast scientific approaches, or to determine logical conclusions. The passages may be accompanied by graphically represented data.

> **Tip:** See Section C.4, "Disciplinary Literacy," for practice in specific content areas.

Note: The practice reading passages in this chapter are shorter than the actual reading passages on the PSAT and the PSAT 10. The passages on the actual PSAT range from about 500 to about 750 words.

C. Focus Skills

The Reading Test passages are designed to be interesting and informative, but quite challenging. The questions following each passage cover a wide range of reading skills. Questions require you to recognize the main idea and/or the writer's main purpose, summarize text, identify rhetorical strategies, analyze the organization of the passage and/or the relationship of a paragraph to the whole, relate graphically presented data, and determine the meaning of words in context. These skills can be organized into four main categories:

- Words in context
- Command of evidence
- Analysis of data in graphics
- Disciplinary literacy

1. Words in Context

The link between vocabulary and reading comprehension is documented in research. It is logical that if you can't understand the key words of a passage, you'll have difficulty comprehending what you're reading. By the time you take the PSAT 10 or the PSAT, you'll have had several years of language arts instruction. Your work in your classes should help you acquire a reasonably well-developed vocabulary. If not, Chapter VII, "Tier 2 Vocabulary," can help. It contains a list of Tier 2 words, those words that have been found to be most useful across a variety of subjects. These aren't obscure words that no one ever uses. They are words that are found frequently in written texts with a complexity on par with that of the PSAT and SAT reading passages. The words on the PSAT are all presented in the context of a passage; thus, you have textual support to help you determine the meaning of the word as it is used in the passage.

Don't rely on *denotation* (the dictionary meaning of a word) alone. The correct response often requires you to consider *connotation* (the suggested meaning or implication of a word).

The best approach to the vocabulary-in-context questions is to follow this method:

- Circle the word in the text.
- Reread the sentence before the one containing the word, the sentence with the word, and the following sentence.
- In your head, think of a word you know that could replace the word and still make sense in the context.
- Replace the word in the text with each of the words in the four answer choices.
- Select the answer choice that is most like the one you thought of and that makes the most sense based on the use of the word in the context.

Note: Some of the choices may fit the context, but they aren't acceptable definitions of the word. Some of the choices may also be synonyms for the word that don't fit in the context of the sentence.

For example, consider the word *clash* in the excerpt below:

One of the most memorable conflicts between religion and science occurred between Galileo Galilei (1564–1642) and the Roman Catholic Church. According to the Church, the Earth is the center of the universe. The Sun, Moon, other planets and stars revolve around the Earth. Galileo, however, argued that the Sun is the center of the solar system; the Earth and other planets revolved around the Sun. The **clash** between Galileo and the Church theologians led to his trial by the Inquisition and subsequent condemnation as a heretic.

The word *clash* has several meanings: It can mean a loud, harsh noise; a conflict; a battle; or a mismatch of colors. Ask yourself: Which one of those meanings fits best in the context of the passage? The context clues—*conflicts between religion and science, led to his trial, condemnation as a heretic*—suggest that *clash* means "conflict" in this context.

Practice

Questions 1–5 are based on the following passage.

Excerpt from *Commodore Paul Jones* by Cyrus Townsend Brady (1912).

      The ship duties in port not being arduous, the young apprentice was permitted to spend the period of the vessel's stay in America on shore under the roof of his kinsman. There he continued his studies with that zeal for knowledge which was one of his distinguishing characteristics, and which never left him in after life; for it is to be noted that he was always a student; indeed, had he not been so, his subsequent
(5) career would have been impossible. It was largely that habit of application, early acquired, that enabled him to advance himself beyond his original station. He especially applied himself to the science of navigation, the intricacies of which he speedily mastered, so that he became subsequently one of the most expert navigators that sailed the sea.

      When his countrymen heard the story of this daring and successful cruise, Paul Jones immediately
(10) became the most famous officer of the new navy. The *éclat* he had gained by his brilliant voyage at once raised him from a more or less obscure position, and gave him a great reputation in the eyes of his countrymen, a reputation he did not thereafter lose. But Jones was not a man to live upon a reputation. He had scarcely arrived at Providence before he busied himself with plans for another undertaking. He had learned from prisoners taken on his last cruise that there were a number of American prisoners, at vari-
(15) ous places, who were undergoing hard labor in the coal mines of Cape Breton Island, and he conceived the bold design of freeing them if possible.

      We are here introduced to one striking characteristic, not the least noble among many, of this great man. The appeal of the prisoner always profoundly touched his heart. The freedom of his nature, his own passionate love for liberty and independence, the heritage of his Scotch hills perhaps, ever made
(20) him anxious and solicitous about those who languished in captivity. It was but the working out of that spirit which compelled him to relinquish his participation in the lucrative slave trade. In all his public actions, he kept before him as one of his principal objects the release of such of his countrymen as were undergoing the horrors of British prisons.

1. As it is used in the passage, the word "zeal" in line 3 most nearly means

    A. respect.
    B. disregard.
    C. inflexibility.
    D. enthusiasm.

2. As it is used in the passage, the word "application" in line 5 most nearly means

    A. claim.
    B. request.
    C. diligence.
    D. submission.

3. As it is used in the passage, the word "obscure" in line 11 most nearly means

    A. incomprehensible.

    B. dark.

    C. unknown.

    D. confused.

4. As it is used in the passage, the word "striking" in line 17 most nearly means

    A. good-looking.

    B. outstanding.

    C. visible.

    D. unusual.

5. As it is used in the passage, the word "objects" in line 22 most nearly means

    A. concerns.

    B. oppositions.

    C. things.

    D. goals.

Answer Explanations

1. **D.** *Zeal* means "enthusiasm" or "passion." Jones had a zeal for knowledge that is supported by the evidence in the passage: *it is to be noted that he was always a student…* Choice A, respect, is a positive word, but it doesn't convey the strong feeling suggested by the context. Choices B and C are both negative words that can't be supported by the context.

2. **C.** *Application* has more than one meaning: It can mean diligence, or it can mean claim, request, or submission, but none of the last three words fits the meaning in context. It was Jones' habit of *application, early acquired, that enabled him to advance himself beyond his original station.* The context suggests Jones applied himself to his studies with hard work ("diligence"), which allowed him to advance in his career.

3. **C.** Depending on the context, *obscure* can mean incomprehensible, dark, unknown, or confused. In this context, *obscure* most nearly means "unknown." Jones didn't have an incomprehensible (Choice A), dark (Choice B), or confused (Choice D) position. He was raised from being unknown to having a great reputation.

4. **B.** *Striking* in this context means "outstanding"; in other contexts, it can mean good-looking (Choice A) or unusual (Choice D), but the context suggests the word refers to Jones' positive characteristic, *not the least noble among many*. The context clue *noble* should help you choose Choice B. There is no discussion of his appearance (Choice A) or his being different from others (Choice D) in this characteristic. Choice C, visible, doesn't make sense in the sentence because *the appeal of the prisoner* is not a visible characteristic.

5. **D.** *Objects* can mean things (Choice C), but the context suggests otherwise. Freeing the prisoners was one of Jones' targets or "goals" (Choice D). Neither Choice A, concerns, nor Choice B, oppositions, fits the context.

2. Command of Evidence

Command of evidence is your ability to understand the passages, to analyze the ideas, to make inferences, and to apply an idea to a similar situation. To answer these questions, you need the following skills:

- Comprehend the information in the passage.
- Identify main ideas and supporting details.
- Infer from what is implied.
- Locate the evidence for a conclusion.
- Find relationships.
- Synthesize (to combine various elements into a new whole).
- Extend ideas to an analogous (similar) situation.
- Understand the structure of a text.
- Evaluate the persuasiveness of an argument.

a. Skills: Comprehend, Find the Main Idea, and Determine the Primary Purpose

To **comprehend the content** of the passages, be an active reader. As you read, consider the writer's position, argument, or purpose. Think about any hypotheses presented, consider the implication of the facts and reasons offered as evidence, and interpret any data provided to support the writer's assertions.

To find the **main idea** of a passage, first ask yourself, "What is this passage about? If I had to summarize it in one sentence, what would I say?" Your answer to these questions is the main idea. If the passage is long and dense and contains several major points, pay particular attention to the topic sentence of each paragraph and the last sentence of the passage. These sentences will frequently give you a good sense of the main or most important idea.

Primary purpose questions ask you to figure out what the writer is trying to accomplish. Think about the writer's presentation of ideas. Ask yourself, "Does this passage present a distinct point of view, either supporting, qualifying, or refuting a position?" In these cases, if the writer's purpose is positive, it may be to defend, to advocate, to support, or to justify; if it's negative, it may be to challenge, to refute, or to question. If the position is mixed—that is, the writer defends under some circumstances and challenges under others—the purpose may be to qualify. A passage may also be objective, simply presenting the ideas without taking a stance. In these cases, the writer's purpose may be to explain, to clarify, or to explicate.

Practice

Questions 6–7 are based on the following passage.

This passage is adapted from *Notes of a Naturalist in South America* by John Ball (published in 1887).

A tour round the South American continent, which was completed in so short a time as five months, may not appear to deserve any special record; yet I am led to hope that this little book may serve to induce others to visit a region so abounding in sources of enjoyment and interest. There is no part of the world where, in the same short space of time, a traveller can view so many varied and impressive aspects

(5) of nature; while he whose attention is mainly given to the progress and development of the social condition of mankind will find in the condition of the numerous states of the continent, and the manners and habits of the many different races that inhabit it, abundant material to engage his attention and excite his interest.

Although, as the title implies, the aim of my journey was mainly directed to the new aspects of (10) nature, organic and inorganic, which South America superabundantly presents to the stranger, I have not thought it without interest to give in these pages the impressions as to the social and political condition of the different regions which I visited, suggested to an unprejudiced visitor by the daily incidents of a traveller's life. In the early period of human history, when voyages and travels were not undertaken from the view of amusement or instruction, or from political or commercial motives, the discovery of (15) adjacent countries was chiefly affected by war, and of distant regions by commerce.

6. According to the author, while the primary purpose of his book is to describe nature in South America, his secondary purpose is to

   A.   criticize a new strategy.
   B.   excite interest in an endeavor.
   C.   explain a physical phenomenon.
   D.   defend an innovative approach.

7. The author's main purpose in the second paragraph of this passage is to

   A.   present details about organic and inorganic nature in South America.
   B.   contrast the political and social conditions of the region.
   C.   rationalize those prejudices that impacted his writing.
   D.   justify his decision to digress from his main focus.

Answer Explanations

6. **B.** This purpose question asks you to think about the author's explanation as to why (other than to describe nature in South America) he wrote the passage. Try to eliminate the most obviously incorrect answer choices first. Is the author criticizing anything? He is not, so cross out Choice A. Choice C is incorrect because the author doesn't explain any particularly unusual physical phenomenon. (Don't be misled by the word *phenomenon*; it is used on the PSAT and SAT to mean any incident, occurrence, or observable fact.) Choice D is incorrect because the author does not state that his approach is innovative (new or creative), nor does he defend it. That leaves Choice B, the correct answer. Your best clue to this answer comes from the end of the first sentence: ...*I am led to hope that this little book may serve to induce others to visit a region*....

7. **D.** The author states his main purpose in the second paragraph when he explains that while his focus was mainly on nature, he felt it worthwhile to digress to share his impressions as to the social and political conditions of the different regions, Choice D. He doesn't present details about nature (Choice A), contrast the political and social conditions of the region (Choice B), or rationalize his prejudices (Choice C). Don't be fooled because he simply mentions organic and inorganic nature, political and social conditions, and prejudices.

b. Skills: Make Inferences, Locate Evidence, and Find Relationships

Inference questions ask you to understand what the author suggests or implies. The answer will not be directly stated in the passage, so you have to "read between the lines." Some questions give you line references for a phrase. For example, a question may ask, "The claim in lines 22–25 suggests primarily that…"

Here are some strategies for answering inference questions:

- First, underline, bracket, or circle the lines. Then, read around the point (the sentences before and after the specific point).
- Don't be tricked into thinking the answers will always be in those lines. Often, the best clue to the answer will be in the line just *before* the lines referred to, and sometimes the best clue will be just *after* the lines referred to.
- Try to *paraphrase* the lines (put them in your own words) to be sure you understand the gist of the lines.

Locate evidence questions ask you to find the lines that best support (or refute or undermine) a given statement. For example, a question may ask, "Which of the following lines is the best evidence to support the claim that string theory is only demonstrable through mathematical equations?" First, be sure to keep in mind exactly what you're looking for: lines that support or lines that disprove. You have to evaluate the sentences in the answer choices and select the one that provides the best evidence. You might find it helpful to bracket all the lines given in the answer choices; then, look carefully at each set of lines to determine which provides the best evidence.

Find relationship questions ask you to analyze and find connections between ideas. Transitional words can provide you with clues by setting up cause and effect (*because, since, as a result, consequently, therefore*), comparison/contrast (*unlike, similarly, in contrast*), or order of importance (*primarily, most importantly, significantly*). Find relationship questions may also ask you to determine the function of a sentence or phrase in relation to the topic as a whole. For example, a question may ask, "In relation to the passage as a whole, the last paragraph serves to…"

Practice

Questions 8–10 are based on the following passage.

The following passage is adapted from the U.S. Government Advisory Council on Historic Preservation (achp.gov).

Within the past generation, historic preservation has evolved from a limited and somewhat insular pursuit into a broad based popular movement with wide support. The reasons for this support are varied. Some desire a tangible sense of permanence and community, while others wish to know about and embrace America's heritage in a direct and personally meaningful way.

(5)   Recognition that historic preservation often is associated with economic successes is an important reason, as is the fact that many see the preservation of historic districts, sites, buildings, structures, and objects as enhancing their quality of life, adding variety and texture to the cultural landscape in which they live and work. Largely because of such highly personal responses, public support for historic preservation has flowed from the bottom up, making it in the truest sense a grassroots movement, not just

(10)   another Government program.

With passage of the National Historic Preservation Act in 1966 (NHPA), Congress made the Federal Government a full partner and a leader in historic preservation. While Congress recognized that national goals for historic preservation could best be achieved by supporting the drive, enthusiasm, and wishes of local citizens and communities, it understood that the Federal Government must set an example through
(15) enlightened policies and practices. In the words of the Act, the Federal Government's role would be to "provide leadership" for preservation, "contribute to" and "give maximum encouragement" to preservation, and "foster conditions under which our modern society and our prehistoric and historic resources can exist in productive harmony."

Indeed, an underlying motivation in passage of the Act was to transform the Federal Government
(20) from an agent of indifference, frequently responsible for needless loss of historic resources, to a facilitator, an agent of thoughtful change, and a responsible steward for future generations.

8. It can be inferred from the passage that the author would agree that

   A. the most important consequence of saving historical buildings is economic prosperity.
   B. the Government has impressed the need to invest in the past upon a somewhat reluctant populace.
   C. wide-ranging support for preserving historical sites is a relatively recent phenomenon.
   D. the Federal Government has historically been at the forefront of any movement to preserve historical artifacts.

9. Which choice presents the best evidence for the answer to the previous question?

   A. Lines 1–2 ("Within the…support.")
   B. Lines 5–8 ("Recognition…work.")
   C. Lines 11–12 ("With passage…preservation.")
   D. Lines 15–18 ("In the words…harmony.'")

10. Which of the following best describes the relationship between "Some" (line 3) and "others" (line 3) on one hand and the Federal Government on the other?

   A. The Federal Government has spearheaded the preservation movement while "Some" and "others" have followed.
   B. The Federal Government has forcefully resisted the position of "Some" and "others."
   C. The Federal Government has responded positively to the preservation movement initiated by "Some" and "others."
   D. The Federal Government has been an indifferent follower of the energetic efforts of "Some" and "others."

Answer Explanations

8. **C.** The author states that the historic preservation movement has evolved only in the past generation, Choice C. Choice A is incorrect because while the author mentions economic success (line 5), he doesn't say it is the most important consequence. Choice B is incorrect because the author makes the point that the people inspired the Federal Government to engage in historical preservation (lines 1–2). Choice D is incorrect because the author indicates that the Federal Government followed the leadership of the populace (the grassroots movement described in lines 8–10).

9. **A.** The first sentence (lines 1–2) offers the best support for question 8. Choices B, C, and D deal with other aspects of the preservation movement.

10. **C.** The author explains that the Federal Government responded to the grassroots (from the bottom up) movement with full support, Choice C: *While Congress recognized that national goals for historic preservation could best be achieved by supporting the drive, enthusiasm, and wishes of local citizens and communities, it understood that the Federal Government must set an example through enlightened policies and practices.* Choice A is incorrect because the Federal Government didn't spearhead the movement. Choice B is incorrect because the Federal Government didn't resist the movement. Choice D is incorrect because the Federal Government was not indifferent to the wishes of the populace.

c. Skills: Synthesize and Extend Reasoning

Synthesis questions ask you to integrate information. You may be asked to draw on more than one source, perhaps from introductory material or from one passage to another in paired reading passages. A typical synthesis question might ask you to consider what the writer of Passage 1 would say about an idea in Passage 2. You might also be asked to find an idea with which both writers would agree or disagree.

Extended reasoning questions require you to extrapolate—that is, to use critical thinking to go beyond what is directly stated in the passage. You must draw conclusions from what you read. These questions will ask you to *infer* (to draw a conclusion from what the author implies). The question may ask you what the author *suggests* or may ask what you can *assume* from the passage. These questions may ask you to apply the reasoning in the passage to a new but analogous situation.

Here are some strategies to consider when answering extended reasoning questions:

- Although the answer will not be directly stated in the passage, always use textual evidence to support your answer.
- Be careful not to allow your own opinions to influence your answer to the question. There will be hints in the passage to guide you to the correct answer choice.

Practice

Questions 11–13 are based on the following passages.

Passage 1 is adapted from the National Park Service website (nps.gov). Passage 2 is written by a citizen concerned about wolf reintroduction.

Passage 1

The gray wolf was present in Yellowstone when the park was established in 1872. Today, it is difficult for many people to understand why early park managers would have participated in the extermination of wolves. After all, the Yellowstone National Park Act of 1872 stated that the Secretary of the Interior "shall provide against the wanton destruction of the fish and game found within said Park." But this
(5) was an era before people, including many biologists, understood the concepts of ecosystem and the interconnectedness of species. At the time, the wolves' habit of killing prey species (mostly deer and sheep) was considered "wanton destruction" of the animals. Between 1914 and 1926, at least 136 wolves were killed in the park; by the 1940s, wolf packs were rarely reported. By the mid-1900s, wolves had been almost entirely eliminated from the 48 states.

(10)   In the 1960s, National Park Service wildlife management policy changed to allow populations to manage themselves. Many suggested at the time that for such regulation to succeed, the wolf had to be a part of the picture. Also in the 1960s and 1970s, national awareness of environmental issues and consequences led to the passage of many laws designed to correct the mistakes of the past and help prevent similar mistakes in the future. One such law was the Endangered Species Act, passed in 1973. The U.S.

(15)   Fish and Wildlife Service is required by this law to restore endangered species that have been eliminated, if possible. By 1978, all wolf subspecies were on the federal list of endangered species for the lower 48 states except Minnesota.

    In 1991, Congress provided funds to the U.S. Fish and Wildlife Service to prepare, in consultation with the National Park Service and the U.S. Forest Service, an environmental impact statement (EIS) on

(20)   restoration of wolves. In June 1994, after several years and a near-record number of public comments, the Secretary of the Interior signed the Record of Decision for the final EIS for reintroduction of gray wolves to Yellowstone National Park and central Idaho.

Passage 2

    Many concerned citizens—including me—oppose the reintroduction of wolves into Yellowstone National Park and other park areas. I don't believe that wolves are an endangered species. Indeed, I have

(25)   done research and found that wolf packs exist in areas all over the world. And, in locales where the wolf populations have been decimated, wolves have naturally migrated in from other, less populated areas. In addition, reintroduction isn't cheap. It comes with extensive costs. Just the process of capturing and reintroducing wolves will cost American taxpayers millions of dollars, not to mention the economic loss to ranchers and livestock raisers when wolves attack sheep and other livestock. I am not alone in my

(30)   objections. Many local citizens resent the government and animal rights activists coming in and interfering in local affairs.

11. Which choice best describes the relationship between the passages?

    A.   Passage 2 remains objective, while Passage 1 takes a strong affirmative position.
    B.   Passage 2 predicts the negative consequences of the objective put forth in Passage 1.
    C.   Passage 1 is critical of conclusions reached in Passage 2.
    D.   Passage 1 refutes the findings expressed in Passage 2.

12. Which situation is most analogous to the objective of the Endangered Species Act (1973)?

    A.   Architects find that in building a new nuclear reactor, they have displaced a flock of rare birds. They set up a garden in the courtyard of the new building to provide adequate nesting grounds for the rare birds.
    B.   Archeologists uncover fossil remains of a previously unknown plant-eating dinosaur and remove the remains to a laboratory for further examination.
    C.   Zoologists introduce a non-native lizard to a remote island. In response, native species adapt to the new inhabitant by building their nests higher in the trees.
    D.   Engineers discover that in dredging the Swifter River to open it to watercraft, they have destroyed all evidence of a plant variety. They remove some plants of this variety from the Roman River and transplant them to the Swifter River.

13. On which point would the authors of both passages agree?

    A. The high cost of reintroducing wolves makes the process a burden on the taxpayer.

    B. Wolf packs present a danger to human beings who camp in Yellowstone National Park.

    C. Wolves are natural predators and may present a danger to livestock.

    D. Wolves are now considered an important part of the ecosystem of Yellowstone National Park.

Answer Explanations

11. **B.** Passage 2 suggests the negative repercussions of wolf reintroduction (high costs, dead livestock) presented in Passage 1, making Choice B correct. Choice A is incorrect because Passage 2 isn't objective (unbiased), and Passage 1 is objective. Choice C is incorrect because Passage 1 doesn't address the conclusions reached in Passage 2. Choice D is incorrect because Passage 1 doesn't refute the findings (nor are there any real findings) expressed in Passage 2.

12. **D.** Choice D presents the situation most analogous to the translocation suggested by the Endangered Species Act: A species is exterminated and then officially reintroduced from another location. The situation in Choice A simply repairs the original location for displaced birds. Choice B doesn't involve any translocation of a living organism. Choice C involves introducing a non-native species rather than translocating a native species.

13. **C.** Both passages state that wolves prey on livestock, making Choice C correct. Choice A is incorrect because Passage 1 doesn't mention the cost to taxpayers. Choice B is incorrect because neither passage mentions wolf attacks on human beings. Choice D is implied in Passage 1 but not in Passage 2.

d. Skills: Understand Structure and Evaluate Persuasiveness

Understand structure questions ask you to recognize the author's organizational plan. The plan will vary according to the author's purpose. Here are some examples:

- In a narrative passage, the author might tell a linear story—chronologically recounting events—or he or she might use flashbacks or flash-forwards to reveal the plot.
- In an expository passage (one that explains), an author might compare and contrast or use a cause-and-effect structure.
- In a persuasive passage, an author might make an assertion, defend the assertion, challenge other points of view, and defend his or her position.

Evaluate persuasiveness questions ask you to ascertain the effectiveness of the author's argument. Ask yourself these questions:

- Is the argument convincing?
- Is the reasoning logical?
- Has the author provided adequate evidence for his or her conclusions?
- Does the argument remain general or are there specific and appropriate examples to prove the claim?
- How does the author make his or her case?

Practice

Questions 14–15 are based on the following passage.

The following passage is the text of a speech given by George Graham Vest (1830–1904), a U.S. senator from Missouri from 1879 to 1903 and one of the leading orators and debaters of his time. Early in his legal career, Vest gave this speech in court while he represented a man who sued another for the killing of his dog.

Gentlemen of the Jury

The best friend a man has in the world may turn against him and become his enemy. His son or daughter that he has reared with loving care may prove ungrateful. Those who are nearest and dearest to us, those whom we trust with our happiness and our good name, may become traitors to their faith. The money that a man has, he may lose. It flies away from him, perhaps when he needs it most. A man's
(5) reputation may be sacrificed in a moment of ill-considered action. The people who are prone to fall on their knees to do us honor when success is with us, may be the first to throw the stone of malice when failure settles its cloud upon our heads.

The one absolutely unselfish friend that man can have in this selfish world, the one that never deserts him, the one that never proves ungrateful or treacherous, is his dog. A man's dog stands by him in pros-
(10) perity and in poverty, in health and in sickness. He will sleep on the cold ground, where the wintry winds blow and the snow drives fiercely, if only he may be near his master's side. He will kiss the hand that has no food to offer. He will lick the wounds and sores that come in encounters with the roughness of the world. He guards the sleep of his pauper master as if he were a prince. When all other friends desert, he remains. When riches take wings, and reputation falls to pieces, he is as constant in his love as the sun in
(15) its journey through the heavens.

If fortune drives the master forth, an outcast in the world, friendless and homeless, the faithful dog asks no higher privilege than that of accompanying him, to guard him against danger, to fight against his enemies. And when the last scene of all comes, and death takes his master in its embrace and his body is laid away in the cold ground, no matter if all other friends pursue their way, there by the grave-
(20) side will the noble dog be found, his head between his paws, his eyes sad, but open in alert watchfulness, faithful and true even in death.

14. During the course of the first two paragraphs, the speaker shifts his focus from

   A. a personal recollection of failed relationships to a general statement of satisfaction with a present relationship.
   B. a reflection on expected relationships to his desire for a new relationship.
   C. a rebuttal of a public failure to a testimony of private success.
   D. a recitation of the failure of traditionally supportive relationships to an explication of a consistently supportive one.

15. The speaker tries to persuade his audience by

   A. belittling the argument of those who disagree with his position.
   B. explaining his position using generalities, while never acknowledging the counterargument.
   C. presenting the antithetical position before presenting his counterargument.
   D. claiming the moral superiority of his position in direct contrast to the baseness of the counterargument.

Answer Explanations

14. **D.** In the first paragraph, the speaker lists traditional relationships (friends, children) that may go bad. He then contrasts these with the one consistently supportive relationship (man and his dog), Choice D. The speaker doesn't recall failed personal relationships because he speaks of "a man" rather than "I." (Choice A). Choice B is incorrect because the speaker doesn't express a desire for a new relationship. Choice C is incorrect because the speaker doesn't rebut a public failure nor testify to a private success.

15. **B.** The speaker never acknowledges that a counterargument (a dog may be disloyal) may exist, and he speaks in sweeping generalities: *A friend may…, a son or daughter may…* (Choice B). He doesn't belittle the opinions of those who disagree with him (Choice A). He doesn't present the antithetical opinion before presenting his counterargument (Choice C). And, he doesn't claim the moral superiority of his position (Choice D).

3. Analysis of Data in Graphics

So much information in today's highly technological world is presented quantitatively in the form of charts, graphs, or diagrams that statistical interpretation skills are deemed essential for college readiness. You're expected to be able to read and interpret statistical data that accompanies the reading passages. To do this, you must carefully examine the graph or chart, not only the data represented on the graph or chart, but also (and equally important) the title, the *x*-axis, and the *y*-axis. You should also consider what is NOT represented on the chart or graph.

Practice

Questions 16–17 are based on the following passage and supplementary material.

The following passage and accompanying graph are adapted from the New York State Department of Environment Conservation website (dec.ny.gov).

     During the last century, human impacts on our planet have led to an increasing and alarming loss of biodiversity. Scientists estimate that current extinction rates exceed those of prehistoric mass extinctions. Loss of biodiversity also means loss of genetic diversity and loss of ecosystems.

     Loss of suitable habitat is the major cause for declines in species populations. Development, wetland fill-
(5) ing, and other activities not only reduce the total amount of habitat, but also fragment remaining forest, grassland, and wetland habitat into patches too small and too isolated to support some animal species.

     In addition, the spread of invasive non-native species has dramatically changed the composition of New York's lands and wildlife, often reducing or replacing native species populations. For example, the chestnut blight fungus from Asia nearly wiped out the American chestnut within 30 years. Now, this
(10) formerly common and tall tree is much reduced in number and in size. While pollution has been greatly reduced over the last 40 years, acid rain, pesticides, and fertilizers still alter the chemical balance of New York's lakes and rivers to the detriment of fish and other aquatic life.

     In the past, unregulated commercial hunting decimated populations of many species, and even led to the extinction of the passenger pigeon, once abundant in New York. Today, turtles and snakes continue
(15) to be poached and collected illegally for the pet trade. Worldwide, populations of many fish species are threatened by overharvesting.

Climate change may cause some species to shift their ranges out of New York State or to higher elevations. Other species may be able to adapt to the new conditions. Those species that cannot move or adapt may eventually be completely extirpated.

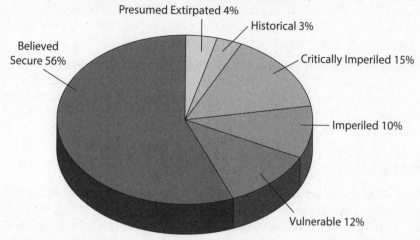

The Six Categories of New York's Biodiversity

Presumed Extirpated 4%

Historical 3%

Believed Secure 56%

Critically Imperiled 15%

Imperiled 10%

Vulnerable 12%

Presumed Extirpated: All known occurrences are gone and there is little chance of finding new populations.
Historical: No occurrences have been reported in the last 15 years, but more survey work is needed. These may still be present within New York or they may be extirpated.
Critically Imperiled: Known at 5 or fewer locations in the state.
Imperiled: Known at 6 to 20 locations.
Vulnerable: Known at 21 to 100 locations.
Believed Secure: Known at more than 100 locations.

16. Which of the following statements does the evidence in both the passage and the chart support?

   A. More than one-half of the fauna and flora in New York State is vulnerable or at risk for extinction.

   B. Some previously extant populations in New York have completely disappeared from the state.

   C. More species are vulnerable than are critically imperiled in New York State.

   D. Human encroachment on habitats is the leading cause of the loss of biodiversity in New York State.

17. Data from the graph indicates that

   A. 12% of the known populations have been decimated by acid rain, pesticides, and fertilizers that alter the chemical balance of New York's lakes and rivers.

   B. more than 10% of the populations have not been seen in New York State for the past 15 years and are presumed extirpated.

   C. in 15 years, more species will be listed as historical or presumed extirpated than are listed as vulnerable.

   D. more populations are known at 5 (or fewer) to 20 locations than are known at 21 to 100 locations.

Answer Explanations

16. **B.** According to the passage, the passenger pigeon, once abundant, is extinct in New York State. The passenger pigeon is an example of one species in the 4% of the population that is presumed extirpated. Choice A is inaccurate based on the evidence in the chart (less than half is vulnerable or at risk). Choice C is also inaccurate based on the evidence in the chart (15% critically imperiled; 12% vulnerable). Choice D cannot be supported by evidence from the graph because the chart doesn't list the causes of population loss.

17. **D.** The categories of critically imperiled (15%) and imperiled (10%), together known at 5 (or fewer) to 20 locations, account for more populations than those categorized as vulnerable (12%), known at 21 to 100 locations, making Choice D correct. Choice A is incorrect because the graph doesn't note the causes of extinction. Choice B is inaccurate; 7% of populations have not been seen in 15 years and/or are presumed extirpated. There is no evidence in the graph to support the prediction in Choice C.

4. Disciplinary Literacy

Disciplinary literacy is the ability to read, write, listen, speak, think critically, and perform in different ways and for different purposes. Each discipline has a specific vocabulary (think "metaphorical language" in literature; "claims," "premises," and "factions" in history/social studies; and "hypothesis formation" and "variables" in science). Thus, while you may be reading to understand character motivation in a fictional excerpt, you're reading to evaluate multiple sources of information in science and social studies. Some of the passages will be paired readings, and some of the history/social studies or science passages will contain information in chart, table, or graph form.

a. Literature

The literature selections will be taken from both classic and contemporary works of literature. They may also be from works of literary criticism (informational writing about works of literature).

Here are some strategies for reading literature passages:

- If the passage is an excerpt from a novel or a short story, try to envision the scene in your imagination.
- Picture the characters, and try to get inside their minds to understand their motivations, their moods, their attitudes, and their interaction with other characters.
- As you read, take note of the author's diction (choice of words). The word choice will reveal the author's tone or attitude toward the characters; does he or she admire them? Despise them? Remain objective?

Practice

Questions 18–20 are based on the following passage.

The following passage is an excerpt from the novel *Emma* (1815) by Jane Austen.

> Mrs. Bates, the widow of a former vicar of Highbury, was a very old lady, almost past every thing but tea and quadrille. She lived with her single daughter in a very small way, and was considered with all the regard and respect which a harmless old lady, under such untoward circumstances, can excite. Her daughter enjoyed a most uncommon degree of popularity for a woman neither young, handsome, rich,

(5)   nor married. Miss Bates stood in the very worst predicament in the world for having much of the public favour; and she had no intellectual superiority to make atonement to herself, or frighten those who might hate her into outward respect. She had never boasted either beauty or cleverness. Her youth had passed without distinction, and her middle of life was devoted to the care of a failing mother, and the endeavour to make a small income go as far as possible. And yet she was a happy woman, and a woman

(10)   whom no one named without good-will. It was her own universal good-will and contented temper which worked such wonders. She loved every body, was interested in every body's happiness, quicksighted to every body's merits; thought herself a most fortunate creature, and surrounded with blessings in such an excellent mother, and so many good neighbours and friends, and a home that wanted for nothing. The simplicity and cheerfulness of her nature, her contented and grateful spirit, were a recommendation to

(15)   every body, and a mine of felicity to herself. She was a great talker upon little matters, which exactly suited Mr. Woodhouse, full of trivial communications and harmless gossip.

18. The author's attitude toward Miss Bates is

    A.   gently admiring.
    B.   mockingly nasty.
    C.   slightly disdainful.
    D.   slavishly worshipful.

19. By describing Miss Bates as having an "uncommon degree of popularity," the narrator implies

    A.   there was no obvious reason for Miss Bates' status in the community.
    B.   Miss Bates' beauty and wealth were universally admired.
    C.   the chief attraction of Miss Bates was her extraordinary intellectual superiority.
    D.   Miss Bates' sense of filial obligation was the quality that most inspired her attractiveness to others.

20. On line 15, the word "mine" most nearly means

    A.   pit.
    B.   excavation.
    C.   source.
    D.   possession.

Answer Explanations

18. **A.** To understand the narrator's attitude toward this character, you must look at the language she uses to describe her. Miss Bates is described as living in a *small way* (line 2), yet she has a simple, cheerful nature and universal good will. Use the process of elimination to cross out choices B and C because they're too negative. Choice D is too strong to be supported by the text; the narrator sees Miss Bates' faults as well as her strengths.

19. **A.** After stating that Miss Bates had an *uncommon degree of popularity*, the narrator implies that this popularity is unexpected, for she was *neither young, handsome, rich, nor married*, characteristics that might justify her popularity. Choice B is incorrect because Miss Bates is neither beautiful nor wealthy. Choice C is incorrect because the narrator says, "she had no intellectual superiority." Choice D is incorrect: While Miss Bates does have a sense of filial responsibility, nowhere does the narrator indicate that this quality is the reason for her popularity.

20. **C.** To answer this vocabulary-in-context question, remember the techniques from section C.1, "Words in Context." Circle the word and use the surrounding context to help you determine the meaning. While a *mine* can be a pit (Choice A) or an excavation (Choice B), neither of these meanings fits the context. Choice C, source, is the best answer because the context suggests her simplicity and cheerfulness gave her (were a source of) happiness. Choice D, possession, doesn't make sense in the context of the passage.

b. History/Social Studies

The history/social studies selection will be taken from important documents in U.S. history and/or writings about important issues in politics and the social sciences. For example, you may read Lincoln's Gettysburg Address, an anthropological discussion of tribal rituals, a linguistic analysis of gender differences, a study of conflicting educational practices, or an economic analysis of inflation.

Here are some strategies for reading history/social studies passages:

- Look for the writer's point of view. Try to ascertain any bias.
- Find the writer's purpose. What is he or she trying to accomplish?
- Evaluate the evidence in the passage: Does it support the writer's claims?
- Consider what information the writer has left out.
- If you're reading a historical document, consider the events at the time of writing.

Practice

Questions 21–23 are based on the following passage.

The following passage is adapted from *Anthropology* by Robert R. Marett (1912).

Anthropology is the whole history of man as fired and pervaded by the idea of evolution. Man in evolution—that is the subject in its full reach. Anthropology studies man as he occurs at all known times. It studies him as he occurs in all known parts of the world. It studies him body and soul together—as a bodily organism, subject to conditions operating in time and space, which bodily organism is in
(5)   intimate relation with a soul-life, also subject to those same conditions. Having an eye to such conditions from first to last, it seeks to plot out the general series of the changes, bodily and mental together, undergone by man in the course of his history. Its business is simply to describe. But, without exceeding the limits of its scope, it can and must proceed from the particular to the general; aiming at nothing less than a descriptive formula that shall sum up the whole series of changes in which the evolution of man
(10)   consists. Simply that all the forms of life in the world are related together; and that the relations manifested in time and space between the different lives are sufficiently uniform to be described under a general formula, or law of evolution.

This means that man must, for certain purposes of science, toe the line with the rest of living things. And at first, naturally enough, man did not like it. He was too lordly. For a long time, therefore, he pre-
(15)   tended to be fighting for the Bible, when he was really fighting for his own dignity. Now-a-days, however, we have mostly got over the first shock to our family pride. We are all Darwinians in a passive kind of way. But we need to Darwinize actively. In the sciences that have to do with plants, and with the rest of the animals besides man, naturalists have been so active in their Darwinizing that the pre-Darwinian stuff is once and for all laid by on the shelf. When man, however, engages on the subject of his noble self,
(20)   the tendency still is to say: We accept Darwinism so long as it is not allowed to count, so long as we may go on believing the same old stuff in the same old way.

21. The author's primary purpose is to

    A. rebut the basic tenets of Darwinism.
    B. define the scope of a field of study.
    C. challenge an existing theory of genesis.
    D. question the scientific basis of religion.

22. It can be inferred that "the first shock to our family pride" (line 16) is the idea that

    A. the body and soul are jointly controlled by the laws of time and space.
    B. anthropology is concerned with mankind in all parts of the world.
    C. man is subject to the same laws of evolution as other living creatures.
    D. mankind has undergone both physical and mental changes through the ages.

23. Which choice best supports the author's claim that a particular method of reasoning is most necessary to accomplish the goal of anthropology?

    A. Lines 3–5 ("It studies…conditions.")
    B. Lines 7–10 ("But, without…consists.")
    C. Line 13 ("This means …things.")
    D. Lines 17–19 ("In the sciences…shelf.")

Answer Explanations

21. **B.** The author's purpose is to explain the scope of anthropology (Choice B). He defines the field in his first paragraph and then goes on to explain the ramifications of his explanation in the second paragraph. Choice A is incorrect because he doesn't argue against the tenets of Darwinism; in fact, he states, *But we [anthropologists] need to Darwinize actively.* He doesn't challenge an existing theory of genesis (Choice C), although he does mention the Bible in the second paragraph. Choice D is incorrect because he doesn't discuss the scientific basis of religion.

22. **C.** The author implies that man is too "lordly" to accept that he is subject to the same laws of evolution as other animals, the Bible notwithstanding. This is the shock to our humanly pride. He states, *This means that man must, for certain purposes of science, toe the line with the rest of living things.* Choices A, B, and D are presented as accepted ideas rather than as radical pronouncements that would affront the pride of "lordly" and "noble" humankind.

23. **B.** In lines 7–10 (*But, without exceeding the limits of its scope, it can and must proceed from the particular to the general; aiming at nothing less than a descriptive formula that shall sum up the whole series of changes in which the evolution of man consists.*), the author sets forth his prescribed methodology (from particular to general) and the goal of anthropology (to create a descriptive formula). Choice A analyzes how anthropology discusses man. Choice C states that man must accept that he is subject to the same laws as all other animals. Choice D supports a Darwinian approach to anthropology.

c. Science

Science selections may address historical foundations for scientific knowledge or current explorations in biology, chemistry, physics, or Earth science. Some science readings will be accompanied by graphs or charts. Some passages may describe experiments or contrast theories.

Here are some strategies for reading science passages:

- Distinguish between fact and opinion in the presentation of information.
- Evaluate the effectiveness of a conclusion based on the evidence in the passage.
- Be able to cite evidence from the text to support an assertion.
- Read the title of any accompanying graphic and consider what information it relays.
- Look carefully at the labels on the x-axis and the y-axis of a graph to be sure you are aware of the variables.
- Use context clues to identify critical information.

As you read, consider the transitional words that the author chooses to establish relationships.

Here are some words that signal contrast:

although	however	rather than
but	in spite of	yet
despite	instead	
even though	nevertheless	

Here are some words that signal similarity:

and	furthermore	likewise
for example	in addition	moreover

Here are some words that signal a cause-and-effect relationship:

as a result	consequently	since
because	hence	therefore

Practice

The following passage is adapted from *Systems Biology for Sustainable Bioenergy* published by the U.S. Department of Energy Genomic Science Program.

Questions 24–27 are based on the following passage.

Properly designed biofuel feedstock[1] systems can be considerably more sustainable than their grain-based counterparts, avoiding competition with food production and potentially delivering ecosystem services not currently provided by existing systems. Realizing this potential is not necessarily straightforward, however. Feedstocks grown on "marginal" lands (i.e., land that is less fertile and more

[1]A feedstock is defined as any renewable, biological material that can be used directly as a fuel, or converted to another form of fuel or energy product.

(5) water stressed and prone to erosion) will be exposed to multiple stressors simultaneously. To achieve reliable and sustainably high yields, bioenergy feedstocks must have the capacity to adapt and maintain productivity even in such challenging environments. In particular, feedstocks need an enhanced capacity to use water and nutrients efficiently, acquire nitrogen and phosphorus from nutrient-depleted soils, and withstand pests and disease. These components interact in ways that cannot always be predicted from
(10) individual factors, yet it is the net effect of all interactions that lends sustainability attributes. Providing climate mitigation and improved air, soil, and water quality requires knowledge of all the organisms and environmental factors that contribute to the sustainability of highly productive ecosystems.

Recent advances in the systems biology of both plants and microbes have the potential to contribute significantly to the understanding of these interacting pieces and therefore to the design of sustainable
(15) biofuel systems. Linking these advances to those in ecosystem science provides an unprecedented opportunity to substantially advance both the fundamental knowledge of systems biology in general and the more specific ability to design sustainable biofuel systems.

Plant productivity, defined as plants' ability to fix carbon dioxide into biomass, is an essential characteristic of sustainable biofuel systems. In most agricultural ecosystems, plant productivity is limited by a deficiency in
(20) resources such as light, water, and nutrients. In particular, plant traits enabling the efficient use of water, nitrogen, and phosphorus are likely to become increasingly important as climate change brings about shifting and potentially volatile precipitation and temperature patterns. Resource-efficient, sustainable agroecosystems are capable of converting valuable inputs such as water and nutrients into valuable outputs with minimal waste.

24. The author indicates which of the following as an advantage of biofuel feedstock systems?

    A. They avoid competition with other non-sustainable energy sources.

    B. They provide nitrogen and phosphorus to the soil.

    C. They are exposed to multiple stressors.

    D. They compensate for deficiencies in existing systems.

25. The author uses the phrase "the net effect" (line 10) to suggest

    A. the way in which air, soil, and water form a mesh.

    B. the cumulative interactions of organisms and environmental factors.

    C. the way in which each individual factor can be used to predict success.

    D. the barrier that must be overcome to achieve sustainability.

26. Which choice provides the best evidence for the answer to the previous question?

    A. Lines 3–4 ("Realizing…however.")

    B. Lines 5–7 ("To achieve…environments.")

    C. Lines 10–12 ("Providing…ecosystems.")

    D. Lines 19–20 ("In most…nutrients.")

27. As it is used in line 10, "lends" most nearly means

    A. loans.

    B. charges.

    C. provides.

    D. borrows.

Answer Explanations

24. **D.** The author states that one of the advantages of feedstock is *delivering ecosystem services not currently provided by existing systems* (lines 2–3), Choice D. He doesn't discuss non-sustainable energy sources (Choice A). The systems acquire nitrogen and phosphorus from the soil, so Choice B is incorrect. Feedstocks are exposed to multiple stressors (Choice C), but this is a drawback, not an advantage.

25. **B.** The author uses the phrase *the net effect* to describe the way all the organisms and environmental factors work together to provide sustainability (lines 10–12), Choice B. He never mentions a mesh of air, soil, and water (Choice A). Choice C is the opposite of what he says: not individual factors, but the interaction of multiple factors. Choice D is incorrect because the author doesn't use the phrase to refer to a barrier to success.

26. **C.** Lines 10–12 (*Providing climate mitigation and improved air, soil, and water quality requires knowledge of all the organisms and environmental factors that contribute to the sustainability of highly productive ecosystems.*) provide the best evidence for the answer to question 25. Choices A, B, and D refer to other aspects of the issue and don't provide any evidence to explain the net effect.

27. **C.** To answer this vocabulary-in-context question, remember the techniques from section C.1, "Words in Context." Circle the word and use the surrounding context to help you determine the meaning. The passage states *it is the net effect of all interactions that lends sustainability attributes.* The author means that the net effect provides sustainability attributes, Choice C. Choice A is a meaning of *lends* that doesn't fit the context here. Choice B (charges) also doesn't fit the context. Choice D (borrows) is an antonym of one meaning of *lends*.

D. Additional Practice

Directions: Carefully read the passage below and answer the questions that follow the passage. Answer the questions based on the content of the passage: both what is stated and what is implied in the passage, as well as any introductory material before the passage and any accompanying graphs or charts.

Note: These practice passages may be shorter than the passages on the actual PSAT.

Questions 1–8 are based on the following passage and supplementary material.

The following passage is adapted from the National Centers for Environmental Information (ncdc.noaa .gov).

How has the climate changed over the past 50 or more years? In what ways and by how much? Many people, including climatologists, have been struggling with these questions for
(5) some time now, not only for scientific interest, but also to aid in policy decisions and to inform the general public. In order to answer these questions, it is important to obtain comprehensive and intuitive information which
(10) allows interested parties to understand the scientific basis for confidence, or lack thereof, in the present understanding of the climate system. One tool, first developed as a framework for quantifying observed changes in climate
(15) within the contiguous United States, is the U.S. Climate Extremes Index (CEI).

The CEI was first introduced in early 1996 with the goal of summarizing and presenting a complex set of multivariate and multidimen-
(20) sional climate changes in the United States so that the results could be easily understood and used in policy decisions made by non-specialists in the field. The contiguous U.S. was selected as the focus for this study in part since

(25) climate change is of great interest to U.S. citizens and policy makers and since climate changes within the U.S. have not been given extensive coverage in intergovernmental or national reports which focus on climate (30) change assessments.

In 2003, two notable modifications were made to the CEI. Indicators in the original CEI summarized trends in temperature, precipitation, and drought data on an annual (35) basis. The revised CEI now includes an experimental tropical system component and is calculated for multiple seasons. The newest indicator documents trends in tropical system activity based on the wind velocity of landfall- (40) ing tropical storm and hurricanes. As of October 2004, CEI calculations begin in 1910 for all periods and are updated within a few weeks after the end of a particular season and include final quality controlled data as well as (45) near-real-time data. In September 2005, the

two components for each of four indicators are plotted separately to help in the identification of trends and variability of each component. In December 2005, a year-to-date season (50) was made available along with the other eight standard seasons. Additions and modifications made to the original CEI are explained in an article entitled "A Revised U.S. Climate Extremes Index," which was published in mid- (55) 2008.

In July 2011, a regional CEI (RCEI) was introduced, which computes the CEI across the 9 U.S. Standard Regions. Year-to-year variations in the regional index have higher (60) amplitude swings and larger/smaller percentages of each region affected by extremes compared with the CEI. There is a good deal of spatial consistency among the RCEI indicators and similar extremes may span across or (65) be absent from a region in any given season.

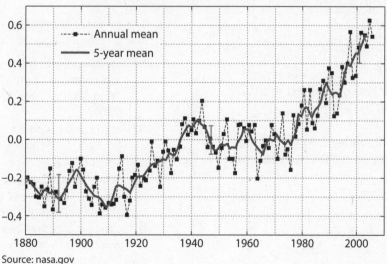

Global-Mean Surface Temperature Anomaly (°C)

Source: nasa.gov

1. The main purpose of the passage is to

   A. garner support for proposed changes to the CEI.

   B. stress the urgency of a scientific issue.

   C. highlight the need to create more tools for controlling climate change.

   D. explain an indicator used in scientific inquiry.

2. In line 13, the word "framework" most nearly means

   A. component.

   B. vector.

   C. structure.

   D. solution.

3. What function does the third paragraph (lines 31–55) serve in the passage as a whole?

   A. It acknowledges the pros and cons of monitoring multidimensional climate change.

   B. It illustrates with detail the distinct components of the plan to monitor global climate changes.

   C. It provides a background overview and justification for the main focus of the passage.

   D. It summarizes the goals of notable climatologists with respect to climate change in the U.S.

4. Which of the following is NOT presented in the passage as a reason for establishing the CEI?

   A. To simplify complex scientific data

   B. To publicize the need for governmental intervention in climatology

   C. To satisfy scientific inquiry

   D. To quantify observations

5. Which choice does the author explicitly state as a 2003 modification of the CEI?

   A. A summary of trends in temperature

   B. An annual measure of precipitation

   C. A computation of changes in wind direction

   D. An indication of trends in tropical system activity

6. Which lines provide the best evidence for the answer to the previous question?

   A. Lines 13–16 ("One tool…Index (CEI).")

   B. Lines 35–37 ("The revised…seasons.")

   C. Lines 40–45 ("As of…data.")

   D. Lines 56–58 ("In July…Regions.")

7. According to the graph, in what year was the 5-year mean temperature the lowest?

   A. 1890

   B. 1900

   C. 1910

   D. 1920

8. The author of the passage would likely interpret the data on the chart as evidence that

   A. fluctuations in the 5-year mean temperatures in the U.S. were greater from 1980 to 1990 than from 1990 to 2000.

   B. the questions posed in the first paragraph of the passage are worth investigating.

   C. temperature change is far less significant an indicator of climate change than trends in precipitation and drought.

   D. spikes in temperature anomalies are far greater than scientists previously predicted.

Questions 9–15 are based on the following passage.

This passage is from the opening chapter of *Great Expectations* by Charles Dickens (1861). In this excerpt, Pip, a 7-year-old orphan boy, is in a church graveyard when he is accosted by an escaped convict.

"Hold your noise!" cried a terrible voice, as a man started up from among the graves at the side of the church porch. "Keep still, you little devil, or I'll cut your throat!"

(5) A fearful man, all in coarse gray, with a great iron on his leg. A man with no hat, and with broken shoes, and with an old rag tied round his head. A man who had been soaked in water, and smothered in mud, and lamed by (10) stones, and cut by flints, and stung by nettles, and torn by briars; who limped, and shivered, and glared, and growled; and whose teeth chattered in his head as he seized me by the chin.

(15) "Oh! Don't cut my throat, sir," I pleaded in terror. "Pray don't do it, sir."

"Tell us your name!" said the man. "Quick!"

"Pip, sir."

"Once more," said the man, staring at me. (20) "Give it mouth!"

"Pip. Pip, sir."

"Show us where you live," said the man. "Pint out the place!"

I pointed to where our village lay, a mile or (25) more from the church.

The man, after looking at me for a moment, turned me upside down, and emptied my pockets. There was nothing in them but a piece of bread. When the church came to (30) itself,—for he was so sudden and strong that he made it go head over heels before me, and I saw the steeple under my feet,—when the church came to itself, I say, I was seated on a high tombstone, trembling while he ate the (35) bread ravenously.

"Now lookee here!" said the man. "Who d'ye live with,—supposin' you're kindly let to live, which I han't made up my mind about?"

"My sister, sir,—Mrs. Joe Gargery,—wife (40) of Joe Gargery, the blacksmith, sir."

"Blacksmith, eh?" said he. And looked down at his leg.

After darkly looking at his leg and me several times, he came closer to my tombstone, (45) took me by both arms, and tilted me back as far as he could hold me; so that his eyes looked most powerfully down into mine, and mine looked most helplessly up into his.

"Now lookee here," he said, "the question (50) being whether you're to be let to live. You know what a file is?"

"Yes, sir."

"And you know what wittles[1] is?"

"Yes, sir."

(55) After each question he tilted me over a little more, so as to give me a greater sense of helplessness and danger.

"You get me a file." He tilted me again. "And you get me wittles." He tilted me again. (60) "You bring 'em both to me." He tilted me again. "Or I'll have your heart and liver out." He tilted me again.

I was dreadfully frightened, and so giddy that I clung to him with both hands, and said, (65) "If you would kindly please to let me keep upright, sir, perhaps I shouldn't be sick, and perhaps I could attend more."

"You bring me, to-morrow morning early, that file and them wittles. You bring the lot to (70) me…You do it, and you never dare to say a word or dare to make a sign concerning your having seen such a person as me, or any person sumever, and you shall be let to live. You fail, or you go from my words in any partickler, no (75) matter how small it is, and your heart and your liver shall be tore out, roasted, and ate… Now, what do you say?"

I said that I would get him the file, and I would get him what broken bits of food I could, (80) and I would come to him early in the morning.

"Say Lord strike you dead if you don't!" said the man.

"Now," he pursued, "you remember what you've undertook, and you get home!"

(85) "Goo-good night, sir," I faltered.

"Much of that!" said he, glancing about him over the cold wet flat.

---

[1]wittles: vittles; food

9. Which choice best describes what happens in the passage?

    A. One character argues with another character who needs help to escape from jail.

    B. One character sentimentally reflects on a dramatic encounter he had when he was younger.

    C. One character makes an urgent demand of another character.

    D. One character unexpectedly pursues another character who threatens him.

10. The mood of the passage is one of

    A. fear and urgency.

    B. sadness and acceptance.

    C. violence and resistance.

    D. giddiness and piety.

11. In line 2, "started" most nearly means

    A. began.

    B. created.

    C. left.

    D. jumped.

12. Why is Pip's brother-in law Joe's occupation so important to the convict?

    A. As the minister of the church, Joe can provide sanctuary to the convict.

    B. Joe's occupation will allow Pip access to a tool the convict needs.

    C. Joe's contacts can help the convict get out of the country.

    D. Joe can provide the food the convict needs to survive in order to escape.

13. Which choice provides the best evidence for the answer to the previous question?

    A. Lines 29–35 ("When…ravenously.")

    B. Lines 39–40 ("My sister…sir.")

    C. Lines 43–48 ("After…into his.")

    D. Lines 63–67 ("I was…more.")

14. In line 67, the word "attend" most nearly means

    A. listen.

    B. join.

    C. appear.

    D. pretend.

15. The tone of the convict's response (line 86) to Pip's remark (line 85) is most likely

    A. gratitude.

    B. fear.

    C. sarcasm.

    D. remorse.

Questions 16–25 are based on the following passages.

Passage 1 is an excerpt from the farewell address given on January 17, 1961, by then President Dwight D. Eisenhower. Passage 2 is an excerpt from a radio address given on February 19, 1983, by then President Ronald Reagan.

Passage 1

A vital element in keeping the peace is our military establishment. Our arms must be mighty, ready for instant action, so that no potential aggressor may be tempted to risk his
(5) own destruction. Our military organization today bears little relation to that known by any of my predecessors in peacetime, or indeed by the fighting men of World War II or Korea.

Until the latest of our world conflicts, the
(10) United States had no armaments industry. American makers of plowshares could, with time and as required, make swords as well. But now we can no longer risk emergency improvisation of national defense; we have been compelled to
(15) create a permanent armaments industry of vast proportions. Added to this, three and a half million men and women are directly engaged in the defense establishment. We annually spend on military security more than the net income of all
(20) United States corporations.

This conjunction of an immense military establishment and a large arms industry is new in the American experience. The total influence—economic, political, even spiritual—is felt in (25) every city, every State house, every office of the Federal government. We recognize the imperative need for this development. Yet we must not fail to comprehend its grave implications. Our toil, resources, and livelihood are all involved; so (30) is the very structure of our society.

In the councils of government, we must guard against the acquisition of unwarranted influence, whether sought or unsought, by the military-industrial complex. The potential for (35) the disastrous rise of misplaced power exists and will persist.

We must never let the weight of this combination endanger our liberties or democratic processes. We should take nothing for granted. (40) Only an alert and knowledgeable citizenry can compel the proper meshing of the huge industrial and military machinery of defense with our peaceful methods and goals, so that security and liberty may prosper together.

(45) Akin to, and largely responsible for, the sweeping changes in our industrial-military posture has been the technological revolution during recent decades. In this revolution, research has become central; it also becomes (50) more formalized, complex, and costly. A steadily increasing share is conducted for, by, or at the direction of the Federal government.

Today, the solitary inventor, tinkering in his shop, has been overshadowed by task forces of (55) scientists in laboratories and testing fields. In the same fashion, the free university, historically the fountainhead of free ideas and scientific discovery, has experienced a revolution in the conduct of research. Partly because of the (60) huge costs involved, a government contract becomes virtually a substitute for intellectual curiosity. For every old blackboard there are now hundreds of new electronic computers.

The prospect of domination of the nation's (65) scholars by Federal employment, project allocations, and the power of money is ever present and is gravely to be regarded.

Yet, in holding scientific research and discovery in respect, as we should, we must also be alert

(70) to the equal and opposite danger that public policy could itself become the captive of a scientific technological elite. It is the task of statesmanship to mold, to balance, and to integrate these and other forces, new and old, within the principles of (75) our democratic system—ever aiming toward the supreme goals of our free society.

Passage 2

"To be prepared for war," George Washington said, "is the most effectual means of preserving the peace." When I reread this (80) quote a few days ago, it brought to mind the current public debate over this administration's efforts to protect the peace by restoring our country's neglected defenses.

Now, I know that this is a hard time to call (85) for increased defense spending. It isn't easy to ask American families who are already making sacrifices in the recession, or American businesses which are struggling to reinvest for the future, and it isn't easy for someone like (90) me who's dedicated his entire political career to reducing government spending.

On the other hand, it's always very easy and very tempting politically to come up with arguments for neglecting defense spending in (95) time of peace. One of the great tragedies of this century was that it was only after the balance of power was allowed to erode and a ruthless adversary, Adolf Hitler, deliberately weighed the risks and decided to strike that (100) the importance of a strong defense was realized too late. That was what happened in the years leading up to World War II. And especially for those of us who lived through that nightmare, it's a mistake that America and the (105) free world must never make again.

I want you to know that members of my administration and I have agonized over the current defense budget. We've trimmed back our plans for rebuilding defense by more than (110) half. We've hunted for savings in nonessential programs. We've weighed economic risks and economic benefits. The defense budget we finally presented is a minimal budget to pro-

tect our country's vital interests and meet our
(115) commitments.

For those who wish to cut it back further, I
have a simple question. Which interests and
which commitments are they ready to aban-
don? Let me make just a few key points about
(120) our defense program.

First, we must develop a responsible and balanced understanding of the danger we face.
Over the past 20 years, the Soviet Union has
accumulated enormous military might, while we
(125) restrained our own efforts to the point where
defense spending actually declined, in real terms,
over 20 percent in the decade of the seventies.

Today, the Soviets out-invest us by nearly 2
to 1. Even with the defense increases of the
(130) past 2 years, they outproduce us substantially
in almost every category of weapons. And in
actions such as the brutal invasion and occupation of Afghanistan, they have demonstrated their willingness to use these weapons
(135) for aggression.

Finally, Soviet military power has spread
around the globe, threatening our access to
vital resources and our sea lines of communi-
cation, undermining our forward line of
(140) defense in Europe and Korea, and challenging
us even at home, here in our own hemisphere.

We must face the facts. If we continue our
past pattern of only rebuilding our defenses in
fits and starts, we will never convince the Soviets
(145) that it's in their interests to behave with restraint
and negotiate genuine arms reductions. We will
also burden the American taxpayer time and
again with the high cost of crash rearmament.
Sooner or later, the bills fall due.

16. Eisenhower's main purpose in this speech in
Passage 1 is to

A. suggest preparation for an imminent
conflict.
B. illustrate the adversarial nature of an
emerging rivalry.
C. convey the necessity of technological
progress.
D. warn of the danger of a trend toward
technology.

17. In line 28, the word "grave" most nearly
means

A. ominous.
B. deadly.
C. heavy.
D. vital.

18. Which of the following ironies is implicit in
the speech in Passage 1?

A. The military-industrial complex could
weaken or destroy the very institutions
and principles it was designed to
protect.
B. Scientific research should be focused
solely on improving human institutions
and should never be politicized.
C. Educational facilities are currently
functioning as subsidiaries of the
Federal government.
D. Scholars are using their knowledge to
design weapons of mass destruction.

19. In Passage 1, Eisenhower views the increasing
Federal employment of scholars as

A. ultimately beneficial.
B. potentially harmful.
C. unequivocally disastrous.
D. clearly innocuous.

20. Which choice provides the best evidence for
the answer to the previous question?

A. Lines 21–23 ("This conjunction…
experience.")
B. Lines 31–34 ("In the councils…
complex.")
C. Lines 55–59 ("In the same fashion…
research.")
D. Lines 64–67 ("The prospect…
regarded.")

21. In Passage 2, Reagan's references to Adolph Hitler (lines 96–101) and "that nightmare" (lines 103–104) mainly have what effect?

    A. They capture the speaker's refusal to accept diplomatic defeat.
    B. They invoke a historical allusion that is only marginally relevant.
    C. They reflect the speaker's pride in American military prowess.
    D. They emphasize the dire consequences of rejecting the speaker's plan.

22. In Passage 2, the purpose of the fourth paragraph (lines 106–115) is to

    A. offer a counterargument to supporters of his plan.
    B. establish the speaker's credentials to make critical decisions.
    C. anticipate and answer expected criticism.
    D. contrast the speaker's good intentions with those of other members of his administration.

23. In line 114, the word "vital" most nearly means

    A. vigorous.
    B. energetic.
    C. crucial.
    D. dynamic.

24. Which choice best describes the relationship between the two passages?

    A. Passage 1 is an impassioned plea for support for the military, while Passage 2 is a more balanced argument.
    B. Passage 1 uses scientific research for support, while Passage 2 presents more anecdotal evidence.
    C. Passage 2 considers only the immediate present, while Passage 1 takes a long view of the consequences of a decision.
    D. Passage 2 cites historical precedent to counter the results of the position espoused in Passage 1.

25. On which of the following points would the speakers of both passages agree?

    A. The defense budget should be the primary allocation in the national budget.
    B. Defending our nation from aggressors is a very costly undertaking.
    C. It is essential to keep reasonable restrictions on Federal employment and project allocations.
    D. The United States spends less than other global powers do on military spending.

Answer Explanations

1. **D.** The author's main purpose is to explain the reasons for creating a Climate Extremes Index (CEI) to aid scientists in their study of climate change, Choice D. Choice A is incorrect because he isn't trying to garner support for proposed changes (several modifications to the CEI have been in existence for some years). Choice B is incorrect because he isn't stressing the urgency of a particular issue. Choice C is incorrect because he doesn't discuss the need to create more tools for controlling climate change.

2. **C.** The word *framework*, as it is used in line 13, most nearly means "structure," Choice C, as it provides a tool to help scientists build a set of computations. Choice A is incorrect because it is not a component or part of a larger whole. Choice B is incorrect because it is not a vector or trajectory. Choice D is incorrect because it doesn't mean a solution or an answer to a problem.

3. **C.** The third paragraph provides a brief historical overview of and suggests the rationale for introducing the CEI, Choice C. Choice A is incorrect because it doesn't present any cons of monitoring climate change. Choice B is incorrect because it doesn't illustrate with detail the components of the plan. Choice D is incorrect because it doesn't summarize goals of notable climatologists (the paragraph doesn't mention climatologists).

4. **B.** The passage doesn't state that the CEI will publicize the need for governmental intervention, Choice B. Lines 17–23 state that one goal of the CEI is to present complex data in a way that can be understood (Choice A). Lines 3–7 state that there is *scientific interest* in knowing the CEI (Choice C). Lines 13–16 indicate that the CEI will quantify *observed changes in climate* (Choice D).

5. **D.** The author states that the 2003 modifications include *trends in tropical system activity* (lines 38–39), Choice D. The summary of trends in temperature and the annual measure of precipitation (choices A and B) are part of the original CEI. The author never discusses changes in wind direction (Choice C).

6. **B.** Lines 35–37, Choice B (*The revised CEI now includes an experimental tropical system component and is calculated for multiple seasons.*), provide the best evidence for the previous question 5. Choices A, C, and D discuss aspects of the CEI other than the 2003 modifications.

7. **C.** The lowest 5-year mean temperatures on the graph are recorded in 1910. The other choices are years with higher 5-year mean temperatures than those shown for 1910.

8. **B.** The data on the graph indicate that the questions posed in the first paragraph of the passage are worth investigating because global mean temperatures have increased steadily (more than one degree) in the last century, Choice B. Choice A is incorrect because the graph displays global data, not U.S. data. Choice C is incorrect because the graph only displays temperature changes. Choice D is incorrect because the passage doesn't discuss a prediction in temperature anomalies.

9. **C.** In the passage the convict demands that Pip bring him food and a file, Choice C. The answer isn't Choice A because the convict has already escaped from jail. Choice B is incorrect because the character (Pip) doesn't sentimentally reflect on this encounter. Choice D is incorrect because although the convict threatens Pip, Pip doesn't pursue him.

10. **A.** The passage is characterized by Pip's fear and the convict's urgency, Choice A. Choice B is not the best answer because although Pip is in a graveyard, he expresses shock and fear rather than sadness and acceptance. Choice C is incorrect because Pip pleads for his life, but he doesn't put up any resistance to the violence of the convict. Choice D is incorrect; while Pip says he feels giddy (mostly from fear), neither character expresses any piety.

11. **D.** In the context of line 2, *started* most nearly means jumped, Choice D. The passage implies the convict has been hiding behind a gravestone when he jumps up and seizes Pip by the chin. Choices A, *began*, B, *created*, and C, *left*, don't fit the context of the passage: *a man started up from among the graves at the side of the church porch.*

12. **B.** Pip's brother-in-law is a blacksmith; Pip will find a file among his tools, which the convict can use to remove his leg irons, Choice B. Choice A is incorrect because Pip's brother-in-law isn't a minister. Choice C is incorrect because the passage doesn't indicate that Pip's brother-in-law has any helpful contacts, nor do we know that the convict wants to leave the country. Choice D is incorrect because Pip's brother-in-law doesn't have to be a blacksmith to provide food; any working person could most likely provide some food.

13. **C.** Lines 43–48, Choice C, provide the best evidence for the answer to the previous question. These lines imply the convict is connecting Joe's occupation as a blacksmith to Pip's being able to get a file that the convict can then use to remove his leg iron: *After darkly looking at his leg and me several times, he came closer to my tombstone, took me by both arms, and tilted me back as far as he could hold me; so that his eyes looked most powerfully down into mine, and mine looked most helplessly up into his.* None of the other choices indicates the convict's understanding that he can use Pip's connections to help him get a tool to file off the leg iron.

14. **A.** Choice A is correct because Pip says, *"If you would kindly please to let me keep upright, sir, perhaps I shouldn't be sick, and perhaps I could attend more."* He means he could listen better if he is upright rather than upside down. The other choices don't fit the context. Choice B is incorrect because Pip is not going to join anyone or anything. Choice C is incorrect because Pip doesn't mean he will appear. Choice D is incorrect because Pip isn't going to pretend.

15. **C.** In line 85, Pip wishes the convict a good night. The convict responds, *"Much of that!"* You can infer that he is being sarcastic, Choice C, as he is cold, wet, muddy, wounded, and hungry as he looks around at the *cold wet flat*. Choices A and D are incorrect because no evidence in the passage suggests the convict feels gratitude or remorse. Choice B is incorrect because while the convict may actually be afraid of getting caught, nowhere in the passage does he express fear.

16. **D.** Eisenhower expresses his concerns about the rise of the military-industrial complex and its consequent emphasis on technology, Choice D. He says, *Yet, in holding scientific research and discovery in respect, as we should, we must also be alert to the equal and opposite danger that public policy could itself become the captive of a scientific technological elite.* Choice A is incorrect because there is no suggestion of an imminent conflict. Choice B is incorrect because Eisenhower doesn't discuss the adversarial nature of an emerging rivalry. Choice C is incorrect because Eisenhower warns against the dangers of technological progress.

17. **A.** When Eisenhower says, *Yet we must not fail to comprehend its grave implications*, the word *its* refers to the rise of the military-industrial complex, a danger he finds ominous or threatening, Choice A. Choice B, deadly, is too strong and specific for the context. Choice C, heavy, is inappropriate for the context because *heavy implications* doesn't make sense in the sentence. Choice D, vital, is too positive a word for the context.

18. **A.** The military-industrial complex arose to protect Americans from danger, yet Eisenhower sees it as a danger in itself, Choice A. Choice B is incorrect because Eisenhower doesn't discuss scientific research being politicized. Choice C is incorrect because educational facilities aren't currently functioning as subsidiaries of the Federal government. Choice D is incorrect; although Eisenhower worries about the uses of scientific research, he doesn't link this concern to the development of weapons of mass destruction.

19. **B.** Eisenhower expresses his fear that with increasing Federal employment of scholars, *a government contract becomes virtually a substitute for intellectual curiosity.* He fears creativity will be stifled as scholars work to fulfill government contracts, Choice B. Choice A is incorrect because he doesn't see this process as beneficial. Choice C is incorrect because *unequivocally disastrous* is too strongly negative to accurately describe his attitude. Choice D is incorrect because the evidence suggests he is apprehensive, so he wouldn't see this process as clearly innocuous (harmless).

20. **D.** Lines 64–67, Choice D, provide the best evidence for the answer to the previous question: *The prospect of domination of the nation's scholars by Federal employment, project allocations, and the power of money is ever present and is gravely to be regarded.* The other choices don't provide evidence about Eisenhower's attitude toward the Federal employment of scholars.

21. **D.** Reagan's references to Hitler and *that nightmare* are designed to reflect the dire consequences that might ensue if Reagan's plan is not followed, Choice D. Choice A is incorrect because the references aren't related to diplomatic defeat. Choice B is incorrect because the references are relevant historical allusions. Choice C is incorrect because the references have little to do with American military prowess.

22. **C.** In the fourth paragraph, Reagan anticipates criticism from some that the defense budget is too high. He defends the fiscal decisions and points out that *The defense budget we finally presented is a minimal budget to protect our country's vital interests and meet our commitments*, Choice C. Choice A is incorrect because Reagan addresses those who will criticize his plan, not supporters. Choice B is incorrect because he doesn't establish his credentials in this paragraph. Choice D is incorrect because he doesn't contrast his good intentions with those of other members of his administration.

23. **C.** In line 114, *vital* most nearly means "crucial," Choice C; in this context, it refers to resources that are essential to national defense. Vital can mean vigorous, Choice A, or energetic, Choice B, or dynamic, Choice D, but none of these choices fits the context.

24. **D.** Passage 1 warns of the dangers of the buildup of military and industrial power; Passage 2 uses George Washington's assertion (*To be prepared for war…is the most effectual means of preserving the peace*) as a springboard for arguments in favor of a strongly funded defense force, making Choice D correct. Choice A is incorrect because Passage 1 isn't a plea for military support. Choice B is incorrect because while Passage 1 alludes to scientific research, it doesn't use scientific research for support. Choice C is incorrect because both passages consider the long view of their respective positions.

25. **B.** Both passages recognize that national defense is necessary but costly, Choice B. Choice A is incorrect because neither passage says the defense budget should be the primary allocation. The speaker of Passage 2 wouldn't agree with Choice C. Choice D is incorrect because Passage 1 doesn't compare the U.S. budget to any other country's budget, and Passage 2 compares the U.S. budget only with the Soviet (Russia) budget.

VI. Evidence-Based Reading and Writing: The Writing and Language Test

The purpose of the PSAT Writing and Language Test is to give you a sense of your readiness to handle the writing you'll be doing in college and/or in your career. You'll be asked to read passages and determine the correctness of the language choices. You'll actually be proofreading and editing the passages just as you proofread and edit your own writing for school. You won't be asked to identify a participial phrase or a gerund; however, you will be asked to recognize correct and effective use of language.

A. The Format of the Writing and Language Test

The format of the PSAT Writing and Language Test is exactly the same as the format of the SAT Writing and Language Test. You'll have 35 minutes to complete 44 questions on four passages in various content areas (humanities, social science, science). Each passage will have some portions underlined, and four alternative choices will be offered or questions will be asked about the underlined portion. Many questions offer you the choice of NO CHANGE; choose NO CHANGE if you think the text is correct as written. In some passages, questions will be asked about the order of sentences and/or paragraphs. In those cases, the sentences and/or the paragraphs will be numbered. In addition, some questions will have a number in the text without an underlined portion. You may be asked whether it is effective to add a piece of information or delete some text at this point. Other questions ask you about a single paragraph, the passage as a whole, or about a chart or graph that accompanies the passage.

On the Writing and Language Test, you'll demonstrate your knowledge of the grammatical conventions of standard written English, your ability to punctuate text correctly, your understanding and interpretation of data, and your awareness of idiomatic English usage (English that is used and accepted as correct by well-educated people). In addition, you'll demonstrate your ability to make correct rhetorical decisions.

What is rhetoric and what is a rhetorical decision? Rhetoric is the art of speaking and writing effectively. It involves the tools of the effective writer: choosing just the right word, knowing when to give a detail and when to omit irrelevant information, arranging ideas in the most effective and logical order, and providing clear and appropriate transitions. A simple way to think of rhetoric is to define it in your mind as the decisions the writer makes to accomplish his or her purpose effectively.

B. Specific Skills Tested on the Writing and Language Test

1. Conventions of Punctuation

a. Apostrophes

An apostrophe is used with nouns to indicate possession and in place of letters in contractions.

i. To Indicate Possession

Singular nouns: The possessive form of singular nouns is made by adding 's to the word.

Example: dog + 's = dog's leash

Before I went for a walk, I searched for the dog's leash.

Example: Simon + 's = Simon's

I found Simon's leash in the back of the closet.

Singular nouns that end in s: In most cases, singular nouns that end in **s** follow the same rule. However, in some cases, it becomes difficult to pronounce the word in its possessive form. In these cases, just the apostrophe alone may be added after the last **s** in the word.

Example: Carlos + 's = Carlos's or Carlos'

Carlos's car is parked behind the school. (or: Carlos' car is parked behind the school.)

Plural nouns: If the plural form of the noun does not end in **s**, form the plural by adding 's.

Example: children + 's = children's

The children's artwork decorated the school.

Plural nouns that end in s: If the plural form of the noun ends in **s**, add only the apostrophe to make it possessive.

Example: drivers + ' = drivers'

The drivers' helmets were painted for the big race.

Joint ownership: When two people own something together, the apostrophe is used only with the name of the last person mentioned.

Example: Sydney and Charlie's house

Indefinite pronouns: The possessive form of indefinite pronouns is formed by adding 's.

Example: everyone + 's = everyone's

The room was quiet because everyone's attention was focused on the stage.

> IMPORTANT: The possessive forms of personal pronouns never require an apostrophe. Never use the apostrophe with these pronouns: *my, his, hers, its, ours, yours, theirs, who*. This situation will appear frequently on the test, and you can quickly eliminate choices that contain *its', yours', theirs', ours', hers',* or *his'*.
>
> *Note:* Who's is the contraction of *who is*; the possessive form of *who* is *whose*.
>
> Example: We should determine who's going on the field trip so we know whose car to take.

ii. In Contractions

In a contraction, the apostrophe indicates that one or more letters have been omitted.

Example: it is = it's (*Note:* This is not the possessive form of *its*, which has no apostrophe.)

Example: who is = who's (*Note:* This is not the possessive of *who*, which is *whose*.)

Example: would have = would've (*Note:* It is never correct to write *would of, could of,* or *should of*.)

Practice

Directions: For the following practice questions, choose the correct word.

1. The DVD (players, players', player's) power cord was so tangled, it took an hour to get it straightened out.

2. I found that it wasn't wise to question the attorney (general's, generals) authority.

3. All of the five caged (wolf's, wolves, wolves') howls could be heard throughout the zoo.

4. I forgot (who's, whose) backpack is blue with orange zippers.

5. In two (years, year's, years') time, all the computers in the school will be replaced.

6. Alex (could of, could've) finished the project if he had budgeted his time more efficiently.

Answer Explanations

1. **player's** The singular possessive of player is *player's*.

2. **general's** The possessive of general is *general's*.

3. **wolves'** The plural possessive of wolf is *wolves'*.

4. **whose** The singular possessive pronoun is *whose*. (*Who's* is the contraction of *who is*.)

5. **years'** The plural possessive of year is *years'*.

6. **could've** The contraction of could have is *could've*. (*Could of* is never correct.)

b. Commas

Commas are used for many purposes:

- To separate items in a series
- Before a conjunction that joins main clauses
- To set off any expressions that interrupt the sentence
- With a direct quotation
- To set off an appositive
- With a non-restrictive clause or phrase
- To set off geographical names, addresses, and dates
- To separate two coordinate adjectives when the word ***and*** can be inserted between them
- To separate contrasting parts of a sentence
- After an introductory phrase or clause

i. Separate Items in a Series

Commas are used to separate items in a series.

> Example: The menu for the July Fourth picnic included hot dogs, hamburgers, grilled vegetables, and ice cream sandwiches. (words in a series)

Example: We struggled to capture the kittens as they scrambled onto the porch, into the vegetable garden, and under the car. (phrases in a series)

Example: My mom informed me that we would be leaving a day earlier than expected, that she would drive the whole way, and that I would have to sit in the back with the dog. (clauses in a series)

ii. Join Main Clauses

Use a comma before a coordinating conjunction that joins main clauses. FANBOYS is an acronym that will help you remember the coordinating conjunctions: For, And, Nor, But, Or, Yet, So.

Example: The colors of the autumn leaves are beautiful, but I prefer the green buds of spring.

iii. Set Off Expressions

Commas are used to set off expressions that interrupt the sentence. Parenthetical expressions are set off with commas.

Example: My algebra final, of course, was the longest test of the day.

Example: My essay on *Julius Caesar*, I think, was the best writing I have done all year.

Words used in direct address are set off with commas.

Example: Luis, please take this message to the main office.

Introductory words are set off with commas.

Example: Yes, you may borrow my phone to call your mom.

iv. Direct Quotation

Commas are used with a direct quotation.

Example: John F. Kennedy reminded all Americans, "The cost of freedom is always high, but Americans have always paid it."

Example: "Do your best," my dad reminded me, "and everything else will fall into place."

v. Set Off an Appositive

Commas are used to set off an appositive. An **appositive** is a word or phrase that follows a noun or pronoun to explain or identify it.

Example: Misty Copeland, a leading American ballet dancer, did not start to dance until she was 13 years old. (In this sentence, *a leading American ballet dancer* is the appositive phrase.)

Note: You do not have to use commas with a one-word appositive that is closely related to the word it modifies.

Example: My uncle David builds houses that rely on solar energy.

Example: The American actor and writer Lin-Manuel Miranda also wrote the rap lyrics for the play *Hamilton*.

vi. Non-Restrictive Clause or Phrase

Commas are used with non-restrictive clauses or phrases. A non-restrictive clause or phrase is not essential to the meaning of the sentence. No commas are needed with restrictive clauses (those that are essential to the meaning of the sentence).

> Example: The tallest boy on the basketball team, the one who came from Russia, scored twenty points last night. (Commas are needed because *the one who came from Russia* is a non-restrictive phrase; it is not essential to the meaning of the sentence.)

> Example: All test-takers who forget to bring picture IDs will be prohibited from taking the test. (No commas are needed because *who forget to bring picture IDs* is a restrictive clause; it is essential to the meaning of the sentence.)

> Example: Morocco, which is a country on the northern coast of Africa, is often used as a film location because of its dramatic desert landscapes. (Commas are needed because *which is a country on the northern coast of Africa* is a non-restrictive clause; it is not essential to the meaning of the sentence.)

If you are not sure if the clause or phrase is essential or non-essential, here are some clues to help you:

- Try leaving out the clause or phrase. Does the sentence still make sense?
- Try moving the clause or phrase to a different position in the sentence. Does the sentence still make sense?

If your answer is *yes* to one or more of these questions, then the clause or phrase is non-restrictive and should be set off with commas.

vii. Geographical Names, Addresses, and Dates

Use commas to set off geographical names, addresses, and dates.

> Example: Abraham Lincoln was shot by John Wilkes Booth on April 14, 1865, in Washington, D.C.

> Example: The spaceship *Voyager 1* was launched on September 5, 1977, to study the outer solar system.

> Example: The Empire State Building is located at 350 Fifth Avenue, New York, NY 10118.

viii. Separate Two Coordinate Adjectives

Use a comma to separate two coordinate adjectives when the word *and* can be inserted between them. **Coordinate adjectives** are paired adjectives that precede and describe the same noun.

> Example: To reach the top of the mountain, the climbers traveled up the steep, rocky path.

In this example, *steep* and *rocky* are coordinate adjectives that precede and describe *path*.

Note: Do not use a comma if you would not use the word *and* between the adjectives.
> **Example:** The climbers wore green wool sweaters. (You would not say "green and wool sweaters.")

ix. Separate Contrasting Parts of a Sentence

Use a comma to separate contrasting parts of a sentence.

Example: All answers on the PSAT should be written in pencil, not in ink.

x. After an Introductory Phrase or Clause

Use a comma after an **introductory adverb clause** that begins with a subordinating conjunction such as *after, although, as, because, before, if, since, though, unless, until, when, whenever, where,* or *while.*

Example: Although I started on Sunday to practice for the dance tryout, I didn't feel completely ready by Friday.

Use a comma after a **participial phrase** (a participle is a form of a verb that functions like an adjective to modify a noun or pronoun).

Example: Running toward home base, Ella could taste her team's victory. (The phrase *Running toward home base* is a participial phrase modifying *Ella.*)

Use a comma after an **infinitive phrase** (to + verb).

Example: To complete the challenge of a marathon, you must run 26 miles.

Use a comma after a long prepositional phrase or a series of prepositional phrases.

Example: On a dark night in the middle of December, the zombies invaded the town.

Practice

Directions: Punctuate the following sentences correctly.

1. The attack on the U.S. Naval Base Pearl Harbor Hawaii on December 7 1941 led to the United States' entry into World War II.

2. No I haven't been to Ann Arbor Michigan but I have spent time in Boca Raton Florida.

3. My new neighbors who moved here from upstate are building a swimming pool in their backyard.

4. After the play Hayley said she loved the dancing not the singing.

5. My cell phone had to be replaced for it had fallen into the water.

6. Unless the competition lasts longer than two hours I can give you a ride home.

7. "The city is blanketed by fog" the flight attendant announced "and we'll be diverted to another airport."

8. To convince the voters to elect him the candidate promised to lower taxes improve roads and raise the minimum wage.

9. The movie which I saw in town last week was a thrilling tale of heroism.

10. Counting on her gymnastic ability Sophie hoped to make the dance company.

Answer Explanations

1. The attack on the U.S. Naval Base, Pearl Harbor, Hawaii, on December 7, 1941, led to the United States' entry into World War II. (Use commas to set off geographical names, addresses, and dates.)

2. No, I haven't been to Ann Arbor, Michigan, but I have spent time in Boca Raton, Florida. (Use a comma after introductory words; use a comma to set off geographical names, addresses, and dates; use a comma between main clauses joined by a coordinating conjunction.)

3. My new neighbors, who moved here from upstate, are building a swimming pool in their backyard. (Use commas to set off non-restrictive clauses or phrases.)

4. After the play Hayley said she loved the dancing, not the singing. (Use a comma to separate contrasting parts of a sentence.)

5. My cell phone had to be replaced, for it had fallen into the water. (Use a comma before a coordinating conjunction that joins main clauses.)

6. Unless the competition lasts longer than two hours, I can give you a ride home. (Use a comma after an introductory adverb clause that begins with a subordinating conjunction.)

7. "The city is blanketed by fog," the flight attendant announced, "and we'll be diverted to another airport." (Use commas with direct quotations.)

8. To convince the voters to elect him, the candidate promised to lower taxes, improve roads, and raise the minimum wage. (Use a comma after an introductory infinitive phrase; use a comma between items in a series.)

9. The movie, which I saw in town last week, was a thrilling tale of heroism. (Use commas to set off a non-restrictive clause.)

10. Counting on her gymnastic ability, Sophie hoped to make the dance company. (Use a comma after a participial phrase.)

c. Colons

The colon indicates a pause in the sentence. It is used before a list; before a long, formal statement; and before an explanatory statement.

i. Before a List

Use a colon before a list of items, including a list that is introduced by the words *the following* or *as follows*.

Example: Don't forget to bring all necessary items to the PSAT: a photo ID, a no. 2 pencil, and a calculator.

Note: Do not use a colon directly after a verb or a preposition.

Example: All outdoor education students are expected to arrive supplied with canteens, sleeping bags, flashlights, and laundry bags. (no colon after the preposition *with*)

Example: All outdoor education students are expected to supply canteens, sleeping bags, flashlights, and laundry bags. (no colon after the verb *supply*)

ii. Before a Long, Formal Statement

Use a colon to introduce a formal quotation. In this case, begin the quotation with a capital letter.

> Example: Mark Antony began his funeral oration for Julius Caesar with the now famous words: "Friends, Romans, countrymen, lend me your ears; I come to bury Caesar, not to praise him."

iii. Before an Explanatory Statement

Use a colon after a main clause when it is followed by a second clause or phrase that offers an explanation or a restatement of the first clause. In this case, if the statement after the colon is a complete clause and is important, you may begin it with a capital letter. (This is not a hard-and-fast rule. You will see it both ways: both with and without the capital letter.)

> Example: There is a good reason to carry a flashlight in your car: You never know when you'll get stuck somewhere and need to signal a passerby. (complete clause after the colon)

> Example: Most bloggers are driven by one desire: to share their thoughts and ideas with others. (phrase after the colon)

Practice

Directions: Rewrite the following practice questions, correcting the punctuation.

1. I have always loved the unifying spirit of John F. Kennedy's words "Let us not seek the Republican answer or the Democratic answer, but the right answer. Let us not seek to fix the blame for the past. Let us accept our own responsibility for the future."

2. A search of the suspect's apartment led to the discovery of several incriminating pieces of evidence a wire-cutter a black ski mask and a roll of duct tape.

3. The concert played to rave reviews in Boston Chicago and Detroit.

4. My least favorite vegetables are cabbage Brussels sprouts and lima beans.

5. Do not forget this important point about punctuation Always begin a sentence with a capital letter.

Answer Explanations

1. I have always loved the unifying spirit of John F. Kennedy's words: "Let us not seek the Republican answer or the Democratic answer, but the right answer. Let us not seek to fix the blame for the past. Let us accept our own responsibility for the future." (Use a colon before a long, formal statement.)

2. A search of the suspect's apartment led to the discovery of several incriminating pieces of evidence: a wire-cutter, a black ski mask, and a roll of duct tape. (Use a colon before a list.)

3. The concert played to rave reviews in Boston, Chicago, and Detroit. (Don't use a colon after the preposition *in*; use a comma with a series.)

4. My least favorite vegetables are cabbage, Brussels sprouts, and lima beans. (Don't use a colon after the verb *are*; use a comma with a series.)

5. Do not forget this important point about punctuation: Always begin a sentence with a capital letter. (Use a colon before an explanatory statement.)

d. Semicolons

A semicolon is used to join main clauses, between main clauses connected by a conjunctive adverb or a connecting phrase, between main clauses if there is a comma within one or both clauses, or between items in a series if there are commas within the series.

i. Join Main Clauses

Use a semicolon between closely related main clauses in a compound sentence when the main clauses are not connected by a conjunction.

> Example: Twenty-four cell phones rang at exactly the same time; the noise was deafening.

ii. Connection between Main Clauses

A semicolon is used between main clauses connected by a conjunctive adverb or a connecting phrase.

> Example: The hamburgers in the new restaurant were overdone and flavorless; however, the milk-shakes were awesome. (***Note:*** Use a semicolon before the conjunctive adverb and a comma after it.)

> Example: Jackson came late to practice today; in fact, he's been late every day this week. (***Note:*** Use a semicolon before the connecting phrase and a comma after it.)

Some common conjunctive adverbs include *indeed, furthermore, however, moreover, besides, consequently, nevertheless, therefore, yet,* and *instead*.

Some common connecting phrases include *in fact, for example, for instance, that is, at the same time,* and *on the other hand*. (***Note:*** Use the semicolon only when these phrases connect two **main** clauses.)

iii. Separate Main Clauses

The semicolon is used between main clauses if there is a comma within one or both clauses, or between items in a series if there are commas within the series.

Use the semicolon for clarity between clauses when there are commas within a clause.

> Example: Some artists paint with oil paints, water colors, or acrylics; but others, for personal reasons, choose to use only chalk.

Use the semicolon for clarity between items in a series that contains a comma.

> Example: The lowest temperatures of the planet have been recorded at Vostok, Antarctica; Verkhoyansk, Russia; and Oymyakon, Russia.

Practice

Directions: Punctuate the following sentences correctly.

1. Before the Red Cross even arrived at the disaster scene volunteers had already begun to hand out necessary items blankets water bottles and snacks.

2. The huge audience for the Super Bowl needless to say has driven up the cost of commercial time to more than one million dollars per 30-second spot.

3. I left Florida and traveled north to Atlanta, Georgia Charlotte, North Carolina Richmond, Virginia and Baltimore, Maryland.

4. I passed my driver's test last week however I haven't had a chance to drive because of the snow.

5. The band was on stage for three hours no one left the room for an instant.

Answer Explanations

1. Before the Red Cross even arrived at the disaster scene, volunteers had already begun to hand out necessary items: blankets, water bottles, and snacks. (Use a comma after an introductory adverbial clause; use a colon before an explanatory statement; and use commas to separate items in a series.)

2. The huge audience for the Super Bowl, needless to say, has driven up the cost of commercial time to more than one million dollars per 30-second spot. (Use commas to set off an interrupter.)

3. I left Florida and traveled north to Atlanta, Georgia; Charlotte, North Carolina; Richmond, Virginia; and Baltimore, Maryland. (Use semicolons for clarity between items in a series that contains commas.)

4. I passed my driver's test last week; however, I haven't had a chance to drive because of the snow. (Use a semicolon before a conjunctive adverb and a comma after it.)

5. The band was on stage for three hours; no one left the room for an instant. (Use a semicolon between closely related main clauses.)

e. Dashes

Use a dash to indicate an important or abrupt break in thought or before a summary.

i. Abrupt Break in Thought

A dash gives the information that is set off for special emphasis or indicates a sudden change in thought.

> Example: If you find this book as helpful as I did—and I hope you do—please recommend it to your friends.
>
> Example: All four of the country music singers—Luke Bryan, Chris Stapleton, Miranda Lambert, and Keith Urban—attended the awards ceremony.

Note: When the dash sets off a part of the sentence, unless the sentence ends with that part, be sure to use a second dash (not a comma, as you'll see in some incorrect answers).

Incorrect: Every site in Paris—the Eiffel Tower, the Louvre, Notre Dame Cathedral, remained permanently etched in my memory.

Correct: Every site in Paris—the Eiffel Tower, the Louvre, Notre Dame Cathedral—remained permanently etched in my memory.

ii. Before a Summary

Use a dash before a summary. In these cases, the dash and the colon are interchangeable. The dash is used after items in a series to indicate a summarizing statement.

Example: Myrna, Susan, Ellen, and I—we were friends forever.

f. Parentheses

Use parentheses to enclose additional material or explanatory information that might be interesting to know but is not of major importance to the text. Information that is enclosed in parentheses can usually be removed from the text without changing the meaning or losing any essential information.

Example: The architecture of the old town (settled more than 200 years ago) was more baroque than classical.

In this sentence, the material is not essential to the main meaning of the sentence, so the parentheses are the proper punctuation.

Punctuation of parentheses can be tricky. Periods and other end punctuation go outside the close of a parenthesis. When the information enclosed in the parentheses is a complete sentence, treat it as such: Start with a capital letter and end with a period. A question mark or exclamation mark, if it is part of the parenthetical material, can go inside a parenthesis, but another punctuation mark is needed to close the sentence.

Example: I wondered who had given away my hiding place (Who knew I was hidden there?).

Example: We left the show after the intermission. (We had already seen all the acts in the second act.)

Practice

Directions: Punctuate the following sentences correctly.

1. During the next month the project isn't due until next June we will assign the research tasks.

2. On our trip to Vietnam, we visited Ho Chi Minh City formerly called Saigon before going to the mountain village of Sapa.

3. The coveted award for best actor none could believe it was given to a 10-year-old girl.

4. Watching our team win the championship game believe me was the most memorable night of the year!

5. Walking through the streets of the old city hushed in the twilight conjured up images of the medieval knights and ladies who strolled there years ago.

6. Broccoli, berries, and citrus fruits fill your plates with these great sources of vitamin C.

Answer Explanations

1. During the next month (the project isn't due until next June), we will assign the research tasks. (Use parentheses to enclose additional material or explanatory information; insert a comma after an introductory phrase.)

2. On our trip to Vietnam, we visited Ho Chi Minh City (formerly called Saigon) before going to the mountain village of Sapa. (Use parentheses to enclose additional material or explanatory information.)

3. The coveted award for best actor—none could believe it—was given to a 10-year-old girl. (Use dashes to indicate an important or abrupt break in thought.)

4. Watching our team win the championship game—believe me—was the most memorable night of the year! (Use dashes to indicate an important or abrupt break in thought.)

5. Walking through the streets of the old city—hushed in the twilight—conjured up images of the medieval knights and ladies who strolled there years ago. (Use dashes to indicate an important or abrupt break in thought.)

6. Broccoli, berries, and citrus fruits—fill your plates with these great sources of vitamin C. (Use a dash after items in a series to indicate a summarizing statement.)

g. Question Marks and Exclamation Marks

Question marks and exclamation marks are end marks that indicate the writer's intention: to ask a question or to make a strong or startling statement.

i. Question Marks

Use a question mark at the end of an interrogative sentence. An interrogative sentence is one that asks a question.

>   Example: What is the date of the PSAT this year?

Do not use a question mark with an indirect question.

>   Example: My mother wonders why I like to rake the leaves in the yard.

ii. Exclamation Marks

Use an exclamation mark after a startling statement or at the end of an exclamatory sentence.

>   Example: Whew! Running the half marathon is exhausting!

Practice

Directions: Punctuate the following sentences.

1. Who are you working with on the media project

2. That was the best game ever

3. Ella wondered if I would help her with the science project

4. We won the state finals in the math competition

5. Oh, no Did I forget to bring a no. 2 pencil to the test

Answer Explanations

1. Who are you working with on the media project? (Use a question mark at the end of an interrogative sentence.)

2. That was the best game ever! (Use an exclamation mark after a startling statement or at the end of an exclamatory sentence.)

3. Ella wondered if I would help her with the science project. (Do not use a question mark with an indirect question.)

4. We won the state finals in the math competition! (Use an exclamation mark after a startling statement or at the end of an exclamatory sentence.)

5. Oh, no! Did I forget to bring a no. 2 pencil to the test? (Use an exclamation mark after a startling statement; use a question mark at the end of an interrogative sentence.)

2. Conventions of Usage in Standard Written English

a. Pronoun Use

i. Pronoun-Antecedent Agreement

Pronouns are words that are used to replace nouns. The noun that the pronoun replaces is called the **antecedent.** Usually, but not always, the antecedent comes before the pronoun.

A pronoun must agree with its antecedent in gender and number. If the antecedent of a pronoun is singular, the pronoun must be singular; if the antecedent is plural, the pronoun must be plural. If the antecedent is feminine, the pronoun must be feminine; if the antecedent is masculine, the pronoun must be masculine.

Example: Jessica gave her speech to the entire student body.

Jessica is the feminine singular antecedent for the feminine singular pronoun *her*.

Example: The seniors thought their team would win the Battle of the Classes.

Seniors is the plural antecedent for the plural pronoun *their*.

If the antecedent refers to both genders, the phrase *his or her* is acceptable to avoid sexist language. When this phrasing is repeated several times in a sentence or paragraph, it may become awkward, though; you can avoid the problem by changing the sentence to the plural form:

Awkward: Each swimmer put his or her feet on his or her starting block.

Better: The swimmers put their feet on their starting blocks.

When indefinite pronouns are antecedents, determine whether they are singular or plural. Here are some singular indefinite pronouns:

anybody	either	neither	one
anyone	everybody	nobody	somebody
each	everyone	no one	someone

Example: Each of the girls in the choir took her part home to study.

Example: Neither of the boys brought his jacket to the field.

Exceptions: Sometimes, with *everyone* and *everybody*, the sense of the sentence is compromised when the singular pronoun is used. In these cases, the plural form is acceptable.

Awkward: Everyone at the performance gasped when he or she saw the lead singer collapse on stage.

Better: Everyone at the performance gasped when they saw the lead singer collapse on stage.

Here are some plural indefinite pronouns:

both	few	many	several

Here are some indefinite pronouns that are either singular or plural, depending on how they're used:

all	most	none	some
any			

For example:

All of the food is gone.	singular in meaning
All of the sandwiches are missing.	plural in meaning

Two or more singular antecedents joined by *or* or *nor* take the singular pronoun.

Example: Either Charlotte or Gabrielle will read her version of the story.

Example: Neither Eli nor Charlie has written his essay for social studies yet.

Every pronoun must clearly refer to a specific antecedent. To avoid vague pronoun reference, be sure you can pinpoint the antecedent of the pronoun. Remember that the antecedent *must* be a noun.

Vague: In our town they like all the lawns to be mowed weekly. (The pronoun *they* has no clear antecedent.)

Better: The town council has suggested that all lawns be mowed weekly.

Vague: The teachers told the students that they would now have to park in the back parking lot. (The pronoun *they* could refer to either the teachers or the students.)

Better: The teachers told the students that the students would now have to park in the back parking lot.

Vague: Louie worked carefully on his practice drill, which pleased his coach. (The word *which* is a vague pronoun because it has no antecedent.)

Better: Louie worked carefully on his practice drill, an effort that pleased his coach.

Or even better: Louie's careful work on his practice drill pleased his coach.

ii. Pronoun Case Errors

If you've ever wondered whether to write *I* or *me*, you've encountered a pronoun case problem. Pronouns change their form depending on how they're used. The different forms of the pronouns are called *cases*. Pronouns have three cases:

- **Nominative:** The nominative case of pronouns is used when the pronoun is the subject or the predicate nominative.
- **Objective:** The objective case is used when the pronoun is the object of a verb or the object of a preposition.
- **Possessive:** The possessive case is used to indicate possession.

Nominative	Objective	Possessive
I	me	my, mine
we	us	our, ours
you	you	your, yours
he	him	his
she	her	her, hers
it	it	its
they	them	their, theirs
who	whom	whose

First, look at the whole sentence and determine what role the pronoun plays in the sentence. Is it the subject? Then use the nominative case. Is it an object of a verb or the object of a preposition? Then choose the objective case. Is the pronoun showing ownership? Then use the possessive case.

Nominative case:
- The pronoun as subject:
    - *She* and *I* want to join the debate team.
    - Jerry and *he* exercised in the gym.
    - *Who* will paint the mural for the entrance to the auditorium?
- The pronoun as *predicate nominative* (a word in the predicate part of the sentence that is linked to the subject):
    - The chairperson must have been *she.*
    - The leaders in the race are Kamal and *he.*

Objective case:

- The pronoun as object of a verb (direct object or indirect object):
  - The school board gave *them* permission to decorate the football field. (*Them* is the indirect object of the verb *gave.*)
  - Delores selected Hayley and *him* to represent the school at the science fair. (*Hayley* and *him* are the direct objects of the verb *selected.*)
- The pronoun as object of a preposition:
  - Michael and Tracy gave the position of treasurer to *her*. (*Her* is the object of the preposition *to.*)
  - With *whom* are you going to the prom? (*Whom* is the object of the preposition *with.*)

Possessive case:

- Use the possessive case to show ownership and to come before a *gerund* (-*ing* form of a verb used as a noun):
  - The problems began with his arriving late to the rehearsal. (*His* is the possessive pronoun used before the gerund *arriving.*)
  - Their coming so quickly averted disaster. (*Their* is the possessive pronoun used before the gerund *coming.*)

Practice

Directions: Select the correct pronoun.

1. The document was sent to Vikram and (I, me).

2. The captains of the team are (she, her) and (I, me).

3. The other students challenged (her, she) answering the question without being recognized by the council president.

4. Either the seniors or (us, we) are going to perform first in the academic challenge.

5. I've known Sarah and (she, her) for as long as I can remember.

6. If anyone wants a ticket to the play, tell (him or her, them) we are all sold out.

7. After finally putting the finishing touches on it, Chris and Olivia shyly brought (his or her, their) poster to the front of the room.

8. Watching the news can keep Judy and (she, her) occupied for hours.

9. Neither of these laptops has (its, their) charger available.

10. It was my grandmother from (who, whom) I received an e-mail this morning.

Answer Explanations

1. **me** The pronoun *I* is incorrect because the nominative pronoun is used for the subject or the predicate nominative. In this sentence, the pronoun *me* is correct; it is the object of the preposition *to*.

2. **she, I** The pronouns *her* and *me* are incorrect because the objective form is used for the object of a verb or the object of a preposition. In this sentence, the pronouns *she* and *I* are correct; they are the compound predicate nominatives.

3. **her** The pronoun *she* is incorrect because the nominative form is used for the subject or the predicate nominative. The pronoun *her* is correct because the possessive pronoun is used before the gerund *answering*.

4. **we** The pronoun *us* is incorrect because the objective form is used for an object of a verb or an object of a preposition. The pronoun *we* is correct because the nominative pronoun is used for the subject or the predicate nominative. In this sentence, *we* is part of the compound subject *the seniors or we*.

5. **her** The pronoun *she* is incorrect because the nominative form is used for the subject or the predicate nominative. The objective pronoun *her* is part of the compound object *Sarah and her*, the objects of the verb *known*.

6. **him or her** The pronoun *anyone* (the antecedent) is singular. The singular objective pronouns *him or her*, not the plural pronoun *them*, must be used to refer to a singular antecedent.

7. **their** The compound subject *Chris and Olivia* (the antecedents) is plural. The plural pronoun *their*, not the singular pronoun *his or her*, must be used to refer to a plural antecedent.

8. **her** The pronoun *she* is incorrect because the nominative pronoun is used for the subject or the predicate nominative. In this sentence, the pronoun *her* is correct because it is the object of the verb *keep*.

9. **its** The pronoun *neither* (the antecedent) is singular. The singular pronoun *its*, not the plural pronoun *their*, must be used to refer to a singular antecedent.

10. **whom** The pronoun *who* is incorrect because the nominative pronoun is used for the subject. The pronoun *whom* is correct because the objective form is used for an object of a verb or an object of a preposition. In this sentence, the pronoun *whom* is the object of the preposition *from*.

b. Agreement

i. Agreement of Subject and Verb

A verb must agree with its subject in number. A singular subject takes the singular form of a verb; a plural subject takes the plural form of the verb.

Singular: The owl hoots in the forest.   one owl

Plural: The owls hoot in the forest.   more than one owl

Note: While most nouns form the plural by adding the letter s, most verbs in their plural form do not end in the letter s.

Phrases may intervene between the subject and the verb. In most cases, ignore the intervening phrase.

Example: The lights in the arena have been turned off. (*In the arena* is a prepositional phrase.)

Intervening prepositional phrases do not affect agreement of subject and verb, so the best approach is to cross out or bracket intervening phrases to help you determine the proper subject-verb agreement. This will avoid confusion.

Note: The subject of a sentence is *never* part of a prepositional phrase.

> Example: The structure of the skulls of prehistoric animals reveals much about their eating habits.
>
> The **structure** [of the skulls of prehistoric animals] reveals much about their eating habits.

Be sure to find the subject and match it with the verb.

> Example: Fishing in the lakes and rivers of the northern territories challenges the most skillful anglers.

Bracket the intervening phrases.

> Example: **Fishing** [in the lakes and rivers of the northern territories] **challenges** the most skillful anglers.
>
> *Fishing* is the singular subject; *challenges* is the singular form of the verb.

Sometimes multiple phrases intervene.

> Example: The sound of the wind blowing through the trees in the mountains reminds me of summer camp.

Follow the same procedure and reread the entire sentence, bracketing the phrases.

> Example: The **sound** [of the wind blowing through the trees in the mountains] **reminds** me of summer camp.
>
> *Sound* is the singular subject; *reminds* is the singular form of the verb.

Intervening parenthetical or explanatory phrases also do not affect agreement of subject and verb, so the best approach is to cross out or bracket intervening phrases. This will avoid confusion.

Bracket the intervening phrase or phrases and match the subject with the verb.

> Example: My cousin, along with five of her friends, plays in a band.
>
> My **cousin**, [along with five of her friends,] **plays** in a band.

> Example: This project, together with my high grades on quizzes, gives me an A for the quarter.
>
> This **project**, [together with my high grades on quizzes,] **gives** me an A for the quarter.

ii. Agreement Problems with Indefinite Pronouns

Singular indefinite pronouns take the singular form of the verb; plural indefinite pronouns take the plural form of the verb.

> *Each* of the dishes on the menu contains vegetables.   singular
>
> *Both* of the dishes on the menu contain vegetables.   plural

Singular subjects joined by the correlative conjunctions *either...or* and *neither...nor* are singular.

Example: Either *Batman* or *Superman is* coming to the rescue of the endangered city.

Plural subjects joined by these correlative conjunctions are plural.

Example: Neither the *superheroes* nor the *aliens were* indestructible.

When one subject is singular and one subject is plural, the verb agrees with the closer subject.

Example: Neither the *aliens* nor *Superman is* indestructible.

Example: Either *Batman* or his *cohorts are* going to defeat the aliens.

iii. Agreement Problems with Inverted Sentences

These sentences are tricky because you encounter the verb before the subject. Again, the key to success is to find the subject, wherever it is in the sentence.

Note: The words *here* and *there* are never subjects.

Example: Through the forest and over the mountains **lie** the **nests** of the rare ibis.

The plural subject *nests* agrees with the plural form of the verb *lie*.

Example: There **are** several rare **birds** that few human beings have ever seen.

The plural subject *birds* agrees with the plural form of the verb *are*.

Be sure to read the whole sentence through to find the subject.

Example: Into the forest **hike** the **bird-watcher and photographer**.

The plural subject *bird-watcher and photographer* agrees with the plural form of the verb *hike*.

Example: Across the hills and over the fields **swoops** the tiny **hummingbird**.

The singular subject *hummingbird* agrees with the singular form of the verb *swoops*.

iv. Noun Agreement

Use a singular noun to refer to a singular noun and a plural noun to refer to a plural noun. Sounds logical, right? Yet, problems do arise:

Incorrect: The women who wanted to become an astronaut prepared to take the physical challenge.

This sentence is incorrect because the plural noun *women* requires the plural noun *astronauts* to be logical.

Correct: The **women** who wanted to become **astronauts** prepared to take the physical challenge.

Here's another example:

Incorrect: Visitors with a cold can't visit friends in the hospital.
Correct: **Visitors** with **colds** can't visit friends in the hospital.

Practice

Directions: Select the best word in the following sentences.

1. Down among the rocks (rest, rests) the baby walrus.

2. The container of vegetables (is, are) no longer in the pantry.

3. Neither the storms nor the wind (was, were) responsible for the fallen trees.

4. A pound of potatoes (is, are) enough for the family.

5. Either scheduling problems or lack of interest (has, have) led to the cancellation of the meeting.

6. Everyone attending the kindergarten parties (is, are) smiling.

Answer Explanations

1. **rests** The subject of the verb *rests* is the singular noun *walrus*.

2. **is** The subject of the verb *is* is the singular noun *container*.

3. **was** With two subjects joined by *neither…nor*, use the subject closer to the verb (*the wind was*).

4. **is** The singular subject *pound* agrees with the singular form of the verb *is*.

5. **has** With two subjects joined by *either…or*, use the subject closer to the verb; in this case, *lack of interest* is singular.

6. **is** The subject of the verb *is* is the singular indefinite pronoun *Everyone*.

c. Comparisons

i. Illogical Comparisons

Use the word *other* or *else* to compare one thing or person to the rest of the group.

> Illogical comparison: The Freedom Tower is taller than any building in New York City. (This is illogical because the Freedom Tower is one of the buildings in New York City.)
>
> Logical comparison: The Freedom Tower is taller than any *other* building in New York City.

ii. Unbalanced Comparisons

Comparisons must be balanced and parallel. Use the word *than* or *as* to balance the sentence.

> Unbalanced: The freshmen wrote as many poems if not more than the juniors.
>
> Balanced: The freshmen wrote as many poems *as*, if not more *than*, the juniors.

iii. Faulty Comparisons

You must compare like things—apples to apples, not apples to oranges.

Faulty: The sneakers at Sneaker Circus are cheaper than Macy's. (In this sentence, you're comparing *sneakers* to *Macy's*.)

Correct: The sneakers at Sneaker Circus are cheaper than the sneakers (or those) at Macy's. (Here you're comparing *sneakers* to *sneakers*.)

Faulty: I like Beyonce's songs better than Justin Bieber. (This sentence compares the *songs* to *Justin Beiber*.)

Correct: I like Beyonce's songs better than Justin Bieber's songs (or those of Justin Bieber). (Here you're comparing *songs* to *songs*.)

Practice

Directions: Correct the comparison errors in the following sentences.

1. The athletes on *American Ninja Warrior* are as good as the Olympics.

2. The weather in Russia is colder than China.

3. Jonathan is a better tennis player than any boy in his class.

4. My mother's chocolate cake is better than your mother.

5. This year's Super Bowl was as exciting, if not more exciting than, last year.

6. The Prius is better than any car on the road.

Answer Explanations

1. The athletes on *American Ninja Warrior* are as good as **those at** the Olympics. (Compare apples to apples: *athletes* to *those*.)

2. The weather in Russia is colder than **the weather in** China. (Compare apples to apples: *weather* to *weather*.)

3. Jonathan is a better tennis player than any **other** boy in his class. (Comparisons must be balanced and parallel.)

4. My mother's chocolate cake is better than your **mother's chocolate cake**. (Compare apples to apples: *cake* to *cake*.)

5. This year's Super Bowl was as exciting as, if not more exciting than, last **year's**. (Comparisons must be balanced: *as exciting as*; compare *this year's* to *last year's*.)

6. The Prius is better than any **other** car on the road. (Comparisons must be balanced and parallel.)

iv. Comparisons of Adjectives and Adverbs

Use the comparative form of the adjective to compare *two* nouns or pronouns. The comparative form is formed in two ways:

- **One-syllable adjectives:** Add *-er*. (This ending is also used for some two-syllable adjectives.) For example:
  - Of the two novels by Harper Lee, *To Kill a Mockingbird* is the longer.
  - Jack is the taller of the two brothers.

- **Most two-syllable-or-more adjectives:** Put the word *more* in front of the word. For example:
  - Max's dog is more intelligent than Ava's dog.

Use the superlative form of the adjective to compare *three or more* nouns or pronouns. The superlative form is formed in two ways:

- **One-syllable adjectives:** Add *-est*. (This ending is also used for some two-syllable adjectives.) For example:
  - Amanda is the sweetest girl in the class.
  - The friskiest kitten in the litter is the black one.

- **Most two-syllable adjectives:** Put the word *most* in front of the word. For example:
  - The deserted island was the most peaceful place on earth.

Here are some irregular comparison forms:

	Comparative	Superlative
good	better	best
bad	worse	worst
little	less or lesser	least
much	more	most
far	farther or further	farthest or furthest

Some adjectives, such as the following, are absolute values and cannot be intensified with *more* or *most*:

complete	round	totally
correct	square	unique
perfect	superior	
preferable	supreme	

v. Adjective/Adverb Confusion

Use an adjective to modify a noun or a pronoun, and use an adverb to modify a verb, an adjective, or another adverb.

Incorrect: The director handled the misplaced scenery so efficient that no one realized the trees were missing. (incorrectly uses the adjective *efficient* to modify the verb *handled*)

Correct: The director handled the misplaced scenery so efficiently that no one realized the trees were missing. (correctly uses the adverb *efficiently* to modify the verb *handled*)

Practice

Directions: Correct the errors in the following sentences.

1. Of all the mountains in Chile, Parinacota is the most highest.

2. Of the two dancers, Karina was the most graceful.

3. Expecting my grandmother to be flustered by the new phone system, I was surprised by how smooth she handled the new equipment.

4. Of the thirty teachers in the school, Ms. North is the more pragmatic when it comes to homework.

5. Because of her amazing work in sculpture, Ronni was voted the most creativest in the exhibition.

6. The committee chose the most perfect theme for the prom.

Answer Explanations

1. Of all the mountains in Chile, Parinacota is the **highest**. (Don't modify the superlative form of an adjective, *highest*, with *most*.)

2. Of the two dancers, Karina was the **more** graceful. (When you're comparing two things, use the comparative form, *more graceful*, rather than the superlative form, *most graceful*.)

3. Expecting my grandmother to be flustered by the new phone system, I was surprised by how **smoothly** she handled the new equipment. (Use an adverb, *smoothly*, rather than an adjective, *smooth*, to modify a verb, *handled*.)

4. Of the thirty teachers in the school, Ms. North is the **most** pragmatic when it comes to homework. (Use the superlative form for comparisons involving more than two.)

5. Because of her amazing work in sculpture, Ronni was voted the most **creative** in the exhibition. (Do not use both *most* and the *-est* superlative form together. In this case, there is no such word as *creativest*.)

6. The committee chose **the perfect** theme for the prom. (The word *perfect* is an absolute and should not be modified with *more* or *most*.)

d. Verb Use

i. Tense

Verbs tell the action or state of being in a sentence. They are also the time words, the principal indicators of tense. As you read, be aware of the tense of the passage and note any inconsistencies.

The six tenses in English are as follows:

- **Present:** Action taking place in the present
- **Past:** Action that has already taken place in the past
- **Future:** Action that will take place in the future

- **Present perfect:** Action that began in the past and continues into the present
- **Past perfect:** Action that began in the past and was completed before some other action
- **Future perfect:** Action that occurs before another action in the future

Present Tense		
	Singular	**Plural**
First person	I call.	We call.
Second person	You call.	You call.
Third person	He/she/it calls.	They call.

Present Perfect Tense		
	Singular	**Plural**
First person	I have called.	We have called.
Second person	You have called.	You have called.
Third person	He/she/it has called.	They have called.

Past Tense		
	Singular	**Plural**
First person	I called.	We called.
Second person	You called.	You called.
Third person	He/she/it called.	They called.

Past Perfect Tense		
	Singular	**Plural**
First person	I had called.	We had called.
Second person	You had called.	You had called.
Third person	He/she/it had called.	They had called.

Future Tense		
	Singular	**Plural**
First person	I will call.	We will call.
Second person	You will call.	You will call.
Third person	He/she/it will call.	They will call.

Future Perfect Tense		
	Singular	**Plural**
First person	I will have called.	We will have called.
Second person	You will have called.	You will have called.
Third person	He/she/it will have called.	They will have called.

Perfect tenses are always formed by using *have*, *has*, or *had* plus the past participle form of the verb. You also have the option of using the progressive form (-*ing*) in each tense to show ongoing action:

- Present progressive: I am calling.
- Past progressive: I was calling.
- Future progressive: I will be calling.
- Present perfect progressive: I have been calling.
- Past perfect progressive: I had been calling.
- Future perfect progressive: I will have been calling.

The present participle is the -*ing* form of the verb. In the case of the verb *to call*, it's *calling*. (These -*ing* forms cannot be verbs alone; they need a helping verb.)

The past participle is the -*ed*, -*d*, -*t*, -*en*, or -*n* form of the verb. In the case of the verb *to call*, it's *called*.

Many verbs have irregular forms:

Present	Past	Past Participle
arise	arose	(have) arisen
become	became	(have) become
bring	brought	(have) brought
catch	caught	(have) caught
do	did	(have) done
drink	drank	(have) drunk
drive	drove	(have) driven
eat	ate	(have) eaten
fall	fell	(have) fallen
fly	flew	(have) flown
lend	lent	(have) lent
ring	rang	(have) rung
sing	sang	(have) sung
swim	swam	(have) swum
write	wrote	(have) written

Often verbs occur in verb phrases with a helping verb and a main verb. Some verbs like *do*, *have*, and *be* can be either main verbs or helping verbs.

Jennifer **does** all the artwork for the newspaper.   main verb

David and Rich **do sing** the duet in the show.   helping verb

Watch for sentences that have illogical shifts in tense or that use incorrect verb forms.

Illogical shift: When Joe **accepted** the medal, he **feels** good.

Correct: When Joe **accepts** the medal, he **feels** good.   present

Or: When Joe **accepted** the medal, he **felt** good.   past

Check the tense of the context to determine whether the sentence should be in the present or past.

Incorrect verb form: The cheering squad was surprised that no one **brang** water.

Correct: The cheering squad was surprised that no one **brought** water.

Incorrect verb form: We thought that everyone **had went** out for dessert after the game.

Correct: We thought that everyone **had gone** out for dessert after the game.

ii. Voice

Verb tenses have active and passive forms. In the **active voice,** the subject of the sentence performs the action.

Example: The committee approved a new plan for restructuring the school day. (*Committee* is the subject; *plan* is the object.)

In the **passive voice,** the object (the receiver of the action) becomes the subject of the sentence.

> Example: A new plan for restructuring the school day was approved by the committee. (*Plan* is the subject; *committee* is the object of the preposition *by*.)

As a general rule, active voice is preferred to passive voice in standard written English. The passive voice is often more awkward and wordy than active voice. Also, it is important to avoid shifts from active to passive within a sentence.

> Example: When the school board met for its annual meeting, a new attendance policy was approved by them. (awkward shift from active to passive)
>
> Better: When the school board met for its annual meeting, it approved a new attendance policy.

Practice

Directions: Write the correct form of the italicized verb in the blank.

1. It had just _____ to snow when we left the gym. *begin*

2. By his own count, Russ will have _____ ten hot dogs. *eat*

3. After we had _____ a theme for the prom, we began to plan the decorations. *choose*

4. When the water pitcher was empty, I realized I had _____ 32 ounces myself. *drink*

5. Although it wasn't very cold, the migrating birds _____ south for the winter last week. *fly*

6. My car has been _____ over 100,000 miles. *drive*

Answer Explanations

1. **begun** To show action that took place before past action, use the past perfect tense.

2. **eaten** To show action that will occur before another action in the future, use the future perfect tense.

3. **chosen** To show action that took place before past action, use the past perfect tense.

4. **drunk** To show action that took place before past action, use the past perfect tense.

5. **flew** This is the simple past tense.

6. **driven** Use the present perfect tense to indicate an action that occurs at an indefinite time in the past.

e. Modification

i. Misplaced Modifiers

Modifiers are words, phrases, or clauses that describe, change, or specify other parts of a sentence. Modifiers are often participial phrases.

> Example: Strolling along the beach, we saw porpoises frolicking out to sea.

Strolling along the beach describes *we*.

Example: When I walked into the classroom, I saw my book lying on the table.

Lying on the table describes *book*.

Sometimes modifiers are infinitive phrases:

Example: To understand the poem, Ketti had to read a little background information on the poet.

To understand modifies *Ketti*.

In English, changes in word order (syntax) lead to changes in meaning. A modifier that is misplaced can cause confusion. For example:

- **Walking through the city, Mike saw his dog eating a hamburger.** In this example, the dog is eating and Mike is walking.
- **Walking through the city eating a hamburger, Mike saw his dog.** Mike is walking and eating when he sees his dog.
- **Mike saw his dog walking through the city eating a hamburger.** Mike is seeing and the dog is walking and eating.

To avoid confusion, always place modifying phrases and clauses as close as possible to the words they modify.

ii. Dangling Modifiers

Dangling modifiers have no word or phrase to modify. The following sentence is confusing:

Incorrect: Looking up from the street, the Space Needle looks enormous.

Who is looking? Certainly not the Space Needle. To correct dangling modifiers, add the missing words or revise the sentence. You might revise this sentence to be:

Correct: Looking up from the street, Shari thought the Space Needle looked enormous.

Practice

Directions: Revise the following sentences to correct the modification errors. Your answers may vary, but be sure to eliminate all modification confusion.

1. Holding on tightly, the ship's deck shifted under our feet.

2. To order online, your credit card should be handy.

3. Flying over the mountains, snow could be seen on the peaks.

4. Gathering up all the loose papers, the briefcase bulged as Seth shoved everything inside.

5. Covered with sticky green sauce, we looked on uneasily as the waiter served the fish.

6. Though only in first grade, the principal was astonished when Harvey solved the quadratic equation.

Answer Explanations

Your answers may vary, but be sure all modification confusion is corrected.

1. Holding on tightly, we felt the ship's deck shift under our feet.

2. To order online, keep your credit card handy.

3. When we flew over the mountains, we could see snow on the peaks.

4. Gathering up all the loose papers, Seth shoved everything inside the bulging briefcase.

5. We looked on uneasily as the waiter served us fish that was covered with sticky green sauce.

6. Though only in first grade, Harvey astonished the principal when he solved the quadratic equation.

f. Parallelism

Parallel ideas should be in the same grammatical form.

When you join ideas using conjunctions, nouns should be joined with nouns, prepositional phrases joined with prepositional phrases, and clauses joined with clauses.

	Unparallel	Parallel
Nouns	The issues on the Congressional agenda were taxation, education, and whether the environmental needed to be protected.	The issues on the Congressional agenda were taxation, education, and environmental protection.
Verb phrases	To improve physical and mental health, everyone should exercise, eat healthily, and they should engage in social interaction.	To improve physical and mental health, everyone should exercise, eat healthily, and engage in social interaction.
Prepositional phrases	The soccer game was rescheduled because it was dark and because of the rain.	The soccer game was rescheduled because of darkness and because of rain. Or: The soccer game was rescheduled because of darkness and rain.
Clauses	Galileo challenged the beliefs that the earth is the center of the universe and it is the sun rotating around the earth.	Galileo challenged the beliefs that the earth is the center of the universe and that the sun rotates around the earth.

Correlative conjunctions (such as *both…and, either…or, neither…nor*, and *not only…but also*), which always occur in pairs, can be tricky: Be sure what comes after the first conjunction is parallel to what comes after the second conjunction.

Unparallel: Julius Caesar not only ignored the soothsayer's warning, but also his wife's dream.

Parallel: Julius Caesar ignored not only the soothsayer's warning, but also his wife's dream.

Unparallel: Alexis went to France, but she toured *neither* the Eiffel Tower *nor* did she visit the Louvre.

Parallel: Alexis went to France, but she toured *neither* the Eiffel Tower *nor* the Louvre.

Practice

Directions: Revise the following sentences to correct the errors in parallelism.

1. Many of the new action films have amazing special effects, supernatural characters, and they have awesome scenery.

2. At the amusement park we can ride the roller coaster, spin on the cyclotron, and we can plummet on the gravity free-fall.

3. I am either going to cook for the party or bring in pizzas.

4. My uncle is a professional landscaper, an accomplished golfer, and he tries to fix things around the house.

5. I like to either read science fiction or fantasy adventure.

Answer Explanations

Your answers may vary slightly.

1. Many of the new action films have amazing special effects, supernatural characters, and awesome scenery.

2. At the amusement park we can ride the roller coaster, spin on the cyclotron, and plummet on the gravity free-fall.

3. I am going to either cook for the party or bring in pizzas.

4. My uncle is a professional landscaper, an accomplished golfer, and an amateur handyman.

5. I like to read either science fiction or fantasy adventure.

g. Sentence Structure

Sentence structure questions concentrate on your understanding of the formation of effective sentences. You must recognize run-on sentences, comma splice errors, and incomplete sentences (sentence fragments).

i. Run-On Sentences and Comma Splice Errors

Two or more complete thoughts joined in one sentence without proper punctuation constitutes a run-on sentence.

Example: The video game didn't make sense to me it didn't come with directions.

A run-on can be corrected in several ways:

- **Break the sentence up into separate sentences:** The video game didn't make sense to me. It didn't come with directions.
- **Join the main clauses with semicolons:** The video game didn't make sense to me; it didn't come with directions.
- **Change one or more of the main clauses to a subordinate clause:** The video game didn't make sense to me because it didn't come with directions.
- **Use a comma and a conjunction:** The video game didn't make sense to me, for it didn't come with directions.
- **Use the semicolon and a conjunctive adverb:** The video game didn't come with directions; consequently, it didn't make sense to me.

The most common run-on occurs when a comma joins two sentences (in what's known as a comma splice):

Example: It is almost seven o'clock, we won't make the start of the concert.

Here are some options to correct this error:

It is almost seven o'clock; we won't make the start of the concert.

It is almost seven o'clock, so we won't make the start of the concert.

It is almost seven o'clock; consequently, we won't make the start of the concert.

ii. Sentence Fragments

Most sentence fragments are phrases or subordinate clauses.

Being around so many young children.	participial phrase
To be around so many young children.	infinitive phrase
Because we are around so many young children.	subordinate clause

To avoid fragments, remember:

- A sentence must have a subject and a verb and express a complete thought.
- No word ending in *-ing* can stand alone as a verb without a helping verb (except one-syllable verbs like *sing* and *ring*).

Practice

Directions: Correct the following sentences.

1. The lifeguard swimming to the rescue of the floundering swimmer.

2. The ocean pulsed with ten-foot waves, the waves are remnants of the tropical storm.

3. Debris floating around the tumultuous sea.

4. We walked along the edge of the beach, the sand was littered with seaweed and broken shells.

5. Seeing the churning up whitecaps in the distance.

6. Misty clouds floating in gray skies.

Answer Explanations

Answers may vary.

1. The lifeguard is swimming to the rescue of the floundering swimmer. (Sentence fragment is missing a verb.)

2. The ocean pulsed with ten-foot waves, remnants of the tropical storm. (Comma splice error.)

3. Debris floated (or is floating) around the tumultuous sea. (Sentence fragment is missing a verb.)

4. We walked along the edge of the beach; the sand was littered with seaweed and broken shells. (Comma splice error.)

5. The spectators see the churning up whitecaps in the distance. (Sentence fragment is missing a subject and a verb.)

6. Misty clouds are floating in gray skies. (Sentence fragment missing the proper verb form.)

3. Rhetoric

Many of the questions on the Writing and Language Test ask you to make choices about word choice, phrasing, adding or deleting material, or the best way to organize a paragraph or express an idea. These rhetoric questions focus on style, writing strategy, and structure. You are asked to make decisions similar to those that writers make when they revise their work.

a. Style

The four passages on the PSAT Writing and Language Test will vary in style. You are expected to note the style (sometimes referred to as the writer's voice) and take it into consideration as you answer questions about the writers' decisions. Many passages are objective and informational; these will have a straightforward and unemotional style. Some passages will refer to information in graphic form.

Example:

Question 1 refers to the passage below.

Recent discoveries of primitive art in the diluvial formations both of France and England have tended to add a fresh interest to the investigation of that "primeval stone-period" which underlies the most ancient memorials of Europe's civilization. The oldest of all written chronicles assigns a period of some duration in the history of the human race, during which man **1** planted a couple of seeds, pursued the chase, and made garments of its spoils, without any knowledge of the working in metals, on which the simplest of all known arts depend. Through such a primitive stage it had already appeared to me probable that all civilized nations had passed, before disclosures of a still older flint-period in the chroniclings of the drift added new significance to the term *primeval*, in its application to the non-metallurgic era of Europe's arts.

1. **A.** NO CHANGE
   B. tilled the ground
   C. stuck some seeds into the earth
   D. farming the soil

In this question, you should note that the excerpt is written in a formal style. Therefore, choices A and C are far too informal for this passage. Choice D, although more formal than Choice A or C, is not parallel to the series of verb phrases: *pursued the chase, and made garments of its spoils…* Choice B, *tilled the ground*, is the best phrasing for the underlined words and most consistent with the style of the paragraph.

In answering style questions, keep in mind that active verbs are preferable to passive ones.

Example: **He planted the crops.** (active verb) is preferable to **The crops were planted by him.** (passive).

b. Writing Strategy

These questions ask you to consider the appropriateness of the writer's strategy in either a portion of the passage or the entire passage. As you read, consider the following questions: Which is the best choice for the writer to accomplish his or her purpose? Which choice shows his or her awareness of the audience? Which choice is more effectively written? Is every piece of information relevant to the focus of the passage?

Example:

Questions 2–3 refer to the passage below.

The Struggle for Survival

[1]

Deer have many natural enemies. It is fortunate that nature has provided for an abundant reproduction in this species. [2] Snow is perhaps most serious of all, since a heavy snowfall may cover the food supply, and certainly hampers the movement of the animals when they must escape predatory coyotes or cougars. Late spring snows, in particular, come at a critical time. At best forage diminishes steadily during the winter months, and when this period is followed by even a short space when food is unavailable, starvation and death strikes the weaker and aged animals.

[2]

(1) Of the predatory animals, the coyote and cougar are most effective. (2) This frequently happens in many parts of the West where the natural enemies of the deer have been exterminated. (3) The fox, wildcat, and bear undoubtedly take an occasional fawn, but cannot be considered dangerous to an adult deer. (4) In view of the powers of rapid reproduction shown by deer, it is well that they have numerous natural enemies; otherwise, wholesale destruction of brush lands and forest reproduction would occur as the animals reached a peak of overpopulation, followed by mass starvation. (5) Predators follow, in most instances, the line of least resistance. (6) As a consequence, it is the weaker, the diseased, or the otherwise unfit animals that tend to be struck down first, and so the fittest survive. [3]

2. At this point, the writer is considering adding the following sentence:

> Most fawns are born during late May and early June, and, while they are able to walk shortly after birth, they spend most of their first several days lying still.

Should the writer add this sentence here?

A. Yes, because it would add a detail that isn't included anywhere in the passage.
B. Yes, because it is essential to understanding the information that follows in the passage.
C. No, because the focus of the passage is the deer's "natural enemies."
D. No, because the detail isn't about deer.

The correct answer is C. The writer shouldn't add the information because the passage is about natural enemies of the deer; thus, choices A and B are incorrect. Choice D is incorrect because the passage is about deer, although not fawns.

c. Organization

Questions on organization deal with the order and coherence of ideas in a passage. One of the keys to achieving coherence is the effective use of transitional words and phrases.

i. Order and Coherence

You will notice as you read the PSAT Writing and Language Test that sometimes the sentences in the passage are numbered, and sometimes the paragraphs are numbered. This numbering tells you that you will encounter questions about order. Use the context clues to help you determine the best order. For example, if a person or place is mentioned by name, ask yourself, "Has this name been introduced or identified?" If the introduction comes later in the passage, then you know you must logically rearrange the order of the sentences. The same holds true for paragraph order. Use logic and look for clues to what happens next within the passage.

Example:

Refer to the previous passage.

3. Which of the following is the best placement for Sentence 2 in Paragraph 2?

   A.   Where it is now
   B.   After Sentence 3
   C.   After Sentence 4
   D.   After Sentence 6

The correct answer is C. The logical placement of this sentence is after Sentence 4. Use the clues in the paragraph to help you arrange the sentences. Sentence 2 begins with *This frequently happens…where the natural enemies of the deer have been exterminated.* That is your clue that you must find the sentence that states what happens to the deer when their enemies have been exterminated. Sentence 4 explains that deer overpopulation leads to starvation. Logic helps you arrange Sentence 2 after Sentence 4.

ii. Transitional Words and Phrases

Transitional words and phrases link ideas and indicate the relationship of ideas within a sentence, a paragraph, or a passage. They are essential tools for a writer who wants to achieve a clear and logical flow of ideas.

Important Transitional Words and Phrases

Words Used to Indicate an Example		Words Used to Show a Result	
For example	Specifically	Consequently	Accordingly
For instance		Hence	Therefore

Words Used to Indicate a Reason		Words Used to Indicate More Information	
As	Since	Besides	Moreover
Because	Due to	In addition	Furthermore

Words Used to Contrast		Words Used to Show Similarity	
Although	While	Another	Again
But	Yet	Similarly	In the same way
However	On the other hand	Likewise	Too
In contrast	Still	Also	Equally
Nevertheless	Despite		
Whereas			

Words Used to Establish Time Relationships		Words Used for Emphasis	
Before	Later	Then	Indeed
During	Soon	Then again	Clearly
After	Next	Once	To be sure
At last	Until	At the same time	Without doubt
At this point	Recently	Assuredly	

Practice

Directions: Select the best transitional word or phrase to fit in the sentences.

1. Floods have ravaged southern West Virginia; _____, the golf tournament scheduled there was canceled for the first time ever.

   A. however
   B. nevertheless
   C. in addition
   D. consequently

2. Beth realized she had missed a step in the dance routine, _____ it was clear the judges didn't consider it a serious deduction.

   A. then
   B. but
   C. likewise
   D. for example

3. In many families, both parents have full-time jobs, _____ in the 1950s only one parent worked outside the home.

    A. then
    B. furthermore
    C. likewise
    D. whereas

4. In recent years, travel abroad has become a much more complicated and inconvenient process; _____, many intrepid travelers continue to fly to exotic locations.

    A. nevertheless
    B. moreover
    C. hence
    D. for example

Answer Explanations

1. **D.** Use *consequently* to show as a result.

2. **B.** Use *but* to show contrast.

3. **D.** Use *whereas* in a subordinate clause to show contrast to the idea of the main clause.

4. **A.** Use *nevertheless* to show contrast.

d. Redundancy

In standard written English, conciseness is a goal. It is best to express your ideas in as few well-chosen words as possible. Always be alert for repetitive and wordy expressions such as the following:

close proximity	large in shape	the future to come
consensus of opinion	new innovations	true fact
due to the fact that	problem that needs a solution	two equal halves
extreme in degree	round in shape	unexpected surprise
important essentials	ten years in age	various different

Example: Alone in the study cubicle for hours, Emma worked on the complex chemistry formula by herself.

At first reading, you may think the sentence is grammatically correct. You'd be almost right. However, if you reread the sentence from the beginning, you'll see the sentence begins with *Alone*. This word makes the phrase *by herself* redundant. You'll have to find a choice that eliminates this redundancy.

Also, be aware of words that are unnecessary to the meaning of the sentence.

Wordy: We drove into the city during rush hour, which is the time when traffic is horrendous.

More concise: We drove into the city during rush hour in horrendous traffic.

Wordy: The lecturer spoke about the various ways and techniques for fixing up and eliminating unnecessary words, so you can shorten the essays you write for class.

More concise: The lecturer suggested methods for editing essays for conciseness.

Practice

Directions: Rewrite the following sentences to avoid redundancies and wordiness. Your answers might be slightly different. Do not worry if this is the case; your goal is to eliminate the redundant expressions.

1. Duane dropped out of school on account of the fact that it was necessary for him to work on the family farm.

2. Before we move forward with the project, there are several important essential contingencies we must consider in the future to come.

3. The cake was round in shape, and the baker divided it into two equal halves.

4. The mayor is hoping for an annual road repair reduction of $50,000 each year.

5. My cousin Helen, who has red hair, was the tallest person who was in the room.

6. The new sofa, so large in size that it wouldn't fit through the door, created a problem that needed a solution.

Answer Explanations

Answers may vary.

1. **Duane dropped out of school because it was necessary for him to work on the family farm.** The words *on account of the fact* are wordy; the same meaning can be conveyed by one word: *because*.

2. **Before we move forward with the project, we must consider several essential contingencies.** The expression *important essential* is redundant; *the future to come* is another wordy expression, and *there are* can be eliminated.

3. **The baker divided the round cake in half.** *Round in shape* and *two equal halves* are redundant expressions.

4. **The mayor is hoping for an annual road repair reduction of $50,000.** Using both *annual* and *each year* is redundant.

5. **My redheaded cousin Helen was the tallest person in the room.** The adjective *redheaded* can replace the whole adjective clause *who has red hair*, and *who was* is unnecessary to the meaning of the sentence.

6. **The new sofa, too large to fit through the door, created a problem.** The expressions *large in size* and a *problem that needed a solution* are wordy. Aim for conciseness and eliminate these unnecessary words.

e. Idioms

Idioms are expressions or verb phrases that are used in English. The problem frequently arises when the incorrect preposition is used with a verb. Unfortunately, there are no rules—you just need to know what is accepted as correct. Usually, you can trust your ears—go with what sounds right.

Here are some common idioms:

abide by	complain about	method of or for
agree to (something)	conform to	object to
agree with (someone)	consists of	opinion of
apply for	depend on	participate in
approve of	differ from	prefer to
argue about (something)	discriminate against	preoccupied with
argue with (someone)	escape from	prohibited from
arrived at	in contrast to	protect from
believe in	insensitive to	relevant to
capable of	insight into	subscribe to
comment on	insist upon	succeeded in

Practice

Directions: Correct the idiom errors in the following sentences.

1. Using the camera on my cell phone, I succeeded to capture the egret in flight.

2. My parents were sure I was capable to do well on the PSAT.

3. I often prefer the book more than the movie version of a novel.

4. I like to read the reviews for their insights upon the themes of the movies I plan to see.

5. Elena was so preoccupied about her upcoming driving test, she forgot to arrange for a ride to the testing site.

Answer Explanations

1. Using the camera on my cell phone, I **succeeded in capturing** the egret in flight.
2. My parents were sure I was **capable of doing** well on the PSAT.
3. I often **prefer the book to** the movie version of a novel.
4. I like to read the reviews for their **insights into** the themes of the movies I plan to see.
5. Elena was so **preoccupied with** her upcoming driving test, she forgot to arrange for a ride to the testing site.

f. Diction and Vocabulary

Diction means "word choice." A diction error occurs when a word is used incorrectly or inappropriately.

On the PSAT Writing and Language Test, diction errors often occur with words that look similar, such as *refer/infer*, *prospective/perspective*, *formally/formerly*, *defensible/defensive*, or *reliable/reliant*. Be alert and careful as you read the sentences. Some incorrect choices will contain nonstandard (unacceptable) expressions.

Vocabulary questions on the Writing and Language Test will measure your ability to understand the meaning of words in context and to recognize words that aren't used correctly.

Here are some commonly misused words:

- *among/between:* Use *between* for two people or things (*between* my brother and me). Use *among* for three or more (*among* all my friends).
- *fewer/less:* Use *fewer* for anything you can count or plural words (*fewer* times at bat). Use *less* for whole quantities or singular words (*less* pain).
- *amount/number:* Use *amount* for whole quantities (*amount* of homework). Use *number* for things you can count (*number* of math problems).
- *being as/being that:* Avoid both these phrases as they are almost never correct; use *because* or *since* instead.
- *irregardless/regardless: Irregardless* is nonstandard; use *regardless* instead.
- *off of/of:* Avoid using *of* with the preposition *off.*
- *reason…is because/reason…is that:* Avoid the expression *the reason* (for something) *is because.* It is a nonstandard expression. The preferable expression is *the reason* (for something) *is that.*
- *there, their, they're: There* indicates location (my brother is *there* now); *their* is the possessive case of they (my brother is at *their* house); *they're* is the contraction of they are (*they're* going to visit my brother).

Practice

Directions: Select the best word or phrase in the following sentences.

1. (Being that there have been, Because of) budget cuts, (less, fewer) scholarship money is available this year.

2. I will go to Indiana University (irregardless, regardless) of any scholarship money I am offered elsewhere.

3. The (amount, number) of students from my town who go to out-of-state colleges is very low.

4. I took my name (off, off of) the list of volunteers for the committee when I realized the meetings were on Saturdays when I help my father.

5. My friends announced that (there, their, they're) going back to (there, their, they're) house, and that we should meet them (there, their, they're).

Answer Explanations

1. **Because of; less:** *Being that* is a nonstandard expression; use *less* to refer to whole quantities.

2. **regardless:** *Irregardless* is a nonstandard expression.

3. **number:** Use *number* for things you can count. (You can count students.)

4. **off:** The phrase *off of* is nonstandard.

5. **they're; their; there:** Use *they're* for the contraction of they are. Use *their* for the possessive of they. Use *there* to indicate location.

g. Quantitative Literacy

The PSAT Writing and Language Test emphasizes literacy across the curriculum by including information presented in graphic form and by asking graphic-based questions.

You might be asked to analyze graphically presented data as part of your rhetorical decision-making. For example: Should the writer include the information? Which wording choice is the most concise and appropriate? What is the best way to synthesize the information from the passage and the chart or graph? What do the data in the graph support?

Practice

Questions 1–2 are based on the following passage and figure.

Civil Service in America

With unbridled courage, zeal, and tenacity, Theodore Roosevelt worked to ensure a hiring system for America's government workers based on fairness and equal access and protection for all—making him the undisputed father of today's Federal Service. Theodore Roosevelt's dedication to civil service reform began in 1881 as a member of the New York Civil Service Reform Association. As a New York State Assemblyman, he had worked hard for passage of the New York State Civil Service Act of 1883, the first state civil service act in the nation. His enthusiasm and perseverance to reform the civil service system thrust him into the national spotlight as he challenged the corrupt style of politics in the state of New York.

Roosevelt's enthusiastic efforts on behalf of reform led then President Benjamin Harrison (1889–1893) to appoint him as U.S. Civil Service Commissioner in 1889. During his term as United States Civil Service Commissioner (1889–1895) the full force of his energy, enthusiasm, and aggressiveness was put to the task of building up the Federal civil service system. He undertook the task of reform with the same honesty and zeal that he showed for all of his endeavors. Commissioner Roosevelt believed his role was to create a civil service system that would attract the best people into government.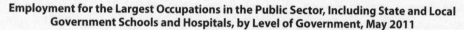

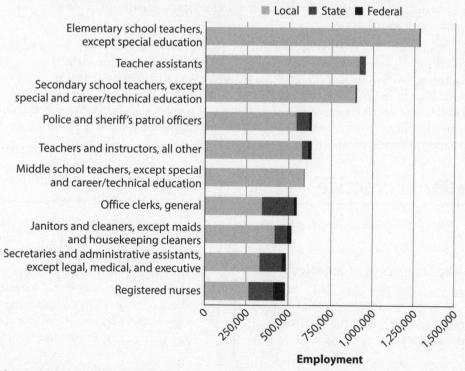

Employment for the Largest Occupations in the Public Sector, Including State and Local Government Schools and Hospitals, by Level of Government, May 2011

Source: U.S. Bureau of Labor Statistics.

1. Which choice offers an accurate interpretation of the data on the bar chart?

    A. From 2011 to the present, the number of federal employees who are registered nurses increased.
    B. More elementary teachers were employed by the federal government than by the state government in the time covered by the chart.
    C. Most middle school teachers in May 2011 were employed by the state governments.
    D. In May 2011, of the occupations listed in the chart, registered nurses are the most evenly distributed throughout local, state, and federal governments.

2. Support for the statement below is provided by which of the following?

    Some workers in New York State took unfair advantage of political patronage to obtain government jobs.

    A. The chart only
    B. The passage only
    C. Both the chart and the passage
    D. Neither the chart nor the passage

Answer Explanations

1. **D.** According to the information on the chart, registered nurses are the only occupation that approaches even distribution throughout local, state, and federal governments (although there are clearly more registered nurses employed by the local governments than the other two governments). So, while the distribution is not even, of the occupations listed, it is the most even. Choice A cannot be determined based on the data in the chart, which covers only May 2011. Choice B is not accurate; fewer elementary teachers were employed by the federal government than by the state governments. Choice C is contradicted by the information in the chart; most middle school teachers were employed by the local government.

2. **B.** It can be inferred from the first sentence of the passage (*With unbridled courage, zeal, and tenacity, Theodore Roosevelt worked to ensure a hiring system for America's government workers based on fairness and equal access and protection for all…*) that Roosevelt had to deal with a corrupt hiring system. This is supported by the information in the last sentence of the first paragraph (*His enthusiasm and perseverance to reform the civil service system thrust him into the national spotlight as he challenged the corrupt style of politics in the state of New York.*). Only the information in the passage, not that in the chart, supports this statement.

C. Additional Practice

Questions 1–10 are based on the following passage and figure.

The Dangers of Domesticity

Since the establishment of the National Park Service in 1916, it has become [1] increasing obvious that the occupation of the national parks by man and wildlife must inevitably result in wildlife problems. The act creating the National Park Service is specific in its [2] language, it says that the Service thus established shall promote and regulate the use of the areas by such means and measures necessary "to conserve the scenery and the natural and historic objects and the wildlife therein and to provide for the enjoyment of the same in such manner and by such means as will leave them unimpaired for the enjoyment of future generations."

The apparent inconsistency [3] presents itself immediately. Natural features must be conserved and protected, they must not be impaired, yet provision must be made for their enjoyment by the millions of visitors [4] whom come to the national parks each year. The course that must be followed, then, is one of permitting modification of the natural scene [5] to loosen restrictions on perpetual enjoyment of "the scenery, the natural and historic objects and the wildlife."

The relations between man and the wildlife of the national parks are complex. Both occupy the parks, with equal rights to that occupancy. It can scarcely be argued that man is not a part of the natural scene; certainly there is nothing essentially unnatural in the progress of our civilization [6] to the dawn of history to the present. In the national parks, however, the *unimpaired* values to be preserved are those of the *primitive natural scene*. Man can strive to maintain these values, unimpaired, because he has the power of reason. Through that power he can recognize the effect of his conflict with nature, and so prevent the destruction of the primitive natural scene by a proper regulation of his acts. [7] Charles Darwin believed we are similar to animals, and merely incrementally more intelligent because of our higher evolution.

Specifically, the wildlife problems now readily recognized in Mount Rainier National Park are those that have developed because of relations between man and mammals. The deer, bear, and raccoon are outstanding examples. In the developed areas of the park many of these animals have become so accustomed to the proximity of man that they no longer exhibit timidity in his presence. They are essentially "wild" animals, yet because of close association with man for several wildlife generations, they may be practically considered as "semi-domestic" animals.

This "semi-domesticity" is a problem in itself. [8] Nevertheless, it is not in keeping with the primitive natural scene. The true wildlife picture is not one of a deer eating from a visitor's hand; that is scarcely more natural than seeing the animal within the fenced enclosure of a zoo. The artificial feeding of any form of wildlife is objectionable for several other reasons. Such feeding encourages an unnatural concentration of the animals in restricted localities, [9] thus decreasing the danger of the spread of any contagious disease or infection. In the case of deer, feeding affects, often disastrously, the normal habit of migration to lower elevations in winter. Deer encouraged to remain in place by feeding, for example, encounter difficult times during the winter months. Natural forage is buried beneath the snow, migratory routes to the lowlands are blocked, and starvation is not unusual.

In every instance, experience has shown that when animals are hand-fed, petted, and tamed, the results have been detrimental to both the animals and to man. The "tamed" animals are often dangerous, or may become so. Even the harmless-appearing deer may, and do, inflict severe injuries by striking with the fore feet or hooking with the antlers, and bears often strike or bite, once they have lost their instinctive fear of man. When any animal becomes dangerous, the only solutions are to eliminate the danger by killing the animal, or to live-trap and remove it to a more isolated section of the park. The latter is often a temporary expedient because the animal is likely to return almost at once to its original home.

10 **White-Tailed Deer, Mule Deer, and Mountain Lion Populations in the U.S. 1944–1973**

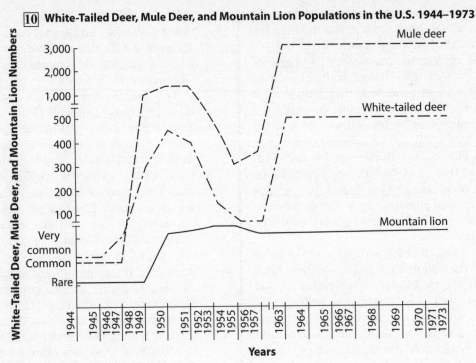

Source: National Park Service (nps.gov).

1. **A.** NO CHANGE
   B. increasingly obviously
   C. obviously increasing
   D. increasingly obvious

2. **A.** NO CHANGE
   B. language; it says
   C. language; they say
   D. language; it says there

3. **A.** NO CHANGE
   B. present itself
   C. presenting itself
   D. presented itself

4. **A.** NO CHANGE
   B. who come
   C. who comes
   D. whom comes

5. Which of the following best supports the concept of "permitting modification" to protect the natural environment?

   A. NO CHANGE
   B. so all visitors can experience
   C. opening up the park to the
   D. only to the degree required to provide for

6. **A.** NO CHANGE
   B. with
   C. from
   D. about

7. The writer is considering deleting the underlined sentence. Should the sentence be kept or deleted?

   A. Kept, because it provides a detail that supports the main topic of the paragraph

   B. Kept, because it sets up the main topic of the paragraph that follows

   C. Deleted, because it brings in a loosely related detail that is not relevant to the main focus of the passage

   D. Deleted, because it repeats information that has been provided in an earlier paragraph

8. A. NO CHANGE
   B. Clearly
   C. Thus
   D. However

9. Which choice most effectively supports the information that precedes it?

   A. NO CHANGE
   B. thus it is not the natural way for animals to concentrate
   C. thus animals are easier for visitors to see in their natural environment
   D. thus increasing the danger of the spread of any contagious disease or infection

10. Which choice offers an accurate interpretation of the data in the chart?

   A. The population of white-tailed deer increased in the early 1950s and decreased in the late 1960s.

   B. At all times represented on the graph, there were fewer white-tailed deer than mule deer.

   C. From 1949 to 1950, all animal populations represented on the graph increased.

   D. No animal population represented on the graph increased in the years 1956–1957.

Answer Explanations

1. **D.** The adverb *increasingly* is needed to modify the adjective *obvious*, Choice D. Choice A incorrectly uses two adjectives, *increasing* and *obvious*, and Choice B incorrectly uses two adverbs, *increasingly* and *obviously*, to modify the pronoun *it*; neither choice makes sense in the context of the sentence. Choice C changes the meaning of the sentence by changing the order of the words; *obviously increasing* has a different meaning from *increasingly obvious*.

2. **B.** Choice B correctly uses the semicolon to connect two closely related main clauses. Choice A contains a comma splice error. Choice C incorrectly uses the plural pronoun *they* to refer to the singular subject *act*. Choice D adds the unnecessary word *there*.

3. **A.** Choice A correctly uses the singular form of the verb *presents* and the singular pronoun *itself* to agree with the singular subject *inconsistency*. Choice B incorrectly uses the plural form of the verb *present*. Choice C incorrectly uses the progressive form of the verb *presenting* without a helping verb. Choice D incorrectly shifts the tense to the past tense verb *presented*.

4. **B.** The subject (nominative) pronoun *who* is needed as the subject of the plural form of the verb *come*, Choice B. Choice A incorrectly uses the objective form *whom*. Choice C incorrectly uses the singular form of the verb *comes*. Since the antecedent of *who* is *millions*, the plural form of the verb is needed here. Choice D incorrectly uses the objective form of the pronoun and the singular form of the verb.

5. **D.** Choice D supports the point of the paragraph that a balance between protecting the natural environment and allowing visitors to enjoy the park must be found. Choices A, B, and C all incorrectly denote loosening the restrictions.

6. **C.** Choice C uses the correct preposition *from* to fit the logic of the sentence, *from the dawn of history to the present*. Choice A incorrectly uses the preposition *to*, which makes no sense in establishing a period of time *from…to*. Choice B incorrectly uses the preposition *with*, which also makes no sense, and Choice D, *about*, is incorrect for the same reason.

7. **C.** The sentence should be deleted (so choices A and B are incorrect) because Charles Darwin's theories about human intelligence are not related the passage's main focus on the dangers inherent in too much contact between human beings and animals in the national parks. Choice D is incorrect because the sentence doesn't repeat information provided in an earlier paragraph.

8. **B.** The transitional word *Clearly* indicates that it is obvious that "semi-domesticity" is not in keeping with the natural scene. One idea *clearly* follows from the other. The rest of the paragraph adds additional evidence for support of this point. Choices A and D incorrectly suggest a contrasting relationship between the ideas in this sentence and the ideas in the preceding sentence. Choice C sets up the illogical sense that this sentence presents a result of the previous sentence.

9. **D.** Choice D best supports the idea that human feeding of "wild" animals causes a serious danger to the animals. Choice A incorrectly states that feeding decreases the danger. Choice B merely repeats the ideas of the first part of the sentence. Choice C is illogical and not relevant to the point being made in this paragraph.

10. **C.** The data show that all the animal populations underwent an increase from 1949 to 1950, Choice C. Choice A is incorrect because the population of white-tailed deer decreased in the early 1950s and remained constant in the late 1960s. Choice B is incorrect because from 1946 to 1947 there were more white-tailed deer than mule deer. Choice D is incorrect because from 1956 to 1957 the population of mule deer increased.

VII. Tier 2 Vocabulary

The PSAT doesn't have a specific vocabulary section, but you are required to determine the meanings of words in context on both the Reading Test and the Writing and Language Test. In addition, the language used in the reading passages is fairly challenging and includes words you will encounter in college and in the workplace. Your knowledge of the Tier 2 words in this chapter will help you read and understand the passages and may even help you find the right word choice in your own writing.

aberration: An abnormality

abet: To aid in the commission (usually of a crime)

abrasive: Rough; coarse

abscond: To depart suddenly and secretly

abstemious: Characterized by self-denial or abstinence

abstruse: Difficult to understand

acquiesce: To comply; to agree; to submit

acumen: Quickness of intellectual insight

admonition: Gentle scolding or warning

aesthetic: Beautiful; relating to the appreciation of art or beauty

affable: Good-natured; easy to approach

agile: Able to move quickly (physically or mentally)

agitate: To move violently; to make someone anxious

alacrity: Cheerful willingness or promptness

alleviate: To relieve; to make less hard to bear

aloof: Reserved; distant

ambiguous: Having a double meaning

ambivalence: Uncertainty; mixed feelings

ameliorate: To relieve; to make better

amiable: Friendly

anecdote: A personal story (often short and humorous)

animosity: Hatred

appease: To soothe

application: Relevance; use of something; formal request

approbation: Approval

arbiter: One who makes a judgment

arbitrary: Based on whim; random

arcane: Difficult to understand; known to only a few

ardor: Passion

articulate: Eloquent; able to express oneself well

assiduous: Unceasing; persistent

assuage: To relieve

astute: Keen in discernment

audacious: Bold; fearless

auspicious: Favorable

austere: Severely simple; strict; harsh

authoritarian: Demanding; despotic

avarice: Greed

banal: Commonplace; trite

belittle: To make seem less significant or worthy

belligerent: Displaying a warlike spirit

benefactor: One who does kindly and charitable acts

beneficent: Charitable

benevolence: An act of kindness or generosity

benign: Good and kind

berate: To scold severely

bewilder: To confuse

boisterous: Lively; rowdy; overexcited

bolster: To support

boorish: Rude

brevity: Briefness

brusque: Curt; brief to the point of rude

burnish: To make brilliant or shining

cajole: To convince by flattering speech

capitulate: To surrender

castigate: To punish

celebratory: Festive; congratulatory

censure: To criticize severely

chagrin: Embarrassment or dismay

circumscribe: To limit or restrict

circumstantial: Based on inference rather than conclusive proof

clash (n): A violent confrontation; a mismatch of colors

clash (v): Conflict; fight; make a loud noise

coerce: To force

cogent: Strongly persuasive

collusion: A secret agreement for a wrongful purpose

compound: To combine; to intensify

comprehensive: All-inclusive; broad in scope

compromise: Meet halfway; expose to danger or disgrace

compunction: Uneasiness caused by guilt or remorse

conciliatory: Tending to reconcile

concord: Harmony

condescension: A snobby and pretentiously kind manner

congenial: Agreeable; friendly

console: To comfort

conspicuous: Clearly visible

constrict: To bind

contemplative: Calm and thoughtful

contemptuous: Scornful; disdainful

contrite: Remorseful

conventional: Usual; conservative

copious: Plentiful

corroboration: Confirmation

credulous: Easily deceived

curtail: To cut off; to cut short

dearth: Scarcity

declaim: Speak formally; proclaim

defame: To harm someone's reputation

defuse: To remove a threat

deleterious: Hurtful

delineate: To outline; to explain

demarcate: To define; to separate

denounce: To condemn; to criticize harshly

deplete: To reduce; to lessen

deride: To ridicule

derivative: Coming from some origin; not original

deter: To frighten away

didactic: Pertaining to teaching

diffidence: Shyness; lack of self-confidence

diligence: Persistent effort

discern: To distinguish; to see clearly

disconsolate: Hopelessly sad

disdain: Scorn; contempt

dissemble: To hide by putting on a false appearance

disseminate: To scatter; to distribute

dissent or dissension: Disagreement

divulge: To tell something previously private or secret

docile: Quiet and easy to control

dogmatic: Stubbornly opinionated; making assertions without evidence

dubious: Doubtful; skeptical; questionable

duplicity: Deceitfulness; dishonesty

ebullient: Showing enthusiasm

eccentric: Odd; unconventional

effervescent: Bubbly; enthusiastic

effrontery: Boldness; audacity

effusive: Gushing; unrestrained in showing feelings

egalitarian: Believing in equality

elucidate: To clarify

elusive: Tending to escape; hard to find or pin down

embellish: To add decoration

enervate: To weaken

engender: To produce

enigma: A riddle or puzzle

enmity: Hatred

equable: Equal; serene

eradicate: To destroy thoroughly

erratic: Irregular

erroneous: Incorrect

evoke: To call or summon forth

exacerbate: To make worse

excavation: Digging out the earth

expedient: Useful; advantageous

explicate: To explain; to clarify

explicit: Clear; unambiguous

expunge: To erase; to remove from a record

extant: Still existing and known

extenuate: To make less severe

extinct: No longer in existence

extol: To praise in the highest terms

extraneous: Irrelevant

facetious: Amusing

facile: Easy

fallacious: Illogical

flaunt: To show off

frenetic: Frantic; frenzied

frivolity: Silly and trivial behavior or activities

frugal: Economical

garrulous: Talkative; chatty

gentility: Refinement; courtesy

germane: Relevant

gregarious: Sociable; outgoing

guile: Duplicity

gullible: Credulous

harbinger: First sign; messenger

heed: Pay attention to

heinous: Odiously sinful

hybrid: Crossbreed; mixture

hyperbole: Exaggeration

hypocrisy: Extreme insincerity

iconoclasm: A challenge to or overturning of traditional beliefs, customs, or values

idiosyncrasy: A habit peculiar to an individual; a quirk

ignominious: Shameful

illicit: Unlawful

illusory: Deceptive; misleading

imminent: About to occur

immutable: Unchangeable

impassive: Unmoved by or not exhibiting feeling

impede: To block; to obstruct

imperious: Insisting on obedience; arrogant

impermanence: Quality of not lasting (lacking permanence)

imperturbable: Calm

impervious: Impenetrable; to be unmoved or unaffected

impetuous: Impulsive

implacable: Incapable of being pacified

implicate: To hint or suggest involvement

implicit: Implied

impromptu: Anything done or said on the spur of the moment

impugn: To oppose or attack; to suggest doubt

inadvertent: Accidental

inane: Silly

incessant: Unceasing

incipient: Initial; beginning of development

incisive: Sharp; perceptive

incite: To rouse to a particular action

incomprehensible: Beyond understanding; inexplicable

incongruous: Unsuitable for the time, place, or occasion; inconsistent

indelible: Permanent; unable to be removed

indigenous: Native

indignant: Angry at unfairness

indiscretion: An unwise action; a tactless lack of judgment

indolence: Laziness

indomitable: Unconquerable

indulgent: Yielding to the desires of oneself or those under one's care

ineffable: Unable to be expressed in words

inept: Not fit or suitable

inevitable: Unavoidable

innocuous: Harmless

inscrutable: Impenetrably mysterious or profound

insinuate: To imply

instigate: To start; to cause trouble

intransigent: Unyielding

intrepid: Fearless and bold

introspection: The act of observing and analyzing one's own thoughts and feelings

inundate: To flood

inveterate: Habitual; firmly established

invincible: Unable to be conquered, subdued, or overcome

iota: Small or insignificant amount

irascible: Prone to anger

irate: Moved to anger

ire: Anger

irksome: Annoying

irrefutable: Certain; undeniable

irresolution: Indecisiveness

itinerant: Wandering

jocular: Inclined to joke

jovial: Merry

judicious: Prudent

juxtaposition: The act of putting side by side

languid: Relaxed

lassitude: Lack of vitality or energy

laudable: Praiseworthy

legacy: A bequest

lethargic: Lacking energy; sluggish

libertarian: One who is tolerant or permissive (n); open-minded (adj)

listless: Inattentive

lithe: Supple

loquacious: Talkative

ludicrous: Ridiculous

malevolence: Ill will

malign: To speak evil of; to slander

malleable: Pliant

mesmerize: To hypnotize

meticulous: Careful; painstaking; fussy

mettle: Courage

microcosm: The world or universe on a small scale

mine (v): To dig out; to make use of a resource

mirth: Laughter; happiness

miser: A stingy person

misnomer: A name wrongly or mistakenly applied

modicum: A small amount

mollify: To soothe

momentous: Highly significant

morose: Gloomy

multifarious: Having great diversity or variety

mundane: Worldly; ordinary

munificent: Extraordinarily generous, especially with money

mutability: Changeability

myriad: A large indefinite number

mystical: Spiritual; magical

nefarious: Wicked or evil

negligent: Careless

nondescript: Having no distinguishing characteristics

noxious: Hurtful

objective: Impartial; neutral

obscure: Hard to understand; indistinct; not known

obsequious: Showing a servile readiness; slavish obedience

obstinate: Stubborn

obstreperous: Boisterous

ominous: Threatening

opportunist: One who takes advantage of something, especially in a devious way

ostentation: A showy display

ostracism: Exclusion from society

pacifism: Belief in peace; nonaggression

palatial: Magnificent; palace-like

paragon: A model of excellence

partisan: Showing partiality to a party or one side of an issue

passivity: Inactiveness; nonparticipation

pedantic: Too concerned with correct rules and accuracy; plodding

pedestrian: Dull; ordinary; humdrum

pejorative: Expressing disapproval

penchant: A strong liking

peremptory: Authoritative; dictatorial

perfunctory: Going through the motions; mechanical

peripheral: Tangential; unimportant; minor

perjury: Lying under oath

permeate: To pervade

pernicious: Harmful; poisonous

perspicacity: Sharp insightfulness or discernment

pertinent: Relevant

perturbation: Mental excitement or confusion

pervasive: Widespread

placate: To calm or appease

platitude: A written or spoken statement that is dull or commonplace

plausible: Believable; reasonable

plethora: Excess; abundance

pluralism: Different groups with different beliefs existing within one society

poignant: Emotionally painful

ponderous: Unusually weighty or forcible

portent: Anything that indicates what is to happen; an omen or sign

pragmatic: Practical

precarious: Perilous; risky; unstable

preclude: To prevent

precocious: Advanced for one's age

predominate: To be chief in importance

premature: Occurring too soon

presage: To foretell

prescience: Knowledge of events before they take place

pretentious: Self-important; showy

prevalent: Widespread

prevaricate: To avoid giving an honest answer; to be deliberately misleading

primordial: Existing at the beginning of time

pristine: Pure; unspoiled

procrastination: Delay

prodigal: Wasteful; extravagant

prodigious: Immense

profound: Showing great perception; having deep meaning

profuse: Produced or displayed in overabundance

prosaic: Unimaginative

provident: Providing for the future

provincial: Unsophisticated; narrow-minded

prudence: Caution

punctilious: Strictly observant of the rules prescribed by law or custom

punitive: As punishment

quandary: A puzzling predicament

quibble: A trivial objection

ramify: To divide or subdivide into branches or subdivisions

recant: To withdraw formally one's belief (in something previously believed or maintained)

recluse: One who lives apart from others or in seclusion

recuperate: To recover

redolent: Having a particular smell; suggesting

relegate: To demote

remorse: Regret

renovate: To restore

repudiate: To refuse to have anything to do with; to reject

repulsive: Grossly offensive

reserve: To set something aside (v); distance or coolness of manner (n)

resilience: The ability to bounce back, cope, or adapt

respite: Interval of rest

reticent: Reserved; unwilling to communicate

revelatory: Revealing an emotion or quality

revere: To respect highly; to worship

ritual: Established pattern of behavior, often ceremonial

sagacious: Wise and perceptive

salutary: Beneficial

sanction (v): To approve authoritatively

sardonic: Scornfully or bitterly sarcastic

scintillating: Dazzling; sparkling

scrupulous: Precise; having moral integrity

secular: Nonreligious

self-effacing: Modest; humble

serenity: Calmness; peacefulness

shrewd: Characterized by skill at understanding and profiting by circumstances

solace: Comfort

solicitous: Considerate; concerned

solvent: Having sufficient funds

somnolent: Sleepy

sophomoric: Immature

soporific: Causing sleep

sordid: Filthy; morally degraded

sparse: Thinly spread

spurious: Not genuine

squalid: Dirty and/or poverty-stricken

stingy: Cheap; unwilling to spend money

subterranean: Underground

subtle: Slight; understated

succinct: Concise

superfluous: More than is needed

suppress: To prevent from being disclosed or published

tacit: Without words; unspoken

taciturn: Quiet; untalkative

tangential: Not central; almost irrelevant

tedious: Boring; monotonous

terse: Brief; concise

timorous: Lacking courage

tractable: Easily led or controlled

tranquil: Calm; peaceful

transitory: Existing for a short time only

trepidation: Fear

trite: Made commonplace by frequent repetition

turbulent: Moving violently

ubiquitous: Being present everywhere

undermine: To subvert in an underhanded way; to weaken

unwarranted: Unjustified

upbraid: To scold

vacuity: Lack of ideas; emptiness

vapid: Dull; uninteresting

vehement: Very eager or urgent

veracity: Truthfulness

verbose: Wordy

vestige: A remaining trace of something gone

vigilant: Alert and watchful

vigorous: Energetic; forceful; strong

vital: Crucial; needed for life; lively

vitiate: To corrupt

vitriolic: Bitter; spiteful

vociferous: Forcefully loud

volatile: Unstable; explosive

voluble: Talkative

voluminous: Large; long; prolific

whimsical: Fanciful; light-hearted; quirky

zealous: Passionate; very enthusiastic

VIII. The Heart of Algebra

The primary focus of the PSAT math sections is "The Heart of Algebra." That title refers to fundamental and essential concepts and skills on which all mathematical reasoning is built. Those include linear expressions and functions, linear equations in one variable, linear inequalities in one variable, graphs of linear equations and inequalities in two variables, and systems of linear equations or of linear inequalities in two variables.

A. Linear Expressions and Functions

Linear expressions in one variable contain a variable, always first degree, with a multiplier or coefficient, and may have a constant added on. The coefficient of the variable is a rate of change or slope. The phrase "linear equation" may refer to an equation that says two linear expressions in one variable are equal, or it may refer to an equation in two variables that can be simplified to $y = mx + b$ form. The graph of a $y = mx + b$ equation is a line, leading to the word "linear" in the name. Function notation is sometimes used to make it easier to talk about what needs to be done. Writing $f(x) = 3x - 2$ lets you ask for $f(-1)$, instead of asking for "the value of the expression $3x - 2$ when $x = -1$."

On the PSAT, you may be asked to:

- Simplify a linear expression to its $mx + b$ form.

  The expression may contain many terms and may even contain quantities in parentheses. Follow the rules for order of operations, or PEMDAS, to simplify what's within parentheses; remove parentheses by using the distributive property; and combine like terms. (***Reminder:*** PEMDAS stands for: **P**arentheses, **E**xponents, **M**ultiplication, **D**ivision, **A**ddition, and **S**ubtraction. Multiplication and division are performed from left to right. Addition and subtraction are also performed from left to right.)

- Evaluate a linear expression given the value of the variable.

  Simplify the expression first, if necessary. Replace the variable with the given value, multiply that value by the rate of change, and add on the constant.

- Evaluate a linear function for a value of the variable.

  This is really just another way of asking you to evaluate the expression.

- Write a linear expression to model a situation.

  Whatever quantity is unknown or changing is the variable, usually labeled x, but any variable could be used. The rate at which that variable is changing is the multiplier, or slope. (Look for clues like "per" or "for each.") Any additional quantity is usually the constant added on.

- Interpret the meaning of parts of the expression.

  The coefficient, or slope, gives the rate of change. It's the increase or decrease in the value of the expression for each change of one unit in the variable. The constant added on is the value of the expression when the variable is zero, or the starting amount.

Practice

1. If $f(x) = \frac{1}{2}x + 7$, what is $f(10)$?

   A. 17.5
   B. 17
   C. 12
   D. 6.5

2. Which of the following is the simplest form of $-3(2x - 7) + 5(3 - 4x)$?

   A. $6 - 26x$
   B. $36 - 26x$
   C. $8 - 12x$
   D. $-4x - 8$

3. When Pat decided he wanted to buy a car, he opened a savings account with an initial deposit. Then he added to the account each week, for w weeks, contributing the same amount each time. The amount in Pat's savings account can be represented by the linear expression $25w + 50$. What is the significance of the 25 in this expression?

   A. Pat contributed $25 to his account each week.
   B. Pat opened the account with an initial deposit of $25.
   C. The car Pat wants costs $2,500.
   D. It will take 25 weeks for Pat to save enough to buy a car.

 4. Samir can work up to 35 hours per week, but wants to reserve some time each week to volunteer at the animal shelter. In a week when Samir spends h hours at the animal shelter, his earnings for the week are represented by $\$12.50(35 - h)$. How much does Samir earn for a week in which he spends 11 hours volunteering?

   A. $137.50
   B. $172.50
   C. $300.00
   D. $426.50

5. Janine noticed that the first stop her train made as she rode to work was at 12th Street, the second stop was at 29th Street, and the third was at 46th Street. She guessed that the train traveled 17 blocks between stops. If Janine's theory is correct, which of these expressions would correctly generate the street of the nth stop on her train?

   A. $12 + n$
   B. $17 + 12n$
   C. $17n + 12$
   D. $17(n - 1) + 12$

6. Luis misses the last bus after practice and has to walk home. His school is 5 miles from his home. He walks toward home at 3 miles per hour. If m represents the number of minutes Luis has walked, then which of the following represents his distance from home?

    A. $-5m + 3$

    B. $5 - 3(60m)$

    C. $5 - 3m$

    D. $5 - 3 \cdot \dfrac{m}{60}$

Answers

1. **C.** If $f(x) = \dfrac{1}{2}x + 7$, $f(10)$ is the value of $\dfrac{1}{2}x + 7$ when x is replaced with 10. $\dfrac{1}{2}(10) + 7 = 5 + 7 = 12$.

2. **B.** To reach the simplest form of $-3(2x - 7) + 5(3 - 4x)$, remove parentheses by distributing and combining like terms: $-3(2x - 7) + 5(3 - 4x) = -6x + 21 + 15 - 20x = -26x + 36$.

3. **A.** The coefficient of the variable w is the rate of change. The 25 represents the amount Pat added to the account each week. His account grew at a rate of $25 per week.

4. **C.** Replace h with 11 in the given expression and simplify: $12.50(35 - 11) = 12.50(24) = 300$. A calculator is helpful, but not absolutely necessary.

5. **D.** The number 12 (for 12th Street) is the starting position, which is the constant term. The rate, or slope, is 17 blocks per stop, so 17 is the coefficient of the variable. But the starting position is 12th Street and at that starting position, the calculation is $17(0) + 12$. That means to get 12th Street for the first stop, you need $17(1 - 1) + 12$. The second stop is $17(2 - 1) + 12 = 29$th Street, and the third stop is $17(3 - 1) + 12 = 46$th Street. In general, the nth stop is $17(n - 1) + 12$.

6. **D.** The starting point is 5 miles from home, so the constant term is 5. The rate at which Luis walks is 3 miles per hour, but notice the variable for the time he walks is in minutes. You have to adjust to make all the units match up. Because the rate is in miles per hour, convert m minutes to a fraction of an hour by dividing m by 60; 3 mph times $\dfrac{m}{60}$ hours will be the distance Luis walked. Take that away from 5 miles. As Luis walks toward home, his distance from home gets smaller. The correct choice is $5 - 3 \cdot \dfrac{m}{60}$.

B. Linear Equations in One Variable

If you set a linear expression in one variable equal to a constant, you create a linear equation. Of course, it's not always that simple. You may have a linear expression equal to another linear expression to start out with, and those expressions may not be in simplest form. You should always begin by simplifying the linear equation as much as possible.

Your real job, when given a linear equation, is to solve the equation. Solving the equation means finding the value of the variable that makes the equation a true statement, or makes both sides of the equation equal. Take the following steps:

1. Simplify the left side. Remove parentheses, combine like terms, and condense the expression to no more than one term involving a variable and one constant term.

2. Simplify the right side in the same way.

3. If both sides have a variable term, add or subtract one variable term from both sides.

4. If both sides have a constant term, add or subtract one constant term from both sides.

5. If the coefficient of the variable is not 1, divide both sides by the coefficient.

If you find that the coefficient of the variable is zero, and the variable term disappears, look at the statement that remains about constants. If it's a true statement, like 4 = 4, then any real number will make the equation true. This is called an identity, and its solution set is the set of real numbers. If the statement that remains is not true, like 0 = 6, then the equation has no solution.

TIP: If the equation contains fractions, you can clear all the fractions by multiplying both sides of the equation by the common denominator of all fractions present. Be sure to distribute and cancel where appropriate.

Practice

1. Solve for z: $\frac{1}{2}z - 3 = \frac{1}{3}z + 1$.
   - **A.** $z = 24$
   - **B.** $z = 19$
   - **C.** $z = 4$
   - **D.** $z = -4.5$

2. If $f(x) = \frac{4 - 3x}{2}$, for what value of x does $f(x) = 11$?
   - **A.** 22
   - **B.** −3
   - **C.** −6
   - **D.** −14.5

3. Solve for x: $5(2x - 3) = 3(3x + 2) - (21 - x)$.
   - **A.** $x = \frac{3}{2}$
   - **B.** $x = \frac{2}{3}$
   - **C.** No solution
   - **D.** $x =$ all real numbers

4. Melanie bought notebooks for \$5 each, but Jeff found the same notebooks on sale at another store for \$3 each. Jeff was able to buy 8 more notebooks than Melanie bought, although they spent the same amount. How many notebooks did Melanie buy?
   - **A.** 4
   - **B.** 8
   - **C.** 12
   - **D.** 16

5. When Brett tried to solve the equation $14w - 3(w - 1) = 58$, he did not get the correct solution. His teacher said that Brett had an error in this line: $14w - 3w - 3 = 58$. What was Brett's error?

   A. He did not add 3 to both sides.
   B. He did not multiply $14w$ by -3.
   C. He made a sign error when distributing.
   D. His work is correct.

6. Which of the following is NOT a correct first step in solving the following equation: $6 - 3(2x - 5) = 4x - 2(5x + 7) - 1$?

   A. $6 - 6x + 15 = 4x - 2(5x + 7) - 1$
   B. $6 - 3(2x - 5) = 4x - 10x - 14 - 1$
   C. $7 - 3(2x - 5) = 4x - 2(5x + 7)$
   D. $3(2x - 5) = 4x - 2(5x + 7) - 1$

Answers

1. **A.** If you deal with the equation just as it is given, subtract $\frac{1}{3}z$ from $\frac{1}{2}z$ by changing both to a common denominator of 6. $\frac{1}{2}z - \frac{1}{3}z - 3 = 1$ becomes $\frac{1}{6}z - 3 = 1$. Add 3 to both sides to get $\frac{1}{6}z = 4$ and divide by $\frac{1}{6}$ (or multiply by 6) to find $z = 24$. If you prefer, multiply the original equation through by 6, the common denominator. $6\left(\frac{1}{2}z - 3\right) = 6\left(\frac{1}{3}z + 1\right)$ becomes $3z - 18 = 2z + 6$. Then subtract $2z$ from both sides to get $z - 18 = 6$. Finally, add 18 to both sides to get $z = 24$.

2. **C.** You're given $f(x) = \frac{4 - 3x}{2}$ and told that $f(x) = 11$, so substitute 11 into the equation and solve for x: $11 = \frac{4 - 3x}{2}$. Multiply both sides by 2 to get $22 = 4 - 3x$, then subtract 4 from both sides to get $18 = -3x$. Divide both sides by -3 to get $-6 = x$.

3. **D.** Simplify first by distributing and combining like terms. Work first on the left side: $5(2x - 3) = 3(3x + 2) - (21 - x)$ becomes $10x - 15 = 3(3x + 2) - (21 - x)$. Then simplify the right side to get $10x - 15 = 9x + 6 - 21 + x$, which simplifies further to $10x - 15 = 10x - 15$. You may recognize as soon as you get to this point, when the two sides are identical, that the solution set is all real numbers, or you may continue solving by subtracting $10x$ from both sides. You're left with $-15 = -15$. All variables have disappeared and the result is true. The solution is all real numbers.

4. **C.** Melanie bought x notebooks for $5 each. Represent that as $5x$. Jeff bought $x + 8$ notebooks for $3 each. Represent that as $3(x + 8)$. Solve the equation $5x = 3(x + 8)$ by distributing to get $5x = 3x + 24$, and then subtracting $3x$ from both sides; this gives you $2x = 24$. Dividing by 2 tells you that $x = 12$. Melanie bought 12 notebooks.

5. **C.** If $14w - 3(w - 1) = 58$ is properly simplified, distributing the multiplication by -3 results in a positive constant: $14w - 3w + 3 = 58$.

6. **D.** In order to solve $6 - 3(2x - 5) = 4x - 2(5x + 7) - 1$, you must first simplify. You could begin simplifying the left side by distributing the -3 (Choice A) or start by distributing the -2 on the right side (Choice B). Choice C adds 1 to both sides, eliminating the -1 from the end of the right side and increasing the constant 6, on the left side, to 7. Choice D subtracts $6 - 3$ on the left side, which is a violation of the order of operations (PEMDAS). The -3 must be multiplied by the expression $2x - 5$ before any addition or subtraction.

C. Linear Inequalities in One Variable

Linear inequalities are a lot like linear equations, except that the two expressions are related by a sign that says one side is larger or smaller than the other (> or <). Some inequalities will also include the possibility that the sides are equal (≥ or ≤).

Inequalities are solved in the same way as equations, with one small but very important change at the last step. If the coefficient that you divide by is negative, the direction of the inequality sign changes; for example, from < to > or from ≥ to ≤.

The solution of an inequality is usually a set of numbers rather than just one number. To make it easier to visualize, the solution set can be graphed on a number line. Use a solid dot for "or equal to" or an open circle if you want to only include numbers less than or greater than the number you're marking. Then shade the numbers you want to include, either to the right of the circle or to the left.

Practice

1. Solve for x: $3x - 7 \geq 5x + 3$.

    A. $x \geq -5$
    B. $x \leq -5$
    C. $x \geq 2$
    D. $x \leq 2$

2. Which of the following graphs shows the solution set of the inequality $7 - 3x < 16$?

    A.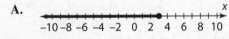

    B.

    C.

    D.

3. The graph below shows the solution set for which of the following inequalities?

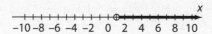

A. $5(2x - 4) \leq 4 - 2x$
B. $2(4 - x) \geq 3x - 2$
C. $-3(x + 4) < 5(x - 4)$
D. $2 + 5x > 2(3x - 1)$

4. Solve for x: $3(2x - 7) - 4(3x + 1) > 5(7 - x)$.

A. $x < -60$
B. $x > -60$
C. $x > 10$
D. $x < 10$

5. The band must raise at least $500 for new uniforms. They organize a fundraiser selling water bottles for $7 each, and receive an anonymous donation of $75. Which of these inequalities could be used to determine the number of water bottles the band must sell?

A. $7b \geq 500$
B. $7b + 75 > 500$
C. $7b + 75 \geq 500$
D. $7b - 75 \leq 500$

 6. Mr. Adams can purchase a car by making a first payment of $2,000 followed by monthly payments of $210 for a period of time, or he can purchase the same car by making a single payment of $12,000. After how many monthly payments will Mr. Adams have paid more for the car than if he had bought it with a single payment?

A. 50 months
B. 48 months
C. 40 months
D. 36 months

Answers

1. **B.** Subtract $5x$ from both sides of $3x - 7 \geq 5x + 3$ to get $-2x - 7 \geq 3$. Add 7 to both sides, producing $-2x \geq 10$. Divide both sides by -2, and remember to reverse the inequality sign, and you have $x \leq -5$.

2. **D.** Solve $7 - 3x < 16$ by subtracting 7 from both sides to get $-3x < 9$, and dividing both sides by -3. That reverses the direction of the inequality, producing $x > -3$. The correct graph has an open circle at -3 and shading to the right.

3. **C.** The graph shows $x > 1$, so the task is to find the inequality that has a solution of $x > 1$. Avoid the temptation to judge by the direction of the inequality because it may flip during solving, but choices A and B can be eliminated, because they include "or equal to" and would have a solid dot. Solve Choice C by distributing to get $-3x - 12 < 5x - 20$, and then subtracting $5x$ from both sides and adding 12 to both sides to get $-8x < -8$. Dividing both sides by -8, and reversing the inequality, gives $x > 1$.

4. **A.** Apply the distributive property to remove parentheses. The inequality $3(2x - 7) - 4(3x + 1) > 5(7 - x)$ becomes $6x - 21 - 12x - 4 > 35 - 5x$. Collect like terms on the left side to get $-6x - 25 > 35 - 5x$. Add $5x$ to both sides, and then add 25 to both sides, and the inequality becomes $-x > 60$. Dividing by -1 reverses the inequality for a solution of $x < -60$.

5. **C.** The band will need $500 or more, so this will be a "greater than or equal to" inequality. Therefore, you can eliminate Choice B. If b is the number of bottles they sell, and each costs $7, they will collect $7b$ dollars for the sale. Add onto that the donation of $75, and $7b + 75 \geq 500$ is the inequality that models the situation.

6. **B.** Write an inequality to compare the amount Mr. Adams would spend after x months on the payment plan to the $12,000 it would cost to buy the car outright. This is $2,000 + 210x > 12,000$. Solve by subtracting 2,000 from both sides, and then dividing both sides by 210. That gives $210x > 10,000$ and then $x > 47.619$. Part of a payment is not possible, so round to 48.

D. Graphs of Linear Equations and Inequalities in Two Variables

A linear expression in one variable can be simplified to the form $mx + b$. When you set that equal to another linear expression in the same variable, or to just a constant, you produce a linear equation in one variable that you can solve, and generally produce a solution that is a single number. Change the equal sign to an inequality sign, and you have a linear inequality in one variable to solve, and your solution will be a set of numbers, a set of values for x, which can be graphed on a number line. But set that linear expression across an equal sign or an inequality sign from a different variable, like y, and you have a linear equation in two variables, $y = mx + b$, or a linear inequality in two variables, like $y < mx + b$. The solutions of these equations and inequalities are sets of ordered pairs (x, y). Those sets contain infinitely many ordered pairs, so rather than a list, a graph on the coordinate plane is the best way to represent the solutions.

The PSAT won't ask you to actually draw those graphs, but it might ask you to select the graph that fits an equation or inequality, or ask you to focus on some detail of the graph. Things to remember about the graph of $y = mx + b$ and its related inequalities:

- Every point that the line passes through is an ordered pair that solves the equation.
- The coefficient of x, denoted by m, is the rate of increase or decrease, the slope of the line.
- Slope is the ratio of the change in y to the change in x. When (x_1, y_1) and (x_2, y_2) are points on the line,
$m = \dfrac{y_2 - y_1}{x_2 - x_1}$.
- The constant term, denoted as b, is the y-intercept of the line, the y-coordinate of the point where the line crosses the y-axis. It is the value of y when x is zero.
- If you know the slope and a point (x_1, y_1) on the line, you can find the equation by substituting into the equation $y - y_1 = m(x - x_1)$ and simplifying.

- Parallel lines have the same slope. Perpendicular lines have slopes whose product is −1.
- For the graph of an inequality, a dotted line indicates that the inequality is strictly less than or strictly greater than, but a solid line includes "or equal to."
- When you shade the plane on one side of the line or the other for an inequality, the shading goes below the line if y is less than $mx + b$ and above the line if y is greater than $mx + b$.

Practice

1. What is the equation of a line that passes through the points (0, 4) and (2, 0)?

   A. $2x + 4y = 0$
   B. $4x + 2y = 0$
   C. $y = -2x + 4$
   D. $y = -4x + 2$

2. The line $y = 3x - 5$ passes through the point $(p, 7)$. What is the value of p?

   A. 3
   B. 4
   C. 8
   D. 16

3. Find the equation of a line that is perpendicular to the line shown below, and has the same y-intercept.

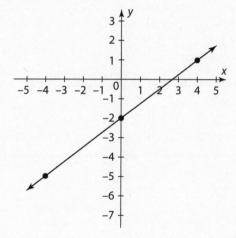

   A. $y = \dfrac{3}{4}x - 2$

   B. $y = \dfrac{4}{3}x - 2$

   C. $y = -\dfrac{4}{3}x - 2$

   D. $y = \dfrac{3}{4}x + \dfrac{1}{2}$

4. What is the y-intercept of a line that passes through the points $(-3, 7)$ and $(5, -1)$?

    A. 5
    B. 4
    C. −5
    D. −6

5. Which of the following inequalities is shown in the graph below?

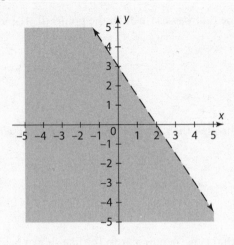

    A. $3x + 2y < 6$
    B. $2x + 3y > 6$
    C. $3x - 2y \geq 6$
    D. $2x - 3y \leq 6$

6. Which of these ordered pairs is a solution of the equation $y = \frac{1}{2}x - 1$ and is in the solution set of $y < 3x - 1$?

    A. $(-4, -3)$
    B. $(-2, -2)$
    C. $(0, -1)$
    D. $(2, 0)$

Answers

1. **C.** Use the given points to find the slope: $m = \frac{4-0}{0-2} = -2$. The y-intercept is 4, so the equation is $y = -2x + 4$.

2. **B.** Every point on the line solves the equation, so if $(p, 7)$ is on the line $y = 3x - 5$, then solving $7 = 3p - 5$ will give the value of p. Add 5 to both sides to get $12 = 3p$, and then divide by 3 to get $p = 4$.

3. **C.** Choose two points on the line and count the rise and run, the vertical and horizontal movement from point to point. The slope is $m = \frac{\text{rise}}{\text{run}} = \frac{3}{4}$. A line perpendicular to this one will have a slope of $-\frac{4}{3}$ and the same y-intercept of -2. The equation is $y = -\frac{4}{3}x - 2$.

4. **B.** Use the given points to find the slope: $m = \dfrac{7+1}{-3-5} = \dfrac{8}{-8} = -1$. The equation is $y - 7 = -1(x + 3)$, which simplifies to $y = -x + 4$. The y-intercept is 4.

5. **A.** Observe first that the line is dotted so the expression will not be an "or equal to" expression, eliminating choices C and D. Also notice that the shading moves downward from the line, so the inequality will be $y <$ an expression in x, eliminating Choice B. That leaves Choice A: $3x + 2y < 6$.

   You can also solve this problem by finding the equation of the line. To find the equation of the line, use two points on the line to calculate the slope. Using the x-intercept, $(2, 0)$, and the y-intercept, $(0, 3)$, the slope is $m = \dfrac{3-0}{0-2} = -\dfrac{3}{2}$. The equation of the line is $y = -\dfrac{3}{2}x + 3$, so the inequality is $y < -\dfrac{3}{2}x + 3$. This does not appear as an answer choice, so consider other forms. Multiply by 2 to get $2y < -3x + 6$, and then add $3x$ to both sides to get $3x + 2y < 6$.

6. **D.** First determine which points fall on the line $y = \dfrac{1}{2}x - 1$. If you test Choice A, you will see it satisfies the equation: $-3 = \dfrac{1}{2}(-4) - 1 = -2 - 1 = -3$. You can avoid testing the others if you note that Choice B is up 1 and right 2 from Choice A, and Choice C is up 1 and right 2 from B, and likewise, the move from C to D fits the slope. All four points fall on the line. To determine which is in the solution set of the inequality, you can sketch the graph of $y < 3x - 1$, or test points in the inequality. However, only Choice D makes the inequality true: $0 < 3(2) - 1$. Note that point $(0, -1)$ is not in the solution set of the inequality because it lies on the dotted line (see graph below).

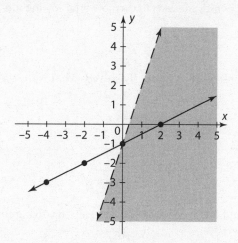

E. Systems of Linear Equations in Two Variables

If you think of a linear equation in two variables as its graphic representation, a line, then it's easy to see that if you have two linear equations, each with the same two variables, one of three things will happen: 1) the two lines will cross in a single point, 2) the two lines will coincide and sit right on top of one another, or 3) the two lines will be parallel and never meet. Two lines that cross form a system that is consistent and has a single ordered pair as its solution. Two lines that coincide are a dependent system, and there are infinitely many ordered pairs in the solution set. Parallel lines are the representation of an inconsistent system, which has no solution.

It's not always desirable to solve a system of equations by looking for the point of intersection on the graph. There are two algebraic methods you can use: the substitution method and the method of elimination.

Substitution Method

If one of the equations is in the form y = an expression (or x = an expression), or if you can easily get one equation to that form, you can use that to substitute into the other equation, making it a one-variable equation. Solve, and then take that value back to the first equation, substitute, and solve for the remaining variable.

Elimination Method

Arrange the two equations in the same format. Most people like $ax + by = c$. Choose the variable you want to eliminate. If you're fortunate, that variable term will have the same coefficient in both equations, or directly opposite coefficients, and you'll be able to eliminate by either adding (if the coefficients are opposite) or subtracting (if they're the same). If the coefficients don't match, you can multiply one or both equations by a constant to make them agree, in much the same way as you create common denominators when adding fractions. Once you've eliminated a variable, solve for the one that remains, and substitute back into one of the equations to find the second variable.

TIP: It may be tempting to think you can find the right answer by checking each choice, and you can, if you must. But plugging answer choices back in is time-consuming, especially with systems, because you must check in both equations. Save that for situations in which you can't find a more efficient method.

Practice

1. When the system of equations below is correctly solved, what is the value of y in the solution?
$$y = 2x - 7$$
$$y = 5x + 2$$
   A. −3
   B. 3
   C. −13
   D. −1

2. Which of the following would NOT be a correct first step in solving the system below?
$$x - 3y = 8$$
$$x + 3y = 2$$
   A. Add the two equations to eliminate the y-terms.
   B. Subtract the two equations to eliminate the x-terms.
   C. Replace x in the second equation with $8 + 3y$.
   D. Replace $3y$ in the second equation with −8.

3. The solution of the system shown below is

$$x - 5y = -9$$
$$x + 3y = -1$$

A. $x = -4, y = 1$
B. $x = 16, y = 5$
C. $x = -4.75, y = 1.25$
D. $x = 2.75, y = -1.25$

4. Which ordered pair is a solution of the system below?

$$\frac{1}{2}x + \frac{1}{3}y = 0$$
$$\frac{2}{3}x + \frac{1}{2}y = -1$$

A. $(2, 3)$
B. $(2.4, -3.6)$
C. $(12, -18)$
D. $(-12, 18)$

5. For the system of equations whose graph is shown below, which of the following is true?

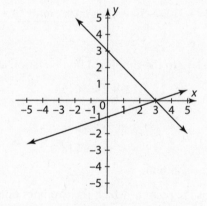

A. The solution is $(0, -1)$.
B. The solution is $(0, 3)$.
C. The solution is $(3, 0)$.
D. The system has no solution.

6. When the system below is solved by graphing, which of the following describes the result?

$$x - 4y = -5$$
$$4x + y = -3$$

A. The graph is a pair of perpendicular lines that intersect at $(-1, 1)$.
B. The graph is a pair of lines that are not perpendicular, but intersect at $(-1, 1)$.
C. The graph is a single line, so the system has infinitely many solutions.
D. The graph is a pair of parallel lines, so the system has no solution.

Answers

1. **C.** Substitute $2x - 7$ for the y in the second equation and solve $2x - 7 = 5x + 2$. Subtract $5x$ from both sides to get $-3x - 7 = 2$, and then add 7 to both sides to get $-3x = 9$. Divide by -3 to find that $x = -3$. Substitute -3 for x in one of the equations to find y: $y = 2(-3) - 7 = -13$.

2. **D.** Adding the two equations is a valid step. It produces $2x = 10$, which can be solved to find $x = 5$; you can then substitute the x-value back in to find y. Likewise, subtracting the equations is valid and produces $-6y = 6$, which allows you to solve for $y = -1$ and then substitute the y-value back in to find x. Choice C is about solving by substitution. Because the first equation is easily transformed from $x - 3y = 8$ to $x = 8 + 3y$, the x in the second equation can be replaced with $8 + 3y$ to create a one-variable equation that can be solved for y. Choice D also suggests a substitution, but replacing $3y$ with -8 is not a valid first step. If $x - 3y = 8$, then $-3y = 8 - x$ and $3y = x - 8$.

3. **A.** Subtract the equations to eliminate x and the result is $-8y = -8$, so $y = 1$. Replace y with 1 in one of the equations and solve for x: $x - 5(1) = -9$ becomes $x = -4$. The solution is $x = -4$, $y = 1$.

4. **C.** This is a good time to clear the fractions. Multiply each equation by 6, the common denominator. $6\left(\dfrac{1}{2}x + \dfrac{1}{3}y\right) = 6(0)$ becomes $3x + 2y = 0$ and $6\left(\dfrac{2}{3}x + \dfrac{1}{2}y\right) = 6(-1)$ becomes $4x + 3y = -6$. More work is required.

$$
\begin{aligned}
3(3x + 2y) &= 3(0) &\text{becomes}& &9x + 6y &= 0 \\
-2(4x + 3y) &= -2(-6) &\text{becomes}& &\underline{-8x - 6y} &= 12 \\
& & & & x &= 12
\end{aligned}
$$

Now substitute the x-value back in to the simplified first equation and solve for y:

$$
\begin{aligned}
3(12) + 2y &= 0 \\
36 + 2y &= 0 \\
2y &= -36 \\
y &= -18
\end{aligned}
$$

The ordered pair $(12, -18)$ is the solution.

5. **C.** The solution of the system is the point at which the two lines intersect. These lines do intersect, so Choice D can be eliminated, and they intersect at a point on the x-axis. The points mentioned in choices A and B are each the y-intercept of one line, so these choices can be eliminated. The point of intersection is Choice C, $(3, 0)$, the x-intercept of both lines.

6. **A.** Start by putting each equation in slope-intercept or $y = mx + b$ form, so that the slopes are easy to read. The line $x - 4y = -5$ can be transformed to $-4y = -5 - x$ or $y = \dfrac{5}{4} + \dfrac{1}{4}x$, so it has a slope of $\dfrac{1}{4}$. The line $4x + y = -3$ becomes $y = -4x - 3$, meaning it has a slope of -4. Because the product of the slopes is -1, the lines are perpendicular. You can verify that the point of intersection is $(-1, 1)$ by checking that this ordered pair balances both equations. For $x - 4y = -5$, $-1 - 4(1) = -5$ checks. For $4x + y = -3$, $4(-1) + 1 = -3$ also checks.

F. Systems of Linear Inequalities in Two Variables

The solution of a system of inequalities is handled graphically. Each inequality is graphed on the same set of axes, and the solution of the system is the set of points the two graphs have in common. This includes the region where the two shaded areas overlap and may include points on the lines (or not), depending on whether the lines are solid or dotted.

Practice

1. Which of the following graphs shows the solution of the system of inequalities below?

$$2x - 5y \leq 10$$
$$3x + 2y < 6$$

A.

B.

C.

D.

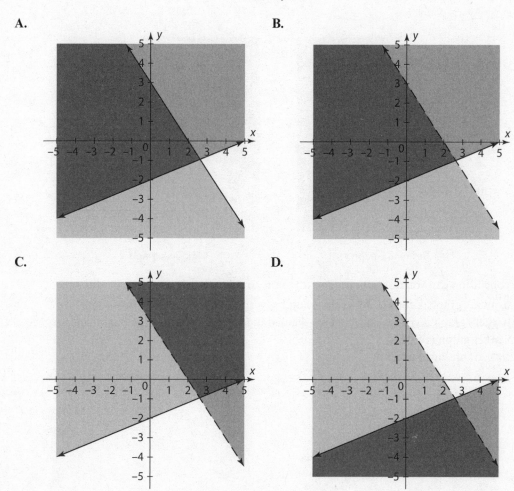

2. The point $(-2, k)$ is in the solution set of the system of inequalities shown below. Which of the following could be a value of k?

$$x - y > -2$$
$$3x + y < 2$$

A. 4
B. 1
C. 0
D. -3

3. Ms. Thompson asked her class to solve the system of inequalities below by graphing. Jasmine and Miguel each drew a graph. Jasmine's graph is on the left, and Miguel's is on the right.

$$y \leq 4 - 2x$$
$$2x - 3y > -3$$

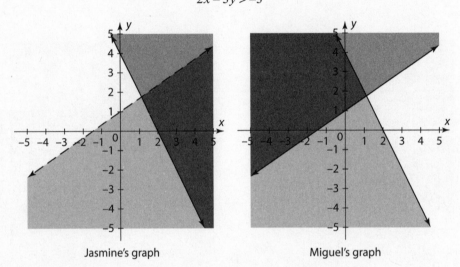

Jasmine's graph   Miguel's graph

What conclusion can you draw about their attempts to solve the system of inequalities?

A. Jasmine's graph is correct. Miguel's graph has a solid line that should be dotted.
B. Miguel's graph is correct. Jasmine has shaded the wrong section of the plane.
C. Neither graph is correct.
D. Both graphs are correct.

4. Caitlin misunderstood the directions for systems of inequalities. She graphed both inequalities correctly but did each one on a separate set of axes instead of graphing both on the same axes. Caitlin's graphs are shown below. If Caitlin had followed the directions correctly, which of the following would be the correct graph?

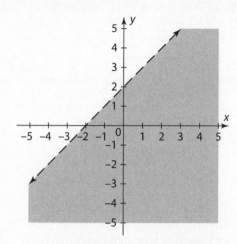

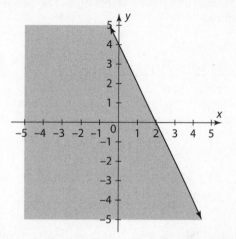

A.

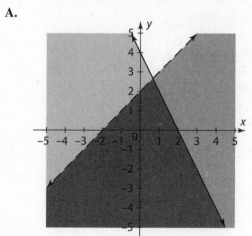

B.

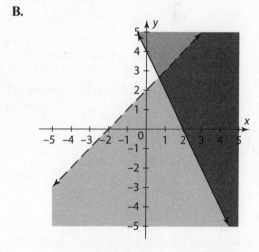

C.

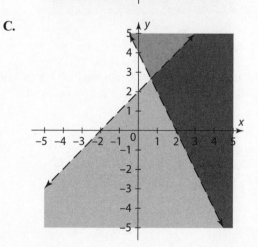

D.

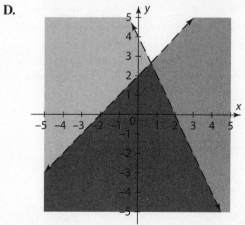

5. Hakan is responsible for providing lunch for a meeting in his office. There must be enough for each of the 14 people to have at least one item, but he must not exceed his budget of $54. He plans to buy a combination of sandwiches for $5 each and salads for $3 each. If x represents the number of sandwiches and y the number of salads, which of the following systems of inequalities models Hakan's situation?

A. $x + y \leq 14$
   $5x + 3y \geq 54$

B. $x + y \leq 54$
   $5x + 3y > 14$

C. $x + y \geq 14$
   $5x + 3y \leq 54$

D. $x + y > 54$
   $5x + 3y \geq 14$

6. Which of the following best describes the graph of the system of inequalities below?
$$3x + y < 7$$
$$y > 1 - 3x$$

A. A pair of solid parallel lines and the shaded area between them
B. A pair of dotted parallel lines and the shaded area between them
C. A pair of dotted lines intersecting at (7, 1) with shading upward from both lines
D. A pair of solid lines that are perpendicular with shading over the entire plane

Answers

1. **B.** Choice A can be eliminated. Both lines are solid, but the second inequality should be a dotted line. The other choices vary in the direction of shading, so transform each inequality to slope-intercept form.

$$2x - 5y \leq 10 \qquad 3x + 2y < 6$$
$$-5y \leq 10 - 2x \qquad 2y < 6 - 3x$$
$$y \geq \frac{2}{5}x - 2 \qquad y < 3 - \frac{3}{2}x$$

Shading should be above the solid line and below the dotted line. Choice C has shading above both lines, and Choice D has shading below both. Choice B is correct.

2. **D.** Transform the inequalities to slope-intercept form for easy graphing. They become $y < x + 2$ and $y < -3x + 2$. The graph is shown below, with the points that result from the possible choices for k. Two points, with positive values for k, fall in a region shaded by only one inequality, so you can eliminate choices A and B. The point with $k = 0$ falls on the line, but the line is dotted and so not part of the solution set, so you can eliminate Choice C as well. Only $k = -3$ creates a point in the solution set.

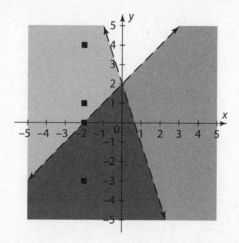

3. **C.** Jasmine's graph has used dotted and solid lines appropriately, but the shading for $y \le 4 - 2x$ is upward and should be downward. Miguel's graph has solid lines for both graphs, but the $2x - 3y > -3$ should have a dotted line. Therefore, neither graph is correct.

4. **A.** One of Caitlin's graphs has a dotted line with a positive slope, and the other a solid line with a negative slope. On both graphs, her shading is below the line. Choice B has the correct lines but the shading is above the solid line instead of below. Choices C and D have both lines dotted. Only Choice A is correct.

5. **C.** If x represents the number of sandwiches and y the number of salads, the total items purchased is $x + y$, and must be 14 or more. One inequality is $x + y \ge 14$; this eliminates choices B and D. Each sandwich costs \$5 and each salad \$3, so $5x + 3y$ represents the total cost and cannot be more than \$54; this inequality is $5x + 3y \le 54$, eliminating Choice A. Choice C is correct.

6. **B.** Put the first inequality in slope-intercept form to compare easily. Thinking of the graphs just as lines for a moment, $y < 7 - 3x$ and $y > 1 - 3x$ will be parallel because they have the same slope, -3. One line has a y-intercept of 7 and the other a y-intercept of 1. They will both be dotted lines, because there is no "or equal to," eliminating choices A and D. The shading for $y < 7 - 3x$ is below the line, and the shading for $y > 1 - 3x$ is above the line, so the overlapping shading will fall between the two lines, Choice B.

IX. Problem Solving and Data Analysis

Problem solving has long been a part of math and testing, but often the problems put forward were firmly in the "when would anyone really want to do this?" category. The changes in the PSAT are aimed in part at making the problems more realistic, more of the kind of thinking we actually need to do in life, as well as in school. Those changes have brought in a lot more of what is called data analysis. You'll be asked to look at information presented in tables, charts, and graphs and to notice patterns, identify relationships, make predictions, and draw conclusions. Some of this may be new to you, but most traces back to familiar ideas.

A. Ratios and Rates

We often compare numbers, and when we do, it's generally in one of two ways. The addition/subtraction comparison makes statements like "A is 4 more than B," while the multiplication/division comparison says things like "P is three times the size of Q" or "X is half of Y." That multiplication/division type of comparison is what leads to ratios and rates.

A ratio is a comparison of two quantities by division. If the student-to-teacher ratio in your school is 15:1, that means that, looking at the school as a whole, the number of students divided by the number of teachers simplifies to 15. It doesn't mean your school has 15 students and 1 teacher. You might have 45 students and 3 teachers, or 1,500 students and 100 teachers, or any other combination that reduces to 15:1.

A rate is also a comparison of quantities by division, but the quantities are measured in different units. (Students and teachers may sound different, but they are all people.) If the plan for the field trip says that there will be 42 students per bus, you're really looking at a rate, because students and buses are very different things. The most common rates are things like 45 miles per hour, 10 feet per second, and 36 inches per yard. These are all unit rates because they compare to 1 hour or 1 second or 1 yard.

Practice

1. In 2015, the United States House of Representatives had 435 members, of whom 84 were women. Which of the following is the ratio of women to men in the 2015 House of Representatives?

   A. 145:118
   B. 28:145
   C. 28:117
   D. 117:28

2. The Modern Language department at Regional High School offers three languages: Spanish, French, and Italian. There are 5 Italian students for every 8 French students, and 4 French students for every 5 Spanish students. What is the ratio of Italian students to Spanish students?

   A. 1:1
   B. 1:2
   C. 2:1
   D. 5:4

157

3. Stephanie made the 308-mile drive from her home to her grandmother's home in 7 hours, 20 minutes. What was her average speed in miles per hour?

   A. 42
   B. 42.8
   C. 44
   D. 70

4. Mr. Caphart's model for the design of the new shopping center uses a scale in which 3 inches represent 20 feet. If the center courtyard is to be a circle with a diameter of 50 feet, what is the diameter of the model courtyard in inches?

   A. 1.5
   B. 6
   C. 7.5
   D. 15

5. Hallie and Howard work in the same office and live in the same apartment complex. They both leave work at exactly 5 pm. Hallie walks home at a rate of 300 feet per minute. Howard drives, but rush hour traffic is badly snarled and he is only able to move at 15 miles per hour. What is the ratio of Howard's speed to Hallie's speed? (1 mile = 5,280 feet)

   A. 1:20
   B. 3:1
   C. 20:1
   D. 22:5

6. Grandma Harriet's birthday cake recipe calls for cups of butter to cups of sugar in a ratio of 2:3, and cups of sugar to cups of flour in ratio of 1:4. How many cups of butter will you need to make Grandma's recipe if you start with 6 cups of flour?

   A. 1
   B. 2
   C. 3
   D. 4

Answers

1. **C.** There are 84 women and 435 – 84 men. The ratio of women to men is 84:(435 – 84), or 84:351, which simplifies to 28:117.

2. **B.** The ratio of Italian students to French students is 5:8, and the ratio of French students to Spanish students is 4:5. Rewrite 4:5 as 8:10 and you can link Italian is to French is to Spanish as 5:8:10. Then remove the French students and the ratio of Italian students to Spanish students is 5:10, which simplifies to 1:2.

3. **A.** Convert 7 hours, 20 minutes to $7\frac{1}{3}$ hours, and divide 308 by $7\frac{1}{3}$. $308 \div 7\frac{1}{3} = \frac{\overset{14}{\cancel{308}}}{1} \cdot \frac{3}{\underset{1}{\cancel{22}}} = 42$. Stephanie's average speed is 42 miles per hour.

4. **C.** If 3 inches represent 20 feet, and 50 feet is 2.5 times 20 feet, the representation of the 50-foot courtyard should be 2.5 times 3 inches, or 7.5 inches.

5. **D.** You're looking for the ratio of 15 miles per hour to 300 feet per minute, but you need to make the units match. You can do that in a variety of ways: miles per hour to feet per minute, or feet per minute to miles per hour, but meeting in the middle avoids both fractions and extremely large numbers.

$$\frac{15 \text{ miles}}{1 \text{ hour}} \times \frac{5{,}280 \text{ feet}}{1 \text{ mile}} = \frac{79{,}200 \text{ feet}}{1 \text{ hour}} \text{ and } \frac{300 \text{ feet}}{1 \text{ minute}} \times \frac{60 \text{ minutes}}{1 \text{ hour}} = \frac{18{,}000 \text{ feet}}{1 \text{ hour}}$$

The ratio is 79,200:18,000, which simplifies to 792:180 = 88:20 = 22:5.

6. **A.** The ratio of butter to sugar is 2:3, and the ratio of sugar to flour is 1:4. Convert 1:4 to 3:12, and link the ratios so butter to sugar to flour is 2:3:12, which means butter to flour is 2:12 or 1:6. For 6 cups of flour, you will need 1 cup of butter.

B. Proportions and Percents

A ratio compares two numbers by division. If a recipe calls for 2 cups of flour for every 1 cup of butter, the ratio of flour to butter is 2:1. But if you have $7\frac{2}{3}$ cups of flour, how much butter do you need? That's where proportions come in.

A proportion is an equation that says two ratios are equal. If 12 students study Mandarin and 60 students study Spanish, the ratio of Mandarin students to Spanish students is 12:60, or 1:5. The equation $\frac{12}{60} = \frac{1}{5}$ is a proportion, a statement that those two ratios are equal. Proportions allow you to solve for a missing number.

If the ratio of flour to butter in a recipe is 2:1 and you have $7\frac{2}{3}$ cups of flour, you can write and solve the proportion:

$$\frac{2}{1} = \frac{7\frac{2}{3}}{b}$$

$$2b = 7\frac{2}{3} = \frac{23}{3}$$

$$b = \frac{23}{6} = 3\frac{5}{6}$$

You can solve any proportion with the same steps you use to solve any other equation, but once you solve a few proportions, you start to notice a pattern. This pattern is commonly called cross-multiplying, and officially called the Means-Extremes Property.

$$\text{If } \frac{a}{b} = \frac{c}{d}, \text{ then } ad = bc.$$

Percent, which means "out of 100," is a way of making comparisons easier. In Martha's family, 9 out of 13 adults voted in the last election. In Shania's family, 11 out of 15 voted. How do these compare? You're asking whether the ratio 9:13 is larger than, smaller than, or the same as the ratio 11:15. To make that easier, use a proportion to change each ratio to a percent.

$$\frac{9}{13} = \frac{x}{100}$$

$$13x = 900$$

$$x = \frac{900}{13} \approx 69\%$$

$$\frac{11}{15} = \frac{y}{100}$$

$$15y = 1,100$$

$$y = \frac{1,100}{15} \approx 73\%$$

A larger percentage of Shania's family voted.

Practice

Use this information for questions 1–2.

Whenever he paints, Eduardo mixes his paints from primary colors. For his latest project, he needs a purple that combines red and blue in a ratio of 5 parts red to 8 parts blue.

1. How many ounces of blue paint will he need to combine with 15 ounces of red paint to produce the correct color?
   A. 8
   B. 13
   C. 24
   D. 39

2. How many ounces of each color will Eduardo need to make 26 ounces of the correct shade of purple?
   A. 5 ounces of red and 21 ounces of blue
   B. 13 ounces of red and 13 ounces of blue
   C. 10 ounces of red and 16 ounces of blue
   D. 18 ounces of red and 8 ounces of blue

3. Maha needs 10 skeins of yarn for every 3 scarves she knits. She plans to make scarves for 14 of her friends. What is the smallest whole number of skeins of yarn Maha will need?
   A. 47
   B. 46
   C. 16
   D. 15

4. In both Maine and New Hampshire, 29% of the state legislators are women. Maine has a total of 186 legislators and New Hampshire has a total of 424 legislators. How many women legislators are there in these two states combined?

   A. 58
   B. 69
   C. 177
   D. 610

5. If P is a positive integer, what is $P\%$ of 400?

   A. 0.04
   B. 0.04P
   C. 4P
   D. 400P

6. A survey showed that 62% of the population said ice cream was their favorite dessert, and of those, 45% identified chocolate as their favorite flavor. What percent of the population identified chocolate ice cream as their favorite dessert?

   A. 17%
   B. 28%
   C. 45%
   D. 107%

Answers

1. **C.** The ratio of red to blue is 5:8. Solve the proportion $\dfrac{5}{8} = \dfrac{15}{x}$ by cross-multiplying: $5x = 120$, and $x = 24$. Eduardo needs 24 ounces of blue paint.

2. **C.** The ratio of red to blue is 5:8, so mixing 5 ounces of red and 8 ounces of blue would yield 13 ounces of the purple. To produce 26 ounces, he must double the batch, using 10 ounces of red and 16 ounces of blue.

3. **A.** Maha uses 10 skeins for 3 scarves but wants 14 scarves. Solve $\dfrac{10}{3} = \dfrac{x}{14}$ by cross-multiplying: $3x = 140$, and $x = 46\dfrac{2}{3}$ skeins. She cannot buy a fraction of a skein, so she will need at least 47 skeins.

4. **C.** Find 29% of 186 and 29% of 424 and add the results, or add 186 + 424 and find 29% of the total. $0.29(186) + 0.29(424) = 0.29(186 + 424) = 0.29(610) = 176.9$. Round to 177.

5. **C.** $P\%$ represents P out of 100 or $\dfrac{P}{100}$. $P\%$ of 400 is $\dfrac{P}{\underset{1}{\cancel{100}}} \cdot \overset{4}{\cancel{400}} = 4P$.

6. **B.** One simple way to deal with percent problems where the whole is not known is to imagine that it is 100. Then 62% of 100 is just 62 people who said ice cream was their favorite dessert and 45% of those 62 preferred chocolate: $0.45(62) = 27.9$, which rounds to 28. Or you can multiply $(0.62)(0.45)$ to get 0.279 and round to 0.28 or 28%.

C. Measurement and Unit Conversions

Proper measuring and units of measurement that work together are crucial to arriving at sensible answers. For example, 10 times 2 may equal 20, but a plant that grows 2 inches per year doesn't grow 20 inches in 10 seconds. You'll need to express 10 seconds as a fraction of a year, or change the rate of 2 inches per year into inches per second.

When the conversion is more than one step, it helps to use a multiplication like this one.

$$\frac{2 \text{ inches}}{1 \text{ year}} \times \frac{1 \text{ year}}{365 \text{ days}} \times \frac{1 \text{ day}}{24 \text{ hours}} \times \frac{1 \text{ hour}}{60 \text{ minutes}} \times \frac{1 \text{ minute}}{60 \text{ seconds}} = \frac{2 \text{ inches}}{31{,}536{,}000 \text{ seconds}} \approx \frac{0.00000006 \text{ inches}}{\text{second}}$$

Conversions on the actual test are unlikely to have so many steps, but what's important is to notice how the process starts with what you know, and each successive multiplication cancels out a unit you don't want and brings in one closer to what you do want. The units that need to be canceled out should be diagonally across the multiplication sign from one another.

Practice

1. A case of paper towels costs $21 and contains 12 rolls, each containing 160 sheets. What is the cost per sheet?

   A. $0.01
   B. $0.06
   C. $0.13
   D. $0.18

2. If 365 days equal 1 year, how many hours are in a year?

   A. 146
   B. 4,380
   C. 8,760
   D. 525,600

3. In preparation for painting, Pam measured the length, width, and height of the room. Pam used a yardstick and recorded the measurements as length of 11 feet 10 inches, width of 8 feet 1 inch, and height of 7 feet 11 inches. She then calculated 2 × height(width + length) to find the square footage to be painted. To the nearest square foot, what is the area Pam needs to paint?

   A. 757
   B. 704
   C. 320
   D. 315

4. In order for an object to break free of Earth's gravity, it must be traveling at a velocity of approximately 11,100 meters per second. What is this escape velocity in kilometers per hour?

    A. 1,110
    B. 6,660
    C. 39,960
    D. 23,976,000

5. The acceleration due to gravity can be measured as 32 feet per second per second. If 1 meter is approximately equal to 3.28 feet, which of the following is the best approximation of the acceleration due to gravity in meters per second per second?

    A. 2.97
    B. 9.76
    C. 104.96
    D. 344.27

6. Record times for men's track events include a time of 3 minutes 26 seconds for the 1,500-meter, and 3 minutes 43 seconds for the mile. If 1 mile is approximately 1,609 meters, what is the speed, in meters per second, recorded by the faster runner?

    A. 6.73 for the 1,500-meter
    B. 7.22 for the mile
    C. 7.28 for the 1,500-meter
    D. 7.81 for the mile

Answers

1. **A.** A case contains 12 rolls of 160 sheets each or $12 \times 160 = 1{,}920$ sheets. $\$21 \div 1{,}920 = \$0.01$ or 1 cent per sheet.

2. **C.** There are 365 days in a year, and each day has 24 hours: $\dfrac{365 \text{ days}}{1 \text{ year}} \times \dfrac{24 \text{ hours}}{1 \text{ day}} = \dfrac{8{,}760 \text{ hours}}{1 \text{ year}}$.

3. **D.** If the measurements all seem just a little bit off, that's really not uncommon, but rounding and estimating will let you eliminate some answer choices (and probably get you close enough in real life). Rounding, a length of 12 feet, a width of 8 feet, and a height of 8 feet plugged into $2 \times \text{height(width + length)}$ gives you $2 \times 8(8 + 12) = 16(20) = 320$. That will let you eliminate choices A and B, which are much larger. To distinguish between choices C and D, you will have to do the actual calculation: $2 \times \text{height(width + length)} = 2\left(7\dfrac{11}{12}\right)\left(8\dfrac{1}{12} + 11\dfrac{10}{12}\right) = 2\left(7\dfrac{11}{12}\right)\left(19\dfrac{11}{12}\right)$. Change to improper fractions and multiply: $\dfrac{2}{1} \cdot \dfrac{95}{12} \cdot \dfrac{239}{12} = \dfrac{45{,}410}{144} = 315\dfrac{50}{144}$. Rounding down to the nearest square foot because $\dfrac{50}{144}$ is less than half, you get 315 square feet.

4. **C.** Change the escape velocity of 11,100 meters per second to 11.1 kilometers per second and then change to kilometers per hour.

$$\frac{11.1 \text{ kilometer}}{1 \text{ second}} \times \frac{60 \text{ seconds}}{1 \text{ minute}} \times \frac{60 \text{ minutes}}{1 \text{ hour}} = \frac{39,960 \text{ kilometers}}{\text{hour}}$$

The escape velocity is approximately 39,960 kilometers per hour.

5. **B.** You want to eliminate feet and replace them with the equivalent in meters.

$\frac{32 \text{ feet}}{1 \text{ second}^2} \times \frac{1 \text{ meter}}{3.28 \text{ feet}} = \frac{32 \text{ meters}}{3.28 \text{ seconds}^2}$. Dividing 32 by 3.28 should give you a number slightly less than

10. The correct answer is 9.76 meters per second per second.

6. **C.** Although often looked upon as equivalent events, the mile is slightly longer than the 1,500-meter, so a direct comparison of times would not be accurate. Instead, find meters per second for each record to allow a fair comparison.

$$\frac{1,500 \text{ meters}}{3 \text{ minutes } 26 \text{ seconds}} = \frac{1,500 \text{ meters}}{206 \text{ seconds}} = 7.28 \text{ meters/second}$$

$$\frac{1 \text{ mile}}{3 \text{ minutes } 43 \text{ seconds}} = \frac{1,609 \text{ meters}}{223 \text{ seconds}} = 7.22 \text{ meters/second}$$

The faster runner was the runner who ran 7.28 meters per second.

D. Scatterplots and a Line or Curve of Best Fit

A scatterplot is a graph that shows the relationship between two variables. It takes its name from the fact that it is a scattering of dots in the coordinate plane. One variable is graphed on the horizontal or x-axis and one on the vertical or y-axis, and each point represents an ordered pair (x, y).

Possible questions about scatterplots include the following:

- Is the association between the two variables positive or negative?
    - If the variables have a positive association, as one increases, the other increases as well. The points generally seem to move upward as you look from left to right.
    - A negative association exists when larger values of one variable are paired with smaller values of the other, causing the points to seem to fall from left to right.
    - Points may appear to fall outside the general pattern. Small variations are natural, but a point that sits significantly outside the pattern is considered an outlier. It may be the result of an unusual occurrence or of an error in recording the data.
- Is the association strong or weak? What is the correlation coefficient?
    - A correlation coefficient of 0 means there is no association, and the plot is just a cloud of random dots.
    - The closer the correlation coefficient is to 1 or –1, the stronger the association.

When the scatterplot shows a pattern that resembles a line, it is common to look for the equation of a line of best fit. Because the data rarely if ever form a perfect line, choosing different points could produce different equations. Finding the line that is truly the best fit is a task best left to calculators and computers, and not one you'd be asked to perform on the PSAT. You should know that a line of best fit passes through the midst of the scattering of points, with a relatively equal number of points above the line and below it, and always passes through the point $(\bar{x}, \bar{y})$, the average x-value and the average y-value. If the scatterplot shows a pattern that is not a line, but can be identified—for example, a parabola or an exponential curve—an equation may be found for the curve of best fit.

The equation of the line of best fit can be used to predict the y-value associated with a certain x-value, even if that point does not appear on the scatterplot. It can be used to estimate the x-value that would produce a certain y. Although the equation could be used to predict values lower or higher than those seen on the scatterplot, this kind of prediction, called extrapolation, is not reliable because the pattern may change when you go beyond the data on the plot.

Practice

1. Which of the following statements most accurately describes the scatterplot below?

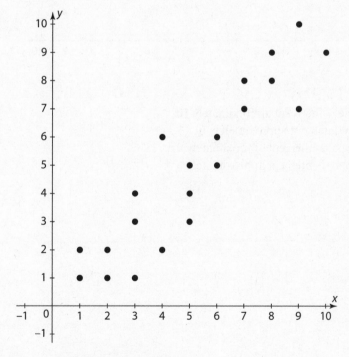

   A. The plot shows a weak negative association.
   B. The variables x and y have no association.
   C. The plot shows a strong positive association.
   D. The variables x and y are related but the association is not linear.

2. Which of the following is true for the line of best fit for the scatterplot below?

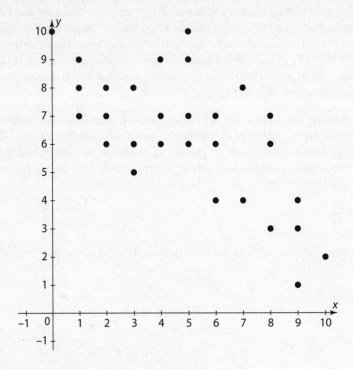

A. Positive slope, y-intercept approximately 10
B. Zero slope, y-intercept approximately 6
C. Negative slope, y-intercept approximately 9
D. Negative slope, y-intercept approximately 6

Use the following information for questions 3–6.

The scatterplot below shows the estimates of the population of one species of gorilla in a national park in Africa in the 40 years following 1975. The line of best fit is shown on the plot.

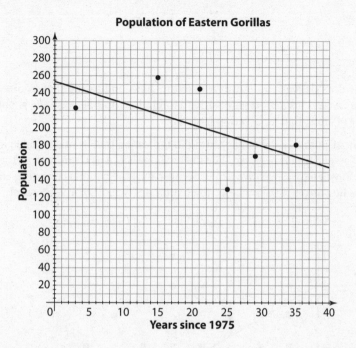

3. Which of the following is the best description of the relationship between the years after 1975 and the gorilla population in that park?

    A.   There is a strong positive association.
    B.   There is a strong negative association.
    C.   There is a moderate positive association.
    D.   There is a weak negative association.

4. In what year are the population data most different from the population predicted by the best-fit line?

    A.   1978
    B.   1990
    C.   1996
    D.   2000

5. The equation of the line of best fit is approximately Population = –2.5 × Years since 1975 + 253. What would this equation predict as the population in 1985?

    A.   206
    B.   228
    C.   248
    D.   740

6. In what year would the line of best fit predict a population of 200 gorillas?

    A.   1921
    B.   1977
    C.   1997
    D.   2021

Answers

1. **C.** The scatter of dots rises as you move from left to right, indicating that as one variable increases, the other increases as well. This denotes a positive association, and because the shape of a line is clear in the arrangement of dots, that association is strong.

2. **C.** This scattering of points falls from left to right, indicating that as one variable increases, the other decreases, so the association is negative. The linear shape is not as clear here, so the association is weaker. The line of best fit will have a negative slope, because the association is negative, eliminating choices A and B. Imagine a line through the midst of the scatter and you'll see a y-intercept of 6 (Choice D) is not feasible.

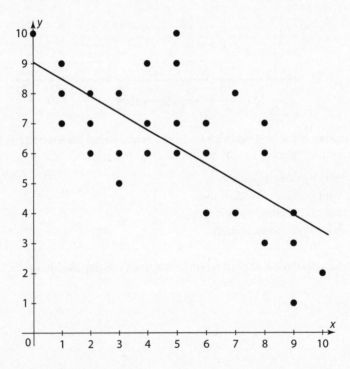

3. **D.** The general trend of the points seems to be decreasing, but there is no linear shape to the plot, so the association is negative but weak.

4. **D.** The point that represents 25 years after 1975 (or the year 2000) falls well below the line of best fit. The best-fit line predicts a population of approximately 190 that year, while the actual point is closer to a population of 130.

5. **B.** 1985 is 10 years after 1975, so replace "Years since 1975" with 10 in Population = –2.5 × Years since 1975 + 253, and you get Population = –2.5 × 10 + 253 = –25 + 253 = 228. The predicted population is 228.

6. **C.** In the equation Population = –2.5 × Years since 1975 + 253, replace Population with 200. Solve the equation 200 = –2.5 × Years since 1975 + 253 by first subtracting 253 from both sides to get –53 = –2.5 × Years since 1975. Then divide both sides by –2.5 to get 21.2 = Years since 1975. Using the model, 21 years brings the population down to 200.5, which is not quite the target of 200. Use 22 years, which brings the number below 200. Adding 22 years to 1975 gives you the year 1997. The line predicts a population of 200 gorillas in 1997.

E. Linear and Exponential Growth

Math uses the word *growth* to describe a situation in which, as one variable (usually time) increases, the other variable also increases. If time, or another independent variable, increases but the dependent variable decreases, the situation is usually referred to as *decay*.

Linear growth describes a situation in which the line of best fit is a line with a positive slope. Linear decay would be represented as a line with a negative slope. Linear growth is increase by addition; for each step along the horizontal axis, the *y*-value increases by a fixed amount. (This is approximately true. Real-life data rarely conform exactly to a pattern.) Each time the *x*-value increases by 1, the *y*-value increases by a positive number and always the same positive number. In the table below, each time *x* increases by 1, *y* increases by 3.

Linear Growth					
x	1	2	3	4	5
y	1	4	7	10	13

Exponential growth is increase by multiplication. Each time the *x*-value increases by 1, the *y*-value is multiplied by a fixed positive number. The larger that multiplier is, the faster the *y*-values increase. In the table below, each time *x* increases by 1, *y* is multiplied by 3. The graph of an exponential growth relationship is a curve that rises gently at first but soon becomes very steep.

Exponential Growth					
x	1	2	3	4	5
y	6	18	54	162	486

Practice

1. Mr. Khan purchases a new copier for his office. The copier is valued at $4,600, and Mr. Khan expects it will depreciate at a rate of 20% per year; that is, it will lose 20% of its value each year. What will be the value of the copier after 2 years?

   A. $1,840
   B. $2,760
   C. $2,944
   D. $7,360

2. A lab technician starts a culture of bacteria with 10 bacteria. The particular bacteria in the culture double every 6 hours. How many bacteria will be in the culture 24 hours after it was started?

   A. 160
   B. 640
   C. 20,000
   D. 160,000

3. Jaime opens a bank account with a deposit of $3,000. He makes no other deposits, but he has all interest earned added to the balance in the account and leaves it to accumulate. If the account earns 2% interest per year, how much money, to the nearest dollar, will be in the account after 5 years?

   A. $3,010
   B. $3,300
   C. $3,312
   D. $6,000

4. The first week of soccer season, Clementine ran 10 miles. Each week she increased her distance by 10%. How far was Clementine running in the fourth week?

   A. 10.4
   B. 11.6
   C. 13.3
   D. 14.6

Use the following information for questions 5–6.

Giselle and Isabella disagree on the model for a growth situation in which you begin with 1 unit and increase by 20% per day. Giselle believes it should be a linear model: $y = 1.2x + 1$, where x is the number of days. Isabella chooses an exponential model: $y = 1.2^x$, with x being the number of days. The graphs of both models are shown on the axes below. The dotted lines connect each of the points of intersection to the point on the exponential curve where $x = 10$.

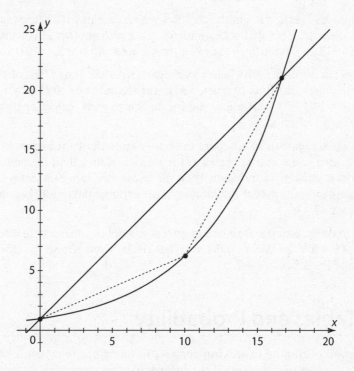

5. For which values of x is the exponential model growing faster than the linear model?

   A. $0 \le x \le 10$
   B. $10 \le x \le 17$
   C. The exponential model always grows faster.
   D. The linear model always grows faster.

6. What is the best approximation of the difference between the two models when $x = 10$?

   A. 2
   B. 5
   C. 7
   D. 10

Answers

1. **C.** If the copier loses 20% of its value, it retains 80% of its value. In the first year, the copier's value declines from \$4,600 to $0.8 \times 4,600 = \$3,680$. In the second year, the value declines from \$3,680 to $0.8 \times 3,680 = \$2,944$. (You can also do this as $\$4,600(0.8)^2 = \$2,944$.)

2. **A.** The bacteria double every 6 hours or 4 times in a 24-hour period. Start with 10 and double 4 times or calculate $10(2)^4 = 10(16) = 160$ bacteria.

3. **C.** If the account earns 2% per year, at the end of a year it contains 102% of what it contained at the beginning of the year: 100% of the beginning balance plus another 2% of that. Calculate $\$3,000(1.02)^5 = \$3,312.24$. To the nearest dollar, the account will contain \$3,312 after 5 years.

4. **C.** If she increases her distance by 10% each week, each week she runs 110% of the previous week's distance. In the first week, she runs 10 miles, and in the second week, $10(1.1) = 11$ miles. In the third week, her distance is $10(1.1)^2 = 12.1$ miles, and for the fourth week, calculate $10(1.1)^3 = 13.31$. By the fourth week, she runs 13.3 miles.

5. **B.** Use the two dotted segments to compare the rate of growth of the exponential curve to the slope of the line. The dotted segment that begins at the y-axis is flatter than the linear model, so the exponential model is growing more slowly than the linear model in this section. The second dotted line is steeper than the linear model, which means the exponential model is growing more quickly in the interval $10 \leq x \leq 17$.

6. **C.** You can only make an estimate from the graph provided, but when $x = 10$, the exponential model appears to say $y \approx 6$, while the linear model says that y is between 12 and 13. Of the choices provided, the best estimate of the difference is 7.

F. Two-Way Tables and Probability

Collecting data is a good beginning in seeking answers to questions, but before you can actually learn anything from data, you need to organize all the information in some way. A two-way table is a method of organizing data based on two characteristics. The two-way table below is organized by gender and age.

	18–35	36–53	54–71	Total
Male	367	133	150	650
Female	391	109	200	700
Total	758	242	350	1,350

The bottom row shows the total of each column and the rightmost column shows row totals. The bottom right corner cell has the total number of data items: 1,350. The two-way table makes it possible to answer both basic probability questions and what are called conditional probability questions.

A basic question might ask: What is the probability that a person chosen at random from this group is female? The probability is the number of females divided by the total number of people, or $\frac{700}{1,350}$, which can be simplified to $\frac{14}{27}$.

An example of a more complicated question might be: What is the probability that a person chosen at random is male and 18 to 35 years old? The denominator is still the total number of people, but now you must use the two-way table breakdown to see that although there are 650 males, there are only 367 males in the required age group. This probability is $\dfrac{367}{1,350}$.

Conditional probability puts a condition or restriction on your choices. It asks about the probability of a certain event occurring if you know that some other event has already occurred. For example, what is the probability that a person chosen at random is between 54 and 71, given that the person is female? Here you're being told that you already know the person is female, so you're not looking at all 1,350 people, but only the 700 females. Looking only at that row of the table, there are 200 females between 54 and 71 out of 700 females. The conditional probability is $\dfrac{200}{700} = \dfrac{2}{7}$.

> TIP: If answers are in fractions, factor and reduce. For decimals and percents, use a calculator.

Practice

1. In a small town, there are 212 registered Republicans, 273 registered Democrats, and 15 registered Independents. If one person is chosen at random from the town, what is the probability that the person is an Independent?

    A. $\dfrac{15}{212}$

    B. $\dfrac{5}{91}$

    C. $\dfrac{3}{97}$

    D. $\dfrac{3}{100}$

2. At the family reunion, Meghan noticed that 12 family members had blond hair, 18 had blue eyes, and 6 had both blond hair and blue eyes. If there were 50 family members at the reunion, what is the probability that a person chosen at random has neither blue eyes nor blond hair?

    A. $\dfrac{2}{5}$

    B. $\dfrac{7}{25}$

    C. $\dfrac{13}{25}$

    D. $\dfrac{18}{25}$

3. Rodney is taking a multiple-choice test in which there are 4 answer choices for each question. After answering all the questions for which he feels confident that he knows the answer, he finds there are 3 questions for which he must guess. If Rodney randomly chooses an answer for each of those 3 questions, what is the probability that he will get all 3 questions correct?

   A. $\dfrac{1}{64}$

   B. $\dfrac{1}{12}$

   C. $\dfrac{1}{4}$

   D. $\dfrac{3}{4}$

Use the information below to answer questions 4–6.

A group of people were surveyed about their interest in sports. They were asked whether or not they had participated in any high school sports. The sample was divided into those who had played one or more sports in high school and those who did not participate in any high school sports. Both groups were then asked which of three professional sports—basketball, baseball, or football—they watched most often. The results are summarized in the table below.

	Basketball	Baseball	Football	Total
Participated in high school sports	150	200	450	800
Did not participate	250	350	350	950
Total	400	550	800	1,750

4. What is the probability that a person selected at random prefers football?

   A. $\dfrac{3}{7}$

   B. $\dfrac{7}{15}$

   C. $\dfrac{8}{15}$

   D. $\dfrac{16}{35}$

5. What is the probability that a person chosen at random prefers baseball and did not participate in high school sports?

   A. $\dfrac{1}{5}$

   B. $\dfrac{7}{11}$

   C. $\dfrac{7}{19}$

   D. $\dfrac{11}{19}$

6. What is the probability that a person selected at random participated in high school athletics, given that their favorite sport is football?

   A. $\dfrac{3}{5}$

   B. $\dfrac{7}{9}$

   C. $\dfrac{9}{16}$

   D. $\dfrac{19}{35}$

Answers

1. **D.** Start with the basic probability of $\dfrac{\text{number of Independents}}{\text{total population}} = \dfrac{15}{212+273+15} = \dfrac{15}{500}$ and simplify: $\dfrac{15}{500} = \dfrac{3}{100}$.

2. **C.** The counting is the key to this question, and a Venn diagram may help.

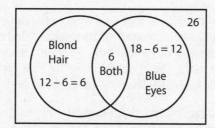

The number of relatives at the reunion with blond hair or blue eyes or both is 6 + 6 + 12 = 24. There were 50 relatives at the reunion, so 50 − 24 = 26 relatives who have neither blond hair nor blue eyes. The probability that a person selected at random has neither is $\dfrac{26}{50} = \dfrac{13}{25}$.

3. **A.** For any question with 4 choices, the probability of choosing the correct answer at random is $\dfrac{1}{4}$. The probability that he chooses correctly on all 3 questions is $\dfrac{1}{4} \times \dfrac{1}{4} \times \dfrac{1}{4} = \dfrac{1}{64}$.

4. **D.** According to the table, 800 people prefer football out of 1,750 people. The probability that a person chosen at random prefers football is $\dfrac{800}{1,750} = \dfrac{80}{175} = \dfrac{16}{35}$.

5. **A.** The number of people who prefer baseball and did not participate in school sports is 350. The probability that a person chosen at random prefers baseball and did not participate in school sports is $\dfrac{350}{1,750} = \dfrac{35}{175} = \dfrac{7}{35} = \dfrac{1}{5}$.

6. **C.** If you know that you're looking only at people who prefer football, you're choosing from the 800 people who watch football most often, rather than the whole group of 1,750. Of those 800, 450 participated in high school sports. The probability that a person chosen at random participated in school sports, given that they prefer football, is $\dfrac{450}{800} = \dfrac{45}{80} = \dfrac{9}{16}$.

G. Statistics

When data are collected to answer some question or test some hypothesis, the data are generally organized into some kind of graph or visual representation. This might be a bar graph if the data are organized into categories or a histogram if the data are numerical data. A histogram is a type of bar graph in which each bar represents a range of numerical values and the height of the bar represents the frequency or number of times values in that range were observed. Once the graph is drawn, the first three questions that are generally asked about the distribution of the data are:

- What is the shape of the distribution?

  If the distribution is highest in the center and drops off at about the same rate on either side, it is roughly symmetrical. If the highest point is to the right or left, the distribution is skewed. If all the bars are about the same size, it's a uniform distribution. Some data will not fit any of these descriptors.

- Where is the center?

  The center tells you something about the average value in the data. You can estimate the center from a graph, or calculate one of three averages: the mean, or arithmetic average; the median, or middle value when data are in order; or the mode, or most common value.

- How large is the spread?

  Ways to measure the spread of the data can be as simple as the range, which is the difference between the highest and lowest value, or as complicated as the standard deviation. On the PSAT, you wouldn't be expected to calculate the standard deviation, but you should understand that it is a measure of spread, and the larger it is, the more spread out the data are. Always compare like to like: range of one data set to range of another, or standard deviation to standard deviation.

Questions about data collection and presentation are asking if you can distinguish reasonable from unreasonable conclusions, sound methods from unsound, and sensible summaries from nonsensical. Ask yourself questions like these:

- How were data gathered?
- Are the people or things on which the data are based really representative of the population of interest?
- Is there bias in the selection of the sample or in the questions asked?
- Is the type of graph used appropriate for the information being presented?
- Is the graph well-labeled?

Practice

1. For the data below, the difference between the mean and the median is

$$16, 18, 19, 20, 30, 45, 55$$

   A. 1
   B. 9
   C. 10
   D. 39

2. Your school wants to determine if cafeteria lunches are appealing to students. Which of the following is an appropriate way to gather information to help make such a determination?

   A. Stand outside the pizza shop across the street at lunch time and ask students why they are not eating in the cafeteria.
   B. At the next faculty meeting, ask teachers to rate school lunch on a scale from 1 (worst) to 5 (best).
   C. Ask the entire freshman class to vote on their three favorite lunches.
   D. Randomly select 10 students from each of the four grades and have those 40 students fill out a questionnaire about what they like and do not like about school lunches.

3. Mr. Swenson gave the same test to his two American history classes. The first class has 14 students and had an average score of 83. The second class has 16 students and had an average score of 81. What was the average score for the combined two classes?

   A. 81.1
   B. 81.9
   C. 82.0
   D. 87.5

Use the information below for questions 4–6.

The same survey question was asked of 20 randomly selected people in a small town and of another group of 20 randomly selected people in a nearby city. The question was "How many times have you moved to a new place of residence in the last 10 years?" Responses are summarized in the two graphs below.

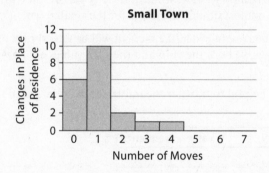
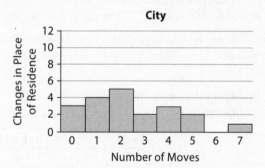

4. Which of the following statements about these two distributions is correct?

   A. The spread of the data collected in the city is wider than the spread of the small-town data.
   B. Both distributions are symmetric.
   C. More people responded to the question in the small town.
   D. The city distribution shows an outlier.

5. Which of the following is the median of the small-town data?

   A. 1
   B. 1.05
   C. 2
   D. 2.45

6. Which of the following is the mean of the city data?

   A. 1
   B. 1.05
   C. 2
   D. 2.45

Answers

1. **B.** The data is presented in order, so the median is the middle value, 20. The mean is the sum of the data values divided by the number of values. $\text{Mean} = \dfrac{16+18+19+20+30+45+55}{7} = \dfrac{203}{7} = 29$. The difference is $29 - 20 = 9$.

2. **D.** Choice A would get opinions from only those who chose not to eat school lunch. They would likely respond with what they didn't like and few, if any, positives. Choice B is inappropriate because the goal is to make the lunches attractive to students, not faculty. The freshman class may not be representative of the school as a whole, and asking them to rank their favorites won't provide any information on what needs to be improved, so Choice C is not a good choice. Only Choice D, which chooses students randomly and includes all grades, is a sensible way to proceed.

3. **B.** If the average of 14 grades was 83, the total of the 14 grades was $14 \times 83 = 1{,}162$. The total of the 16 grades in the other section was $16 \times 81 = 1{,}296$. Adding $1{,}162 + 1{,}296$ gives a total of 2,458 for the $14 + 16 = 30$ students. Divide 2,458 by 30 to get the average of 81.9.

4. **A.** Values in the small-town survey vary from 0 to 4, a range of 4, while in the city survey, they vary from 0 to 7, a range of 7. The range for the city is almost double the range for the small town.

5. **A.** Twenty people were questioned, so when the data are in order, the median will be the average of the 10th and 11th values. There are 6 zeros and 10 ones, so both the 10th and the 11th values are ones. The median is 1.

6. **D.** To find the mean for the city data, it might be helpful to transfer the information in the graph to a frequency table.

Value	Frequency	Value × Frequency
0	3	0
1	4	4
2	5	10
3	2	6
4	3	12
5	2	10
6	0	0
7	1	7
Total	20	49

Multiply each value by the frequency, or number of times that value was recorded. Three zeros are worth zero, four ones are worth four, five twos are worth 10, and so on, as shown in the last column. Add the products for a total of 49, and divide by 20 to get a mean of 2.45.

X. Passport to Advanced Math

The questions that are categorized as "Passport to Advanced Math" are generally questions about algebra, but they step beyond "The Heart of Algebra" and move toward the techniques that are used in areas of mathematics like calculus. No actual calculus is involved. This is the math that is your passport. It's what you need to get to advanced math. Much of it can be managed with skills from "The Heart of Algebra" applied in new ways to new situations.

A. Equivalent Expressions and Isolating Variables

If *equivalent expressions* sounds like a description of an equation and *isolating variables* sounds like solving equations, you may wonder how these questions are different from basic algebra skills. The fundamental manipulations are the same, but the situations may be more complex. The equation may be a literal equation, with few if any numbers, and several letters representing variables and constants. If you're asked to isolate one of those letters, your job is to focus on that letter as your variable, and treat the others as numbers. Apply your equation-solving skills to get that key letter all alone on one side. It may be a bit messy, because there will be few like terms or nice opportunities to simplify, but it's the same process as solving basic algebra equations.

Practice

1. If an object is launched upward from the ground, its height in feet t seconds after launch is $h = vt - 16t^2$, where v is the velocity with which the object is launched. Which of the following is a formula for the velocity in terms of the height and time?

   A. $v = t - 16t^2 - h$

   B. $v = \dfrac{h}{t} + 16t$

   C. $v = ht + 16t^2$

   D. $v = \dfrac{h}{t} - \dfrac{h}{16t^2}$

2. The perimeter of a rectangle is $P = 2l + 2w$, and the area is $A = lw$. Which of the following expresses the area in terms of the perimeter and the width?

   A. $A = w(2l + 2w)$
   B. $A = w(2P + 2w)$
   C. $A = w(P - 2w)$
   D. $A = 0.5w(P - 2w)$

3. If $\Delta = \heartsuit + 2\Omega$ and $\heartsuit = 3\otimes - \Delta$, which of the following is equal to $\otimes$?

   A. $\dfrac{2}{3}(\Delta - \Omega)$

   B. $2\Delta + 2\Omega$

   C. $6\Delta - 6\Omega$

   D. $\dfrac{2\Omega}{3}$

179

4. All of the following are equivalent to $2(ax - b) + a - 3(c - bx)$ EXCEPT

    A. $(2a + 3b)x + a - 2b - 3c$

    B. $2ax - 2b - 3(c - bx) + a$

    C. $2ax - 2b - 3c - 3bx + a$

    D. $a(2x + 1) + 3(bx - c) - 2b$

5. Solve for x: $ax + by = c$.

    A. $x = c - by - a$

    B. $x = \dfrac{c}{a} - by$

    C. $x = \dfrac{c}{aby}$

    D. $x = \dfrac{c - by}{a}$

6. Which of the following results when y is isolated in the equation $ax - by = cx + dy$?

    A. $y = \dfrac{x(a - c)}{b + d}$

    B. $y = \dfrac{ax - c}{-b}$

    C. $y = \dfrac{ax - b}{c + d}$

    D. $y = \dfrac{x(b + d)}{a - c}$

Answers

1. **B.** Solve the equation $h = vt - 16t^2$ for v. Add $16t^2$ to both sides to get $h + 16t^2 = vt$, and then divide by t. The result is $v = \dfrac{h + 16t^2}{t} = \dfrac{h}{t} + \dfrac{16t^2}{t} = \dfrac{h}{t} + 16t$.

2. **D.** Solve $P = 2l + 2w$ for l by subtracting $2w$ from both sides to get $P - 2w = 2l$ and then dividing by 2 to get $l = \dfrac{P - 2w}{2} = \dfrac{P}{2} - \dfrac{2w}{2} = 0.5P - w$. Substitute that into the area formula: $A = (0.5P - w)w$. Simplify to get $A = 0.5Pw - w^2$. That form is not an answer choice, so consider alternate forms. Factor out the common factor of w to get $A = w(0.5P - w)$ and you're closer. Factor out $0.5w$ instead to get $A = 0.5w(P - 2w)$.

3. **A.** Don't let the strange symbols frighten you. They just act as variables. Start with $\heartsuit = 3\otimes - \Delta$ and isolate $\otimes$. $\heartsuit = 3\otimes - \Delta$ becomes $3\otimes = \heartsuit + \Delta$ or $\otimes = \dfrac{\heartsuit + \Delta}{3}$, but that's not a choice. No choice involves $\heartsuit$, so solve $\Delta = \heartsuit + 2\Omega$ for $\heartsuit$. You get $\heartsuit = \Delta - 2\Omega$, and you can substitute for the $\heartsuit$ in $\otimes = \dfrac{\heartsuit + \Delta}{3}$, as follows: $\otimes = \dfrac{\heartsuit + \Delta}{3} = \dfrac{(\Delta - 2\Omega) + \Delta}{3} = \dfrac{2\Delta - 2\Omega}{3} = \dfrac{2(\Delta - \Omega)}{3} = \dfrac{2}{3}(\Delta - \Omega)$.

4. **C.** There are many ways to rewrite $2(ax - b) + a - 3(c - bx)$, so use the answer choices to guide you. Choices A and D show a lot of regrouping. Start with the simpler options. Distribute the 2 to eliminate the first set of parentheses: $2(ax - b) + a - 3(c - bx) = 2ax - 2b + a - 3(c - bx)$. This confirms that Choice B is equivalent. Distribute the -3 over the second set of parentheses: $2ax - 2b + a - 3(c - bx) = 2ax - 2b + a - 3c + 3bx$. Choice C has a sign error and is therefore NOT equivalent. Confirm that choices A and D are equivalent. Choice A groups the terms including an x as follows; it is equivalent:

$$2ax - 2b + a - 3c + 3bx = 2ax + 3bx + a - 2b - 3c = (2a + 3b)x + a - 2b - 3c$$

Choice D chooses to group terms with a and terms with 3 as follows; it too is equivalent:

$$2ax - 2b + a - 3c + 3bx = 2ax + a + 3bx - 3c - 2b = a(2x + 1) + 3(bx - c) - 2b$$

5. **D.** To solve $ax + by = c$ for x, keep your focus on x as the variable and treat everything else as a constant. Subtract by from both sides, and divide by a. $ax + by = c$ becomes $ax = c - by$ and finally $x = \dfrac{c - by}{a}$.

6. **A.** To isolate y, begin by moving all terms with y to one side and all terms without y to the other side. $ax - by = cx + dy$ becomes $ax - cx = by + dy$. Factor out the y on the right side: $ax - cx = y(b + d)$. Divide both sides by $b + d$: $y = \dfrac{ax - cx}{b + d}$. That exact form is not a choice, but factoring out the x in the numerator will produce Choice A: $y = \dfrac{x(a - c)}{b + d}$.

B. Compositions of Functions and Transformations

The more you move toward advanced math, the more you see the language of functions. A function is a relationship between two quantities, referred to as the independent and dependent variables or as inputs and outputs. While the relationship is often defined by an equation, a better image is that a function is a device that matches inputs with outputs. A function assigns a single output to each input. The equation is one way to explain that assignment rule. It could also be shown in a chart, a list, or a graph, or simply described in words.

A composition of functions can be thought of as one function taking an input, determining the proper output, and then handing that output to another function. The second function takes that value as its input and follows its particular rule to assign an output. A doubling function, one that multiplies every input by 2, might take a 3 and assign an output of 6. If it then hands that 6 to a function whose job is to add 3 to every input, the second function sees an input of 6 and assigns an output of 9. The composition of those two functions is a new function that takes the original input of 2 and assigns the final output of 9.

It's not as complicated as it may sound. Let $f(x) = 2x$, the doubling function, and $g(x) = x + 3$, the function that adds 3. We want a function that doubles, and then adds 3:

$$g(f(x)) = g(2x) = 2x + 3$$

Note that order matters. If we had found $f(g(x))$, that would add 3 and then double, and that would take an input of 2, add 3 to get 5, and then double to get 10. Changing the order of the functions changes the results. The first function to do its work goes inside the parentheses.

Whenever you look at a category of things, like functions, one of the things you look for is what they all have in common. One thing all functions have in common is that their graphs respond the same way to certain changes in the equation. In general, these are called transformations, and they fall into several categories: translation (shifting left, right, up, or down), reflection (flipping horizontally or vertically), and scale change (stretching or shrinking horizontally or vertically). To make these a little easier to understand, let's use y rather than $f(x)$, and look at some examples using different types of functions.

Translation is an adding/subtracting change. Adding or subtracting a constant to or from the x moves the graph left or right: to the left if you add and to the right if you subtract. Adding or subtracting a constant to or from the y moves the graph up if you subtract and down if you add. Be aware that it's common to isolate y, so you may need to rearrange to see the translation. Let's use $y = x^2$ as the starting graph and look at $y = (x + 3)^2$, $y = (x - 1)^2$, $y + 2 = x^2$, and $y - 4 = x^2$.

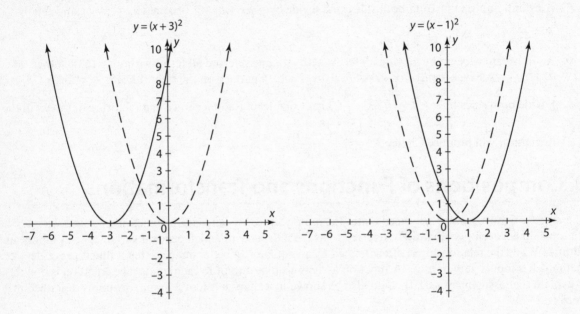

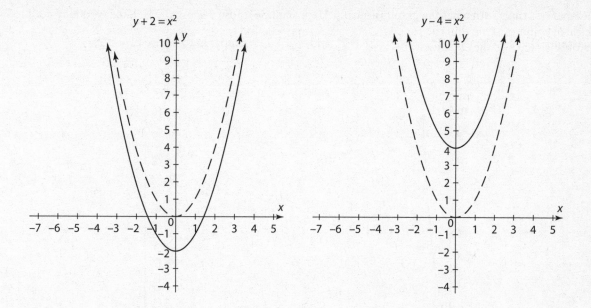

Reflection is a sign change. Changing the sign of x mirrors the graph across the y-axis, while changing the sign of y flips the graph across the x-axis. Let's use $y = x - 3$ as the base equation and look at $y = -x - 3$ and $-y = x - 3$.

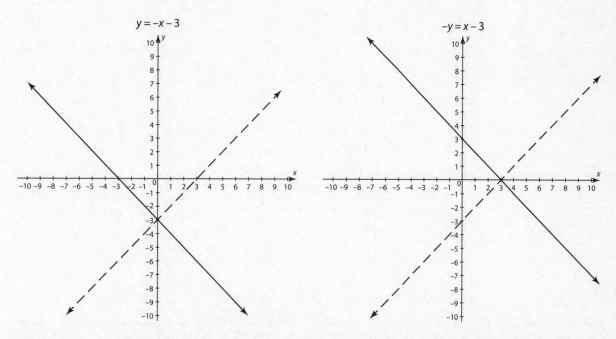

Scale change is a multiplication/division change. Multiplying x by a number greater than 1 compresses the graph toward the y-axis, but multiplying by a number less than 1 stretches the graph out from the y-axis. Multiplying y by a number greater than 1 compresses the graph toward the x-axis, and multiplying y by a number less than 1 stretches the graph vertically. Here again, because y is usually isolated, you may need to rearrange. Let's look at $y = 2^{3x}$, $y = 2^{\frac{1}{3}x}$, $3y = 2^x$, and $\frac{1}{3}y = 2^x$, compared to a base of $y = 2^x$.

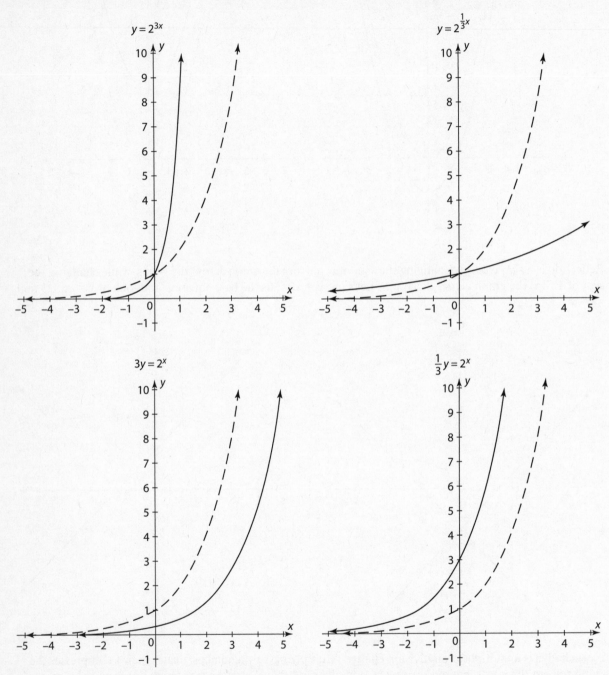

Practice

1. The graph below shows the result of applying transformations to the graph of $y = x^2$. What is the equation of the graph shown?

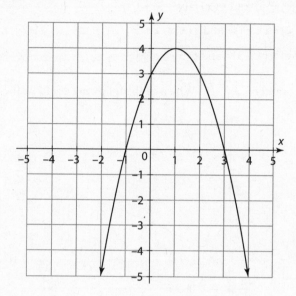

    A. $y = -x^2 + 4$

    B. $y = -x^2 - 1$

    C. $y = -(x - 1)^2 + 4$

    D. $y = (x + 1)^2 - 4$

2. If the graph of the line $y = 2x - 1$ is translated 4 units left and 3 units down, what is the equation of the resulting graph?

    A. $y = 2x - 3$

    B. $y = 2x - 4$

    C. $y = 3x - 4$

    D. $y = 2x + 4$

3. If $f(x) = \dfrac{1}{2}x$ and $g(x) = x^2$, then $g(f(x)) =$

    A. $\dfrac{1}{2}x^2$

    B. $\dfrac{1}{2}x^3$

    C. $\dfrac{1}{4}x^2$

    D. $\dfrac{1}{8}x^3$

4. The function $h(x) = (x-3)^2 + 1$ can be created by the composition of two functions. Which of these describes a composition that produces $h(x) = (x-3)^2 + 1$?

    A. $f(g(x))$ with $f(x) = x^2 - 3$ and $g(x) = x + 1$

    B. $g(f(x))$ with $f(x) = x^2$ and $g(x) = (x-3) + 1$

    C. $f(g(x))$ with $f(x) = (x+1)^2$ and $g(x) = x - 3$

    D. $g(f(x))$ with $f(x) = (x-3)^2$ and $g(x) = x + 1$

5. The figure below is the graph of $y = \sqrt{x}$. Which of the following could be the graph of $y = 2\sqrt{x+1} + 3$?

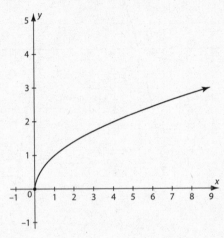

A.

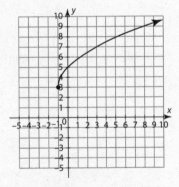

C.

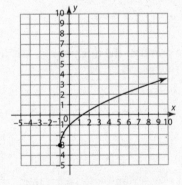

B.

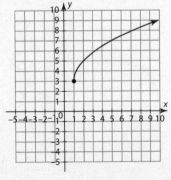

D.

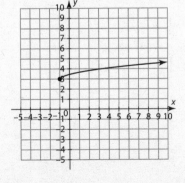

6. Which of these functions is the composition $f(g(x))$ with $f(x) = x^2 + 4$ and $g(x) = 1 - \sqrt{x}$?

   A. $h(x) = 3 - x$

   B. $h(x) = 1 - \sqrt{x^2 + 4}$

   C. $h(x) = 5 + x$

   D. $h(x) = 5 - 2\sqrt{x} + x$

Answers

1. **C.** The parabola opens down, which means there's been a vertical flip, so there must be a negative multiplier, eliminating Choice D. There is a shift right and up, so choices A and B can be eliminated; they do not show a horizontal shift. The parabola has been flipped, shifted 1 unit right, and shifted 4 units up. The correct equation is $y = -(x - 1)^2 + 4$.

2. **D.** Shifts left and down will not change the slope of the line, so eliminate Choice C. Focus on the y-intercept $(0, -1)$. It moves 4 units left to $(-4, -1)$ and then down 3 units to $(-4, -4)$. The result is a line with a slope of 2 that passes through $(-4, -4)$. Use $y - (-4) = 2(x - (-4))$ and simplify to get $y + 4 = 2(x + 4)$ or $y = 2x + 4$. Alternately, sketch the graph and do the translation.

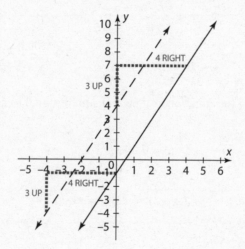

3. **C.** If $f(x) = \dfrac{1}{2}x$ and $g(x) = x^2$, then $g(f(x)) = g\left(\dfrac{1}{2}x\right) = \left(\dfrac{1}{2}x\right)^2 = \dfrac{1}{4}x^2$.

4. **D.** The function you want to create takes x, subtracts 3 from it, squares the result, and adds 1. Examine each of the choices to see which composition might create that. Remember the inner function works first. Choice A adds 1 first, then squares, and then subtracts 3: $f(g(x)) = f(x + 1) = (x + 1)^2 - 3$. Choice B squares first, then subtracts, and then adds: $g(f(x)) = g(x^2) = (x^2 - 3) + 1$. Choice C subtracts 3 first, then adds, and finally squares: $f(g(x)) = f(x - 3) = ((x - 3) + 1)^2$. Choice D is the correct choice: $g(f(x)) = g((x - 3)^2) = (x - 3)^2 + 1$.

5. **A.** The graph of $y = 2\sqrt{x+1} + 3$ is shifted 1 unit left, stretched vertically and shifted up 3 units. Eliminate Choice B because it shifts right, not left. Eliminate Choice D because it is compressed vertically, not stretched. Choice C shifts down instead of up. Only Choice A correctly shifts left and up; Choice A is correct.

6. **D.** If $f(x) = x^2 + 4$ and $g(x) = 1 - \sqrt{x}$, $f(g(x)) = f(1 - \sqrt{x}) = (1 - \sqrt{x})^2 + 4$. Remember to use the FOIL rule when squaring $1 - \sqrt{x}$: $f(g(x)) = (1 - \sqrt{x})^2 + 4 = 1 - 2\sqrt{x} + (\sqrt{x})^2 + 4 = 5 - 2\sqrt{x} + x$.

C. Solving Quadratic Equations

You had some experience with solving quadratic equations in "The Heart of Algebra" chapter. These questions look at more complicated equations and more advanced techniques for solving them. The techniques for solving quadratic equations include:

- **Factoring:** Rewrite the equation as the product of two linear factors, equal to zero. Set each factor equal to zero and solve.

$$x^2 = 5x - 6$$
$$x^2 - 5x + 6 = 0$$
$$(x - 2)(x - 3) = 0$$

$$x - 2 = 0 \qquad\qquad x - 3 = 0$$
$$x = 2 \qquad\qquad\qquad x = 3$$

- **Square root method:** Rewrite the equation as a perfect square, equal to a constant. Take the square root of both sides and solve.

$$x^2 - 6x + 9 = 12$$
$$(x - 3)^2 = 12$$
$$\sqrt{(x - 3)^2} = \pm\sqrt{12} = \pm 2\sqrt{3}$$

$$x - 3 = 2\sqrt{3} \qquad\qquad x - 3 = -2\sqrt{3}$$
$$x = 3 + 2\sqrt{3} \qquad\qquad x = 3 - 2\sqrt{3}$$

- **Completing the square:** This method grew out of the square root method. It manipulates the equation by adding a constant to both sides so that the equation can be written as a perfect square equal to a constant. For simple equations like the one below, it's not too difficult, but it can get messy for more complicated equations, which is what leads to the next method, the quadratic formula.

$$x^2 - 6x = 2$$
$$x^2 - 6x + 9 = 2 + 9$$
$$(x - 3)^2 = 11$$
$$x - 3 = \pm\sqrt{11}$$
$$x = 3 \pm \sqrt{11}$$

- **Quadratic formula:** Some very patient person took the form of a quadratic equation, $ax^2 + bx + c = 0$, and very carefully solved that literal equation by completing the square. They arrived at this formula for the solutions: $x = \dfrac{-b \pm \sqrt{b^2 - 4ac}}{2a}$.

$$x^2 - 6x = 2$$
$$x^2 - 6x - 2 = 0$$
$$a = 1 \ b = -6 \ c = -2$$
$$x = \frac{-b \pm \sqrt{b^2 - 4ac}}{2a} = \frac{-(-6) \pm \sqrt{(-6)^2 - 4(1)(-2)}}{2(1)}$$
$$x = \frac{6 \pm \sqrt{36 + 8}}{2} = \frac{6 \pm \sqrt{44}}{2} = \frac{6 \pm 2\sqrt{11}}{2} = 3 \pm \sqrt{11}$$

- **Graphing:** In theory, you can solve a quadratic by graphing the equation and finding its x-intercepts. In practice, that's not really useful unless the equation has integer solutions (in which case other methods are faster), or you have a lot of time and graph paper that lets you set a scale of 10 boxes for 1 unit (not really practical on the PSAT), or you have a graphing calculator (possible, if you have one, and it's a calculator section; see the Appendix for the how-to).

Practice

1. If the equation $x^2 - 4 = 3x$ is solved by using the quadratic formula, the first step is

   A. $x = \dfrac{-4 \pm \sqrt{(4)^2 - 4(1)(3)}}{2(1)}$

   B. $x = \dfrac{0 \pm \sqrt{(0)^2 - 4(1)(4)}}{2(1)}$

   C. $x = \dfrac{-(-3) \pm \sqrt{(-3)^2 - 4(1)(-4)}}{2(1)}$

   D. $x = \dfrac{-3 \pm \sqrt{(3)^2 - 4(1)(4)}}{2(4)}$

2. Which of the following is true about the solution(s) of the equation $x^2 - 5x + 4 = 0$?

   A. The equation has no real solution.
   B. The equation has a single positive solution.
   C. The equation has two solutions, one positive and one negative.
   D. The equation has two solutions, both positive.

3. Solve for x: $x^2 + 15 = 6 - 6x$.

   A. $x = 3$
   B. $x = -3$
   C. $x = 3$ or $x = -3$
   D. No solution

4. If the equation $3x^2 + 24x + 48 = 75$ is solved by the square root method, which of the following is the result?

   A. $x = \pm 1$
   B. $x = \pm 5\sqrt{3}$
   C. $x = \pm 5$
   D. $x = 1, x = -9$

5. An object is dropped from a 100-foot cliff. The height of the object after t seconds is given by the equation $h = -16t^2 + 100$. At what time, to the nearest tenth of a second, is the object 20 feet off the ground?

   A. 1.1
   B. 2.2
   C. 2.5
   D. 8.9

6. The area of a circle with radius r is $A = \pi r^2$. To the nearest tenth of an inch, what is the radius of a circle with an area of 50 square inches?

   A. 2.3
   B. 4.0
   C. 7.1
   D. 15.9

Answers

1. **C.** To solve $x^2 - 4 = 3x$ with the quadratic formula, first move all terms to one side and set equal to zero: $x^2 - 3x - 4 = 0$. Identify $a = 1$, $b = -3$, and $c = -4$. Write the quadratic formula $x = \dfrac{-b \pm \sqrt{b^2 - 4ac}}{2a}$ and replace a, b, and c with the appropriate values: $x = \dfrac{-(-3) \pm \sqrt{(-3)^2 - 4(1)(-4)}}{2(1)}$.

2. **D.** If it's possible to solve a quadratic equation by factoring, that's usually the fastest method, so try to factor $x^2 - 5x + 4 = 0$. The left side factors to $(x - 1)(x - 4) = 0$. Setting each factor equal to 0 and solving gives you $x = 1$ and $x = 4$, two positive solutions.

3. **B.** Move all terms to one side, set equal to zero, and $x^2 + 15 = 6 - 6x$ becomes $x^2 + 6x + 9 = 0$. Factor the left side and you have $(x + 3)(x + 3) = 0$. Set each factor equal to zero and solve. Both factors give you $x = -3$.

4. **D.** The equation $3x^2 + 24x + 48 = 75$ doesn't look like a great candidate for solving by the square root method, but take a moment to simplify. Divide through the entire equation by 3, and you have $x^2 + 8x + 16 = 25$, and both sides are perfect squares: $(x + 4)^2 = 5^2$. Taking the square root of both sides gives you $x + 4 = \pm 5$. If $x + 4 = 5$, then $x = 1$, and if $x + 4 = -5$, then $x = -9$.

5. **B.** The object is 20 feet off the ground when $h = 20$, so substitute: $20 = -16t^2 + 100$. Subtract 100 from both sides to get $-80 = -16t^2$, and divide both sides by -16 to get $t^2 = 5$. With a calculator, you can find $t \approx 2.2$, but if you don't have a calculator available, you can estimate. You know $2^2 = 4$ and $3^2 = 9$, so t is between 2 and 3. You need to decide between Choice B and Choice C, and a little bit of multiplying tells you Choice C is too big. The correct answer is Choice B, 2.2.

6. **B.** With an area of 50 square inches, $A = \pi r^2$ becomes $50 = \pi r^2$. Divide both sides by π to get $r^2 = \dfrac{50}{\pi} \approx 15.915$, and then take the square root: $r \approx \sqrt{15.915} \approx 3.989$. A calculator is a plus, but estimate if you must. Fifty divided by a number a little more than 3 should give you something close to 16, because 3 times 16 is 48, and the square root of 16 is 4.

D. Systems of Equations Consisting of One Linear and One Non-Linear Equation

The techniques for solving systems that include one linear and one non-linear equation are not really different from the methods you used for linear systems. The algebra involved may get a little more complicated, and you will likely be finding more than one solution.

- The system may be solved by locating the points of intersection on the graph. Because the non-linear graph curves, there may be two (or more) points of intersection.

- To solve by substitution, you'll find it easiest to isolate one variable in the linear equation, and then substitute into the non-linear. Solve for one variable in the non-linear equation, probably getting more than one solution, and plug each solution back into the linear equation to find the second number in each ordered pair.

- Solving by elimination is theoretically possible, but usually looks a lot like substitution.

Practice

1. Which of the following is the solution set of the system graphed below?

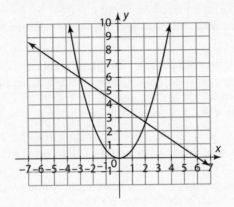

   A. {(0, 4), (6, 0)}
   B. {(0, 4), (2, 2.67)}
   C. {(−3, 6), (2, 2.67)}
   D. {(−3, 6), (6, 0)}

2. Which of the following is the solution set of the system below?

$$y = 5 - x^2$$
$$y = x + 3$$

   A. {(−2, 1), (0, 3)}
   B. {(−3, 0), (1, 4)}
   C. {(0, 5), (−3, 0)}
   D. {(−2, 1), (1, 4)}

3. Which of the following statements about the system below is true?

$$y = 4x + 7$$
$$y = (x + 2)^2 + 3$$

   A. The system has no solution.
   B. The system has one solution: (0, 7).
   C. The system has one solution: (−2, 3).
   D. The system has two solutions: (0, 7) and (−2, 3).

4. If the equation $y = -x - 3$ is graphed on the same axes with the graph below, how many solutions will the resulting system have?

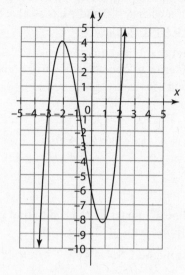

A. 0
B. 1
C. 2
D. 3

5. Which of these systems has the largest number of ordered pairs in its solution set?

A. $y = 4 - x^2$
   $y = -4$

B. $y = 4 - x^2$
   $y = 4$

C. $y = 4 - x^2$
   $x = -2$

D. $y = 4 - x^2$
   $x = 2$

6. How many ordered pairs are solutions of the system below?

$$x + y + 2 = 0$$
$$y = (x - 3)^2 + 4$$

A. 0
B. 1
C. 2
D. 3

Answers

1. **C.** The line intersects the parabola in two points. One point is (–3, 6), representing a solution of $x = -3$, $y = 6$. The other intersection occurs when $x = 2$ and y has a value between 2 and 3. From the answer choices provided, the best choice is C, {(–3, 6), (2, 2.67)}.

2. **D.** To solve the system, use the fact that both equations have isolated y, and substitute to get the equation $5 - x^2 = x + 3$. Move all terms to one side equal to 0 and you have $0 = x^2 + x - 2$. The equation can be solved by factoring.

$$x^2 + x - 2 = 0$$
$$(x - 1)(x + 2) = 0$$

$$x - 1 = 0 \qquad\qquad x + 2 = 0$$
$$x = 1 \qquad\qquad\qquad x = -2$$

   Plug each x-value back into the linear equation $y = x + 3$ to find y. If $x = 1$, $y = 1 + 3 = 4$. If $x = -2$, $y = -2 + 3 = 1$. Therefore, the solution set is {(–2, 1), (1, 4)}.

3. **B.** Substitution looks like the best method. Solve $4x + 7 = (x + 2)^2 + 3$ by first simplifying.

$$4x + 7 = (x + 2)^2 + 3$$
$$4x + 7 = x^2 + 4x + 4 + 3$$
$$4x + 7 = x^2 + 4x + 7$$
$$0 = x^2$$

   Without any further work, it's clear $x = 0$ is the only solution for x, and when $x = 0$, $y = 4(0) + 7 = 7$.

4. **D.** Because a graph is provided, the quickest way to answer this question is to graph $y = -x - 3$ and see how many points of intersection are produced. Start with a y-intercept of –3, and count out a slope of –1. Extend carefully so the line doesn't bend. You should see three points of intersection, and thus three solutions. There is no need to determine their coordinates.

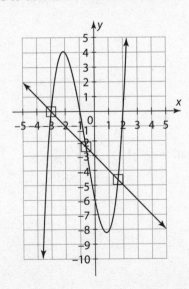

5. **A.** All choices involve the same quadratic equation, and thus all produce the same parabola when graphed. Each choice involves a different linear equation, either horizontal or vertical. A sketch is likely the quickest method.

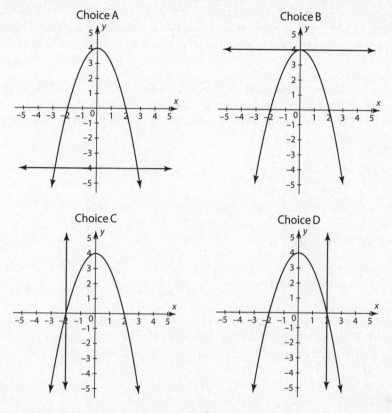

Choices B, C, and D each show one point of intersection. Only Choice A shows two points of intersection, and thus the largest number of ordered pairs in its solution set.

6. **A.** Solve $x + y + 2 = 0$ for y: $y = -x - 2$. Substitute to get $-x - 2 = (x - 3)^2 + 4$. Simplify and collect terms:

$$-x - 2 = (x - 3)^2 + 4$$
$$-x - 2 = x^2 - 6x + 9 + 4$$
$$-x - 2 = x^2 - 6x + 13$$
$$0 = x^2 - 5x + 15$$

The quadratic does not factor, so try the quadratic formula with $a = 1$, $b = -5$, and $c = 15$.

$$x = \frac{-b \pm \sqrt{b^2 - 4ac}}{2a} = \frac{-(-5) \pm \sqrt{(-5)^2 - 4(1)(15)}}{2(1)} = \frac{5 \pm \sqrt{25 - 60}}{2} = \frac{5 \pm \sqrt{-35}}{2}$$

Because the square root of -35 is not a real number, this equation has no real solutions, Choice A.

E. Arithmetic Operations on Polynomials

You've done many arithmetic operations on algebraic expressions; don't let the label "polynomial" intimidate you. A polynomial is an algebraic expression that has a particular form. It is made up of terms called monomials, each of which is a coefficient multiplied by a power of a variable. The exponents must be non-negative integers. When the exponent is zero, the term becomes just the coefficient, and so it looks like, and is, a constant.

When the monomials are added or subtracted and simplified, they form polynomials. A polynomial with two terms is a binomial, and one with three terms is a trinomial. The general pattern of a polynomial is $a_n x^n + a_{n-1} x^{n-1} + \cdots + a_2 x^2 + a_1 x + a_0$ (but that really doesn't help much). Examples are better:

- Monomial: $-3x^4$ or $\dfrac{1}{2}t^7$
- Binomial: $3x - 2$ or $w^4 + 8w^2$
- Trinomial: $x^2 - 5x + 4$ or $9z^{12} - 5z^6 + 2z^2$
- Polynomial: $6t^5 + 8t^3 - 7t^2 + 9t - 11$ or $a^{11} - 9a^{10} + 7a^6 - 5a^4 + 3a^2 - 12a - 17$

To add or subtract polynomials, simply combine like terms:

$$\left(9x^{12} - 5x^6 + 2x^2 + 1\right) + \left(7x^6 - 5x^4 + 3x^2 - 12x - 17\right) = 9x^{12} + \left(-5x^6 + 7x^6\right) - 5x^4 + \left(2x^2 + 3x^2\right) - 12x + (1-17)$$
$$= 9x^{12} + 2x^6 - 5x^4 + 5x^2 - 12x - 16$$

The method of multiplying polynomials depends on the size of the polynomials involved, but each method comes down to this: Multiply each term of the first polynomial times each term of the second polynomial, and then combine like terms. The different methods are ways of organizing that work so that nothing is missed.

- Distributive property:
$$-3x^4(9x^{12} - 5x^6 + 2x^2) = -3x^4(9x^{12}) - 3x^4(-5x^6) - 3x^4(2x^2) = -27x^{16} + 15x^{10} - 6x^6$$
- FOIL method (first terms, outside terms, inside terms, last terms):
$$(3x + 5)(-2x^2 + x^3) = 3x(-2x^2) + 3x(x^3) + 5(-2x^2) + 5(x^3) = -6x^3 + 3x^4 - 10x^2 + 5x^3 = 3x^4 - x^3 - 10x^2$$
- Vertical arrangement:

$$
\begin{array}{r}
x^2 + 4x - 7 \\
2x - 3 \\
\hline
-3x^2 - 12x + 21 \\
2x^3 + 8x^2 - 14x + 0 \\
\hline
2x^3 + 5x^2 - 26x + 21
\end{array}
$$

Like multiplication, division can be organized in different ways, but it comes down to dividing term by term.

- Monomial divisor:
$$\frac{4x^2 - 12x}{2x} = \frac{4x^2}{2x} - \frac{12x}{2x} = 2x - 6$$

- Long division:

$$\begin{array}{r} 2x+5 \\ 3x-1\overline{\smash{\big)}6x^2+13x-5} \\ \underline{6x^2-2x} \\ 15x-5 \\ \underline{15x-5} \end{array}$$

Practice

1. The length of a rectangle is $3z^2 + 5z + 4$ and the width is $z^2 - 2z - 9$. Which of the following is the perimeter of the rectangle?

   A. $8z^2 + 14z - 26$
   B. $2z^2 + 7z + 13$
   C. $4z^2 + 3z - 5$
   D. $8z^2 + 6z - 10$

2. Find the area of a triangle with a base of $n^2 - 2$ and a height of $4n + 3$.

   A. $A = 4n^3 + 3n^2 - 8n - 6$

   B. $A = 2n^3 + \dfrac{3}{2}n^2 - 4n - 3$

   C. $A = 4n^2 - 5n - 6$

   D. $A = \dfrac{7}{2}n^3 - 4n - 3$

3. Simplify $\dfrac{2x^2 - x - 15}{x - 3}$.

   A. $2x + 5$
   B. $2x - 5$
   C. $x + 5$
   D. $x - 5$

4. The product of $(2x - 3)(x + 2)(x - 1)$ is

   A. $2x^3 - 5x^2 - 7x + 6$
   B. $2x^2 - x - 3$
   C. $2x^3 - x^2 - 7x + 6$
   D. $4x^2 - 10x + 6$

5. If long division is used to divide $3x^3 - x^2 - 12x + 6$ by $(3x - 1)$, the remainder is

   A. 0
   B. 1
   C. 2
   D. 3

6. If the product of $(2x + 3)(x - 5)$ is subtracted from the product of $3x(2x^2 - 3x + 4)$, the result is

   A. $8x^2 - 16x + 5$
   B. $4x^3 - 2x^2 + 27x$
   C. $6x^3 - 7x^2 + 5x - 15$
   D. $6x^3 - 11x^2 + 19x + 15$

Answers

1. **D.** The perimeter is $P = 2l + 2w$. Replace l and w with the given information, then distribute and combine like terms: $2(3z^2 + 5z + 4) + 2(z^2 - 2z - 9) = 6z^2 + 10z + 8 + 2z^2 - 4z - 18 = 8z^2 + 6z - 10$.

2. **B.** The area of a triangle is $A = \dfrac{1}{2}bh$. Substitute to get $A = \dfrac{1}{2}(n^2 - 2)(4n + 3)$, and simplify by

   FOILing and then distributing the $\dfrac{1}{2}$:

   $$A = \frac{1}{2}(n^2 - 2)(4n + 3) = \frac{1}{2}(4n^3 + 3n^2 - 8n - 6) = 2n^3 + \frac{3}{2}n^2 - 4n - 3$$

3. **A.** Before jumping into long division, check to see if the numerator can be factored:

   $\dfrac{2x^2 - x - 15}{x - 3} = \dfrac{(2x + 5)(x - 3)}{x - 3}$. Cancel $x - 3$ and the quotient is $2x + 5$.

4. **C.** Choose two factors and FOIL:

   $$(2x - 3)(x + 2)(x - 1) = (2x - 3)(x^2 + 2x - x - 2) = (2x - 3)(x^2 + x - 2)$$

   Then use vertical form (or lots of distributing) to do the final multiplication:

   $$\begin{array}{r} x^2 + x - 2 \\ 2x - 3 \\ \hline -3x^2 - 3x + 6 \\ 2x^3 + 2x^2 - 4x + 0 \\ \hline 2x^3 - x^2 - 7x + 6 \end{array}$$

5. **C.** Use long division, being careful about signs. Remember to subtract, not just combine like terms. The remainder is 2.

   $$\begin{array}{r} x^2 - 4 \\ 3x - 1 \overline{) 3x^3 - x^2 - 12x + 6} \\ \underline{3x^3 - x^2} \\ 0 - 12x + 6 \\ \underline{-12x + 4} \\ 2 \end{array}$$

6. **D.** To simplify $3x(2x^2 - 3x + 4) - (2x + 3)(x - 5)$, first perform the multiplications:

$$3x\left(2x^2 - 3x + 4\right) - (2x + 3)(x - 5)$$
$$6x^3 - 9x^2 + 12x - (2x + 3)(x - 5)$$
$$6x^3 - 9x^2 + 12x - \left[2x^2 - 10x + 3x - 15\right]$$

The subtraction sign between the first expression and the second must affect everything that follows it, so it's wise to keep the second product in grouping symbols to remind you to distribute the subtraction sign.

$$6x^3 - 9x^2 + 12x - \left[2x^2 - 7x - 15\right]$$
$$6x^3 - 9x^2 + 12x - 2x^2 + 7x + 15$$
$$6x^3 - 11x^2 + 19x + 15$$

F. Zeros and Factors of Polynomials

When you think about a polynomial expression or a polynomial equation in one variable, one of the first things you investigate is whether the polynomial can be factored. If you can factor a polynomial, evaluating is easier and dividing by another polynomial may be easier, as is solving an equation that equates that polynomial to zero. Each factor can be set equal to zero and those smaller equations solved to find the solution set of the polynomial equation.

- If $x - c$ is a factor of a polynomial, then $x = c$ is a zero of the polynomial.
- The zeros of the polynomial are the solutions of the equation created by setting the polynomial equal to zero.
- The zeros of the polynomial are the x-intercepts of its graph.

To find possible rational zeros of a polynomial, try factors of the constant term divided by factors of the lead coefficient. If the highest power term is $5x^3$ and the constant term is 6, try $\frac{1}{1}, \frac{2}{1}, \frac{3}{1}, \frac{6}{1}$ and $\frac{1}{5}, \frac{2}{5}, \frac{3}{5}, \frac{6}{5}$, and remember each possibility might be positive or negative.

> **TIP:** If you're stumped for factors and have a graphing calculator, graph the polynomial and look at its x-intercepts. If they're integers or simple rational numbers, you can work backward to the factors.

To see if a possible solution is actually a zero, you can plug in to see if it makes the polynomial equal to zero, or divide the polynomial by the factor that corresponds to the possible solution. If the remainder is zero, the divisor $x - c$ is a factor and c is a zero.

Practice

1. If the polynomial $2x^3 - x^2 - 2x + 1$ can be factored to $(2x - 1)(x^2 - 1)$, what is the solution set of $2x^3 - x^2 - 2x + 1 = 0$?

    A. $\left\{ \dfrac{1}{2}, 1 \right\}$

    B. $\{1, -1\}$

    C. $\left\{ \dfrac{1}{2}, -1, 1 \right\}$

    D. $\left\{ \dfrac{1}{2}, 0, 1 \right\}$

2. Which of the following is the correct factorization of $x^3 - 7x^2 - 4x + 28$?

    A. $(x - 7)(x - 2)(x - 2)$
    B. $(x - 7)(x - 2)(x + 2)$
    C. $(x - 7)(x + 2)(x + 1)$
    D. $(x + 7)(x - 1)(x + 2)$

3. What is the solution set of the equation $x^3 + 5x^2 + 8x + 4 = 0$?

    A. $\{2, -2\}$
    B. $\{0, -1, -2\}$
    C. $\{2, -1, -2\}$
    D. $\{-1, -2\}$

4. How many distinct solutions does the equation $x^3 - 9x = 0$ have?

    A. 0
    B. 1
    C. 2
    D. 3

5. If the polynomial equation $y = (x - 2)^3$ is graphed, how many x-intercepts will the graph have?

    A. 0
    B. 1
    C. 2
    D. 3

6. Which of the factors of $x^3 - 2x^2 - x + 2$ is also a factor of $x^2 + 3x + 2$?

    A. $x - 2$
    B. $x + 2$
    C. $x + 1$
    D. $x - 1$

Answers

1. **C.** If $2x^3 - x^2 - 2x + 1 = (2x - 1)(x^2 - 1) = 0$, you can set each factor equal to 0 and solve. Solving $2x - 1 = 0$, you get $2x = 1$ and $x = \dfrac{1}{2}$. The second factor can be set equal to 0 and solved by the square root method, or actually be factored further to $(x + 1)(x - 1) = 0$; setting those factors equal to 0 gives solutions of $x = -1$ and $x = 1$.

2. **B.** You could attack the problem by multiplying out the answer choices, but that takes time. First, try to eliminate answer choices. The constants from the three factors in an answer choice must multiply to 28, which eliminates choices C and D. Checking signs also eliminates Choice A, which gives a constant term of -28.

   If you don't spot those shortcuts, start by plugging small factors of 28 into the polynomial to see what makes the polynomial equal 0. You should find that $x^3 - 7x^2 - 4x + 28 = 1^3 - 7(1^2) - 4(1) + 28$ does not equal 0, but $x^3 - 7x^2 - 4x + 28 = 2^3 - 7(2^2) - 4(2) + 28$ does equal 0. That means $x = 2$ is a zero and $x - 2$ is a factor. Divide $x^3 - 7x^2 - 4x + 28$ by $x - 2$, using long division:

$$
\begin{array}{r}
x^2 - 5x - 14 \\
x - 2 \overline{)\,x^3 - 7x^2 - 4x + 28} \\
\underline{x^3 - 2x^2} \\
-5x^2 - 4x \\
\underline{-5x^2 + 10x} \\
-14x + 28 \\
\underline{-14x + 28}
\end{array}
$$

   Finally, factor the quadratic: $x^3 - 7x^2 - 4x + 28 = (x - 2)(x^2 - 5x - 14) = (x - 2)(x - 7)(x + 2)$.

3. **D.** This is a question for which plugging in answer choices intelligently could save time. The various choices include 0, ± 1, and ± 2. You can probably see that $x = 0$ makes $x^3 + 5x^2 + 8x + 4 = 4$, not 0, so you can eliminate Choice B. Several choices involve $x = -2$, so try dividing by $x + 2$:

$$
\begin{array}{r}
x^2 + 3x + 2 \\
x + 2 \overline{)\,x^3 + 5x^2 + 8x + 4} \\
\underline{x^3 + 2x^2} \\
3x^2 + 8x \\
\underline{3x^2 + 6x} \\
2x + 4 \\
\underline{2x + 4}
\end{array}
$$

   Now you know $x^3 + 5x^2 + 8x + 4 = (x + 2)(x^2 + 3x + 2)$, and you can factor the quadratic to get $x^3 + 5x^2 + 8x + 4 = (x + 2)(x + 2)(x + 1)$. If the factors are set equal to zero and solved, there will be a solution of $x = -2$ (appearing twice) and a solution of $x = -1$.

4. **D.** $x^3 - 9x = 0$ can be factored as $x^3 - 9x = x(x^2 - 9) = x(x + 3)(x - 3) = 0$. Setting each factor equal to zero and solving produces three distinct solutions: $x = 0$, $x = -3$, and $x = 3$.

5. **B.** The number of x-intercepts of the graph is the number of solutions of the equation. $y = (x - 2)^3$ or $y = (x - 2)(x - 2)(x - 2)$ has three identical solutions, so only one x-intercept.

6. **C.** $x^2 + 3x + 2$ is easier to factor than $x^3 - 2x^2 - x + 2$, so start with $x^2 + 3x + 2 = (x + 1)(x + 2)$. You can divide $x^3 - 2x^2 - x + 2$ by these factors to see if either is a factor, or you can see if $x = -1$ or $x = -2$ will make $x^3 - 2x^2 - x + 2 = 0$. $(-1)^3 - 2(-1)^2 - (-1) + 2 = -1 -2 + 1 + 2 = 0$, so $x + 1$ is a factor of both.

G. Arithmetic Operations on Rational Expressions

A rational expression is the ratio of two polynomials. It's sometimes called an algebraic fraction because it has the form of a fraction, but instead of the numerator and denominator being just constants, they may be polynomials of any number of terms, as long as the denominator is not zero. Operations on rational expressions follow the same rules as operations on fractions.

- To simplify, factor the numerator and denominator (if possible) and cancel any factor that appears in both:

$$\frac{x^2 - 2x}{x^2 - 4} = \frac{x(x-2)}{(x+2)(x-2)} = \frac{x}{x+2}$$

- To add or subtract, you must have a common denominator, and then you add or subtract the numerators. After you add or subtract, you may be able to simplify:

$$\frac{4}{x-3} - \frac{3}{x+1} = \frac{4(x+1)}{(x-3)(x+1)} - \frac{3(x-3)}{(x-3)(x+1)} = \frac{4x+4-3x+9}{(x-3)(x+1)} = \frac{x+13}{x^2-2x-3}$$

- To multiply, multiply numerator by numerator and denominator by denominator. Factoring all numerators and denominators first, and canceling where possible, makes the job easier:

$$\frac{x^2-1}{x^2+4x+3} \cdot \frac{x^2+6x+9}{x^2-2x+1} = \frac{(x+1)(x-1)}{(x+1)(x+3)} \cdot \frac{(x+3)(x+3)}{(x-1)(x-1)} = \frac{x+3}{x-1}$$

- To divide, multiply the first rational expression by the reciprocal of the second:

$$\frac{x^2-9}{x^2-4x} \div \frac{x+3}{x} = \frac{x^2-9}{x^2-4x} \cdot \frac{x}{x+3} = \frac{(x+3)(x-3)}{x(x-4)} \cdot \frac{x}{x+3} = \frac{x-3}{x-4}$$

Practice

1. Find the sum of $\dfrac{x}{x-2}$ and $\dfrac{1}{x+3}$ in simplest form.

   A. $\dfrac{x+1}{2x+1}$

   B. $\dfrac{x+2}{x+3}$

   C. $\dfrac{x^2-x-6}{(x-2)(x+3)}$

   D. $\dfrac{x^2+4x-2}{(x-2)(x+3)}$

2. The difference of $\dfrac{5}{x+1}-\dfrac{3}{x}$ is

   A. $\dfrac{2x-3}{x(x+1)}$

   B. $\dfrac{2x+3}{x(x+1)}$

   C. $\dfrac{1}{x+1}$

   D. $\dfrac{1}{x}$

3. In simplest form, the product of $\dfrac{x^2-4}{x^2+6x}$ and $\dfrac{x^2+3x}{x^2+5x+6}$ is

   A. $\dfrac{-2}{x^2+5x+6}$

   B. $\dfrac{x-2}{2(x+3)}$

   C. $\dfrac{x-2}{x+6}$

   D. $-\dfrac{1}{3}$

4. The quotient of $\dfrac{4x}{x^2-9}$ and $\dfrac{x^2}{x^2+6x+9}$ is

   A. $-\dfrac{4}{x}$

   B. $\dfrac{x(x-3)}{4(x+3)}$

   C. $\dfrac{4(x+3)}{x(x-3)}$

   D. $\dfrac{12}{x-3}$

5. The difference of the product $\dfrac{3x}{x^2+2x-15}\cdot\dfrac{x+5}{x^2-x}$ and the quotient $\dfrac{x^2+3x+2}{x-3}\div\dfrac{x^2+x-2}{4}$ is

   A. $\dfrac{-4x-1}{(x-3)(x-1)}$

   B. $\dfrac{7-4x}{(x-3)(x-1)}$

   C. $\dfrac{12}{(x-3)(x-1)}$

   D. $\dfrac{12x-1}{(x-3)(x-1)}$

6. If the difference of $\dfrac{2}{x+1}$ and $\dfrac{3}{x-1}$ is divided by their sum, the simplest form of the result is

   A. $\dfrac{-x+1}{5x+1}$

   B. $\dfrac{-(x+5)}{5x+1}$

   C. $-\dfrac{5}{6}$

   D. $-\dfrac{1}{5}$

Answers

1. **D.** To add, you need a common denominator. Multiply the numerator and denominator of the first expression by the denominator of the second, and multiply the numerator and denominator of the second expression by the denominator of the first: $\dfrac{x}{x-2}+\dfrac{1}{x+3}=\dfrac{x(x+3)}{(x-2)(x+3)}+\dfrac{1(x-2)}{(x+3)(x-2)}$

   Distribute to remove parentheses, and then combine like terms in the numerators:

   $\dfrac{x^2+3x+x-2}{(x-2)(x+3)}=\dfrac{x^2+4x-2}{(x-2)(x+3)}$.

2. **A.** Transform both expressions to a common denominator. When distributing, remember that the subtraction sign affects the entire second numerator: $\dfrac{5}{x+1}-\dfrac{3}{x}=\dfrac{5x-3x-3}{x(x+1)}=\dfrac{2x-3}{x(x+1)}$.

3. **C.** Before multiplying, always factor numerators and denominators and look for opportunities to cancel: $\dfrac{x^2-4}{x^2+6x}\cdot\dfrac{x^2+3x}{x^2+5x+6}=\dfrac{\cancel{(x+2)}(x-2)}{\cancel{x}(x+6)}\cdot\dfrac{\cancel{x}\cancel{(x+3)}}{\cancel{(x+2)}\cancel{(x+3)}}=\dfrac{x-2}{x+6}$.

4. **C.** Begin a division problem by inverting the divisor (if you start factoring, you may forget!):

   $$\dfrac{4x}{x^2-9}\div\dfrac{x^2}{x^2+6x+9}=\dfrac{4x}{x^2-9}\cdot\dfrac{x^2+6x+9}{x^2}$$

   Then factor and cancel where possible. Finish by multiplying numerator by numerator and denominator by denominator:

   $$\dfrac{4x}{x^2-9}\cdot\dfrac{x^2+6x+9}{x^2}=\dfrac{4\cdot\cancel{x}}{\cancel{(x+3)}(x-3)}\cdot\dfrac{\cancel{(x+3)}(x+3)}{x\cdot\cancel{x}}=\dfrac{4(x+3)}{x(x-3)}$$

5. **A.** Find the product by factoring, canceling, and then multiplying numerator by numerator and denominator by denominator:

   $$\dfrac{3x}{x^2+2x-15}\cdot\dfrac{x+5}{x^2-x}=\dfrac{3\cancel{x}}{\cancel{(x+5)}(x-3)}\cdot\dfrac{\cancel{x+5}}{\cancel{x}(x-1)}=\dfrac{3}{(x-3)(x-1)}$$

   Find the quotient by first inverting the divisor, then factoring, canceling, and multiplying:

   $$\dfrac{x^2+3x+2}{x-3}\div\dfrac{x^2+x-2}{4}=\dfrac{x^2+3x+2}{x-3}\cdot\dfrac{4}{x^2+x-2}=\dfrac{\cancel{(x+2)}(x+1)}{x-3}\cdot\dfrac{4}{(x-1)\cancel{(x+2)}}=\dfrac{4x+4}{(x-3)(x-1)}$$

   Finally, perform the subtraction. You have a common denominator, so just focus on numerators:

   $$\dfrac{3}{(x-3)(x-1)}-\dfrac{4x+4}{(x-3)(x-1)}=\dfrac{3-(4x+4)}{(x-3)(x-1)}=\dfrac{-4x-1}{(x-3)(x-1)}$$

6. **B.** The question asks you to find the simplest form of $\left(\dfrac{2}{x+1}-\dfrac{3}{x-1}\right)\div\left(\dfrac{2}{x+1}+\dfrac{3}{x-1}\right)$. Focus on the expressions in the parentheses first. Luckily, both will end up with the same denominator.

$$\left(\frac{2}{x+1}-\frac{3}{x-1}\right)=\frac{2x-2-3(x+1)}{(x+1)(x-1)}=\frac{2x-2-3x-3}{x^2-1}=\frac{-x-5}{x^2-1}$$

$$\left(\frac{2}{x+1}+\frac{3}{x-1}\right)=\frac{2x-2+3x+3}{(x+1)(x-1)}=\frac{5x+1}{x^2-1}$$

$$\left(\frac{2}{x+1}-\frac{3}{x-1}\right)\div\left(\frac{2}{x+1}+\frac{3}{x-1}\right)=\frac{-x-5}{x^2-1}\div\frac{5x+1}{x^2-1}=\frac{-x-5}{x^2-1}\cdot\frac{x^2-1}{5x+1}=\frac{-(x+5)}{5x+1}$$

H. Rational Exponents and Radicals

Radicals, or roots, are the inverses of powers. A square root is the inverse of a square; a cube root is the inverse of a cube. If $a^2=b$, then a is the square root of b. That's often written as $a=\sqrt{b}$. The same kind of statement can be made for any power and corresponding root, so in general, if $a^n=b$, then $a=\sqrt[n]{b}$. The little number in the crook of the radical sign is called the index and tells you what power is involved.

- To simplify a square root, write the radicand, the number under the radical, as the product of a perfect square and another factor. You want that second factor to be as small as possible. Take the root of the perfect square and leave the other factor under the radical:

$$\sqrt{48}=\sqrt{4\cdot12}=\sqrt{16\cdot3}=\sqrt{16}\cdot\sqrt{3}=4\sqrt{3}$$

- To add or subtract radicals, remember that radicals act like variables. You can only add like radicals, just as you can only add like terms; then you add or subtract the coefficients and keep the radical as is:

$$3\sqrt{2}+5\sqrt{2}=8\sqrt{2}$$
$$\sqrt{12}-\sqrt{3}=\sqrt{4\cdot3}-\sqrt{3}=2\sqrt{3}-\sqrt{3}=\sqrt{3}$$

- For multiplying or dividing, remember inside with inside, outside with outside:

$$2\sqrt{7}\cdot3\sqrt{2}=2\cdot3\sqrt{7}\sqrt{2}=6\sqrt{14}$$
$$\frac{10\sqrt{20}}{5\sqrt{5}}=\frac{10}{5}\cdot\frac{\sqrt{20}}{\sqrt{5}}=2\sqrt{\frac{20}{5}}=2\sqrt{4}=2\cdot2=4$$

- To rationalize the denominator or remove a radical from a denominator, multiply both the numerator and the denominator by the radical if the denominator is a single term:

$$\frac{3}{2\sqrt{5}}=\frac{3}{2\sqrt{5}}\cdot\frac{\sqrt{5}}{\sqrt{5}}=\frac{3\sqrt{5}}{2\cdot5}=\frac{3\sqrt{5}}{10}$$

- If the denominator is a sum or difference, multiply the numerator and denominator by the conjugate of the denominator. The conjugate of $a + b$ is $a - b$, and the conjugate of $a - b$ is $a + b$:

$$\frac{6}{2+\sqrt{2}} = \frac{6}{2+\sqrt{2}} \cdot \frac{2-\sqrt{2}}{2-\sqrt{2}} = \frac{6(2-\sqrt{2})}{4+2\sqrt{2}-2\sqrt{2}-2} = \frac{6(2-\sqrt{2})}{4-2} = \frac{6(2-\sqrt{2})}{2} = 3(2-\sqrt{2}) = 6-3\sqrt{2}$$

Rational exponents are rational numbers used as exponents, extending the idea of an exponent. Rational numbers include integers and fractions, and the fractional exponent is the new piece. Rational exponents give you a way to express a root by means of an exponent. The exponent $\frac{1}{2}$ represents the square root. If $a^2 = b$, and b is non-negative, then $a = b^{\frac{1}{2}}$, and similar statements can be made for any power and corresponding root. The advantage is that all the rules of exponents apply, and that often makes it easier to simplify. It also means you can express both a root and a power in one exponent: $\left(\sqrt{x}\right)^3 = \left(x^{\frac{1}{2}}\right)^3 = x^{\frac{3}{2}}$. Remember that a rational exponent is always $\frac{\text{power}}{\text{root}}$.

Practice

1. Express $\sqrt{63}$ in simplest radical form.

    A. $3\sqrt{21}$

    B. $7\sqrt{3}$

    C. $21\sqrt{3}$

    D. $3\sqrt{7}$

2. Find the sum of $\sqrt{8} + \sqrt{18} + \sqrt{48} + \sqrt{288}$.

    A. $72\sqrt{2} + 4\sqrt{3}$

    B. $17\sqrt{2} + 4\sqrt{3}$

    C. $76\sqrt{5}$

    D. $21\sqrt{5}$

3. Simplify $\dfrac{\sqrt{108x^5}}{\sqrt{27}} \cdot \dfrac{\sqrt{45}}{\sqrt{75x^4}}$.

    A. $6x$

    B. $\sqrt{2x}$

    C. $\dfrac{6x}{\sqrt{3}}$

    D. $\dfrac{2\sqrt{15x}}{5}$

4. Find the simplest form of $8^{\frac{1}{3}} + 27^{\frac{2}{3}}$.

    A. 5
    B. 9
    C. 11
    D. 25

5. Which of the following is NOT equivalent to $4^{\frac{5}{2}}$?

    A. 2^5
    B. $4\sqrt{64}$
    C. $\sqrt{1,024}$
    D. $\sqrt[5]{16}$

6. Express $\left(16x^4\right)^{\frac{3}{2}} \cdot \left(27x^9\right)^{\frac{2}{3}}$ in simplest form.

    A. $576x^{12}$
    B. $576x^{36}$
    C. $73x^{12}$
    D. $73x^6$

Answers

1. **D.** The largest perfect square that is a factor of 63 is 9, so express the square root in factored form, then take the square root of each factor: $\sqrt{63} = \sqrt{9 \cdot 7} = \sqrt{9}\sqrt{7} = 3\sqrt{7}$.

2. **B.** Only like radicals can be added, so begin by simplifying each radical so that you can see which are like, then add the coefficients of the like radicals:

$$\sqrt{8} + \sqrt{18} + \sqrt{48} + \sqrt{288} = 2\sqrt{2} + 3\sqrt{2} + 4\sqrt{3} + 12\sqrt{2} = 17\sqrt{2} + 4\sqrt{3}$$

3. **D.** You can approach this multiplication by first simplifying each of the radicals:

$$\frac{\sqrt{108x^5}}{\sqrt{27}} = \frac{\sqrt{36 \cdot 3 \cdot x^4 \cdot x}}{\sqrt{9 \cdot 3}} = \frac{6x^2\sqrt{3}\sqrt{x}}{3\sqrt{3}} = 2x^2\sqrt{x}$$

$$\frac{\sqrt{45}}{\sqrt{75x^4}} = \frac{\sqrt{9 \cdot 5}}{\sqrt{25 \cdot 3 \cdot x^4}} = \frac{3\sqrt{5}}{5x^2\sqrt{3}}$$

Multiply, canceling where possible:

$$2x^2\sqrt{x} \cdot \frac{3\sqrt{5}}{5x^2\sqrt{3}} = \frac{6\sqrt{5x}}{5\sqrt{3}} \cdot \frac{\sqrt{3}}{\sqrt{3}} = \frac{6\sqrt{15x}}{15} = \frac{2\sqrt{15x}}{5}$$

4. **C.** Because the exponents have a denominator of 3, indicating a third root, express 8 and 27 as third powers of smaller numbers. Rewrite 8 as 2^3 and 27 as 3^3 and rewrite $8^{\frac{1}{3}} + 27^{\frac{2}{3}}$ as $\left(2^3\right)^{\frac{1}{3}} + \left(3^3\right)^{\frac{2}{3}}$. To raise a power to a power, multiply the exponents:

$$\left(2^3\right)^{\frac{1}{3}} + \left(3^3\right)^{\frac{2}{3}} = 2 + 3^2 = 2 + 9 = 11$$

5. **D.** $4^{\frac{5}{2}}$ can be seen as the square root of 4, raised to the fifth power, or the square root of the fifth power of 4. The square root of 4 is 2. Raising 2 to the fifth power gives $2^5 = 2 \cdot 2 \cdot 2 \cdot 2 \cdot 2 = 32$, so Choice A is equivalent. Because $\sqrt{4 \cdot 4 \cdot 4 \cdot 4 \cdot 4} = 2 \cdot 2\sqrt{4 \cdot 4 \cdot 4} = 4\sqrt{64}$, Choice B is equivalent. Taking the square root of the fifth power of 4 can be expressed as $\sqrt{4 \cdot 4 \cdot 4 \cdot 4 \cdot 4} = \sqrt{1,024}$, so Choice C is equivalent. Choice D, however, shows $\sqrt[5]{16} = \sqrt[5]{4^2} = 4^{\frac{2}{5}}$, and that is not equivalent.

6. **A.** Simplify each factor before multiplying: $\left(16x^4\right)^{\frac{3}{2}} = 16^{\frac{3}{2}} \cdot \left(x^4\right)^{\frac{3}{2}} = 4^3 \cdot x^6$ and $\left(27x^9\right)^{\frac{2}{3}} = 27^{\frac{2}{3}} \cdot \left(x^9\right)^{\frac{2}{3}} = 3^2 \cdot x^6$. Then $\left(4^3 \cdot x^6\right)\left(3^2 \cdot x^6\right) = 64 \cdot 9 \cdot x^{12} = 576x^{12}$.

I. Rational and Radical Equations

A rational equation is an equation that contains one or more rational expressions. At first glance, it may seem that lots of common denominators will have to be found, but there is a shortcut.

To solve a rational equation:

- Factor all denominators.
- Determine the simplest common denominator for all rational expressions in the equation.
- Multiply each term of the equation by the common denominator, canceling when possible.
- Solve the resulting equation, and be sure to check your solutions in the original equation.

$$\frac{5}{x+1} + \frac{1}{x-2} = \frac{21}{x^2 - x - 2}$$

$$\frac{5}{x+1} + \frac{1}{x-2} = \frac{21}{(x+1)(x-2)}$$

$$(x+1)(x-2)\left(\frac{5}{x+1}\right) + (x+1)(x-2)\left(\frac{1}{x-2}\right) = (x+1)(x-2)\left(\frac{21}{(x+1)(x-2)}\right)$$

$$5(x-2) + x + 1 = 21$$
$$5x - 10 + x + 1 = 21$$
$$6x - 9 = 21$$
$$6x = 30$$
$$x = 5$$

A radical equation is one that contains one or more radicals, whether expressed as radicals or by means of rational exponents.

To solve a radical equation:

- Isolate the radical. If there is more than one radical, isolate one.
- Raise both sides of the equation to the power that corresponds to the root. Square both sides if you have a square root, raise both sides to the third power if you have a cube root. Be careful to raise the entire side of the equation to the power. Do not treat terms separately.
- If any radical remains, isolate it and repeat the previous step.
- Solve the resulting equation, and be certain to check any solutions in the original equation. Extraneous solutions are common.

$$\sqrt{5x+1} = x+1$$
$$\left(\sqrt{5x+1}\right)^2 = (x+1)^2$$
$$5x+1 = x^2 + 2x + 1$$
$$0 = x^2 - 3x$$
$$0 = x(x-3)$$

$x = 0$ $\qquad\qquad$ $x - 3 = 0$

Check $\qquad\qquad\qquad$ $x = 3$

$\sqrt{5(0)+1} = 0+1$ $\qquad$ Check

$\sqrt{1} = 1$ $\qquad\qquad$ $\sqrt{5(3)+1} = 3+1$

$\qquad\qquad\qquad\qquad$ $\sqrt{16} = 4$

Practice

1. Solve for x: $\dfrac{3}{x+2} + \dfrac{1}{x-2} = 1$.

   A. $x = 4$
   B. $x = 0, x = 4$
   C. $x = 1.25$
   D. $x = -1.5, x = 5.5$

2. Solve for x: $\sqrt{3x-5} = 4$.

   A. $x = 3$
   B. $x = 3, x = -3$
   C. $x = 7$
   D. No solution

3. Solve for x: $\dfrac{2}{x+3}+\dfrac{3}{x+1}=2$.

   A. $x = 2, x = -2$
   B. $x = -1.8$
   C. $x = -2.5, x = 1$
   D. $x = 2.5, x = -1$

4. Solve for x: $9-\sqrt{2-7x}=5$.

   A. $x = -2$

   B. $x=\dfrac{12}{49}$

   C. $x=-\dfrac{18}{7}$

   D. $x=-\dfrac{2}{7}$

5. Solve for x: $\sqrt{4x+3}+5\sqrt{3}=8\sqrt{3}$.

   A. $x = 7.5$
   B. $x = 6$
   C. $x = 1.5$
   D. $x = 0.75$

6. Solve for x: $\dfrac{5}{x-4}-\dfrac{3}{x-2}=\dfrac{6x+2}{x^2-6x+8}$.

   A. $x = 0$
   B. $x = -6$
   C. $x = 12$
   D. $x = -1$

Answers

1. **B.** Multiply through the equation by $(x + 2)(x - 2)$, then solve:

$$\cancel{(x+2)}(x-2)\left(\frac{3}{\cancel{x+2}}\right)+(x+2)\cancel{(x-2)}\left(\frac{1}{\cancel{x-2}}\right)=(x+2)(x-2)(1)$$
$$3x-6+x+2=x^2-4$$

Collect like terms and move terms to one side to get $x^2 - 4x = 0$. Factor and solve: $x(x - 4) = 0$, so $x = 0$ and $x = 4$. Check in the original equation.

2. **C.** The radical is isolated, so you can square both sides: $\left(\sqrt{3x-5}\right)^2 = 4^2$ becomes $3x - 5 = 16$. Add 5 to get $3x = 21$ and then divide by 3 to get $x = 7$. Check the solution of $x = 7$ in the original equation.

3. **C.** To solve $\dfrac{2}{x+3} + \dfrac{3}{x+1} = 2$, multiply through by $(x + 3)(x + 1)$ to clear denominators:

$$\cancel{(x+3)}(x+1)\left(\frac{2}{\cancel{x+3}}\right) + (x+3)\cancel{(x+1)}\left(\frac{3}{\cancel{x+1}}\right) = (2)(x+3)(x+1)$$
$$2x + 2 + 3x + 9 = 2\left(x^2 + x + 3x + 3\right)$$
$$5x + 11 = 2x^2 + 8x + 6$$

Bring all terms to one side equal to zero, and factor:

$$5x + 11 = 2x^2 + 8x + 6$$
$$0 = 2x^2 + 3x - 5$$
$$0 = (2x + 5)(x - 1)$$

$$2x + 5 = 0 \qquad\qquad\qquad x - 1 = 0$$
$$2x = -5 \qquad\qquad\qquad\qquad x = 1$$
$$x = -2.5$$

4. **A.** Isolate the radical before you try to eliminate it:

$$9 - \sqrt{2 - 7x} = 5$$
$$-\sqrt{2 - 7x} = -4$$
$$\sqrt{2 - 7x} = 4$$

Then square both sides and solve the resulting equation:

$$\left(\sqrt{2 - 7x}\right)^2 = 4^2$$
$$2 - 7x = 16$$
$$-7x = 14$$
$$x = -2$$

5. **B.** Isolate the first radical by subtracting $5\sqrt{3}$ from both sides:

$$\sqrt{4x+3}+5\sqrt{3}=8\sqrt{3}$$
$$\sqrt{4x+3}=3\sqrt{3}$$

Then square both sides to remove the radicals:

$$\left(\sqrt{4x+3}\right)^2=\left(3\sqrt{3}\right)^2$$
$$4x+3=9\cdot 3$$
$$4x+3=27$$

Solve the resulting equation and check in the original:

$$4x=24$$
$$x=6$$

6. **A.** Start by factoring the denominator of the last rational expression. Often it will factor to the product of the other two denominators, but check, don't assume:

$$\frac{5}{x-4}-\frac{3}{x-2}=\frac{6x+2}{x^2-6x+8}=\frac{6x+2}{(x-4)(x-2)}$$

Multiply through by $(x-4)(x-2)$ and then solve:

$$\cancel{(x-4)}(x-2)\left(\frac{5}{\cancel{x-4}}\right)-(x-4)\cancel{(x-2)}\left(\frac{3}{\cancel{x-2}}\right)=\cancel{(x-4)(x-2)}\left(\frac{6x+2}{\cancel{(x-4)(x-2)}}\right)$$
$$5(x-2)-3(x-4)=6x+2$$
$$5x-10-3x+12=6x+2$$
$$2x+2=6x+2$$
$$0=4x$$
$$x=0$$

Check the solution of $x=0$ in the original equation.

XI. Additional Topics in Math

Earlier versions of the PSAT said the math section focused on arithmetic, algebra, and geometry. Arithmetic is in the middle of everything, of course, but as you can see, the revisions have put a strong focus on algebra, and added much more data analysis. That pushes geometry to a smaller portion of the test, but it hasn't gone away. The category of questions labeled "Additional Topics in Math" includes critical ideas from geometry and their extension into trigonometry, and one more bit of algebra.

A. Volume, Area, and Perimeter

The different ways in which objects are measured are part of many problems to be solved. Specifically, the PSAT includes questions about the perimeter and area of a two-dimensional, or plane, figure and the volume of a solid (a three-dimensional figure). The goal of these questions is not to find out if you know the formula. Remember that formulas are given to you. Expect questions that ask you to compare or combine measurements of different figures or that ask you to imagine what happens if certain changes are made. You want to understand why the formulas are what they are, why they work, and not just what to plug in.

- **Perimeter:** The distance around a two-dimensional figure, measured in linear units, like meters or feet. (The equivalent in a circle is called circumference.)
- **Area:** The space inside a two-dimensional figure, measured in square units. Finding area usually involves multiplying two dimensions, like base and height.
- **Volume:** The space occupied by a three-dimensional object, measured in cubic units. (The space inside a three-dimensional object is technically its capacity, but capacity and volume are often used interchangeably.) Finding volume involves multiplying three measurements, like length, width, and height, or multiplying the area of a base by a height.
- **Surface area:** The total of the areas of the individual surfaces of a three-dimensional figure, measured in square units.

Practice

1. A rectangle has an area of 112 square feet. If the length is tripled and the width is doubled, what is the area of the new rectangle in square feet?

   A. 168
   B. 336
   C. 672
   D. 1,344

2. What is the volume, in cubic inches, of a rectangular box that is 2.5 feet long, 1 foot wide, and 18 inches deep?

   A. 77,760

   B. 6,480

   C. 540

   D. 45

3. A cylinder is placed in a rectangular box with a square base that is 10 centimeters on each side. The cylinder and the box are exactly the same height, 20 centimeters, and the diameter of the cylinder's base is equal to the side of the square. Which of these represents the amount of empty space in the box? (Volume of a cylinder: $V = \pi r^2 h$)

   A. $1,500\pi$

   B. $2,000 - 500\pi$

   C. $4,000 - 400\pi$

   D. $2,000 - 2,000\pi$

4. The area of the figure below is best represented by

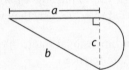

   A. $\dfrac{1}{2}ac + \dfrac{1}{2}\pi c^2$

   B. $\dfrac{1}{2}ac + \dfrac{1}{4}\pi c^2$

   C. $\dfrac{1}{2}ab + \dfrac{1}{2}\pi c^2$

   D. $\dfrac{1}{2}ac + \dfrac{1}{8}\pi c^2$

5. The number of feet in the perimeter of a rectangular garden is equal to the number of square feet in its area. If the length is 3 feet more than the width, what is the area of the garden in square feet?

   A. 4

   B. 10

   C. 18

   D. 40

6. Find the surface area, in square centimeters, of a cylinder with a diameter of 18 centimeters and a height of 30 centimeters. ($S.A. = 2\pi r^2 + 2\pi rh$)

   A. 576π

   B. 702π

   C. $1,728\pi$

   D. $2,430\pi$

Answers

1. **C.** The area of the original rectangle is the product of its length and width: $A = lw$. Replace the length with 3 times l and the width with 2 times w and simplify: $A = (3l)(2w) = 6lw$. The new area is 6 times the original: $6 \times 112 = 672$.

2. **B.** Convert all dimensions to inches first: 2.5 feet = 30 inches, 1 foot = 12 inches, and 18 inches is fine as is. Then multiply: $30 \times 12 \times 18 = 6,480$ cubic inches.

3. **B.** The volume of the box is $l \times w \times h$ or $10^2 \cdot 20 = 2,000$. The cylinder has a diameter of 10 and so its radius is 5; its height is 20. The volume of the cylinder is $\pi r^2 h = \pi \left(\dfrac{10}{2}\right)^2 (20) = 500\pi$. The empty space in the box is $2,000 - 500\pi$.

4. **D.** The area of the triangular portion is half the product of the base and the height. Using c and a as the base and height, respectively, the triangular section has an area of $\dfrac{1}{2}ac$. The semicircle has a radius equal to half of c. The area of the semicircle is half of π times the radius squared, or $\dfrac{1}{2}\pi\left(\dfrac{c}{2}\right)^2$. The total area is $\dfrac{1}{2}ac + \dfrac{1}{2}\pi\left(\dfrac{c}{2}\right)^2 = \dfrac{1}{2}ac + \dfrac{1}{2}\pi\left(\dfrac{c^2}{4}\right) = \dfrac{1}{2}ac + \dfrac{1}{8}\pi c^2$.

5. **C.** Set the formula for the perimeter equal to the formula for the area: $2l + 2w = lw$. Replace l with $w + 3$. Simplify, and solve the resulting quadratic equation by factoring:

$$2(w+3) + 2w = w(w+3)$$
$$4w + 6 = w^2 + 3w$$
$$w^2 - w - 6 = 0$$
$$(w-3)(w+2) = 0$$

$$w - 3 = 0 \qquad\qquad w + 2 = 0$$
$$w = 3 \qquad\qquad w = -2$$

Negative results are unreasonable, so the width is 3, the length is $3 + 3 = 6$, and the area is $3 \times 6 = 18$.

6. **B.** Use the surface area formula with $r = 9$ and $h = 30$:

$$S.A. = 2\pi r^2 + 2\pi rh = 2\pi(9)^2 + 2\pi(9)(30) = 162\pi + 540\pi = 702\pi$$

B. Pythagorean Theorem

If it sometimes seems as though the Pythagorean theorem turns up everywhere you look, it's a mark of how powerful and important that right triangle relationship is. The Pythagorean theorem says that if a and b are the lengths of the legs of a right triangle, then the length of the hypotenuse, c, can be found with the rule $c^2 = a^2 + b^2$.

You can use the Pythagorean theorem to find the length of the hypotenuse if you know the lengths of both legs, or to find the length of a leg if you know the length of one leg and the length of the hypotenuse.

Things to remember:

- It doesn't matter which leg you call a or which you call b, but the hypotenuse must always be c. The hypotenuse is always the longest side.
- If you're finding the hypotenuse, add $a^2 + b^2$ before taking the square root.
- If you're finding a side, either substitute in what you know and then solve for what you don't know, or rearrange first: $c^2 = a^2 + b^2$ becomes $a^2 = c^2 - b^2$ or $b^2 = c^2 - a^2$.
- Note that $\sqrt{a^2 + b^2}$ does NOT equal $a + b$, $\sqrt{c^2 - a^2}$ does NOT equal $c - a$, and $\sqrt{c^2 - b^2}$ does NOT equal $c - b$.
- Many square roots are irrational. Look at answer choices before you grab your calculator. Does the question want the simplest radical form or a decimal approximation?
- Pythagorean triples are sets of three integers that fit the Pythagorean theorem, like 3, 4, and 5 or 5, 12, and 13. Although the side lengths of many right triangles are not Pythagorean triples, test questions will often use triples to make the arithmetic easier.
- Multiples of Pythagorean triples are also Pythagorean triples. Because 3, 4, 5 is a triple, so are 6, 8, 10, and 30, 40, 50, and 300, 400, 500, and any set of positive integers of the form $3n$, $4n$, $5n$.

Practice

1. Find the length, in centimeters, of the shorter leg of a right triangle if the hypotenuse measures 50 centimeters and the longer leg measures 48 centimeters.

   A. 2
   B. 4
   C. 14
   D. 69

2. When carpenters build a rectangular frame, they often attach a diagonal brace to prevent the frame from tilting. To the nearest tenth of a foot, how long should the brace be to reach from one corner to the diagonally opposite corner of a frame that measures 3 feet by 5 feet?

   A. 2.1
   B. 4.0
   C. 5.8
   D. 8.0

3. An 80-foot flagpole is to be erected and held steady by a 100-foot cable from the top of the pole to a stake in the ground. If the cable is to be pulled tight, how far from the base of the pole, in feet, should the cable be staked down?

   A. 5
   B. 20
   C. 60
   D. 128

4. Baseball is played on a diamond, which is a square, 90 feet on each side. The pitcher's mound is on the line connecting home to 2nd base, 60 feet from home. How far is the pitcher's mound from 2nd base to the nearest foot?

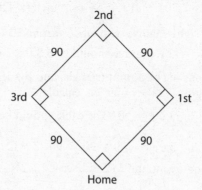

   A. 30
   B. 60
   C. 67
   D. 108

5. The Chamber of Commerce built a small park on a street corner in the business district. The property was a rectangle 40 feet by 50 feet, and the builders added a walkway connecting diagonally opposite corners. If a shopper takes the new path rather than walking along two sides at the edge of the park, how much shorter is the walk to the nearest foot?

   A. 4
   B. 26
   C. 60
   D. 64

6. In the figure below, what is the total length of the path made up of segments a, b, c, and d to the nearest tenth?

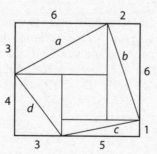

   A. 10.6
   B. 13.4
   C. 20.0
   D. 23.1

Answers

1. **C.** The hypotenuse measures 50 centimeters and the longer leg 48 centimeters, so the other leg measures $\sqrt{50^2 - 48^2} = \sqrt{2,500 - 2,304} = \sqrt{196} = 14$ centimeters. The shorter leg is 14 centimeters long.

2. **C.** To find the hypotenuse of a right triangle with legs 3 feet and 5 feet long, calculate $\sqrt{3^2 + 5^2} = \sqrt{9 + 25} = \sqrt{34} \approx 5.8$ feet. The brace should be 5.8 feet long.

3. **C.** The 80-foot flagpole forms one leg of a right triangle, and the 100-foot cable forms the hypotenuse. To find the distance along the ground, the other leg, calculate: $\sqrt{100^2 - 80^2} = \sqrt{10,000 - 6,400} = \sqrt{3,600} = 60$. The cable should be staked down 60 feet from the pole.

4. **C.** The distance from home to 2nd base is $\sqrt{90^2 + 90^2} = 90\sqrt{2} \approx 127.28$. The pitcher's mound is 60 feet from home, so the distance from the mound to 2nd base is $127.28 - 60 \approx 67.28$ feet or 67 to the nearest foot.

5. **B.** The walk around two sides of the rectangular park is $40 + 50 = 90$ feet. The diagonal, corner to corner, is the hypotenuse of a right triangle whose length is equal to $\sqrt{40^2 + 50^2} = \sqrt{1,600 + 2,500} = \sqrt{4,100} \approx 64.03$ feet. Taking the diagonal route is a savings of $90 - 64.03 \approx 25.97$ or 26 feet.

6. **D.** Each path is the hypotenuse of a right triangle, so their lengths can be found using the Pythagorean theorem. Then add the individual lengths to find the total.

$$a + b + c + d =$$
$$\sqrt{3^2 + 6^2} + \sqrt{2^2 + 6^2} + \sqrt{1^2 + 5^2} + \sqrt{3^2 + 4^2} =$$
$$\sqrt{9 + 36} + \sqrt{4 + 36} + \sqrt{1 + 25} + \sqrt{9 + 16} =$$
$$\sqrt{45} + \sqrt{40} + \sqrt{26} + \sqrt{25} =$$
$$6.71 + 6.32 + 5.10 + 5 = 23.13$$

C. Congruence and Similarity

Arithmetic and algebra compare numerical expressions using two basic relationships: equality and inequality. Geometry compares figures using the two basic relationships of congruence and similarity. Two figures are congruent if they have the same shape and size. You can match them up to show pairs of equal-sized angles and pairs of sides the same length. Examine $\triangle ABC$ and $\triangle XYZ$ below. If $\triangle ABC \cong \triangle XYZ$, then $\angle A \cong \angle X$, $\angle B \cong \angle Y$, and $\angle C \cong \angle Z$, and $AB = XY$, $BC = YZ$, and $AC = XZ$.

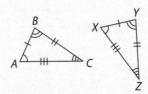

The minimum information you need to be certain two triangles are congruent can be remembered by these acronyms:

- SSS: Three sides of one triangle are equal in length to the three corresponding sides of the other triangle.
- SAS: Two sides and the angle included between them are equal to the corresponding parts of the other.
- ASA: Two angles and the side that connects them are equal to the corresponding parts of the other.
- AAS: Two angles and a side not included between them are equal to the corresponding parts of the other.
- HL: Only in right triangles: The hypotenuse and one leg are equal to the corresponding parts of the other.

Two figures are similar if they are the same shape but different sizes. The corresponding angles will still have the same measurement, but the sides, rather than being the same size, will be in proportion, meaning one figure will be an enlargement (or reduction) of the other. Examine $\triangle RST$ and $\triangle JKL$ below. If $\triangle RST \sim \triangle JKL$, $\angle R \cong \angle J$, $\angle S \cong \angle K$, and $\angle T \cong \angle L$, but $\dfrac{RS}{JK} = \dfrac{ST}{KL} = \dfrac{RT}{JL}$.

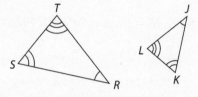

If you know two figures are similar and know the lengths of some sides, you may be able to find the length of a missing side by setting up and solving a proportion. If $ST = 12$ centimeters, $RT = 20$ centimeters, and $JL = 35$ centimeters, you can find the length of $\overline{KL}$:

$$\frac{ST}{KL} = \frac{RT}{JL}$$
$$\frac{12}{x} = \frac{20}{35}$$
$$20x = 12 \cdot 35 = 420$$
$$x = \frac{420}{20} = 21$$

Practice

1. Which of the following is a true statement about $\triangle ABC$ and $\triangle XYZ$ below?

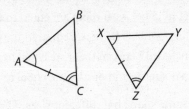

A. $\triangle ABC \cong \triangle XYZ$ by SSS
B. $\triangle ABC \cong \triangle XYZ$ by SAS
C. $\triangle ABC \cong \triangle XYZ$ by ASA
D. There is not enough information to determine if the triangles are congruent.

2. $\triangle PQR$ is similar to $\triangle DEF$. $PQ = 12$, $PR = 18$, and $DF = 27$. Find the length of $\overline{DE}$.

A. 8
B. 12
C. 18
D. 40.5

3. Right triangle $\triangle RST$ has $\overline{RS} \perp \overline{ST}$, and $ST = 72$. If $\triangle RST \cong \triangle JKL$ and $JL = 78$, how long is $\overline{JK}$?

A. 30
B. 66
C. 72
D. 78

4. In $\triangle LEG$, I is the midpoint of $\overline{LE}$ and T is the midpoint of $\overline{LG}$. If segment $\overline{IT}$ is drawn, $\triangle LIT \sim \triangle LEG$. If $LE = 16$ and $IT = 11$, find the length of $\overline{EG}$.

A. 5.5
B. 22
C. 44
D. 88

5. Reference the diagram below. If $\triangle ACT \cong \triangle DOG$, what is the measure of $\angle O$?

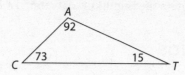

A. 15
B. 19
C. 58
D. 73

6. In $\triangle EAR$, $EA = 36$, $ER = 48$, and $AR = 60$. If $\triangle EAR \sim \triangle LID$, the ratio $\dfrac{LI}{ID}$ is equal to

A. $\dfrac{3}{4}$

B. $\dfrac{3}{5}$

C. $\dfrac{4}{5}$

D. $\dfrac{5}{3}$

Answers

1. **C.** $\angle A = \angle X$, $\angle C = \angle Z$ and the included sides, $AC = XZ$. $\triangle ABC \cong \triangle XYZ$ by ASA.

2. **C.** Set up the ratio $\dfrac{PQ}{DE} = \dfrac{PR}{DF}$ and substitute the known lengths to get $\dfrac{12}{x} = \dfrac{18}{27}$. Solve by

cross-multiplying: $18x = 12 \cdot 27$ and $x = \dfrac{\overset{2}{\cancel{12}} \cdot \overset{9}{\cancel{27}}}{\underset{\cancel{x}}{\cancel{18}}} = 18$.

3. **A.** $\angle S$ is the right angle so $\overline{ST}$, which measures 72, is a leg, and the congruence statement

$\triangle RST \cong \triangle JKL$ indicates that $\overline{ST}$ corresponds to $\overline{KL}$. Therefore, $ST = KL = 72$. $JL = 78$ and

corresponds to $\overline{RT}$, so $JL = RT = 78$ are the hypotenuses. To find the measure of $\overline{JK}$, a leg, calculate:

$\sqrt{78^2 - 72^2} = \sqrt{6,084 - 5,184} = \sqrt{900} = 30$. $\overline{JK}$ measures 30.

4. **B.** If $\triangle LIT \sim \triangle LEG$, then $\dfrac{LI}{LE} = \dfrac{IT}{EG} = \dfrac{LT}{LG}$. You know that $IT = 11$, $LE = 16$, and because I is the

midpoint of $\overline{LE}$, $LI = 8$. Solve the proportion $\dfrac{8}{16} = \dfrac{11}{x}$ by cross-multiplying to get $8x = 16 \times 11 = 176$,

and $x = 22$.

5. **D.** If $\triangle ACT \cong \triangle DOG$, then $\angle O = \angle C$, and from the diagram $\angle C = 73°$, so $\angle O = 73°$.

6. **B.** Use the proportion and substitute the lengths of $\overline{EA}$ and $\overline{AR}$: $\dfrac{LI}{ID} = \dfrac{EA}{AR} = \dfrac{36}{60} = \dfrac{6}{10} = \dfrac{3}{5}$.

D. Trigonometric Ratios

When triangles are similar, their sides are in proportion. When right triangles are similar, you can group them into families according to the size of the acute angle in them. Many right triangles of different sizes have the same acute angle and are all similar, as illustrated below.

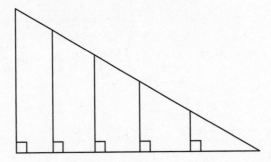

This allows you to say that the ratio of a particular pair of sides is the same number for any right triangle with that acute angle. The ratio of the side opposite a 30° angle to the hypotenuse will always be 1:2, for example.

The three most common ratios are given names: sine, cosine, and tangent. For any acute angle, $\angle A$, in a right triangle,

$$\sin(\angle A) = \frac{\text{opposite}}{\text{hypotenuse}}$$

$$\cos(\angle A) = \frac{\text{adjacent}}{\text{hypotenuse}}$$

$$\tan(\angle A) = \frac{\text{opposite}}{\text{adjacent}}$$

These ratios can be used to find the length of a side if you know another side and the angle, or to find the angle if you know two sides. You'll need a calculator to find the values of the ratios.

Suppose $\triangle ABC$ is a right triangle, with right angle $\angle B$. If $\angle A$ measures 50° and side $\overline{AB}$ measures 8 inches, how long is hypotenuse $\overline{AC}$? You know the length of the side adjacent to $\angle A$, and you want to know the length of the hypotenuse, so use $\cos(\angle A) = \dfrac{\text{adjacent}}{\text{hypotenuse}}$:

$$\cos(50°) = \frac{8}{x}$$

Use your calculator to find $\cos(50°) \approx 0.6428$:

$$0.6428 = \frac{8}{x}$$
$$0.6428x = 8$$
$$x = \frac{8}{0.6428} \approx 12.446$$

The hypotenuse measures approximately 12.45 inches.

> **TIP:** When using a calculator, be sure it's set to degree mode when working with angles measured in degrees. Later, you'll want to switch to radian mode, but always check that your calculator is set correctly.

If $\triangle RST$ is a right triangle with right angle $\angle S$ and you know that legs $RS = 25$ centimeters and $ST = 14$ centimeters, you can find the measure of $\angle R$:

$$\tan(\angle R) = \frac{ST}{RS} = \frac{14}{25} = 0.56$$

> **TIP:** Express trig ratios as decimals or fractions, whichever is convenient.

Use your calculator to find the angle measurement. Type $\boxed{2nd}$ $\boxed{tan}$ and $\tan^{-1}($ will appear on the screen. Then type 0.56 or 14/25 and type the final). Press ENTER. $\angle R \approx 29.25°$.

Remember that there are two families of right triangles called special right triangles. The isosceles right triangle, or 45°–45°–90° triangle, has two legs of equal length and a hypotenuse that's equal to a leg times the square root of 2. That makes the trig ratios for 45° easy to remember.

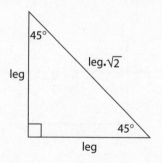

$$\sin(45°) = \frac{\text{leg}}{\text{leg} \times \sqrt{2}} = \frac{1}{\sqrt{2}} = \frac{\sqrt{2}}{2}$$

$$\cos(45°) = \frac{\text{leg}}{\text{leg} \times \sqrt{2}} = \frac{1}{\sqrt{2}} = \frac{\sqrt{2}}{2}$$

$$\tan(45°) = \frac{\text{leg}}{\text{leg}} = 1$$

The other special right triangle is the 30°–60°–90° right triangle. It has a hypotenuse, a short leg that is half as long as the hypotenuse, and a leg that is half the hypotenuse times the square root of 3. It gives you an easy way to remember the trig ratios for 30° and for 60°.

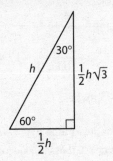

$$\sin(30°) = \frac{\frac{1}{2}h}{h} = \frac{1}{2}$$

$$\cos(30°) = \frac{\frac{1}{2}h\sqrt{3}}{h} = \frac{1}{2}\sqrt{3}$$

$$\tan(30°) = \frac{\frac{1}{2}h}{\frac{1}{2}h\sqrt{3}} = \frac{1}{\sqrt{3}} = \frac{\sqrt{3}}{3}$$

$$\sin(60°) = \frac{\frac{1}{2}h\sqrt{3}}{h} = \frac{1}{2}\sqrt{3}$$

$$\cos(60°) = \frac{\frac{1}{2}h}{h} = \frac{1}{2}$$

$$\tan(60°) = \frac{\frac{1}{2}h\sqrt{3}}{\frac{1}{2}h} = \sqrt{3}$$

Practice

Use the figure below for questions 1–3.

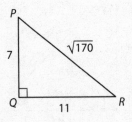

1. $\tan(\angle R) =$

   A. $\sin(\angle P)$
   B. $\cos(\angle P)$
   C. $\tan(\angle P)$
   D. None of the above

2. $\cos(\angle R) =$

   A. $\dfrac{7}{11}$

   B. $\dfrac{7\sqrt{170}}{170}$

   C. $\dfrac{11\sqrt{170}}{170}$

   D. $\dfrac{\sqrt{170}}{7}$

3. To the nearest degree, what is the measure of $\angle P$?

   A. $28°$
   B. $32°$
   C. $50°$
   D. $58°$

4. In right triangle $\triangle ABC$ with hypotenuse $\overline{AC}$, $\sin(\angle C) = 0.45$ and $AC = 40$. The length of $\overline{AB}$ is

   A. 11
   B. 18
   C. 85
   D. 88

5. In right triangle $\triangle XYZ$, leg $\overline{XY}$ measures 12 inches and hypotenuse $\overline{XZ}$ is 24 inches. What is the measure of $\angle X$?

   A. $30°$
   B. $45°$
   C. $50°$
   D. $60°$

6. If $\triangle LMN$ is an isosceles right triangle with $LM = MN$ and hypotenuse $LN = 50$ centimeters, what is the measure of $\overline{LM}$?

   A. 25
   B. 50
   C. $25\sqrt{2}$
   D. $50\sqrt{2}$

Answers

1. **D.** $\tan(\angle R) = \dfrac{7}{11}$, but $\sin(\angle P) = \dfrac{11}{\sqrt{170}}$, $\cos(\angle P) = \dfrac{7}{\sqrt{170}}$, and $\tan(\angle P) = \dfrac{11}{7}$. None of these answer

   choices are equal to $\tan(\angle R) = \dfrac{7}{11}$.

2. **C.** $\cos(\angle R) = \dfrac{QR}{PR} = \dfrac{11}{\sqrt{170}}$. In simplest radical form, $\dfrac{11}{\sqrt{170}} = \dfrac{11}{\sqrt{170}} \cdot \dfrac{\sqrt{170}}{\sqrt{170}} = \dfrac{11\sqrt{170}}{170}$.

3. **D.** To find the measure of $\angle P$, set up a ratio: $\tan(\angle P) = \dfrac{11}{7}$. Use your calculator to find

   $\tan^{-1}\left(\dfrac{11}{7}\right) \approx 57.53°$. To the nearest degree, $\angle P$ measures $58°$.

4. **B.** By definition, $\sin(\angle C) = \dfrac{AB}{AC}$. Substitute known values to get $\sin(\angle C) = \dfrac{AB}{AC} = \dfrac{x}{40} = 0.45$. Solve for

   x: $x = 40(0.45) = 18$.

5. **D.** Leg $\overline{XY}$ is adjacent to $\angle X$. The ratio of the adjacent side to the hypotenuse is the cosine:

   $\cos(\angle X) = \dfrac{XY}{XZ} = \dfrac{12}{24} = \dfrac{1}{2}$. Use your calculator or the special right triangle values to find

   $\cos^{-1}\left(\dfrac{1}{2}\right) = 60°$.

6. **C.** $\triangle LMN$ is an isosceles right triangle with legs $LM = MN$ meeting at right angle $\angle M$. The measure of

   $\angle L$ = the measure of $\angle N = 45°$. $\sin(\angle N) = \dfrac{LM}{LN} = \dfrac{x}{50}$ and $\sin(\angle N) = \sin(45°) = \dfrac{\sqrt{2}}{2}$. Solve $\dfrac{x}{50} = \dfrac{\sqrt{2}}{2}$.

   for x by cross-multiplying to get $2x = 50\sqrt{2}$ and $x = 25\sqrt{2}$.

E. Geometry of the Circle

There is quite a bit of vocabulary connected to the circle, especially names for lines or line segments that touch or cut the circle in different ways.

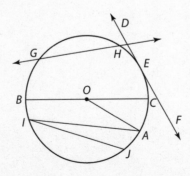

Reference the diagram above as you review the following definitions:

- **Radius:** The distance from the center to the circle, or a line segment that connects the center to a point on the circle ($\overline{OA}$).
- **Diameter:** A line segment through the center of the circle with its endpoints on the circle, or the length of that segment ($\overline{BC}$).
- **Tangent:** A line that touches the circle in only one point ($\overline{DF}$). A radius drawn to the point of tangency is perpendicular to the tangent.
- **Secant:** A line that cuts through the circle at two points ($\overline{GH}$).
- **Chord:** A line segment that has its endpoints on the circle, or the portion of a secant that is inside the circle ($\overline{IJ}$). The diameter is the longest chord in the circle ($\overline{BC}$).
- **Arc:** A portion of the circumference of the circle ($\overset{\frown}{AC}$).
- **Central angle:** An angle whose vertex is the center of the circle and whose sides are radii ($\angle AOC$).
- **Sector:** The portion of the area of the circle defined by the central angle and its arc.
- **Inscribed angle:** An angle whose vertex is a point of the circle and whose sides are chords ($\angle JIA$).

You should also know the following formulas:

- **Circumference:** $C = \pi d = 2\pi r$
- **Length of an arc:** $\dfrac{\text{degrees in central angle}}{360} \cdot 2\pi r$
- **Area of a circle:** $A = \pi r^2$
- **Area of a sector:** $\dfrac{\text{degrees in central angle}}{360} \cdot \pi r^2$

Practice

1. The radius of circle O is 14 centimeters, and central angle $\angle DOT$ measures 84°. What is the length of arc $\overset{\frown}{DT}$?

    A. 2.5π
    B. 6π
    C. $\dfrac{98\pi}{15}$
    D. $\dfrac{686\pi}{15}$

Use the figure below for questions 2–4.

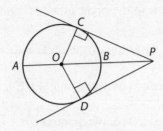

2. In circle O, diameter $\overline{AB}$ is 10 inches long and is extended 8 inches beyond the circle to point P. Two tangents are drawn to the circle from point P: one to point C and one to point D. Radii $\overline{OC}$ and $\overline{OD}$ are drawn, forming right angles at C and D. Find PD to the nearest tenth.

   A. 9.4
   B. 12.0
   C. 12.8
   D. 13.9

3. If $\angle OPC$ measures $20°$, find the length of arc $\overset{\frown}{BD}$.

   A. $\dfrac{5\pi}{9}$

   B. $\dfrac{25\pi}{18}$

   C. $\dfrac{35\pi}{18}$

   D. $\dfrac{175\pi}{36}$

4. If $\angle OPC$ measures $20°$, what is the area of sector AOD?

   A. $\dfrac{5\pi}{9}$

   B. $\dfrac{25\pi}{18}$

   C. $\dfrac{175\pi}{36}$

   D. $\dfrac{275\pi}{36}$

5. If the radius of the larger circle in the figure below is 8 inches, and the central angles measure as marked, find the total area of the shaded regions.

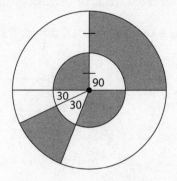

A. $\dfrac{76\pi}{3}$

B. 32π

C. $\dfrac{128\pi}{3}$

D. 64π

6. In circle O, the area of sector AOB is 45π. If the radius of the circle is 15 centimeters, find the measure of central angle $\angle AOB$.

A. $5°$
B. $45°$
C. $72°$
D. $1{,}080°$

Answers

1. **C.** The length of the arc is a fraction, $\dfrac{84}{360} = \dfrac{7}{30}$, times the circumference of the circle, $2\pi(14)$. Simplify where possible as you multiply: $\dfrac{84}{360} \cdot 2\pi(14) = \dfrac{7}{\cancel{30}_{15}} \cdot \cancel{28}^{14}\pi = \dfrac{98\pi}{15}$.

2. **B.** $OD = 5$ and $OP = 5 + 8 = 13$. Use the Pythagorean theorem to find PD:

$$OD^2 + PD^2 = OP^2$$
$$5^2 + x^2 = 13^2$$
$$x^2 = 169 - 25 = 144$$
$$x = \sqrt{144} = 12$$

3. **C.** If $\angle OPC = 20°$ and $\angle PCO = 90°$, the central angle $\angle POC = 70°$. The arc length is a fraction of the circumference: $\dfrac{70}{360} \cdot 10\pi = \dfrac{70\pi}{36} = \dfrac{35\pi}{18}$.

4. **D.** The sector is defined by central angle $\angle AOD$. $\overline{AB}$ is a diameter and $\angle POC = 70°$, so $\angle AOD = 180°$ $- 70° = 110°$. The area of the sector is a fraction of the area of the circle: $\dfrac{110}{360} \cdot 25\pi = \dfrac{275\pi}{36}$.

5. **A.** The radius of the large circle is 8 and the radius of the small circle is 4.

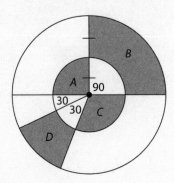

If the four shaded regions are labeled as shown above, you can calculate each area:

A: $\dfrac{90}{360} \cdot 4^2 \pi = 4\pi$

B: $\dfrac{90}{360} \cdot 8^2 \pi - \dfrac{90}{360} \cdot 4^2 \pi = 16\pi - 4\pi = 12\pi$

C: $\dfrac{120}{360} \cdot 16\pi = \dfrac{16\pi}{3}$

D: $\dfrac{30}{360} \cdot 64\pi - \dfrac{30}{360} \cdot 16\pi = \dfrac{64\pi}{12} - \dfrac{16\pi}{12} = \dfrac{48\pi}{12} = 4\pi$

Add the individual areas: $4\pi + 12\pi + \dfrac{16\pi}{3} + 4\pi = 20\pi + \dfrac{16\pi}{3} = \dfrac{60\pi}{3} + \dfrac{16\pi}{3} = \dfrac{76\pi}{3}$.

6. **C.** Set up the calculation using a variable for the degree measure of the angle, over 360, times the area of the circle. Set that equal to the known area of the section. Solve the resulting equation:

$$\frac{x}{360} \cdot \pi \cdot 15^2 = \frac{\overset{45}{\cancel{225}} \pi x}{\underset{72}{\cancel{360}}} = \frac{45\pi x}{72} = 45\pi$$

$$\cancel{45\pi}\, x = 72\left(\cancel{45\pi}\right)$$

$$x = 72$$

F. Radians, Degrees, and Arc Lengths

In geometry, it's traditional to measure angles in degrees, a system of measurement that divides a full rotation, or circle, into 360 units. Measurement in other units is possible, however, and one of the most commonly used is radians. A radian is the measure of a central angle whose arc length is equal to the radius of the circle. The circumference of the circle is $2\pi r$, so there will be 2π, or a little more than 6, radians in a full rotation.

> TIP: Read carefully, and understand the difference between arc measure and arc length. Arc measure is the number of the degrees in the arc, which is the number of degrees in its central angle. Arc measure is the same whether the circle is large or small. Arc length is measured in centimeters or inches, or other units of length. The same central angle cuts off arcs with the same degree measure in different circles, but has a longer arc length in a large circle, with a large radius, and a shorter arc length in a small circle.

To convert between degrees and radians, use a simple proportion based on part of whole:

$$\frac{\text{degrees}}{360} = \frac{\text{radians}}{2\pi}$$

What is the degree measure equivalent to $\dfrac{3\pi}{4}$ radians?

Fill in what you know and solve for the other:

$$\frac{d}{360} = \frac{\frac{3\pi}{4}}{2\pi}$$

$$2\pi d = \frac{3\pi}{4} \cdot 360 = 270\pi$$

$$d = \frac{270\pi}{2\pi} = 135°$$

When you look at arc length and area of a sector with angles measured in radians, you notice a convenient result. If you use the symbol θ to represent the measure of the central angle in radians, and 2π radians in a full rotation, you get:

$$\text{Arc length: } \frac{\theta}{2\pi} \cdot 2\pi \cdot r = \theta r$$

$$\text{Area of sector: } \frac{\theta}{2\pi} \cdot \pi \cdot r^2 = \frac{\theta r^2}{2}$$

Radian measurement allows you to talk about the size of an angle or an arc in real numbers, and that makes it easier to talk about functions based on trig ratios. First, you need to expand the definitions of sine, cosine, and tangent beyond acute angles in right triangles to angles of any size. To do that, start with a circle with a radius of 1, called a unit circle, in the coordinate plane, centered on the origin. Then draw a central angle with the positive x-axis as one of its sides. Drop a perpendicular from the point where the side of the angle crosses the circle to the x-axis.

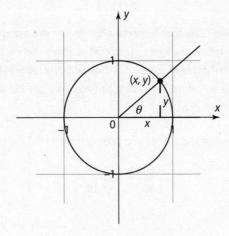

The right triangle formed has a central angle, θ, at the origin, for which you can find the sine, cosine, and tangent if you know the coordinates (x, y) of that point where the side of the angle crosses the circle. These new definitions allow you to see sine, cosine, and tangent as functions of any real number, θ.

$$\sin(\theta) = \frac{y}{1}$$

$$\cos(\theta) = \frac{x}{1}$$

$$\tan(\theta) = \frac{y}{x}$$

Practice

1. An angle that measures 120° is equivalent to what radian measure?

   A. $\dfrac{\pi}{6}$

   B. $\dfrac{\pi}{3}$

   C. $\dfrac{2\pi}{3}$

   D. $\dfrac{3\pi}{4}$

2. In a circle of diameter 18 centimeters, find the length of the arc of a central angle of $\dfrac{5\pi}{6}$ radians.

   A. 15π

   B. $\dfrac{5\pi}{2}$

   C. $\dfrac{15\pi}{2}$

   D. $\dfrac{45\pi}{2}$

3. $\angle A$ measures $\dfrac{5\pi}{3}$ radians. $\angle B$ measures $280°$. Which of the following is true?

   A. $\angle A$ is larger than $\angle B$.
   B. $\angle A$ is smaller than $\angle B$.
   C. $\angle A$ is the same size as $\angle B$.
   D. It is impossible to compare the angles.

4. If a central angle of $\dfrac{\pi}{3}$ radians defines a sector with an area of 24π, what is the radius of the circle?

   A. 8
   B. 12
   C. 24
   D. 72

5. A central angle $\angle AOB$ is drawn with side $\overline{OA}$ on the positive x-axis. Side $\overline{OB}$ crosses a unit circle at $(0.8, 0.6)$. What is the value of $\tan(\angle AOB)$?

   A. 0.6
   B. 0.75
   C. 0.8
   D. $1.\overline{3}$

6. $\cos\left(\dfrac{\pi}{4}\right) =$

   A. $\dfrac{1}{2}$

   B. $\dfrac{\sqrt{2}}{2}$

   C. $\sqrt{2}$

   D. $\dfrac{\sqrt{3}}{2}$

Answers

1. **C.** Use $\dfrac{\text{degrees}}{360} = \dfrac{\text{radians}}{2\pi}$, with degrees = 120°. Then, $\dfrac{120}{360} = \dfrac{\text{radians}}{2\pi}$ or $\dfrac{1}{3} = \dfrac{\text{radians}}{2\pi}$ can be solved by

   cross-multiplying: 3 radians $= 2\pi$ so radians $= \dfrac{2\pi}{3}$.

2. **C.** If the diameter is 18, the radius is half of that, or 9. The arc length is the product of the radian

   measure of the angle times the radius: $\dfrac{5\pi}{\cancel{6}_2} \cdot \cancel{9}^3 = \dfrac{15\pi}{2}$.

3. **A.** Convert one of the angles to the other measuring system. $\dfrac{d}{360} = \dfrac{\frac{5\pi}{3}}{2\pi}$ becomes

   $2\pi d = \dfrac{5\pi}{3} \cdot 360 = 5\pi \cdot 120$ or $2\pi d = 600\pi$, so $d = 300°$. Since $\angle A$ at $\dfrac{5\pi}{3}$ radians is equivalent to 300°, it

   is larger than $\angle B$ at 280°.

4. **B.** The area of the sector is the measure of the angle, over 2π, times the area of the circle.

   $\dfrac{\frac{\pi}{3}}{2\pi} \cdot \cancel{\pi} r^2 = 24\pi$ becomes $\dfrac{\pi r^2}{6} = 24\pi$. Isolate r^2 and then take the square root of both sides: $\pi r^2 = 144\pi$

   and $r^2 = 144$, so $r = 12$.

5. **B.** Substitute and simplify: $\tan(\angle AOB) = \dfrac{y}{x} = \dfrac{0.6}{0.8} = \dfrac{6}{8} = \dfrac{3}{4} = 0.75$.

6. **B.** Draw an angle of $\dfrac{\pi}{4}$ radians in standard position, with the vertex at the origin, the initial side along

   the positive x-axis, and the terminal side of length 1. Drop a perpendicular from the terminal side to
   the x-axis. The right triangle formed is isosceles, so you can use the measurements of a 45°–45°–90°

   triangle. The adjacent side measures $\dfrac{\sqrt{2}}{2}$ and the hypotenuse measures 1. Therefore,

   $$\cos\left(\dfrac{\pi}{4}\right) = \dfrac{x}{1} = \dfrac{\frac{\sqrt{2}}{2}}{1} = \dfrac{\sqrt{2}}{2}.$$

G. Circles in the Coordinate Plane

When a circle is drawn in the coordinate plane, it can be described by an equation that says: For every point (x, y) on the circle, $(x - h)^2 + (y - k)^2 = r^2$. In that equation, h and k are the coordinates of the center of the circle (h, k) and r is the radius. If the circle is centered at the origin $(0, 0)$, the equation simplifies to $x^2 + y^2 = r^2$.

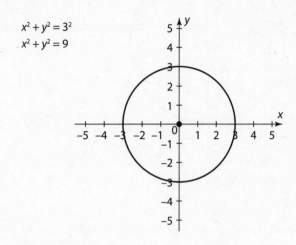

$$x^2 + y^2 = 3^2$$
$$x^2 + y^2 = 9$$

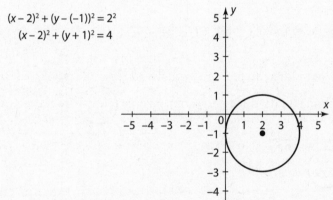

$$(x - 2)^2 + (y - (-1))^2 = 2^2$$
$$(x - 2)^2 + (y + 1)^2 = 4$$

Practice

1. Which of the following points is the center of the circle whose equation is $(x + 4)^2 + (y - 7)^2 = 9$?

   A. $(4, -7)$

   B. $(-4, 7)$

   C. $(-1, 10)$

   D. $(7, -4)$

2. Which of the following is the equation of the circle shown below?

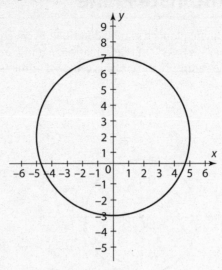

A. $(x - 5)^2 + (y + 3)^2 = 49$
B. $x^2 + (y + 2)^2 = 25$
C. $x^2 + (y - 2)^2 = 25$
D. $(x + 5)^2 + (y - 7)^2 = 9$

3. Which of the graphs below is the graph of $(x - 4)^2 + (y + 3)^2 = 4$?

A.

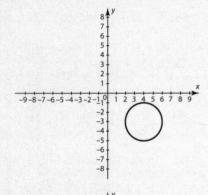

C.

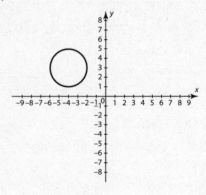

B.

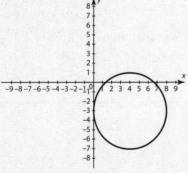

D.

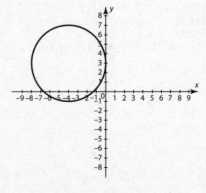

4. Which of these points does NOT lie on the circle whose equation is $x^2 + y^2 = 25$?

   A. (3, 4)
   B. (–4, 3)
   C. (0, –5)
   D. (0, 0)

5. Which of the following is the equation of a circle of radius 8, centered at (–7, –1)?

   A. $(x - 7)^2 + (y - 1)^2 = 8$
   B. $(x - 7)^2 + (y - 1)^2 = 64$
   C. $(x + 7)^2 + (y + 1)^2 = 64$
   D. $(x + 7)^2 + (y + 1)^2 = 8$

6. If the line $y = x$ and the circle $(x - 2)^2 + (y - 3)^2 = 25$ are graphed on the same set of axes, they intersect at

   A. (6, 6) and (–1, –1)
   B. (2, 2) and (3, 3)
   C. (–2, –2) and (–3, –3)
   D. (–6, –6) and (1, 1)

Answers

1. **B.** Compare the equation $(x + 4)^2 + (y - 7)^2 = 9$ to the standard form $(x - h)^2 + (y - k)^2 = r^2$ and identify h and k, the coordinates of the center. $(x - (-4))^2 + (y - (7))^2 = 9$, so $h = -4$ and $k = 7$. The center is (–4, 7).

2. **C.** The circle shown is shifted up, but not left or right, so choices A and D can be eliminated because both have horizontal shifts. Choices B and C both have a radius of 5, but Choice B shifts the circle down, while Choice C shifts up. Choice C is correct.

3. **A.** The equation $(x - 4)^2 + (y + 3)^2 = 4$ or $(x - (4))^2 + (y - (-3))^2 = 2^2$ indicates the circle has a radius of 2 and is centered at (4, –3). Choices A and C have the correct radius, but only Choice A has the correct center.

4. **D.** You could sketch a graph of the circle, or simply test points in the equation algebraically. Testing Choice A, $3^2 + 4^2 = 25$, so Choice A is not the correct answer. For Choice B, $(-4)^2 + 3^2 = 25$, so it too is incorrect. Testing Choice C, $0^2 + (-5)^2 = 25$; incorrect. Now look at Choice D; it will not fit, a fact you might spot more quickly by realizing (0, 0) is the center of the circle, not a point on the circle. The answer is Choice D.

5. **C.** Start with the standard form of the equation $(x - h)^2 + (y - k)^2 = r^2$. Substitute the given information and simplify:

$$(x - (-7))^2 + (y - (-1))^2 = 8^2$$
$$(x + 7)^2 + (y + 1)^2 = 64$$

6. **A.** You could sketch the graphs, or solve the system algebraically. First, because $y = x$, replace y with x in the equation of the circle $(x - 2)^2 + (y - 3)^2 = 25$. Simplify and solve for x:

$$(x-2)^2 + (x-3)^2 = 25$$
$$x^2 - 4x + 4 + x^2 - 6x + 9 = 25$$
$$2x^2 - 10x + 13 = 25$$
$$2x^2 - 10x - 12 = 0$$
$$2(x^2 - 5x - 6) = 0$$

Solve the quadratic equation by factoring:

$$x^2 - 5x - 6 = 0$$
$$(x - 6)(x + 1) = 0$$

$$x - 6 = 0 \qquad\qquad x + 1 = 0$$
$$x = 6 \qquad\qquad x = -1$$
$$y = 6 \qquad\qquad y = -1$$

The graphs intersect at (6, 6) and (–1, –1).

H. Complex Numbers

The subject of complex numbers really fits in with the algebra of square roots and quadratic equations. You learned that there is no real number that is the square root of a negative number. But if you agree to define the square root of –1 as a number represented by the symbol i, you can create a system of numbers in which there is a square root of a negative number.

$$i = \sqrt{-1} \quad i^2 = -1 \quad i^3 = -i \quad i^4 = 1$$

Imaginary numbers are multiples of i, numbers of the form bi, where b is a real number and i is the square root of –1. Complex numbers are numbers of the form $a + bi$, where a is a real number and bi is an imaginary number. Examples of complex numbers include $3 + 5i$, $-2 + 3i$, $6 - 7i$, and $\sqrt{3} - \dfrac{1}{2}i$.

Arithmetic with complex numbers is similar to arithmetic with radicals because i is a square root.

For addition and subtraction, combine the real parts and combine the imaginary parts. Remember to apply any subtraction sign to the entire complex number that follows it.

$$(4 - 7i) + (5 + 9i) = (4 + 5) + (-7i + 9i) = 9 + 2i$$
$$(8 - 5i) - (3 - 2i) = (8 - 3) + (-5i - (-2i)) = 5 - 3i$$

Multiply complex numbers by using the FOIL method and changing i^2 to -1.

$$(2+5i)(3-i) = 6-2i+15i-5i^2 = 6+13i-5(-1) = 11+13i$$

$$(5-4i)(5+4i) = 25+20i-20i-16i^2 = 25-16(-1) = 25+16 = 41$$

The conjugate of $a + bi$ is $a - bi$. The product of a complex number and its conjugate is always a real number.

Dividing complex numbers is essentially the same process as rationalizing a denominator. Multiply both the numerator and the denominator by the conjugate of the denominator.

$$\frac{3+2i}{5-3i} = \frac{(3+2i)}{(5-3i)} \cdot \frac{(5+3i)}{(5+3i)} = \frac{15+9i+10i+6i^2}{25+15i-15i-9i^2} = \frac{15+19i-6}{25+9} = \frac{9+19i}{34} = \frac{9}{34} + \frac{19}{34}i$$

Practice

1. Which of the following is the simplest form of $5i + 3i^2 - 2i^3 + 2i^4$?

    A. $2i$
    B. -2
    C. $-1 + 7i$
    D. $-3 + 2i$

2. The solution of $3x^2 + 48 = 0$ is

    A. $x = \pm 4\sqrt{3}$
    B. $x = \pm 4i\sqrt{3}$
    C. $x = \pm 4$
    D. $x = \pm 4i$

3. The quotient $\dfrac{2-5i}{1+i}$ is equal to

    A. $-1.5 - 3.5i$
    B. $-3 - 7i$
    C. 0
    D. Undefined

4. If the expression $(2 - 9i)(3 + 4i) - (5 - 6i)(3 + 4i)$ is correctly simplified, the result is

    A. $-21 - 21i$
    B. $3 - 21i$
    C. 3
    D. $51 - 57i$

5. The difference between $2i(3 - 4i)$ and $2(3 - 4i)$ is

    A. $2 + 14i$

    B. $14 + 14i$

    C. $2 + 2i$

    D. $2i$

6. Suppose $2 + 5i$ is added to the conjugate of $3 - 2i$, and $3 - 2i$ is added to the conjugate of $2 + 5i$. What is the product of the two sums?

    A. $16 + 30i$

    B. $32 + 16i$

    C. 74

    D. 24

Answers

1. **C.** Simplify: $5i + 3i^2 - 2i^3 + 2i^4 = 5i + 3(-1) - 2(-i) + 2(1) = 5i - 3 + 2i + 2 = -1 + 7i$.

2. **D.** Isolate x^2 on one side: $3x^2 + 48 = 0$ becomes $3x^2 = -48$ and then $x^2 = -16$. Take the square root of both sides and simplify the radical: $x = \pm\sqrt{-16} = \pm\sqrt{16(-1)} = \pm\sqrt{16}\sqrt{-1} = \pm 4i$.

3. **A.** Multiply the numerator and denominator by the conjugate of the denominator:

$$\frac{(2-5i)}{(1+i)} \cdot \frac{(1-i)}{(1-i)} = \frac{2-2i-5i+5i^2}{1-i^2} = \frac{2-7i-5}{1+1} = \frac{-3-7i}{2} = -\frac{3}{2} - \frac{7}{2}i$$

This can also be written as $-1.5 - 3.5i$, Choice A.

4. **B.** Use the FOIL method to perform each multiplication:

$$(2-9i)(3+4i)-(5-6i)(3+4i) = (6+8i-27i-36i^2)-(15+20i-18i-24i^2)$$
$$= (6-19i+36)-(15+2i+24)$$
$$= (42-19i)-(39+2i)$$

Now you can subtract:

$$(42-19i)-(39+2i) = (42-39)+(-19i-2i)$$
$$= 3-21i$$

5. **A.** Use the distributive property to perform each multiplication, then combine real terms and combine imaginary terms:

$$2i(3-4i)-2(3-4i) = (6i-8i^2)+(-6+8i)$$
$$= (6i+8)+(-6+8i)$$
$$= (8-6)+(6i+8i)$$
$$= 2+14i$$

6. **C.** The conjugate of $3 - 2i$ is $3 + 2i$. $(2 + 5i) + (3 + 2i) = 5 + 7i$. The conjugate of $2 + 5i$ is $2 - 5i$. $(3 - 2i) + (2 - 5i) = 5 - 7i$. Multiply the results using the FOIL method. Because you are multiplying conjugates, the result is a real number:

$$(5+7i)(5-7i) = 25-35i+35i-49i^2$$
$$= 25+49$$
$$= 74$$

XII. Full-Length Practice Test with Answer Explanations

The total time for the entire exam is 2 hours and 45 minutes.

Answer Sheet

Section 1: Reading Test

1 Ⓐ Ⓑ Ⓒ Ⓓ
2 Ⓐ Ⓑ Ⓒ Ⓓ
3 Ⓐ Ⓑ Ⓒ Ⓓ
4 Ⓐ Ⓑ Ⓒ Ⓓ
5 Ⓐ Ⓑ Ⓒ Ⓓ

6 Ⓐ Ⓑ Ⓒ Ⓓ
7 Ⓐ Ⓑ Ⓒ Ⓓ
8 Ⓐ Ⓑ Ⓒ Ⓓ
9 Ⓐ Ⓑ Ⓒ Ⓓ
10 Ⓐ Ⓑ Ⓒ Ⓓ

11 Ⓐ Ⓑ Ⓒ Ⓓ
12 Ⓐ Ⓑ Ⓒ Ⓓ
13 Ⓐ Ⓑ Ⓒ Ⓓ
14 Ⓐ Ⓑ Ⓒ Ⓓ
15 Ⓐ Ⓑ Ⓒ Ⓓ

16 Ⓐ Ⓑ Ⓒ Ⓓ
17 Ⓐ Ⓑ Ⓒ Ⓓ
18 Ⓐ Ⓑ Ⓒ Ⓓ
19 Ⓐ Ⓑ Ⓒ Ⓓ
20 Ⓐ Ⓑ Ⓒ Ⓓ

21 Ⓐ Ⓑ Ⓒ Ⓓ
22 Ⓐ Ⓑ Ⓒ Ⓓ
23 Ⓐ Ⓑ Ⓒ Ⓓ
24 Ⓐ Ⓑ Ⓒ Ⓓ
25 Ⓐ Ⓑ Ⓒ Ⓓ

26 Ⓐ Ⓑ Ⓒ Ⓓ
27 Ⓐ Ⓑ Ⓒ Ⓓ
28 Ⓐ Ⓑ Ⓒ Ⓓ
29 Ⓐ Ⓑ Ⓒ Ⓓ
30 Ⓐ Ⓑ Ⓒ Ⓓ

31 Ⓐ Ⓑ Ⓒ Ⓓ
32 Ⓐ Ⓑ Ⓒ Ⓓ
33 Ⓐ Ⓑ Ⓒ Ⓓ
34 Ⓐ Ⓑ Ⓒ Ⓓ
35 Ⓐ Ⓑ Ⓒ Ⓓ

36 Ⓐ Ⓑ Ⓒ Ⓓ
37 Ⓐ Ⓑ Ⓒ Ⓓ
38 Ⓐ Ⓑ Ⓒ Ⓓ
39 Ⓐ Ⓑ Ⓒ Ⓓ
40 Ⓐ Ⓑ Ⓒ Ⓓ

41 Ⓐ Ⓑ Ⓒ Ⓓ
42 Ⓐ Ⓑ Ⓒ Ⓓ
43 Ⓐ Ⓑ Ⓒ Ⓓ
44 Ⓐ Ⓑ Ⓒ Ⓓ
45 Ⓐ Ⓑ Ⓒ Ⓓ

46 Ⓐ Ⓑ Ⓒ Ⓓ
47 Ⓐ Ⓑ Ⓒ Ⓓ

Section 2: Writing and Language Test

1 Ⓐ Ⓑ Ⓒ Ⓓ
2 Ⓐ Ⓑ Ⓒ Ⓓ
3 Ⓐ Ⓑ Ⓒ Ⓓ
4 Ⓐ Ⓑ Ⓒ Ⓓ
5 Ⓐ Ⓑ Ⓒ Ⓓ

6 Ⓐ Ⓑ Ⓒ Ⓓ
7 Ⓐ Ⓑ Ⓒ Ⓓ
8 Ⓐ Ⓑ Ⓒ Ⓓ
9 Ⓐ Ⓑ Ⓒ Ⓓ
10 Ⓐ Ⓑ Ⓒ Ⓓ

11 Ⓐ Ⓑ Ⓒ Ⓓ
12 Ⓐ Ⓑ Ⓒ Ⓓ
13 Ⓐ Ⓑ Ⓒ Ⓓ
14 Ⓐ Ⓑ Ⓒ Ⓓ
15 Ⓐ Ⓑ Ⓒ Ⓓ

16 Ⓐ Ⓑ Ⓒ Ⓓ
17 Ⓐ Ⓑ Ⓒ Ⓓ
18 Ⓐ Ⓑ Ⓒ Ⓓ
19 Ⓐ Ⓑ Ⓒ Ⓓ
20 Ⓐ Ⓑ Ⓒ Ⓓ

21 Ⓐ Ⓑ Ⓒ Ⓓ
22 Ⓐ Ⓑ Ⓒ Ⓓ
23 Ⓐ Ⓑ Ⓒ Ⓓ
24 Ⓐ Ⓑ Ⓒ Ⓓ
25 Ⓐ Ⓑ Ⓒ Ⓓ

26 Ⓐ Ⓑ Ⓒ Ⓓ
27 Ⓐ Ⓑ Ⓒ Ⓓ
28 Ⓐ Ⓑ Ⓒ Ⓓ
29 Ⓐ Ⓑ Ⓒ Ⓓ
30 Ⓐ Ⓑ Ⓒ Ⓓ

31 Ⓐ Ⓑ Ⓒ Ⓓ
32 Ⓐ Ⓑ Ⓒ Ⓓ
33 Ⓐ Ⓑ Ⓒ Ⓓ
34 Ⓐ Ⓑ Ⓒ Ⓓ
35 Ⓐ Ⓑ Ⓒ Ⓓ

36 Ⓐ Ⓑ Ⓒ Ⓓ
37 Ⓐ Ⓑ Ⓒ Ⓓ
38 Ⓐ Ⓑ Ⓒ Ⓓ
39 Ⓐ Ⓑ Ⓒ Ⓓ
40 Ⓐ Ⓑ Ⓒ Ⓓ

41 Ⓐ Ⓑ Ⓒ Ⓓ
42 Ⓐ Ⓑ Ⓒ Ⓓ
43 Ⓐ Ⓑ Ⓒ Ⓓ
44 Ⓐ Ⓑ Ⓒ Ⓓ

Section 3: Math Test – No Calculator

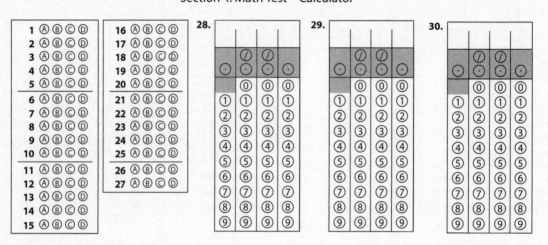

Section 4: Math Test – Calculator

Section 1: Reading Test

47 questions

60 minutes

Directions: Read the passages or pair of passages that follow and answer the questions by filling in the appropriate circle on your answer sheets. Select the best answer based on what is directly stated or implied in the passage or in any accompanying information including introductory material and/or graphics (tables, charts, or graphs).

Questions 1–9 are based on the following passage.

This passage is adapted from *Jane Eyre* (1847), a novel by British author Charlotte Brontë. The protagonist, Jane Eyre, the governess at Thornfield Hall, who is walking back to the Hall on a cold winter's day, narrates this passage.

It was very near, but not yet in sight; when, in addition to the tramp, tramp, I heard a rush under the hedge, and close down by the hazel stems glided a great dog, whose black and

(5) white colour made him a distinct object against the trees…

The horse followed,—a tall steed, and on its back a rider….only a traveller taking the short cut to Millcote. He passed, and I went on; a few

(10) steps, and I turned: a sliding sound and an exclamation of "What the deuce is to do now?" and a clattering tumble, arrested my attention. Man and horse were down; they had slipped on the sheet of ice which glazed the causeway. The

(15) dog came bounding back, and seeing his master in a predicament, and hearing the horse groan, barked till the evening hills echoed the sound, which was deep in proportion to his magnitude. He snuffed round the prostrate group, and then

(20) he ran up to me; it was all he could do,—there was no other help at hand to summon. I obeyed him, and walked down to the traveller, by this time struggling himself free of his steed. His efforts were so vigorous, I thought he could not

(25) be much hurt; but I asked him the question—

"Are you injured, sir?"

I think he was swearing, but am not certain; however, he was pronouncing some formula which prevented him from replying to me directly.

(30) "Can I do anything?" I asked again.

"You must just stand on one side," he answered as he rose, first to his knees, and then to his feet. I did; whereupon began a heaving, stamping, clattering process, accom-

(35) panied by a barking and baying which removed me effectually some yards' distance; but I would not be driven quite away till I saw the event. This was finally fortunate; the horse was re-established, and the dog was silenced

(40) with a "Down, Pilot!" The traveller now, stooping, felt his foot and leg, as if trying whether they were sound; apparently something ailed them, for he halted to the stile whence I had just risen, and sat down.

(45) I was in the mood for being useful, or at least officious, I think, for I now drew near him again.

"If you are hurt, and want help, sir, I can fetch some one either from Thornfield Hall or

(50) from Hay."

"Thank you: I shall do: I have no broken bones,—only a sprain," and again he stood up and tried his foot, but the result extorted an involuntary "Ugh!"

(55) Something of daylight still lingered, and the moon was waxing bright: I could see him plainly. His figure was enveloped in a riding cloak, fur collared and steel clasped; its details were not apparent, but I traced the general

(60) points of middle height and considerable breadth of chest. He had a dark face, with

GO ON TO THE NEXT PAGE

stern features and a heavy brow; his eyes and gathered eyebrows looked ireful and thwarted just now; he was past youth, but had not
(65) reached middle-age; perhaps he might be thirty-five. I felt no fear of him, and but little shyness. Had he been a handsome, heroic-looking young gentleman, I should not have dared to stand thus questioning him against
(70) his will, and offering my services unasked. I had hardly ever seen a handsome youth; never in my life spoken to one. I had a theoretical reverence and homage for beauty, elegance, gallantry, fascination; but had I met those
(75) qualities incarnate in masculine shape, I should have known instinctively that they neither had nor could have sympathy with anything in me, and should have shunned them as one would fire, lightning, or anything else that
(80) is bright but antipathetic.

If even this stranger had smiled and been good-humoured to me when I addressed him; if he had put off my offer of assistance gaily and with thanks, I should have gone on my
(85) way and not felt any vocation to renew inquiries: but the frown, the roughness of the traveller, set me at my ease: I retained my station when he waved to me to go, and announced—

"I cannot think of leaving you, sir, at so late
(90) an hour, in this solitary lane, till I see you are fit to mount your horse."

He looked at me when I said this; he had hardly turned his eyes in my direction before.

"I should think you ought to be at home
(95) yourself," said he….

1. Which choice best summarizes the passage?

   A. An inconsequential encounter occurs, leading to frivolous ramifications.

   B. An unexpected discovery follows a violent confrontation.

   C. A chance meeting foreshadows a more profound relationship.

   D. A preordained skirmish begins between forces of good and evil.

2. Jane is summoned to help by

   A. the traveller.

   B. the dog.

   C. her own conscience.

   D. a neighbor.

3. What does the passage suggest are Jane's impressions of the stranger?

   A. He is pleasant and good-natured.

   B. He is classically handsome yet shy.

   C. He is the personification of elegance and gallantry.

   D. He is stern and angry.

4. Which choice provides the best evidence for the answer to the preceding question?

   A. Lines 61–66 ("He had…thirty-five.")

   B. Lines 67–70 ("Had he…unasked.")

   C. Lines 70–72 ("I had hardly…one.")

   D. Lines 72–80 ("I had a…antipathetic.")

5. In line 42, the word "sound" most nearly means

   A. deep and peaceful.

   B. not damaged.

   C. sensible.

   D. completely acceptable.

6. In line 87, the word "station" most nearly means

   A. position.

   B. post.

   C. class.

   D. rank.

7. Jane indicates she would have obeyed the traveler's dismissal of her aid if he had

   A. been less badly injured.

   B. yelled at her rudely.

   C. been more cheerful and grateful.

   D. insisted she leave immediately.

8. Which choice provides the best evidence for the answer to the preceding question?

   A. Lines 27–29 ("I think…directly.")
   B. Lines 51–54 ("Thank you…Ugh!")
   C. Lines 66–67 ("I felt…shyness.")
   D. Lines 81–86 ("If even…inquiries:")

9. Which of the following best describes the impression each character has of the other?

   A. Jane is immediately infatuated; the traveler seems to dislike her.
   B. Jane responds sympathetically to his roughness; the traveler barely notices Jane.
   C. Jane is shocked by his uncouth appearance; the traveler is touched by her sympathy.
   D. Jane is aloof and distant; the traveler tries to ingratiate himself.

Questions 10–18 are based on the following passage and table.

This is an excerpt from *A Field Study of the Kansas Ant-Eating Frog* by Henry S. Fitch.

Ordinarily the ant-eating frog stays beneath the soil surface, in cracks or holes or beneath rocks. Probably it obtains its food in such situations, and rarely wanders on the surface. The
(5) occasional individuals found moving about above ground are in most instances flushed from their shelters by the vibrations of the observer's footsteps. On numerous occasions I have noticed individuals, startled by nearby footfalls, dart
(10) from cracks or under rocks and scuttle away in search of other shelter. Such behavior suggests that digging predators may be important natural enemies. The gait is a combination of running and short hops that are usually only an inch or
(15) two in length. The flat pointed head seems to be in contact with the ground or very near to it as the animal moves about rapidly and erratically. The frog has a proclivity for squeezing into holes and cracks, or beneath objects on the ground.
(20) The burst of activity by one that is startled lasts for only a few seconds. Then the frog stops abruptly, usually concealed wholly or in part by some object. Having stopped it tends to rely on concealment for protection and may allow close
(25) approach before it flushes again.

Less frequently, undisturbed individuals have been seen wandering on the soil surface. Such wandering occurs chiefly at night. Diurnal wandering may occur in relatively cool weather when
(30) night temperatures are too low for the frogs to be active. Wandering above ground is limited to times when the soil and vegetation are wet, mainly during heavy rains and immediately afterward. Pitfalls made from gallon cans buried
(35) in the ground with tops open and flush with the soil surface were installed in 1949 in several places along hilltop rock outcrops where the frogs were abundant. The number of frogs caught from day to day under varying weather-
(40) conditions provided evidence as to the factors controlling surface activity. After nights of unusually heavy rainfall, a dozen frogs, or even several dozen, might be found in each of the more productive pitfalls. A few more might be
(45) caught on the following night, and occasional stragglers as long as the soil remained damp with heavy dew. Activity is greatest on hot summer nights. Below 20° C there is little surface activity but individuals that had body temperatures as
(50) low as 16° C have been found moving about.

Frogs uncovered in their hiding places beneath flat rocks often remained motionless, depending on concealment for protection, but if further disturbed, they made off with the
(55) running and hopping gait already described. Although they were not swift, they were elusive because of their sudden changes of direction and the ease with which they found shelter. When actually grasped, a frog would
(60) struggle only momentarily, then would become limp with its legs extended. The viscous dermal secretions copiously produced by a frog being handled made the animal so slippery that after a few seconds it might slide from the
(65) captor's grasp, and always was quick to escape when such an opportunity was presented.

GO ON TO THE NEXT PAGE

The following table shows the number of sites at which each frog species was heard per route taken by the surveyors. Chart adapted from www.michigan.gov.

Trends of Michigan Frogs and Toads 1996–2002			
Species	Mean (number of sites ÷ route)	Trend	95% Confidence Interval for Trend Value
Wood Frog	3.7	0.08	−0.74 to 0.90
W. Chorus Frog	4.8	0.16↑	−0.02 to 0.35
Spring Peeper	9.0	0.04	−0.16 to 0.24
N. Leopard Frog	1.2	−0.07	−0.24 to 0.11
Pickerel Frog	0.1	−0.01	−0.05 to 0.04
American Toad	4.1	−0.06	−0.59 to 0.47
E. Gray Treefrog	7.4	0.02	−0.49 to 0.53
Fowler's Toad	0.3	−0.16↑	−0.34 to 0.01
Cope's Gray Treefrog	0.2	−0.01	−0.51 to 0.49
Blanchard's Cricket Frog	0.1	−0.02	−0.09 to 0.06
Mink Frog	0.0	0.0	−0.02 to 0.02
Green Frog	6.1	0.06	−0.52 to 0.65
Bullfrog	1.4	0.08	−0.06 to 0.21

10. In line 6, "flushed" most nearly means

    A. embarrassed.
    B. chased.
    C. reddened.
    D. swatted.

11. The author mentions the frog's startle response (lines 8–11) to conclude that

    A. the frog is a very timid creature.
    B. the frog's hearing is acute.
    C. the frog has exceptionally sharp reflexes.
    D. the frogs are afraid of burrowing creatures.

12. Which choice provides the best evidence for the answer to the preceding question?

    A. Lines 3–4 ("Probably…surface.")
    B. Lines 8–11 ("On numerous…shelter.")
    C. Lines 11–13 ("Such…enemies.")
    D. Lines 18–19 ("The frog…ground.")

13. The passage indicates that the frog can escape, even when gripped in the captor's hand, by

    A. becoming limp and extending its legs.
    B. secreting a substance to make its skin spiky.
    C. hopping swiftly away.
    D. biting the captor's hand.

14. According to the passage, the frog is most likely to wander above ground

    A. on a dry, warm evening.
    B. on a cold winter's night.
    C. on a summer afternoon during a drought.
    D. on a warm, rainy night.

15. Which choice provides the best evidence for the answer to the preceding question?

   A. Lines 26–27 ("Less…surface.")
   B. Lines 47–48 ("Activity…nights.")
   C. Lines 51–55 ("Frogs…described.")
   D. Lines 56–59 ("Although …shelter.")

16. In line 44, "productive" most nearly means

   A. fruitful.
   B. creative.
   C. diligent.
   D. dynamic.

17. It can be inferred from the passage that moles, a species that digs extensive underground tunnels, are

   A. likely to be prey for the ant-eating frog.
   B. never found in the same habitat as ant-eating frogs.
   C. a species that might be an ant-eating frog predator.
   D. capable of using camouflage to elude predators.

18. According to the data in the chart, the species showing the most fluctuation in number of sites per route are

   A. the W. (Western) Chorus frog and the Fowler's toad.
   B. the Pickerel frog and the Mink frog.
   C. the Spring Peeper and the Green frog.
   D. the Wood frog and the Bullfrog.

Questions 19–28 are based on the passage below.

This passage is excerpted from Gloria Steinem's testimony before the Senate, Committee on the Judiciary, *The "Equal Rights" Amendment: Hearings before the Subcommittee on Constitutional Amendments of the Committee on the Judiciary*, 91st Cong., 2d sess., May 5, 6, and 7, 1970.

I hope this committee will hear the personal, daily injustices suffered by many women—professionals and day laborers, women housebound by welfare as well as by
(5) suburbia. We have all been silent for too long. But we won't be silent anymore.

The truth is that all our problems stem from the same sex-based myths. We may appear before you as white radicals or the
(10) middle-aged middle class or black soul sisters, but we are all sisters in fighting against these outdated myths. Like racial myths, they have been reflected in our laws. Let me list a few.

That woman are biologically inferior to
(15) men. In fact, an equally good case can be made for the reverse. Women live longer than men, even when the men are not subject to business pressures. Women survived Nazi concentration camps better, keep cooler heads in
(20) emergencies currently studied by disaster-researchers, are protected against heart attacks by their female sex hormones, and are so much more durable at every stage of life that nature must conceive 20 to 50 percent more males in
(25) order to keep the balance going.

Another myth, that women are already treated equally in this society. I am sure there has been ample testimony to prove that equal pay for equal work, equal chance for advance-
(30) ment, and equal training or encouragement is obscenely scarce in every field, even those— like food and fashion industries—that are supposedly "feminine."

A deeper result of social and legal injustice,
(35) however, is what sociologists refer to as "Internalized Aggression." Victims of aggression absorb the myth of their own inferiority, and come to believe that their group is in fact second class.

(40) Women suffer this second-class treatment from the moment they are born. They are expected to be, rather than achieve, to function biologically rather than learn. A brother, whatever his intellect, is more likely to get the
(45) family's encouragement and education money,

GO ON TO THE NEXT PAGE

251

while girls are often pressured to conceal ambition and intelligence, to "Uncle Tom."

Another myth, that American women hold great economic power. Fifty-one percent of (50) all shareholders in this country are women. That is a favorite male-chauvinist statistic. However, the number of shares they hold is so small that the total is only 18 percent of all the shares. Even those holdings are often (55) controlled by men.

Similarly, only 5 percent of all the people in the country who receive $10,000 a year or more, earned or otherwise, are women. And that includes the famous rich widows. The (60) constantly repeated myth of our economic power seems less testimony to our real power than to the resentment of what little power we do have.

Another myth, that children must have full-(65) time mothers.

The truth is that most American children seem to be suffering from too much mother, and too little father. Part of the program of Women's Liberation is a return of fathers to (70) their children. If laws permit women equal work and pay opportunities, men will then be relieved of their role as sole breadwinner. Fewer ulcers, fewer hours of meaningless work, equal responsibility for his own chil-(75) dren: these are a few of the reasons that Women's Liberation is Men's Liberation too.

Another myth, that the women's movement is not political, won't last, or is somehow not "serious."

(80) We are 51 percent of the population; we are essentially united on these issues across boundaries of class or race or age; and we may well end by changing this society more than the civil rights movement. That is an apt paral-(85) lel. We, too, have our right wing and left wing, our separatists, gradualists, and Uncle Toms. But we are changing our own consciousness, and that of the country.

Finally, I would like to say one thing about (90) this time in which I am testifying.

Women are not more moral than men. We are only uncorrupted by power. But we do not want to imitate men, to join this country as it is, and I think our very participation will (95) change it. Perhaps women elected leaders— and there will be many of them—will not be so likely to dominate black people or yellow people or men; anybody who looks different from us.

19. What is the speaker's purpose in this speech?

   A. To prove that women are superior to men

   B. To condemn acts of sexism and misogyny

   C. To advocate for passage of the Equal Rights Amendment

   D. To represent the Civil Rights movement

20. According to the speaker, what is the basis of women's issues in society?

   A. Discriminatory laws

   B. Lack of constitutional protection

   C. Male dominance

   D. Sex-based myths

21. The speaker claims she speaks for

   A. middle-class white radicals.

   B. professional black women.

   C. stay-at-home mothers.

   D. all women, regardless of race or social class.

22. In line 17, the word "subject" most nearly means

   A. someone treated or acted upon.

   B. the topic of discussion.

   C. a particular course of study.

   D. someone ruled by another.

23. The speaker explains "Internalized Aggression" (lines 36–39) as

    A. harmful stereotypes within a female sub-group.
    B. the self-fulfilling acceptance of inherent inferiority.
    C. a tendency to direct hostility toward oneself
    D. a second-class attitude that stems from aggression.

24. The speaker believes the myth of women's economic power stems from

    A. the 51 percent of female-controlled stock shares.
    B. the number of rich widows.
    C. male antipathy toward any female economic authority.
    D. female aggression in the business world.

25. Which choice provides the best evidence for the answer to the previous question?

    A. Lines 49–50 ("Fifty-one percent…women.")
    B. Lines 52–54 ("However…shares.")
    C. Lines 59–63 ("The constantly…have.")
    D. Lines 70–72 ("If laws…breadwinner.")

26. The speaker uses the term "Men's Liberation" (line 76) to

    A. mock the use of the phrase "Women's Liberation."
    B. declaim the advantages to men of equal rights for women.
    C. espouse more freedom for men.
    D. support the suggestion that men are freer than women.

27. Which choice provides the best evidence for the answer to the previous question?

    A. Lines 52–54 ("However…shares.")
    B. Lines 66–68 ("The truth…father.")
    C. Lines 70–72 ("If laws…breadwinner.")
    D. Lines 92–95 (But we…change it.")

28. In lines 84–85, the word "parallel" most nearly means

    A. distance.
    B. interval.
    C. configuration.
    D. comparison.

Questions 29–39 are based on the following passage.

This passage is adapted from a speech made on April 7, 2016, by Jessica Rich, Director of the Bureau of Consumer Protection (ftc.gov).

Digital marketing and consumer data are overtaking the era of TV, print, and radio advertising. From Facebook to YouTube, from text messages to tweets, timing and con-
(5) text are everything. Brands are looking to connect with the right consumer at just the right moment. To do that, they rely on a high-tech, personalized experience—one that uses detailed data about who consumers are, what
(10) they do, and where they go to make predictions about their likely behavior.

There's no question that consumers have benefitted enormously from this explosive growth. Every day, we encounter new products
(15) and services once left only to the imagination—smart cars, smart homes, wearables, smart-TVs, everything you can think of. Personalization can save us time and provide other conveniences. And for businesses, there
(20) are many new opportunities for innovative and cost-effective advertising.

But these changes also pose immense challenges for consumer protection. Today, commerce comes at us from every direction, at
(25) every minute—through the smartphones we

GO ON TO THE NEXT PAGE

carry with us everywhere and the many connected devices all around us. Data-driven predictions determine the information we receive and the offers we get. And, increasingly, con(30) sumers become the marketers, as they're enlisted in campaigns on social media to tout products and services to their friends and acquaintances.

Adding to these challenges, many of the (35) technologies that drive these advances now have small screens or no screens at all. And many of the companies that receive and use our personal information are behind the scenes, completely invisible to us. As a result, it's harder (40) to rely on some of the traditional tools we've all used to protect consumers, such as disclosures to avoid deception and privacy policies to describe data practices. And it's extremely hard for consumers to protect themselves.

(45) The FTC has made significant shifts in its consumer protection agenda to address these challenges. The FTC's goal is to make clear that despite and amidst the vast changes we're seeing in the marketplace, the fundamental (50) principles of consumer protection still apply: Tell the truth, the *full* truth. In your business decisions, weigh any harms you might impose on consumers very carefully. Don't help others deceive or harm consumers. These principles (55) are timeless, and we expect companies to abide by them across all of their business models—old and new.

Let me start with the topic of deceptive advertising. The rise of mobile and other new (60) platforms have provided a host of new ways to deliver advertising to consumers. To keep pace with these developments, the FTC has spent significant resources developing our investigatory tools and bringing enforcement actions (65) that involve new technologies. Today, I'll highlight three topics in particular—deceptive health claims, deceptive endorsements, and native advertising.

Deceptive health and safety claims have (70) been, and remain, one of the FTC's top enforcement priorities. These claims raise particular concerns because, if they're false, they

can cause real harm to consumers. Thanks (or perhaps no thanks) to the smartphone explo(75) sion, we're seeing these types of deceptive claims all over the mobile platform.

The second area that I want to highlight is deceptive endorsements. Today, everyone's a salesman—the doctor on TV, the blogger you (80) follow, your friends on Facebook. Given the ubiquity of reviews, blogs, and infomercials, we're seeing deceptive endorsements just about everywhere. For decades, the Commission has made clear—through its cases and Endorsement (85) Guides—that while testimonials and endorsements are a common and accepted form of marketing, there are certain rules you need to follow to make sure they're not deceptive. One is that if the person making the endorsement or (90) testimonial has been paid or has other material connections to the advertiser, you need to disclose that fact.

We have similar concerns about my next topic—native advertising—by which I mean the (95) use of formats that make advertising or promotional messages look like objective content. The Commission recently issued an Enforcement Policy Statement and accompanying guidance on native advertising. The policy statement (100) explains how established truth-in-advertising principles apply to different ad formats, including native ads that look like surrounding nonadvertising content. It affirms that ads and marketing messages that promote the benefits (105) and attributes of goods and services should be identifiable as advertising to consumers.

The takeaway for advertisers? When designing your marketing campaigns and hiring other companies to implement them, you must (110) make clear that advertising is advertising.

29. Which choice best describes the speaker's overall attitude toward personalization?

A. Appreciation
B. Ambivalence
C. Astonishment
D. Disdain

30. In line 11, the word "likely" most nearly means

   A. expected.
   B. pleasing.
   C. promising.
   D. plausible.

31. What function does the second paragraph (lines 12–21) serve in the passage as a whole?

   A. It acknowledges the positive ramifications of a phenomenon whose undesirable consequences will be enumerated later in the passage.
   B. It illustrates in detail the argument posed in the preceding paragraph.
   C. It gives a historical overview that serves to place the current situation in context.
   D. It advocates continuing a practice for which the passage provides mostly favorable data.

32. In line 22, the word "pose" most nearly means

   A. model.
   B. impersonate.
   C. question.
   D. present.

33. According to the passage, the speaker believes that privacy protection for consumers is difficult because

   A. consumers are constantly upgrading their technology.
   B. predictions are more and more likely to be data-driven.
   C. companies are operating out of public view.
   D. the technology marketplace is a virtual marketplace.

34. Which choice provides the best evidence for the answer to the preceding question?

   A. Lines 5–7 ("Brands…moment.")
   B. Lines 27–29 ("Data-driven…we get.")
   C. Lines 36–39 ("And many…to us.")
   D. Lines 54–57 ("These principles…new.")

35. When the speaker refers to "new platforms" in lines 59–60, she is talking about

   A. the raised area from which she is speaking.
   B. electronic hardware and operating systems.
   C. the policy of a political party.
   D. a public statement of principles.

36. According to the passage, which choice best describes the current situation in digital marketing?

   A. It will eventually be eclipsed as TV and print claim the larger share of the advertising market.
   B. Its operations are so deceptive that the FTC is no longer able to investigate and enforce protective rules.
   C. Because of insufficient revenue, it must rely on deceptive claims to boost sales.
   D. As an industry, it has not always strictly adhered to the principles of truth in advertising.

37. Which of the following best describes the steps the FTC has taken in response to current trends in digital advertising?

   A. It has shied away from addressing such an ethically questionable domain.
   B. It has increased fact-finding and policing resources.
   C. It has made significant cutbacks in consumer protection.
   D. It has relinquished its authority in favor of self-policing by the advertising industry.

GO ON TO THE NEXT PAGE

38. Which choice provides the best evidence for the answer to the preceding question?

   A.   Lines 22–23 ("But these…protection.")
   B.   Lines 29–33 ("And, increasingly… acquaintances.")
   C.   Lines 39–43 ("As a…practices.")
   D.   Lines 61–65 ("To keep…technologies.")

39. It can be inferred that the last paragraph of the passage is intended to be

   A.   a punishment for those advertisers who engage in deceptive practices.
   B.   an admonition urging the advertising industry to engage in transparency.
   C.   a highlight of the main points of the passage.
   D.   a reiteration of current trends in the digital advertising industry.

Questions 40–47 are based on the following two passages about the Arctic region.

Passage 1 is adapted from a White House report on the Arctic (Whitehouse.gov). Passage 2 is adapted from "An Unrecognizable Arctic" by Megan Scudellari (climate.nasa.gov).

Passage 1

While the Arctic region has experienced warming and cooling cycles over millennia, the current warming trend is unlike anything previously recorded. The reduction in sea ice
(5) has been dramatic, abrupt, and unrelenting. The dense, multi-year ice is giving way to thin layers of seasonal ice, making more of the region navigable year-round. Scientific estimates of technically recoverable conventional
(10) oil and gas resources north of the Arctic Circle total approximately 13 percent of the world's undiscovered oil and 30 percent of the world's undiscovered gas deposits, as well as vast quantities of mineral resources, including rare
(15) earth elements, iron ore, and infrastructure development in the region. As portions of the Arctic Ocean become more navigable, there is

increasing interest in the viability of the Northern Sea Route and other potential
(20) routes, including the Northwest Passage, as well as in development of Arctic resources.

For all of the opportunities emerging with the increasing accessibility and economic and strategic interests in the Arctic, the opening
(25) and rapid development of the Arctic region presents very real challenges. On the environmental front, reduced sea ice is having an immediate impact on indigenous populations as well as on fish and wildlife. Moreover, there
(30) may be potentially profound environmental consequences of continued ocean warming and Arctic ice melt. These consequences include altering the climate of lower latitudes, risking the stability of Greenland's ice sheet,
(35) and accelerating the thawing of the Arctic permafrost in which large quantities of methane— a potent driver of climate change—as well as pollutants such as mercury are stored. Uncoordinated development—and the conse-
(40) quent increase in pollution such as emissions of black carbon or other substances from fossil fuel combustion—could have unintended consequences on climate trends, fragile ecosystems, and Arctic communities. It is imperative
(45) that the United States proactively establish national priorities and objectives for the Arctic region.

The U.S. approach to the Arctic region must reflect our values as a nation and as a
(50) member of the global community. We will approach holistically our interests in promoting safety and security, advancing economic and energy development, protecting the environment, addressing climate change, and
(55) respecting the needs of indigenous communities and Arctic state interests. To guide our efforts, we have identified the several principles to serve as the foundation for U.S. Arctic engagement and activities.

(60) We will safeguard peace and stability by working to maintain and preserve the Arctic region as an area free of conflict, acting in concert with allies, partners, and other interested parties. This principle will include

(65) United States action, and the actions of other interested countries, in supporting and preserving international legal principles of freedom of navigation and overflight and other uses of the sea related to these freedoms, (70) unimpeded lawful commerce, and the peaceful resolution of disputes. The United States will rely on existing international law, which provides a comprehensive set of rules governing the rights, freedoms, and uses of the world's (75) oceans and airspace, including the Arctic.

We will make decisions using the best available information by promptly sharing—nationally and internationally—the most current understanding and forecasts based on (80) up-to-date science and traditional knowledge.

We will pursue innovative arrangements to support the investments in scientific research, marine transportation infrastructure requirements, and other support capability and (85) capacity needs in this region. The harshness of the Arctic climate and the complexity associated with developing, maintaining, and operating infrastructure and capabilities in the region necessitate new thinking on public- (90) private and multinational partnerships.

Passage 2

Though the effects of climate change may be most visible with ice and water, one of the most dramatic coming effects of global warming is on land, within the solid, cement-like perma- (95) frost beneath Alaska and Western Canada. Permafrost is layer upon layer of frozen soil, some of which has formed over thousands of years from compacted dead plants, and it is chock-full of carbon. There are an estimated (100) 1,700 billion metric tons of carbon tucked away in northern permafrost—more than twice the carbon currently in the atmosphere.

As the planet warms, permafrost thaws and releases portions of that carbon into the air, as (105) both carbon dioxide and methane (methane being a greenhouse gas twenty-two times more powerful at trapping heat than carbon dioxide).

Today, scientists are trying to identify when and how significantly that thawing will occur.

(110) "We're looking for harbingers of what could be a massive release of carbon from thawing permafrost soils of the high latitudes of the Northern Hemisphere," said Charles Miller, a NASA research scientist and the (115) principal investigator of the airplane-based mission Carbon in Arctic Reservoirs Vulnerability Experiment (CARVE).

With CARVE, NASA researchers are flying around the Alaskan Arctic in a small plane, (120) taking measurements of temperature, carbon dioxide, oxygen, and the amount of moisture at the ground level. In 2013, the CARVE team flew every day for two weeks per month from May until October, swooping low to take mea- (125) surements of the Alaskan surface to determine how fast and where the permafrost was melting. "We want to get into the mud—to record the most local signals that we can," Miller said. The project has already made one (130) sobering observation: There is more methane in the local air earlier in the year, and it is sustained longer throughout the summer, than current models expected.

What the CARVE team finds will help scien- (135) tists predict what might happen to permafrost in other parts of the globe, such as in Antarctica or the Andes Mountains. "Because we expect changes to happen largest and first in Arctic, the Arctic acts as an early warning system for (140) the entire planet," Miller said. Within a few decades, the Arctic will be unrecognizable to any explorers who had seen it in centuries past. Scientists are already seeing the signs.

40. The author of Passage 1 indicates that Arctic warming could have which positive effect?

A. Altering the climate of lower latitudes
B. Respecting the needs of indigenous people
C. Increasing recoverable gas and oil resources
D. Closing the Northwest Passage

GO ON TO THE NEXT PAGE

41. Which choice provides the best evidence for the answer to the previous question?

    A. Lines 6–8 ("The dense…year-round.")
    B. Lines 8–16 ("Scientific estimates… region.")
    C. Lines 16–21 ("As portions…resources.")
    D. Lines 26–29 ("On the…wildlife.")

42. In line 73, the word "comprehensive" most nearly means

    A. understandable.
    B. complete.
    C. legible.
    D. restrictive.

43. According to the author of Passage 1, "new thinking" (line 89) is needed because

    A. new laws must be written to deal with unexpected climate changes.
    B. the U.S. alone must deal with the entire problem of climate change.
    C. the ecosystem of the Arctic is complex and fragile.
    D. up-to-date scientists and traditional knowledge are inadequate to deal with the crisis.

44. According to the author of Passage 2, NASA researchers are determining the speed and location of permafrost melting by

    A. estimating degree of change using previous years' models.
    B. flying in low over the ground 14 days each month for 6 months.
    C. having ground teams take biweekly measurements.
    D. identifying thawing patterns in other locations such as Antarctica and the Andes Mountains.

45. In line 110, the word "harbingers" most nearly means

    A. streaks.
    B. announcers.
    C. details.
    D. indications.

46. Which of the following choices best states the positions of the two passages on the most serious effects of global warming in the Arctic?

    A. Passage 1 believes the most serious effects of global warming manifest themselves in the sea ice, while Passage 2 believes that the land effects are most dangerous.
    B. Passage 1 presents the argument that the increased navigability resulting from the reduction in sea ice offsets the detrimental effects of global warming, while Passage 2 expresses concern about the increase in permafrost.
    C. Passage 1 advocates addressing the ramifications of global warming piece by piece, while Passage 2 argues in favor of a holistic approach.
    D. Passage 1 predicts that the United States will take a leading role in safeguarding the delicate Arctic ecosystem, while Passage 2 contends that Arctic warming is a global problem requiring international partnerships.

47. Both passages explicitly refer to

    A. changes in the Arctic mud.
    B. the effect of global warming on fish and wildlife.
    C. the dangers of increased methane emissions.
    D. the viability of the Northern Sea Route.

IF YOU FINISH BEFORE TIME IS CALLED, CHECK YOUR WORK ON THIS SECTION ONLY. DO NOT WORK ON ANY OTHER SECTION IN THE TEST.

Section 2: Writing and Language Test

44 questions

35 minutes

Directions: The Writing and Language Test consists of a series of passages accompanied by a number of questions. As you answer the questions, think about how the passage may be revised to improve the expression of ideas, the grammatical constructions including mechanics and usage, the sentence structure, and the punctuation. Some passages will be accompanied by a chart or a graph to which you will refer as you answer the questions.

Some questions will ask you to consider an underlined portion; some will ask you to look at a specific location in the passage; and some questions will ask you about the passage as a whole.

Read each passage before you begin to answer the questions; then, look for the most effective and grammatically correct answer to each question. Many questions offer the option of NO CHANGE. If you think the most effective choice is to leave the underlined portion as it is, choose NO CHANGE.

Questions 1–11 are based on the following passage.

This passage was adapted from State of Michigan website (michigan.gov).

Understanding the Ecosystem

Ecosystems change over time. Even habitats that have been ☐1 damaged bad or destroyed may restore themselves, or new habitats may be created instead. Part of the process of habitat creation or restoration is the succession of plant communities. For example, ☐2 there are empty fields, many of which are visible along quiet county roads. Later, perennial plants invade, followed by shrubs and trees, which some day may make a forest. Natural disturbances may also cause the succession to move backwards, such as a fire returning a forest to bare ground.

As ☐3 lakes' age, over thousands of years they may fill with sediments and grow warm and shallow. Eventually cattails and other wetland plants may invade, and the lake could become a marsh, or swamp. Someday, it may turn into upland habitat and may later support a forest. Nothing remains static in the world, and that is why the composition of ecosystems ☐4 are always changing.

Many observers think of ecosystems as a hierarchical arrangement, where one system fits naturally within another. ☐5 Whereas, the rotting log ecosystem may be part of a larger complex of lowland evergreens, embedded in a northern hardwood forest ecosystem, ☐6 which stretches from Wisconsin to the southern Michigan ecosystem, all of which are modified by the Great Lakes ecosystem. Taken logically to its conclusion, planet Earth is an ecosystem. There are other ways to look at this fascinating phenomenon, too. Looking at cover types or wildlife habitats, for example, offers another ☐7 view through which to view ecosystems on the scale of landscapes. In this way, ecosystems can be wetlands, woodlands, grasslands, brushlands, or farmlands.

☐8 In Michigan, each part of the state is dominated by different landscapes, each of which functions differently, and will respond differently to management. Biologists and ecologists have divided Michigan into four major geographic ☐9 landscapes, the southern

GO ON TO THE NEXT PAGE

Lower Peninsula, the northern Lower Peninsula, the eastern Upper Peninsula, and the western Upper Peninsula.

In summary, ecosystems involve relationships between plant and animal communities and [10] it's environments. For this reason, everything in the natural world is part of an ecosystem. No ecosystem stands [11] alone. This is because it is part of a larger natural order to which it both contributes and is dependent upon. Learning to look at how your land fits into local neighborhoods, area landscapes, and regional ecosystems will help you to understand and appreciate your part of the big picture.

1. **A.** NO CHANGE
   B. damaged bad and destroyed
   C. damaging and destroying
   D. badly damaged or destroyed

2. Which choice provides the most logical and relevant detail?

   A. NO CHANGE
   B. a once-bare crop field left fallow for years will first support annual weeds and flowers
   C. sometimes a farmer will plant corn for several years and then will plant wheat
   D. shrubs and trees can spring up, filling in a once barren wasteland

3. **A.** NO CHANGE
   B. lake's age
   C. lakes age
   D. lakes aged

4. **A.** NO CHANGE
   B. is always changing
   C. are changing always
   D. are being changed

5. **A.** NO CHANGE
   B. In contrast,
   C. Yet,
   D. For example,

6. **A.** NO CHANGE
   B. who stretched
   C. that has stretched
   D. which stretch

7. **A.** NO CHANGE
   B. sign
   C. lens
   D. way

8. Which choice presents the best introductory sentence for this paragraph?

   A. Michigan offers scenic routes and hundreds of miles of trails for naturalists and nature lovers.
   B. Michigan is a Midwestern U.S. state bordering four of the Great Lakes.
   C. The entire planet Earth is an ecosystem.
   D. Ecosystems also vary geographically.

9. **A.** NO CHANGE
   B. landscapes: the southern Lower Peninsula
   C. landscapes; the southern Lower Peninsula
   D. landscapes. The southern Lower Peninsula

10. **A.** NO CHANGE
    B. its
    C. their
    D. there

11. Which choice most effectively combines the sentences at the underlined portion?

    A. NO CHANGE
    B. alone, which is the reason that it is part
    C. alone, being that it is part
    D. alone, as it is part

Questions 12–22 are based on the following passage and supplementary material.

This passage was adapted from Centers for Disease Control and Prevention (cdc.gov).

Are We Getting the Sleep We Need?

Sleep is increasingly recognized **12** for importance to public health, with sleep insufficiency linked to motor vehicle crashes, industrial disasters, and medical and other occupational errors. Unintentionally falling asleep, nodding off while driving, and **13** to have difficulty performing daily tasks because of sleepiness all may contribute to these hazardous outcomes. Persons experiencing sleep insufficiency are also more likely to suffer from chronic diseases such as hypertension, diabetes, depression, and obesity, as well as from cancer, increased mortality, and reduced quality of life and productivity. Sleep insufficiency **14** may have been caused by broad scale societal factors such as round-the-clock access to technology and **15** work schedules, sleep disorders such as insomnia or obstructive sleep apnea also play an important role. An estimated 50–70 million U.S. adults have sleep or wakefulness disorder. Notably, snoring is a major indicator of obstructive sleep apnea.

In recognition of the importance of sleep to the nation's health, CDC surveillance of sleep-related behaviors has increased in recent years. Additionally, the Institute of Medicine encouraged collaboration between CDC and the National Center on Sleep Disorders Research. **16** Two new reports on the prevalence of unhealthy sleep behaviors and self-reported sleep-related difficulties among U.S. adults provide further evidence that **17** insignificant sleep is an important public health concern.

The National Health and Nutrition Examination Survey (NHANES) introduced the Sleep Disorders Questionnaire in 2005 for participants 16 years of age and older. This analysis was conducted using data from the last two survey cycles (2005–2006 and 2007–2008) to include 10,896 respondents aged 20 years or younger. A short sleep duration **18** was found to be more common among adults ages 20 to 39 years (37.0%) or 40 to 59 years (40.3%) than among adults aged 60 years or older (32.0%), and among non-Hispanic blacks (53.0%) compared to non-Hispanic whites (34.5%), Mexican-Americans (35.2%), or those of other race/ethnicity (41.7%). Adults **19** whom reported sleeping less than the recommended 7 to 9 hours per night were more likely to have difficulty performing many daily tasks.

How much sleep we need varies between individuals but generally changes as we age. The National Institutes of Health suggests that school-age children need at least 10 hours of sleep daily, teens need 9 to10 hours, and adults need 7 to 8 hours. **20** Humans spend about a third of their lives sleeping, but some animals don't sleep at all. According to data from the National Health Interview Survey, nearly 30% of adults reported an average of less than 6 hours of sleep per day in 2005–2007. In 2009, only 31% of high school students reported getting at least 8 hours of sleep on an average school night.

(1) The promotion of good sleep habits and regular sleep is known as sleep hygiene. (2) First of all, go to bed at the same time each night and rise at the same time each morning. (3) Secondly, plan your mealtimes to avoid large meals shortly before bedtime. (4) There are significant choices we can make to improve sleep. (5) Finally, avoid caffeine, alcohol, and nicotine close to bedtime. (6) Changing these behaviors can lead to better sleep and better overall health. **21**

GO ON TO THE NEXT PAGE

22 **Self-Reported Sleep-Related Difficulties Among Adults ≥ 20 Years, 2005–2006 and 2007–2008**

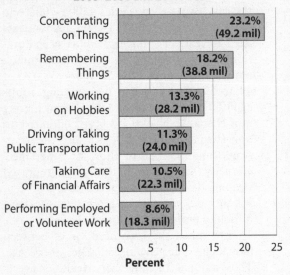

12. **A.** NO CHANGE
    B. as important to
    C. importantly as
    D. as importantly as

13. **A.** NO CHANGE
    B. difficulty having a performance of
    C. having a difficult performance of
    D. having difficulty performing

14. **A.** NO CHANGE
    B. may be causing
    C. may be caused by
    D. could have caused

15. **A.** NO CHANGE
    B. work schedules, and sleep
    C. work schedules, but sleep
    D. work schedules, hence sleep

16. At this point, the writer is considering adding the following information (omitting the period after "Research").

    > to support development and expansion of adequate surveillance of the U.S. population's sleep patterns and associated outcomes.

    Should the writer make this addition here?

    A. Yes, because it adds detail that clarifies the reason for the action in the first half of the sentence.
    B. Yes, because it acknowledges the role of sleep in maintaining good physical health.
    C. No, because it offers information that isn't relevant to the first half of the sentence.
    D. No, because it undermines the passage's claim about personal privacy.

17. **A.** NO CHANGE
    B. insufficient
    C. inordinate
    D. inevitable

18. **A.** NO CHANGE
    B. found
    C. were found
    D. is found

19. **A.** NO CHANGE
    B. whom are reporting
    C. who are reporting
    D. who reported

20. The writer is considering deleting this sentence. Should the writer make this change?

    A. Yes, because it introduces information that is irrelevant at this point in the passage.
    B. Yes, because it introduces information that is contradicted by the previous sentence.
    C. No, because it provides a smooth transition to the following sentence.
    D. No, because it provides a specific example in support of the central argument.

21. To make this paragraph most logical, Sentence 4 should be placed

    A. where it is now.
    B. after Sentence 1.
    C. after Sentence 2.
    D. after Sentence 5.

22. Which choice offers an accurate interpretation of the data on the chart?

    A. More than 5 million more people report having sleep-related difficulties working on hobbies than report having sleep-related difficulties driving or taking public transportation.
    B. The number of people who reported sleep-related difficulties taking care of financial affairs and performing employed or volunteer work is greater than the number of people who reported sleep-related difficulties concentrating on things.
    C. More people experienced sleep-related concentration difficulties than experienced all of the other difficulties combined.
    D. More people experienced sleep-related memory difficulties and difficulties performing employed or volunteer work than experienced sleep-related concentration difficulties.

Questions 23–33 are based on the following passage.

This passage was adapted from *Fundamental Change*, a publication of the U.S. Department of Education (www2.ed.gov).

Race to the Top

A strong education opens doors to opportunity, and all children with dreams and determination should have the chance to reach their full potential. With this recognition, in 2009, President Obama and the Department of Education announced a Race to the Top for American education.

The program offered unprecedented 23 resources—$4 billion, to states that committed to reshaping 24 its education systems and ensuring every student would graduate college- and career-ready, regardless of disability, race, zip code, or family income. 25 Because this program provided a larger sum of discretionary funding for education than had been available to states ever before, Race to the Top was not just about the money. It was about ensuring that every child in America—especially our most vulnerable—can thrive.

26 The program represented a groundbreaking approach to federal grantmaking. It called for the best ideas to improve teaching and learning from educators and leaders in states and communities throughout the country. The program enabled states and districts to expand upon effective and promising practices already in existence that were tailored to 27 one-of-a-kind, unique, local contexts.

In addition to building on what works, Race to the Top encouraged and supported state and local leadership on tough education reforms, which catalyzed deep thinking—and legislative activity—in states about improving how students are prepared for success in school and in life.

Even in states that did not win awards, the work to develop an application and establish the conditions for positive change unleashed an incredible amount of courage and creativity at the local level.

28 To break from a status quo that has traditionally denied disadvantaged students access to high standards, great teachers and leaders, and outstanding schools, an innovative, all-hands-on-deck approach is necessary. As a result, Race to the Top acknowledged the importance of collaboration 29 —from administrators, to teachers, to unions, to parents and communities, to elected officials.

Race to the Top asked a lot of states—from establishing rigorous student achievement standards, to developing and supporting teachers and leaders, to leveraging data

GO ON TO THE NEXT PAGE

systems to inform and enhancing instruction, to turning around the lowest-performing schools. But if we are to change the odds for our most vulnerable students and ensure a world-class education for every child, we must ask a lot $\boxed{30}$ of themselves. This work is complex and interconnected. And this work is far from done. Too many students, especially in underserved groups and communities, lack access to a quality education and supportive, well-resourced schools.

Despite the challenges, there are encouraging signs of progress. Over the course of the Obama $\boxed{31}$ administration's six years; America's schools' have experienced positive change—and America's students have made gains. The high school graduation rate is at the highest point ever recorded. Dropout rates are down sharply for low-income and minority students; and, since 2008, college enrollment for African-Americans and Hispanics has increased by more than a million.

Ensuring that all students can access life-changing opportunity through education will require sustained effort. $\boxed{32}$ The real lessons from Race to the Top will be measured. We will look at the program's long-term impacts on student learning. There is no silver bullet solution or singular approach to improving education; states are taking multiple paths, and they are learning from each other in this work.

Race to the Top demonstrated that teachers, principals, administrators and others were—and still are—eager to work urgently and collaboratively to solve their most pressing education challenges. At the federal level, our hope is that bold blueprints for education reform both inspired and supported by Race to the Top will continue to be implemented in states across America $\boxed{33}$ for the achieving of all students.

23. **A.** NO CHANGE
　　B. resources; $4 billion, to states
　　C. resources—$4 billion—to states
　　D. resources: $4 billion—to states

24. **A.** NO CHANGE
　　B. their
　　C. those
　　D. these

25. **A.** NO CHANGE
　　B. Unless
　　C. Since
　　D. Although

26. The writer wants to link the previous paragraph with this paragraph at this point. Which choice best accomplishes this goal?

　　A. Then and now,
　　B. Looking ahead to the future,
　　C. Considering the outcome,
　　D. Making hard choices,

27. **A.** NO CHANGE
　　B. one-of-a-kind, and unique, and local contexts
　　C. one-of-a-kind, local and unique contexts
　　D. unique local contexts

28. **A.** NO CHANGE
　　B. Breaking it from a status quo
　　C. If you break from a status quo
　　D. Taking a brake from a status quo

29. The writer is considering ending the sentence at this point and deleting the underlined portion of the sentence. Should the writer make this change?

　　A. Yes, because the information is not specifically relevant to the main focus of the sentence and paragraph.
　　B. Yes, because the information is redundant as it is included earlier in the paragraph.
　　C. No, because the underlined portion identifies those who engage in collaboration.
　　D. No, because the underlined portion explains why there is a need for collaboration.

30. **A.** NO CHANGE
    B. of ourselves
    C. about ourselves
    D. of himself or herself

31. **A.** NO CHANGE
    B. administrations six years', America's schools
    C. administration's six years, Americas' schools
    D. administration's six years, America's schools

32. Which choice most effectively combines the underlined sentences?

    A. We will look at the program's long-term impacts on student learning if we want to do the measuring of the impact of Race to the Top.
    B. Measuring the real lessons from Race to the Top, it will be necessary to look at the program's long-term impacts on student learning.
    C. The real lessons from Race to the Top, measured in the program's impacts on student learning, will be looked at in the program's long-term impacts on student learning.
    D. The real lessons from Race to the Top will be measured in the program's long-term impacts on student learning.

33. **A.** NO CHANGE
    B. so that all students can achieve
    C. and in this way it will be possible for all students to achieve
    D. making sure that achievement is possible for all students

Questions 34–44 are based on the following passage and supplementary material.

This passage was adapted from the website of the Department of Agriculture (blogs.usda.gov).

Hoopla about Healthy Eating

Squeals of excitement and laughter [34] competing with the sounds of power saws, drills, and hammers at the Hungry Valley Child Care Center in Sparks, Nevada, as Reno-Sparks Indian Colony (RSIC) teens were handed power tools [35] including power saws and drills to assist with building a hoop house, a polyethylene tunnel in which plants and soil are warmed by incoming solar radiation.

[36] Part of their life skills learning, the teens helped members of the National Association of Resource Conservation & Development Councils (NARC&DC) [37] who were attending their national conference in Reno, erect a 14′ × 26′ hoop house, with guidance from University of Nevada Cooperative Extension Federally Recognized Tribal Extension Program staff and assistance from United States Department of Agriculture's Natural Resources Conservation Service (USDA/NRCS). More than 70 youth employment workers, community volunteers, and education department staff were there to assist. [38]

"The purpose of this demonstration project is to highlight the efficiency and effectiveness of hoop houses and to show community members and historically underserved landowners [39] how easy and impactful installation of such a structure has in a producer's operations," said Andrew Gordon, executive director of NARC&DC. "This project is also designed to help our members learn about how to increase historically underserved community use of hoop houses from NRCS program participation through EQIP; recommended crops; agencies and organizations available to assist; and [40] other essential information to accommodate a successful hoop house grower experience."

"The demonstration project showed how hoop houses can improve food supply and extend growing seasons for producers," said

GO ON TO THE NEXT PAGE

San San Tin, the Reno-Sparks Indian Colony education manager. "The young children at the Child Care and Head Start programs will have an opportunity to learn healthy eating habits by growing 41 it's own fruits and vegetables in their garden. By being involved in the process of planting, nurturing, and seeing their fruits and vegetables grow, they will be more likely to try eating foods that are healthy."

42 According to the USDA: most American Indian reservations—including Hungry Valley, are located in areas with limited access to food. Furthermore, the United States Department of Health & Human Services reports that Native American diets and food practices have changed more (for the worse) 43 than any ethnic group in the United States. For about the last 200 years, most aspects of the lifestyles of Great Basin Native Americans have changed, including cooking and eating patterns.

For complex reasons, Native Americans have experienced high rates of poverty and unemployment, and families often struggle to put enough food, much less healthy food, on their table. One reason is that healthy and fresh foods tend to be more expensive and are often simply unavailable in low-income and rural communities.

"It is very important for Tribal members, young and old, to see that they can have an impact on what they eat," USDA StrikeForce West Regional Coordinator Sharon Nance said. "In Nevada, the StrikeForce Initiative for Rural Growth and Opportunity—which addresses specific challenges associated 44 with rural poverty's targeted at Tribes. So after conference attendees learned about StrikeForce efforts as part of their conference, it was great for them to then assist NRCS in placing a hoop house with a local Tribe to enrich their community."

Average Expenditures for Farmers Using Hoop Houses

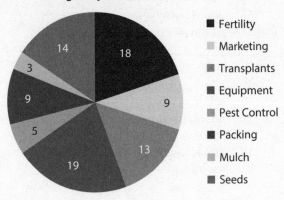

34. **A.** NO CHANGE
    B. competing against
    C. competed with
    D. competed for

35. The writer wants this detail to emphasize the newness of this experience for the teens. Which choice best accomplishes this goal?

    A. NO CHANGE
    B. which were handled with great care
    C. for the first time in their lives
    D. which they enthusiastically put to work

36. **A.** NO CHANGE
    B. As part of their life skills learning
    C. Learning of their life skills
    D. Being part of the life skills learning

37. **A.** NO CHANGE
    B. whom was attending
    C. whom were in attendance
    D. who was attending

38. At this point, the writer is considering adding the following sentence.

> This program also works with farmers to obtain clearances for pest control materials for use with specific crops.

Should the writer make this addition here?

   A. Yes, because it further explains the assistance provided by the USDA.

   B. Yes, because it introduces an important aspect of agriculture.

   C. No, because it distracts from the focus of the paragraph by adding irrelevant material.

   D. No, because it reiterates a point made earlier in the paragraph.

39. **A.** NO CHANGE

   B. how it is easy to install and impact

   C. that the installation can be both easy and impactful of

   D. the ease of installation and impact

40. Which choice most accurately and effectively incorporates the information on the chart?

   A. NO CHANGE

   B. associated costs

   C. likelihood of success

   D. profits to be made

41. **A.** NO CHANGE

   B. its

   C. our

   D. their

42. **A.** NO CHANGE

   B. According to the USDA, most American Indian reservations,

   C. Accordingly, to the USDA, most American Indian reservations,

   D. In accordance with the findings of the USDA, most American Indian reservations:

43. **A.** NO CHANGE

   B. then any ethnic group

   C. then any other ethnic group

   D. than any other ethnic group

44. **A.** NO CHANGE

   B. with rural poverty, is targeted at Tribes

   C. with rural poverty—is targeted at Tribes

   D. for rural poverty are targeted at Tribes

IF YOU FINISH BEFORE TIME IS CALLED, CHECK YOUR WORK ON THIS SECTION ONLY. DO NOT WORK ON ANY OTHER SECTION IN THE TEST.

Section 3: Math Test – No Calculator

17 questions

25 minutes

Turn to Section 3 of your answer sheet to answer the questions in this section.

Directions: For **questions 1–13,** solve each problem, choose the best answer from the choices provided, and fill in the corresponding circle on your answer sheet. For **questions 14–17,** solve the problem and enter your answer in the grid on the answer sheet. Please refer to the directions before question 14 on how to enter your answers in the grid. You may use any available space in your test booklet for scratch work.

NOTES:

1. The use of a calculator is not permitted.
2. All variables and expressions used represent real numbers unless otherwise indicated.
3. Figures provided in this test are drawn to scale unless otherwise indicated.
4. All figures lie in a plane unless otherwise indicated.
5. Unless otherwise indicated, the domain of a given function f is the set of all real numbers x for which $f(x)$ is a real number.

REFERENCE:

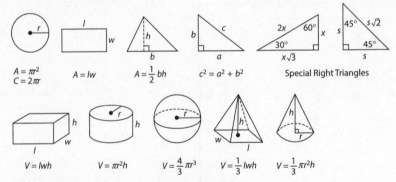

$A = \pi r^2$
$C = 2\pi r$

$A = lw$

$A = \frac{1}{2}bh$

$c^2 = a^2 + b^2$

Special Right Triangles

$V = lwh$

$V = \pi r^2 h$

$V = \frac{4}{3}\pi r^3$

$V = \frac{1}{3}lwh$

$V = \frac{1}{3}\pi r^2 h$

The number of degrees of arc in a circle is 360.

The number of radians of arc in a circle is 2π.

The sum of the measures in degrees of the angles of a triangle is 180.

1. Gretchen's cleaning service charges $50 per hour for a two-person team and an additional fee of $10 if the client requests hypoallergenic cleaning products. Assuming that you request hypoallergenic cleaning products, which of the following could you use to determine what you will pay to employ Gretchen's service for x hours?

   A. $50(x + 2) + 10$
   B. $50x + 10$
   C. $50x + (2 + 10)$
   D. $2(50x) + 10$

2. If $3a - b = -3a$ and $a \neq 0$, what is the value of $\dfrac{b}{a}$?

   A.   6
   B.   3
   C.   1
   D.   0

3. Which of the following ordered pairs (x, y) represents the solution of the system of equations below?

   $$\frac{1}{2}x + \frac{1}{3}y = 1$$
   $$x - \frac{1}{4}y = -\frac{7}{2}$$

   A. $(-2, 0)$
   B. $(4.4, -3.6)$
   C. $(4.4, 1.0\overline{6})$
   D. $(-2, 6)$

4. In $\triangle ABC$ below, $AB = BC$. Segment $\overline{BD}$ is the perpendicular bisector of side $\overline{AC}$, and segment $\overline{DE}$ is perpendicular to side $\overline{AB}$. $AE = 9$ and $AC = 30$. Find the length of $\overline{BD}$.

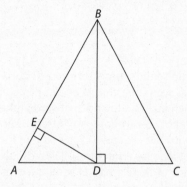

   A.   10
   B.   15
   C.   20
   D.   25

5. Juliana is planning an event at which each of the 100 people attending will be given either a water bottle or a coffee mug as a souvenir. She has determined that the two items are equally attractive to attendees. She can purchase water bottles for $2 each and coffee mugs for $2.50 each. If Juliana wants to spend her entire budget of $240 for exactly 100 souvenirs, how many of each item can she purchase?

   A.   80 water bottles and 20 coffee mugs
   B.   180 water bottles and 20 coffee mugs
   C.   180 water bottles and 100 coffee mugs
   D.   20 water bottles and 80 coffee mugs

GO ON TO THE NEXT PAGE

6. The quadratic equation $x^2 - 7x + 12 = 0$ has two solutions: $x = a$ and $x = b$. $a > b$ and neither solution is 0. What is the value of $2a + 3b$?

   A.   1
   B.   6
   C.   17
   D.   18

7. Justin's landscaping service will lay down grass seed for a charge of $25 per square foot, which includes the price of seed and the cost of labor. Elise's company offers a similar service but charges $15 per square foot for the seed plus a flat fee of $300 for labor. For which of these areas, in square feet, is Justin's service less expensive?

   A.   25
   B.   32
   C.   38
   D.   41

8. During a hurricane, meteorologists investigated the relationship between the average sustained wind speeds, in miles per hour, and the high tide levels, measured in feet. They described the relationship with the equation Tide Level = 0.1 × Wind Speed + 5.

   In this equation, what does 5 represent?

   A.   The speed of the wind during the storm
   B.   The number of feet the tide level increases for each 10-mph increase in wind speed
   C.   The tide level when there is no wind
   D.   The number of wind speed readings taken during the storm

9. The top of a beginner's ski slope is 525 feet higher than the base of the lodge. The slope is straight and drops 16 feet for every 100 feet a skier travels down its length. If Tammy can ski down the slope at 15 feet per second, how much higher than the base of the lodge is she k seconds after she leaves the top?

   A. $525 - 16k$
   B. $525 - 15k$
   C. $525 - 2.4k$
   D. $525 - 240k$

10. Given the function defined by $f(x) = 2 - 3x - x^2$, find $f(-1)$.

   A. $f(-1) = 4$
   B. $f(-1) = 6$
   C. $f(-1) = 0$
   D. $f(-1) = -2$

11. Simplify $\dfrac{a}{b}\left(ab - \dfrac{b^2c}{a} \right)$, assuming $a \neq 0$ and $b \neq 0$.

   A. $a^2 - c$
   B. $a^2 - bc$
   C. $a - bc$
   D. $a^2 - b^2c$

12. In the polynomial $p(x) = 2(x^2 - 5x + 3) - 2(k + x)$, k is a constant. If $p(x)$ is divisible by $2x$, find the value of k.

   A. -6
   B.   6
   C.   3
   D. -5

13. The graph of the equation $y = x^2 - bx + c$ passes through the point $(3, 2)$. If b and c are constants, which of the following must be true?

   A. $c = 3 - 2b$
   B. $c = 2b - 1$
   C. $c = 4 - 6b$
   D. $c = 3b - 7$

Directions for Student-Produced Response Questions (grid-ins): Questions 14–17 require you to solve the problem and enter your answer by carefully marking the circles on the special grid. Examples of the appropriate way to mark the grid follow.

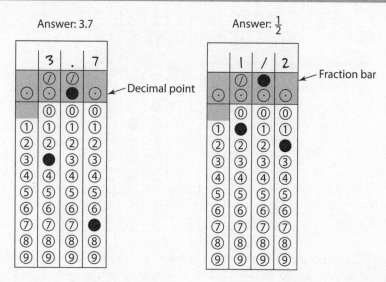

Do not grid in mixed numbers in the form of mixed numbers. Always change mixed numbers to improper fractions or decimals.

Answer: $1\frac{1}{2}$

GO ON TO THE NEXT PAGE

Space permitting, answers may start in any column. Each grid-in answer below is correct.

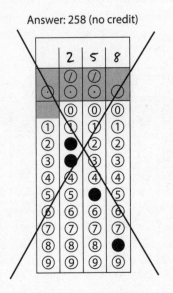

Note: Circles must be filled in correctly to receive credit. Mark only one circle in each column. No credit will be given if more than one circle in a column is marked. Example:

Always enter the most accurate decimal value that the grid will accommodate. For example, an answer such as .8888… can be gridded as .888 or .889. Gridding this value as .8, .88, or .89 is considered inaccurate and, therefore, not acceptable. The acceptable grid-ins of $\frac{8}{9}$ are:

Answer: $\frac{8}{9}$

Be sure to write your answers in the boxes at the tops of the circles before doing your gridding. Although writing out the answers above the columns is not required, it is very important to ensure accuracy. Even though some problems may have more than one correct answer, grid only one answer. Grid-in questions contain no negative answers.

14. For what value of z is $7 - \frac{z}{3} = -5$?

15. What is the value of x if $6(2 - x) - 3(2x + 1) = 5$?

16. If $a \neq 0$ and $b \neq 0$, what is the value of
$$\frac{(3a)^2 \, b^2}{18 (ab)^2} ?$$

17. If $x - 3$ is a factor of $x^2 + kx - 12k$, where k is a constant, what is the value of k?

IF YOU FINISH BEFORE TIME IS CALLED, CHECK YOUR WORK ON THIS SECTION ONLY. DO NOT WORK ON ANY OTHER SECTION IN THE TEST.

Section 4: Math Test – Calculator

31 questions

45 minutes

Turn to Section 4 of your answer sheet to answer the questions in this section.

Directions: For **questions 1–27,** solve each problem, choose the best answer from the choices provided, and fill in the corresponding circle on your answer sheet. For **questions 28–31,** solve the problem and enter your answer in the grid on the answer sheet. Please refer to the directions before question 28 on how to enter your answers in the grid. You may use any available space in your test booklet for scratch work.

NOTES:

1. The use of a calculator **is permitted.**
2. All variables and expressions used represent real numbers unless otherwise indicated.
3. Figures provided in this test are drawn to scale unless otherwise indicated.
4. All figures lie in a plane unless otherwise indicated.
5. Unless otherwise indicated, the domain of a given function f is the set of all real numbers x for which $f(x)$ is a real number.

REFERENCE:

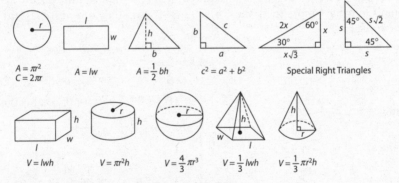

$A = \pi r^2$
$C = 2\pi r$

$A = lw$

$A = \frac{1}{2}bh$

$c^2 = a^2 + b^2$

Special Right Triangles

$V = lwh$

$V = \pi r^2 h$

$V = \frac{4}{3}\pi r^3$

$V = \frac{1}{3}lwh$

$V = \frac{1}{3}\pi r^2 h$

The number of degrees of arc in a circle is 360.

The number of radians of arc in a circle is 2π.

The sum of the measures in degrees of the angles of a triangle is 180.

1. Marco joins a gym that charges a one-time $5 membership fee and $10 per month for the use of the facility. Which of the following could be used to find the total amount, T, that Marco spends on the gym over x months?

   A. $T = 15x$
   B. $T = 5x + 10$
   C. $T = 10x + 5$
   D. $T = 10(x + 5)$

2. Each PTA member contributed 2 dozen cupcakes to the bake sale. The PTA sold individual cupcakes as well as multi-packs containing 4 cupcakes. At the end of the sale, all cupcakes had been sold and they found that they sold 80 individual cupcakes and 34 multi-packs. Which of the following calculations could be used to determine how many dozen cupcakes were contributed?

   A. $\dfrac{80 + 34(4)}{12}$

   B. $\dfrac{80(4) + 34}{12}$

   C. $80(4) + 34(12)$

   D. $\dfrac{80}{12} + 34(4)$

3. Traffic through a particular tollbooth is monitored on the weekdays. The changes in volume of traffic for one week are shown in the line graph below. The largest change for consecutive days, in absolute value, occurs between which two days?

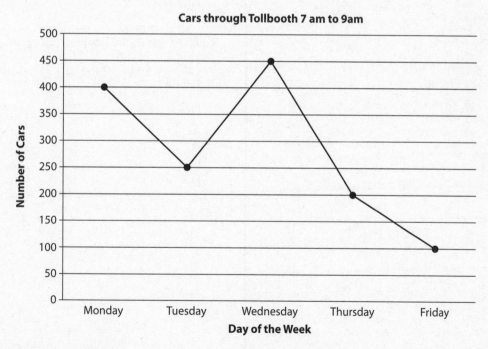

Cars through Tollbooth 7 am to 9am

Number of Cars / Day of the Week

   A. Monday to Tuesday
   B. Tuesday to Wednesday
   C. Wednesday to Thursday
   D. Thursday to Friday

GO ON TO THE NEXT PAGE

4. The area of a triangle can be found using the formula $A = \dfrac{1}{2}bh$, where A is the area of the triangle in square units, b is the length of the base, and h is the height measured perpendicular to the base. Which of the following gives a formula for the height of the triangle in terms of the area and the base?

A. $h = A - \dfrac{1}{2}b$

B. $h = \dfrac{A}{2b}$

C. $h = \dfrac{2A}{b}$

D. $h = 2Ab$

5. Which ordered pair represents the solution of the system of equations below?

$$3x - y = -10$$
$$x + 2y = 13$$

A. $\left(\dfrac{33}{7}, \dfrac{29}{7}\right)$

B. $(-1, 7)$

C. $(-6.6, 9.8)$

D. $(-7, 10)$

6. The school cafeteria buys ketchup in 5-gallon drums and repackages it in 2-ounce serving containers. What is the maximum number of serving containers that can be filled from one 5-gallon drum? (32 ounces = 1 quart; 4 quarts = 1 gallon)

A. 10

B. 80

C. 320

D. 640

7. Whitney's new car is claimed to travel 30 miles on a gallon of gas when driven at highway speed (usually 50 to 70 mph). If Whitney drives at 60 miles per hour and, at the end of the trip, finds she has used 11 gallons of gas, how many hours did she drive?

A. 2.7

B. 5.5

C. 11

D. 22

8. The slope of the line connecting the points $\left(\dfrac{1}{4}, \dfrac{1}{3}\right)$ and $\left(\dfrac{1}{2}, \dfrac{1}{k}\right)$ is $\dfrac{2}{3}$. Find the value of k.

A. 1

B. 2

C. 3

D. 4

9. Mr. Jensen's research team looked at 25 towns across the country. In each town, they determined the percent of residents with a college education and the percent whose annual incomes were below the national median income. The results of their research are shown in the scatterplot below. The point representing one town stood out from the rest because it fell significantly below the line of best fit (not shown). Which of the following is true about that town?

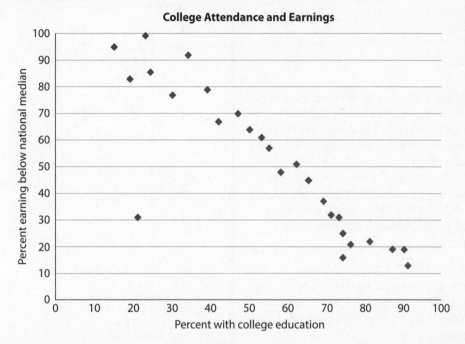

College Attendance and Earnings

A. 20% of the residents have a college education and 30% earn less than the national median income.
B. 30% of the residents have a college education and 20% earn less than the national median income.
C. 80% of the residents have a college education and 10% earn less than the national median income.
D. 20% of the residents have a college education and 80% earn less than the national median income.

GO ON TO THE NEXT PAGE

10. Exactly 51% of the voters in a recent city election voted for the incumbent mayor. Which of the following could be the total number of townspeople who cast votes in the election?

    A.   350
    B.   450
    C.   475
    D.   600

11. Each of the students who compete in athletics at the high school must have a physical exam by the school doctor. The doctor examines a set number of students each day until all have been seen. The equation below can be used to model the number of students, y, who still need physicals x days after the examinations begin. What does it mean to say that the ordered pair (7, 136) is a solution of the equation?

$$18x + y = 262$$

    A.   The doctor examines 7 students per day until 136 students have been examined.
    B.   After 7 days, 136 students still need to be examined.
    C.   It will take 7 more days to examine the remaining 136 students.
    D.   If 7 students are examined each day, it will take 136 days to complete the physicals.

12. Which of the scatterplots below shows an association that is linear and positive? (A positive association between two variables is one in which higher values of one variable correspond to higher values of the other variable.)

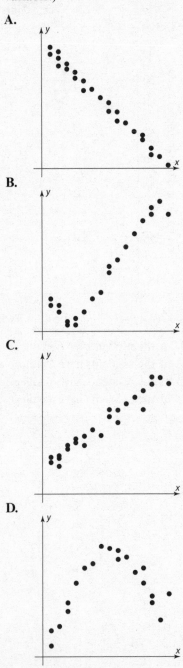

13. The histogram below shows the results of rolling a pair of dice 100 times and recording the sum of the numbers shown on the top surfaces. Which of the following could be the mean and the median of this distribution?

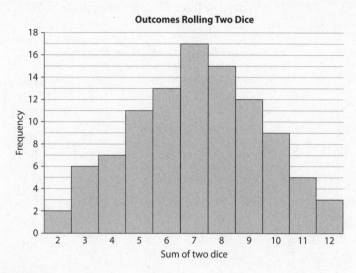

Outcomes Rolling Two Dice

A. mean: 7, median: 7
B. mean: 7, median: 10
C. mean: 10, median: 7
D. mean: 4, median: 10

Questions 14–16 refer to the following information.

A survey of 900 randomly selected adults aged 30 to 39 was taken to collect information about gender and education level. The data are shown in the table below.

Education and Gender			
	College Degree	No College Degree	Total
Male	212	130	342
Female	397	161	558
Total	609	291	900

14. Which of the following is closest to the percent of respondents who are women with a college degree?

A. 18%
B. 44%
C. 62%
D. 71%

15. The total population of the United States aged 30 to 39 in 2016 was 40,141,741. If the data from the survey were used to estimate information about this group of the population, which of the following is the best estimate of the number of men with no college degree?

A. 5,798,251
B. 7,180,911
C. 12,979,163
D. 17,932,737

16. Based on the survey data, if one person is chosen at random, how many times more likely is it that the person is a woman with a college degree than a man with a college degree? (Round to the nearest hundredth.)

A. 1.15
B. 1.24
C. 1.63
D. 1.87

GO ON TO THE NEXT PAGE

17. Melanie can purchase five different brands of rice in her local market. Brands A, B, C, D, and E are of equal quality but are packaged in boxes containing different numbers of servings at different prices per box. The graph below shows the number of servings in each box. The per-box prices are $1.70, $2.70, $7.70, $4.50, and $5.80 for brands A, B, C, D, and E, respectively. Which brand offers the lowest price per serving?

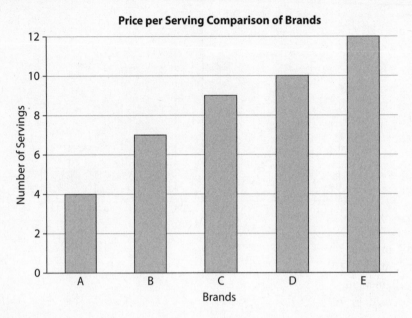

A. Brand A
B. Brand B
C. Brand C
D. Brand E

18. △*ABC* with altitude $\overline{BD}$ is shown below. If base $\overline{AC}$ is halved and altitude $\overline{BD}$ is doubled, how will the area of the resulting triangle compare to the area of △*ABC*?

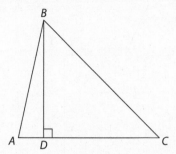

   A.   The area of △*ABC* is doubled.
   B.   The area of △*ABC* is unchanged.
   C.   The area of △*ABC* is cut in half.
   D.   The area of △*ABC* is divided by 4.

19. Celine began her clothing line by producing two dresses. In her first year, she manufactured 400 day dresses and 150 evening dresses. Her plan for year two is to increase production of day dresses by 75% and production of evening dresses by 20%. If Celine activates this plan, by what percent will her total production increase?

   A.   35%
   B.   55%
   C.   60%
   D.   95%

20. Jason used a random generator to produce 50 random integers between 1 and 10. The results are shown in the table below. Find the mean of the 50 integers.

Random Integer	1	2	3	4	5	6	7	8	9	10
Frequency	9	4	6	6	2	2	3	4	3	11

   A.   4.50
   B.   5.00
   C.   5.42
   D.   5.50

21. The function *f* has the graph shown below. What is the minimum value of the function on the interval $-2 \leq x \leq 2$?

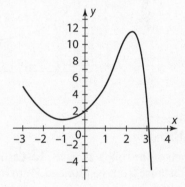

   A.   −5
   B.   −1
   C.   0
   D.   1

GO ON TO THE NEXT PAGE

Use the scatterplot and information below for questions 22–24.

The plot relates the distance of the planets (and dwarf planet Pluto) from the sun, measured in Astronomical Units (AU), to the orbital velocity of the planet in kilometers per second. An equation ($V = 29.731d^{-0.5}$) was determined to relate the distance, d, and the orbital velocity, V, and its graph has been added to the plot. (1 AU is approximately 150 million kilometers.)

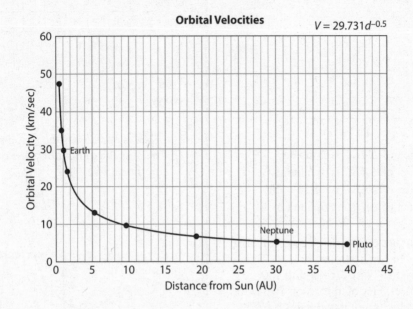

22. Which of the following is the best estimate of the distance from Neptune to Pluto in kilometers?

    A. 66,667 kilometers
    B. 15 million kilometers
    C. 1.5 billion kilometers
    D. 15 billion kilometers

23. The group of planets with orbital velocities greater than 20 kilometers per second have distances from the sun that are

    A. not more than 2 AU.
    B. more than 5 AU.
    C. not more than 10 AU.
    D. more than 30 AU.

24. Imagine that a planet were discovered to be orbiting our sun at a distance of 50 AU. Assuming the relationship described by the equation is valid for larger distances, what is the most reasonable prediction of the new planet's orbital velocity? (Round to the nearest hundredth of a kilometer per second.)

    A. 0.03
    B. 2.97
    C. 4.20
    D. 9.40

25. Carlos wants to create a garden along the side of his home, and he wants the length to be 1 foot more than twice the width. Because he is placing the garden at the side of the house, he only needs to fence three sides, one length and two widths. If he wants the garden to have an area of 78 square feet, how many feet of fencing will he need for the three sides?

    A. 25
    B. 32
    C. 55
    D. 78

26. In right triangle $\triangle RST$, leg $\overline{RS}$ measures 5 inches and leg $\overline{ST}$ measures 12 inches. Which of the following must be true?

    A. $\cos(\angle R) = \dfrac{5}{12}$

    B. $\sin(\angle R) = \dfrac{12}{5}$

    C. $\tan(\angle R) = \dfrac{5}{13}$

    D. $\sin(\angle R) = \dfrac{12}{13}$

27. The solution of the system of inequalities below can be represented by a shaded region on the graph.

$$3x - y \geq 5$$
$$2x + 3y \geq 18$$

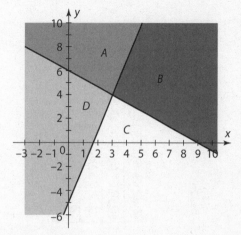

Which region or regions represent the solution of the system?

    A. A
    B. B
    C. A and B
    D. B and C

GO ON TO THE NEXT PAGE

Directions for Student-Produced Response Questions (grid-ins): Questions 28–31 require you to solve the problem and enter your answer by carefully marking the circles on the special grid. Examples of the appropriate way to mark the grid follow.

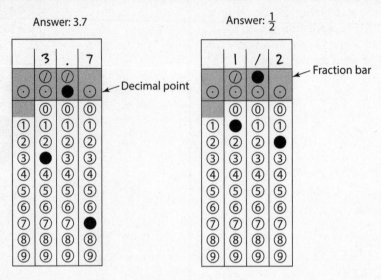

Answer: 3.7 — Decimal point

Answer: $\frac{1}{2}$ — Fraction bar

Do not grid in mixed numbers in the form of mixed numbers. Always change mixed numbers to improper fractions or decimals.

Answer: $1\frac{1}{2}$

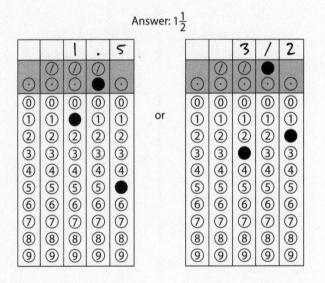

or

Space permitting, answers may start in any column. Each grid-in answer below is correct.

Answer: 123

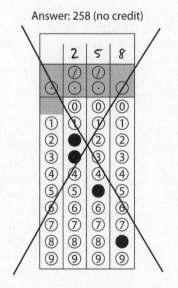

Note: Circles must be filled in correctly to receive credit. Mark only one circle in each column. No credit will be given if more than one circle in a column is marked. Example:

Answer: 258 (no credit)

GO ON TO THE NEXT PAGE

Always enter the most accurate decimal value that the grid will accommodate. For example, an answer such as .8888... can be gridded as .888 or .889. Gridding this value as .8, .88, or .89 is considered inaccurate and, therefore, not acceptable. The acceptable grid-ins of $\frac{8}{9}$ are:

Answer: $\frac{8}{9}$

Be sure to write your answers in the boxes at the tops of the circles before doing your gridding. Although writing out the answers above the columns is not required, it is very important to ensure accuracy. Even though some problems may have more than one correct answer, grid only one answer. Grid-in questions contain no negative answers.

28. The point $(3, -3.5)$ is the vertex of the parabola below. What is the value of t?

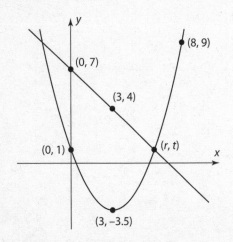

29. Mr. Caputo and Ms. Sand are taking 60 of their students on a field trip to the Museum of Art. The students will be divided into groups of seven or eight and each group must be accompanied by at least one adult. In addition to the two teachers, nine parent volunteers are available to accompany the students. If all the students are present and every one of the adults accompanies a group, how many groups can have two adults?

Use the following information for questions 30 and 31.

The area of a circle with radius r is $A = \pi r^2$.

The area of a rectangle with length l and width w is $A = lw$.

The area of an ellipse (oval) with major axis $2a$ and minor axis $2b$ is $A = \pi ab$.

30. As shown below, an ellipse is inscribed in a rectangle so that the sides of the rectangle are tangent to the ellipse. The area of the ellipse is 21π. If a and b are integers, what is the area of the rectangle?

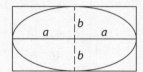

31. The area of a circle with radius of 4 divided by the area of an ellipse with major axis of 8 and a minor axis of 4 produces what number?

IF YOU FINISH BEFORE TIME IS CALLED, CHECK YOUR WORK ON THIS SECTION ONLY. DO NOT WORK ON ANY OTHER SECTION IN THE TEST.

Answer Key

Section 1: The Reading Test

1. C	13. A	25. C	37. B
2. B	14. D	26. B	38. D
3. D	15. B	27. C	39. B
4. A	16. A	28. D	40. C
5. B	17. C	29. B	41. B
6. A	18. A	30. A	42. B
7. C	19. C	31. A	43. C
8. D	20. D	32. D	44. B
9. B	21. D	33. C	45. D
10. B	22. A	34. C	46. A
11. D	23. B	35. B	47. C
12. C	24. C	36. D	

Section 2: The Writing and Language Test

1. D	12. B	23. C	34. C
2. B	13. D	24. B	35. C
3. C	14. C	25. D	36. B
4. B	15. C	26. A	37. A
5. D	16. A	27. D	38. C
6. A	17. B	28. A	39. D
7. C	18. A	29. C	40. B
8. D	19. D	30. B	41. D
9. B	20. A	31. D	42. B
10. C	21. B	32. D	43. D
11. D	22. D	33. B	44. C

Section 3: Math Test – No Calculator

1. B (HA)
2. A (PAM)
3. D (HA)
4. C (ATM)
5. D (HA)
6. C (PAM)
7. A (HA)
8. C (HA)
9. C (HA)

10. A (PAM)
11. B (PAM)
12. C (PAM)
13. D (PAM)
14. 36 (HA)
15. $\frac{1}{3}$ (HA)
16. $\frac{1}{2}$ (PAM)
17. 1 (PAM)

(HA) – The Heart of Algebra

(PSDA) – Problem Solving and Data Analysis

(PAM) – Passport to Advanced Math

(ATM) – Additional Topics in Math

Section 4: Math Test – Calculator

1. C (HA)
2. A (HA)
3. C (PSDA)
4. C (PAM)
5. B (HA)
6. C (PSDA)
7. B (PSDA)
8. B (HA)
9. A (PSDA)
10. D (PSDA)
11. B (HA)
12. C (PSDA)
13. A (PSDA)

14. B (PSDA)
15. A (PSDA)
16. D (PSDA)
17. B (PSDA)
18. B (PSDA)
19. C (PSDA)
20. C (PSDA)
21. D (PAM)
22. C (PSDA)
23. A (PSDA)
24. C (HA)
25. A (PAM)
26. D (ATM)

27. B (HA)
28. 1 (PAM)
29. 3 (HA)
30. 84 (PAM)
31. 2 (PAM)

(HA) – The Heart of Algebra

(PSDA) – Problem Solving and Data Analysis

(PAM) – Passport to Advanced Math

(ATM) – Additional Topics in Math

Answer Explanations

Section 1: The Reading Test

1. **C.** The passage depicts a chance encounter between Jane and an unknown man. The detailed description of the man and Jane's reaction to him suggest this meeting will be a significant one in her life, Choice C. The confrontation between Jane and the man doesn't suggest anything frivolous (Choice A), and it isn't violent (Choice B). Jane's lack of fear in the man's presence and her insistence on helping him suggest their relationship might include conflicts, but doesn't suggest a skirmish between forces of good and evil (Choice D).

2. **B.** Jane says the dog *ran up to me; it was all he could do,—there was no other help at hand to summon*, Choice B. None of the other choices are supported by the text.

3. **D.** Jane describes the stranger as having *stern features and a heavy brow* that looked *ireful*, Choice D. She does not describe him as good-natured (Choice A), classically handsome (Choice B), or elegant and gallant (Choice C).

4. **A.** The lines that provide evidence for the previous answer are lines 61–66 (*He had a dark face, with stern features and a heavy brow; his eyes and gathered eyebrows looked ireful and thwarted just now; he was past youth, but had not reached middle-age; perhaps he might be thirty-five.*). The other lines don't provide evidence to support the previous answer.

5. **B.** As it is used in line 42, the word *sound* most nearly means "not damaged," Choice B. The traveler checks his leg to see if it is injured. None of the other meanings are supported by the context.

6. **A.** As it is used in line 87, the word *station* most nearly means "position," Choice A. Jane stays in place, in the same position, when the traveler waves her away. None of the other meanings are supported by the context.

7. **C.** Jane responds to the traveler's grouchy dismissal of her help by standing her ground. She says she would have left if he had been more pleasant, Choice C. There is no indication her decision is based on his degree of injury (Choice A), his yelling at her (Choice B), or his insistence on her leaving (Choice D).

8. **D.** Lines 81–86 support the answer to the previous question (*If even this stranger had smiled and been good-humoured to me when I addressed him; if he had put off my offer of assistance gaily and with thanks, I should have gone on my way and not felt any vocation to renew inquiries…*), Choice D. The other lines don't provide evidence to support the previous answer.

9. **B.** Jane responds sympathetically to the traveler (*I cannot think of leaving you…*), but the traveler barely notices Jane (*he had hardly turned his eyes in my direction…*), Choice B. There is no evidence Jane is immediately infatuated (Choice A), nor is the traveler touched by her sympathy (Choice C). Jane isn't aloof and distant, and the traveler doesn't try to ingratiate himself (Choice D).

10. **B.** In line 6, *flushed* most nearly means "chased," Choice B. The frogs were chased from their shelters by the ground vibrations of the footsteps. There is no evidence that the frogs were embarrassed (Choice A), reddened (Choice C), or swatted (Choice D).

11. **D.** The author explains that the frogs *scuttle away* when they sense the vibrations of footsteps. He concludes that their fear of vibrations stems from their fear of burrowing predators, whose movements would cause vibrations. The frog may be timid (Choice A), but this isn't the conclusion stated in the passage. The frog's hearing acuteness (Choice B) and sharp reflexes (Choice C) are not discussed in the passage.

12. **C.** Lines 11–13 support the answer to the previous question (*Such behavior suggests that digging predators may be important natural enemies.*), Choice C. The other lines don't provide evidence to support the previous answer.

13. **A.** According to the passage, when the frog is grasped, it becomes limp and extends its legs so it might slip from its captor's grasp, Choice A. The frog's skin becomes slippery, not spiky (Choice B). The frog must slip out of the captor's hands before it can hop away (Choice C). There is no evidence that the frog bites the captor's hands (Choice D).

14. **D.** According to the passage, the frogs wander chiefly at night, mainly during rain, when it is not too cool, Choice D. Choice A is incorrect because the frogs prefer rainy nights. Choice B is incorrect because the frogs prefer warm nights. Choice C is incorrect because the frogs prefer wet nights.

15. **B.** Lines 47–48 support the answer to the previous question (*Activity is greatest on hot summer nights.*), Choice B. The other lines don't provide evidence to support the previous answer.

16. **A.** In line 44, *productive* most nearly means "fruitful," because these are the places where the frogs are most abundant, Choice A. There is no evidence that the pitfalls are creative (Choice B), diligent (Choice C), or dynamic (Choice D).

17. **C.** The most likely predators of the frog referred to in the passage are those that burrow, so moles might prey on ant-eating frogs, Choice C. Choice A is incorrect because there is no evidence in the passage that frogs eat moles. Choice B is incorrect because the habitat of the mole is not mentioned in the passage. Choice D is incorrect because the mole's use of camouflage is not mentioned in the passage.

18. **A.** According to the data on the chart, the Western Chorus frog (0.16) and the Fowler's toad (–0.16) show the most fluctuation in number of sites per route. None of the other choices can be supported by the data on the chart.

19. **C.** The speaker's main argument is that the passage of the Equal Rights Amendment is necessary to correct the social and legal injustices suffered by women, Choice C (note the introductory information that indicates she presented this speech at Senate "Equal Rights" hearings). While in this excerpt from a longer speech she doesn't specifically mention the Equal Rights Amendment, her argument is structured around debunking myths about women that prevent their having equal rights under the law. She doesn't try to prove that women are superior to men (Choice A); she doesn't condemn acts of sexism and misogyny (Choice B); and she doesn't attempt to represent the Civil Rights movement (Choice D).

20. **D.** In lines 7–8 the speaker states, *The truth is that all our problems stem from the same sex-based myths.* While the speaker may believe women are subject to discriminatory laws (Choice A), lack of constitutional protection (Choice B), and male dominance (Choice C), she doesn't specifically present any of these choices as the basis of women's issues.

21. **D.** The speaker uses language that indicates she speaks for all women (see lines 1–5). She doesn't speak only for middle-class white radicals (Choice A), professional black women (Choice B), or stay-at-home mothers (Choice C).

22. **A.** In line 17, the context indicates that *subject* most nearly means someone treated or acted upon: … *men are not subject to business pressures.* It doesn't mean the topic of discussion (Choice B), a particular course of study (Choice C), or someone ruled by another (Choice D).

23. **B.** The speaker explains the term *Internalized Aggression* as the belief of victims who accept the myth of their own inferiority, Choice B. It isn't a harmful stereotype within a female sub-group (Choice A), although it is harmful. It isn't a tendency to direct hostility toward oneself (Choice C) because it is an acceptance of inferiority, and it isn't a second-class attitude that stems from aggression (Choice D).

24. **C.** The speaker believes the myth of female economic power comes from male antipathy toward any female economic authority, Choice C. She explains that women may hold more shares of the market, but their shares are of lesser value than those of men, so Choice A is incorrect. Choice B is incorrect because rich widows who are part of the 5 percent of people who receive $10,000 a year have little economic power. She doesn't mention female aggression in the business world, so Choice D is incorrect.

25. **C.** The best evidence for the answer to the previous question is in lines 59–63, Choice C: *The constantly repeated myth of our economic power seems less testimony to our real power than to the resentment of what little power we have.* The other lines don't provide evidence to support the previous answer.

26. **B.** When the speaker says, *…Women's Liberation is Men's Liberation too,* she states that giving women their right to equal pay will free men from the responsibility of being the sole breadwinner in the family, thus pointing out the advantages to men, Choice B. She isn't mocking the use of the phrase "Women's Liberation" (Choice A) or espousing more freedom for men (Choice C); she believes they already have more freedom. While she does believe men are freer than women (Choice D), she doesn't use the term to support that suggestion.

27. **C.** The best evidence for the answer to the previous question is in lines 70–72: *If laws permit women equal work and pay opportunities, men will then be relieved of their role as sole breadwinner.* The other lines don't provide evidence to support the previous answer.

28. **D.** In lines 84–85, the word *parallel* most nearly means "comparison," Choice D. The speaker makes an apt (appropriate) comparison between the equal rights movement and the civil rights movement, pointing out the similarities between the two movements. The context indicates she doesn't use the word to mean distance (Choice A), interval (Choice B), or configuration (Choice C).

29. **B.** The speaker has mixed feelings about personalization. She says *consumers have benefitted enormously*, but the changes have come with *immense challenges for consumer protection.* The best choice to describe the speaker's attitude is ambivalence, Choice B. While she has some appreciation (Choice A), this isn't the best choice because it doesn't indicate her misgivings. She doesn't display astonishment (Choice C) or disdain (Choice D).

30. **A.** In line 11, the word *likely* most nearly means "expected" (Choice A) because the word is used to describe typical behavior. It doesn't mean pleasing (Choice B) or promising (Choice C) because the behavior may or may not be positive. It doesn't mean plausible (Choice D) because the context doesn't support the behavior being believable.

31. **A.** In the second paragraph, the speaker lists several benefits of the personalized experience, citing smart cars, smart homes, wearables, etc. Then, later in the passage, she discusses the undesirable consequences of personalization, making Choice A correct. The second paragraph doesn't illustrate the argument in the preceding paragraph (Choice B), or give a historical overview (Choice C), or advocate continuing a practice for which the passage provides mostly favorable data (Choice D). In fact, most of the remainder of the passage discusses the harmful ramification of personalized advertising.

32. **D.** In line 22, the word *pose* most nearly means "present" because the changes present challenges for the consumer, Choice D. The changes don't model (Choice A), or impersonate (Choice B), or question (Choice C) challenges for the consumer.

33. **C.** The speaker states that many companies that receive and use personal information are *invisible*, making it difficult to maintain privacy protection, Choice C. By operating out of public view, the companies evade the FTC overview. Choice A is incorrect because consumers upgrading their technology is not causing privacy problems. Choice B is incorrect because data-driven predictions don't cause privacy problems. Choice D is incorrect because the virtual marketplace doesn't cause problems with privacy protection.

34. **C.** The best evidence for the answer to the previous question is in lines 36–39, Choice C: *And many of the companies that receive and use our personal information are behind the scenes, completely invisible to us.* The other lines don't provide evidence to support the previous answer.

35. **B.** The *new platforms* the speaker refers to are new electronic hardware and operating systems, Choice B. The speaker refers to *the rise of mobile and other new platforms* as ways of delivering advertising to consumers. It is clear from the context that she doesn't refer to the raised area from which she is speaking (Choice A), or the policy of a political party (Choice C), or a public statement of principles (Choice D), although *platform* can have these meanings in a different context.

36. **D.** As the speaker enumerates different types of deceptive advertising, her belief that the advertising industry has not always strictly adhered to the principles of truth in advertising is apparent, Choice D. Choice A is incorrect because it is the opposite of what she says in the first sentence of the passage. Choice B is incorrect because the FTC is investigating and enforcing the rules. There is no evidence in the passage to support Choice C.

37. **B.** The speaker describes the actions of the FTC in response to the growth of deceptive advertising. The FTC has investigated (increased fact-finding) and brought enforcement actions against those found guilty of deceptive advertising, Choice B. It hasn't shied away from addressing these unethical practices (Choice A). It hasn't made cutbacks in consumer protection (Choice C). It hasn't relinquished its authority in favor of self-policing (Choice D).

38. **D.** The best evidence for the answer to the previous question is in lines 61–65, Choice D: *To keep pace with these developments, the FTC has spent significant resources developing our investigatory tools and bringing enforcement actions that involve new technologies.* The other lines don't provide evidence to support the previous answer.

39. **B.** The last paragraph suggests the speaker is warning the advertising industry to *make clear that advertising is advertising*. In other words, to be transparent about its intentions, Choice B. She doesn't suggest punishment (Choice A), highlight the main point of her speech (Choice C), or reiterate current trends (Choice D).

40. **C.** The author of Passage 1 indicates that melting sea ice has made the region more navigable year-round. This development means an increase in technically recoverable resources of oil and gas, Choice C. The author doesn't discuss the positive effect of Arctic warming on the climate of lower latitudes (Choice A); rather, this is presented as a challenge to the environment. The author discusses the importance of respecting the needs of the indigenous communities (Choice B), but not as a positive effect of Arctic warming. The author discusses the positive effect of opening, not closing, the Northwest Passage (Choice D).

41. **B.** The best evidence for the answer to the previous question is in lines 8–16: *Scientific estimates of technically recoverable conventional oil and gas resources north of the Arctic Circle total approximately 13 percent of the world's undiscovered oil and 30 percent of the world's undiscovered gas deposits, as well as vast quantities of mineral resources, including rare earth elements, iron ore, and infrastructure development in the region.* The other lines don't provide evidence to support the previous answer.

42. **B.** In line 73, the word *comprehensive* most nearly means "complete," Choice B. International law will provide a complete set of rules governing the Arctic. It doesn't mean understandable (Choice A); *comprehensible* means understandable. It doesn't mean legible (Choice C) because nothing in the context suggests the laws must be easy to read. There is no sense from the context that *comprehensive* means restrictive (Choice D).

43. **C.** The author states that *new thinking* is necessary because the Arctic ecosystem is fragile due to the harshness of the climate and the complexity of the infrastructure, Choice C. The author doesn't state that new laws must be written (Choice A); the U.S. will rely on existing international laws. Choice B is incorrect because the author specifically states that preserving the Arctic will be an international effort. Choice D is incorrect because nothing in the passage purports the inadequacy of up-to-date scientists and knowledge.

44. **B.** According to the passage, NASA researchers in a small plane fly low over the land, taking measurements every day for two weeks each month from May until October, Choice B. They don't estimate the change using previous years' models (Choice A). They don't take biweekly measurements (Choice C). They don't determine the speed and location of permafrost melting in the Arctic by identifying thawing patterns in other cold locations (Choice D). They use measurements from the Arctic to predict melting in these other regions.

45. **D.** In line 110, the word *harbingers* most nearly means "indications," Choice D. Scientists are looking for indications or signs of a massive release of carbon. They aren't looking for streaks (Choice A), announcers (Choice B), or details (Choice C).

46. **A.** Choice A best states the positions of the two passages on the most serious effects of global warming in the Arctic. Passage 1 focuses on the effects of melting sea ice, while Passage 2 focuses on the melting permafrost. Choice B is incorrect because while Passage 1 recognizes the positive effect of melting sea ice, this doesn't offset the dangers. Also, Passage 2 is concerned about the melting of permafrost rather than an increase in permafrost. Choice C is incorrect because Passage 1 advocates a holistic approach, while Passage 2 focuses on permafrost. Choice D is incorrect because the U.S. favors an international approach, while Passage 2 doesn't mention international partnerships.

47. **C.** Both passages refer to the dangers of increased methane emissions, Choice C. Passage 1 refers to methane as a *potent driver of climate change* (line 37), while Passage 2 identifies methane as a powerful greenhouse gas (lines 105–107). Choice A is incorrect because only Passage 2 refers to Arctic mud. Choice B is incorrect because only Passage 1 refers to fish and wildlife. Choice D is incorrect because only Passage 1 refers to the viability of the Northern Sea Route.

Section 2: The Writing and Language Test

1. **D.** The adverb *badly* (Choice D), rather than the adjective *bad* (choices A and B), is needed here to modify the adjective *damaged*. Choice C is incorrect because it changes the meaning of the sentence; the habitats aren't doing the destroying.

2. **B.** Choice B presents the most logical and relevant detail. Choice A is vague and without detail. Choice C brings in an irrelevant farmer. Choice D is redundant because shrubs and trees are mentioned in the next sentence.

3. **C.** Choice C is correct because it uses the plural *lakes*, rather than the possessive forms *lakes'* or *lake's*, and the correct verb form *age*. Choice A incorrectly uses the plural possessive form *lakes'*, and Choice B incorrectly uses the singular possessive form *lake's*. Choice D incorrectly uses the past tense form of the verb *aged*, which doesn't agree with the other present tense verbs in the sentence, *may fill* and *grow*.

4. **B.** Choice B is correct because it uses the proper singular verb form *is changing* to agree with the singular subject *composition*. Choices A, C, and D incorrectly use the plural verb form *are changing*.

5. **D.** Choice D is correct because it provides a transitional phrase, *For example*, that accurately represents the relationship between the two sentences connected by the transitional phrase. The rotting log ecosystem is an example of a hierarchical arrangement. Choices A, B, and C are incorrect because each provides a transition that doesn't accurately represent the relationship between the two sentences.

6. **A.** Choice A is the correct answer because it provides the correct pronoun *which* and the correct present tense of the verb *stretches*, which is consistent with the other present tense verbs in the sentence. Choice B uses the incorrect pronoun *who* to refer to an ecosystem and the past tense verb *stretched*. Choice C uses the incorrect present perfect tense *that has stretched*. Choice D incorrectly uses the plural form of the verb *stretch*.

7. **C.** Choice C is correct because it provides the best word to fit the phrase that follows it: *through which to view*. Choice A is illogical and redundant: *view through which to view*. Choices B and D are illogical in this sentence.

8. **D.** Choice D is the best introductory sentence for the paragraph because the paragraph explains and gives examples of the different landscapes in the state. Choices A and B aren't relevant to the content of the paragraph. Choice C is much too general.

9. **B.** Choice B is correct because it utilizes proper punctuation for items listed in a series. Choices A, C, and D are incorrect because they fail to recognize that the series should be preceded by a colon. Choice D also makes the items in the series into a sentence fragment.

10. **C.** Choice C uses the correct plural pronoun *their* to refer to *plant and animal communities*. Choice A incorrectly uses the contraction *it's*. Choice B incorrectly uses the singular pronoun *its*. Choice D incorrectly uses the adverb *there* instead of the pronoun *their*.

11. **D.** Choice D is the correct answer because it effectively combines the two sentences into a coherent and grammatically correct sentence. Choices A and B are unnecessarily wordy. Choice C uses the awkward phrase *being that*.

12. **B.** Choice B is correct because it provides a coherent and grammatically correct sentence. Choice A uses the awkward and idiomatically incorrect expression *for importance to*. Choice C uses an illogical comparison between sleep and public health. Choice D is also illogical because sleep isn't recognized importantly.

13. **D.** Choice D is correct because it utilizes a verb phrase that is parallel to the other verb phrases in a series (*falling, nodding, having*). Choice A uses a non-parallel infinitive, *to have*, instead of the gerund, *having*. Choice B uses illogical syntax (word order) that changes the meaning of the sentence. Choice C uses the awkward and illogical phrase *having a difficult performance of*.

14. **C.** Choice C is correct because it is in the present tense, the logical tense for the sentence. Choice A illogically uses the present perfect tense. Choices B and D change the meaning by making insufficiency cause societal factors.

15. **C.** Choice C is correct because it uses a comma and a coordinating conjunction to fix the comma splice error in the sentence. Choice A is incorrect because it is a comma splice error. Choice B also uses a comma and a coordinating conjunction, but *and* doesn't provide the correct logic that *but* provides. Choice D is incorrect because *hence* doesn't provide the logical transition between the two ideas in the sentence.

16. **A.** Choice A is the correct answer because the information provides a detail that clarifies the reason for the collaboration between the CDC and the National Center on Sleep Disorders Research. The other choices are inaccurate.

17. **B.** Choice B is correct because it uses the correct word choice; *insufficient* fits the meaning of the sentence better than *insignificant* (Choice A), *inordinate* (Choice C), and *inevitable* (Choice D).

18. **A.** No change is needed because the sentence is correct as it is. The other choices use incorrect verb forms or tenses.

19. **D.** Choice D is correct because it uses the nominative (subject) pronoun *who* rather than the objective pronoun *whom* (choices A and B). Choice C incorrectly uses the present progressive tense rather than the correct past tense.

20. **A.** The writer should delete the sentence because it is irrelevant at this point in the passage, and it interrupts the flow of the statistical evidence of sleep insufficiency. The other choices offer inaccurate or incorrect reasons.

21. **B.** Choice B is correct because Sentence 4 should come before all the choices *we can make to improve sleep*. The choices begin with Sentence 2, so the most logical placement for Sentence 4 is after Sentence 1. None of the other choices create a coherent sequence of ideas.

22. **D.** Choice D is correct because it is the only choice that represents an accurate interpretation of the data on the chart. Choice A is inaccurate because the difference is 4.2 million rather than *more than 5 million*. Choice B is inaccurate because the number of people who reported sleep-related difficulties taking care of financial affairs and performing employed or volunteer work (40.6 million) isn't greater than the number of people who reported sleep-related difficulties concentrating on things (49.2 million). Choice C is inaccurate because fewer people experienced sleep-related concentration difficulties (49.2 million) than experienced all of the other difficulties combined (over 100 million).

23. **C.** Choice C is correct because the *$4 billion* is an interrupter; an interrupter is set off, either by commas or by dashes, for a more dramatic effect. Choice A incorrectly uses the dash and the comma. Choice B incorrectly uses the semicolon and the comma. Choice D incorrectly uses the colon and the dash.

24. **B.** Choice B correctly uses the plural pronoun *their* to refer to the plural antecedent *states*. Choice A incorrectly uses the singular pronoun *its*. Choice C incorrectly uses the demonstrative pronoun *those* and Choice D incorrectly uses the demonstrative pronoun *these* rather than the possessive pronoun *their*.

25. **D.** The correct conjunctive adverb to fit the logic of the two clauses in the sentence is Choice D because a contrast is needed between providing a larger sum and the Race being not just about money. Choices A and C are incorrect because the two clauses don't have a cause-and-effect relationship. The relationship is not one of dependence, so Choice B is incorrect.

26. **A.** Choice A is the only transitional phrase that provides a link to show that the program is ongoing. Choice B is illogical because the paragraph is in the past tense. Choice C is incorrect because no outcome has been discussed. Choice D is incorrect because the paragraph is not about making choices.

27. **D.** Choice D eliminates the redundant wording *one-of-a-kind, unique*. All the other choices are redundant.

28. **A.** No change is needed because the sentence is correct as it is. Choice B includes the vague pronoun *it*. Choice C includes the unnecessary pronoun *you*. Choice D uses the incorrect homonym (a word that sounds the same but is spelled differently) *brake*.

29. **C.** The underlined information identifies the collaborators, which is relevant information. It doesn't explain why there is a need (Choice D), nor is it irrelevant (Choice A) or redundant (Choice B).

30. **B.** The subject of the sentence, the first person plural pronoun *we*, requires the first person plural reflexive pronoun *ourselves* (Choice B) rather than the third person plural reflexive pronoun *themselves* (Choice A) or the third person singular reflexive pronouns *himself or herself* (Choice D). Choice C uses the incorrect preposition *about*, which changes the meaning of the sentence.

31. **D.** Choice D uses the correct possessive form of the noun *administration's* and the correct use of the comma after *years*. Choice A incorrectly uses a semicolon after *years* and incorrectly adds an apostrophe to *schools*. Choice B incorrectly omits the apostrophe on *administrations* and adds one to *years*. Choice C incorrectly adds an apostrophe after the "s" in *Americas*.

32. **D.** Choice D most effectively combines the two sentences. Choice A uses the awkward phrase *if we want to do the measuring*. Choice B has a modification error: *Measuring* doesn't modify *it*. Choice C uses awkward and repetitive phrasing (*impacts on student learning* appears twice).

33. **B.** Choice B is correct because *so that* conveys the meaning of the relationship between implementation and achievement. Choice A uses the awkward phrase *for the achieving of all students*. Choices C and D are excessively wordy.

34. **C.** Choice C correctly uses the verb phrase *competed with* to create a complete sentence. Choices A and B are sentence fragments because the "ing" form of the verb cannot be used without a helping verb. Choice D uses the incorrect preposition *for*, which changes the meaning of the sentence.

35. **C.** Choice C best emphasizes the newness for the teens because it says *for the first time in their lives*. None of the other choices emphasize that this is a first-time experience for the teens.

36. **B.** Choice B corrects the awkward wording by adding the subordinating conjunction *As* to the beginning of the sentence. Choices A, C, and D are awkward or illogical.

37. **A.** The underlined portion is correct as it is. Choices B and C incorrectly use the objective pronoun *whom* rather than the nominative pronoun *who*. Choice D incorrectly uses the singular verb *was* rather than the plural verb *were* to agree with the plural subject *members*.

38. **C.** Choice C is correct; the writer should not add the information because it is irrelevant and detracts from the focus of the paragraph. It doesn't explain USDA assistance relevant to hoop houses (Choice A). Choice B is incorrect because the information about agriculture isn't relevant to this passage. Choice D is incorrect because it doesn't reiterate a point made earlier in the paragraph.

39. **D.** Choice D is the best choice because it creates a logical subject for the verb *has*: *the ease of installation and impact such a structure has in a producer's operations*. Choices A, B, and C change the meaning of the sentence by creating illogical syntax (word order).

40. **B.** Choice B most accurately and effectively incorporates the information on the chart. The chart presents information on the farmers' expenditures. Only Choice B refers to money spent by the farmers.

41. **D.** Choice D is correct because the plural possessive pronoun *their* is needed to refer to the plural subject *children*. Choice A incorrectly uses the contraction *it's*. Choice B incorrectly uses the singular possessive pronoun *its*. Choice C incorrectly uses the first person plural possessive pronoun *our*.

42. **B.** Choice B is correct because it uses the correct phrasing *According to the USDA* and correctly uses commas after *USDA* and after *reservations.* Choice A incorrectly uses a colon and a dash. Choice C incorrectly uses *Accordingly*. Choice D is wordy and incorrectly uses a colon after *reservations*.

43. **D.** Choice D uses the correct word *than* and the logical comparison *than any other ethnic group*. The word *other* is necessary; otherwise, you are comparing ethnic groups to themselves, as do choices A and B (which also incorrectly uses *then* rather than *than*). Choice C incorrectly uses *then* rather than *than*.

44. **C.** Choice C correctly uses the dash to set off the interrupting phrase (notice the dash earlier in the sentence). Choice A is a sentence fragment; there is no verb for the subject *StrikeForce Initiative for Rural Growth and Opportunity*. Choice B incorrectly uses a comma rather than a dash. Choice D omits the necessary dash and uses the incorrect plural verb *are* rather than the singular verb *is* to agree with the singular subject.

Section 3: Math Test – No Calculator

1. **B.** For x hours at \$50 per hour, you would pay \$$50x$. Then add \$10 for the hypoallergenic cleaning products. Your cost is $50x + 10$. (*The Heart of Algebra*)

2. **A.** Add $3a$ to both sides of the equation to get $6a - b = 0$. Add b to both sides: $6a = b$. Find the value of $\dfrac{b}{a}$ by dividing both sides by a: $\dfrac{b}{a} = 6$. (*Passport to Advanced Math*)

3. **D.** Multiply the top equation by 6 and multiply the bottom equation by 8. The system becomes:

$$3x + 2y = 6$$
$$8x - 2y = -28$$

Add the equations to get $11x = -22$, and divide by 11 to get $x = -2$. Plugging -2 in for x in the top equation gives you $-6 + 2y = 6$. Add 6 to both sides to get $2y = 12$, and divide by 2 to get $y = 6$. The solution is $(-2, 6)$. (*The Heart of Algebra*)

4. **C.** Segment $\overline{BD}$ bisects side $\overline{AC}$, so $AD = DC = 15$. $AE = 9$. Using the Pythagorean relationship in right triangle $\triangle AED$ will show that $ED = 12$:

$$AE^2 + ED^2 = AD^2$$
$$9^2 + ED^2 = 15^2$$
$$ED = \sqrt{225 - 81} = \sqrt{144} = 12$$

$\triangle AED$ is similar to $\triangle ADB$ or to $\triangle CDB$ and the scale factor is 9:15.

$$\frac{ED}{BD} = \frac{9}{15}$$
$$15 \cdot ED = 9 \cdot BD$$
$$15 \cdot 12 = 9 \cdot BD$$
$$BD = \frac{180}{9} = 20$$

(*Additional Topics in Math*)

5. **D.** Let W = number of water bottles and C = number of coffee mugs. In order to have one item for each attendee, $W + C = 100$, or $C = 100 - W$. To spend the entire $240, $2W + 2.50C = 240$. Substitute $100 - W$ for C in the budget equation: $2W + 2.50(100 - W) = 240$. Simplify to get $2W + 250 - 2.50W = 240$ or $-0.50W = -10$. Then divide by -0.50 to find $W = 20$. If she purchases 20 water bottles, Juliana will need 80 coffee mugs. (*The Heart of Algebra*)

6. **C.** $x^2 - 7x + 12 = (x - 4)(x - 3) = 0$ means $x - 4 = 0$ gives a solution of $x = 4$, and $x - 3 = 0$ gives a solution of $x = 3$. The larger value, 4, is a and 3 is b, so $2a + 3b = 2(4) + 3(3) = 8 + 9 = 17$. (*Passport to Advanced Math*)

7. **A.** Let x = the number of square feet to be seeded. Justin will charge $25x$ and Elise will charge $15x + 300$. To find out when $25x < 15x + 300$, subtract $15x$ from both sides: $10x < 300$, which means that $x < 30$. The only choice less than 30 is Choice A, 25 square feet. (*The Heart of Algebra*)

8. **C.** The 5 in this linear equation is the y-intercept, the value of y when $x = 0$. Choice A is incorrect. The wind speed occurs as a variable. Choice B describes a rate of change or slope. In this equation, that is 0.1. Choice D is irrelevant. (*The Heart of Algebra*)

9. **C.** Tammy's height above the base of the lodge starts at 525 feet and drops 16 feet for every 100 feet she skis. That looks like an equation of $h = 525 - 0.16d$, where h is how high she is and d is the distance she has skied. But the question asks you to relate the height to the time she has skied. Use her speed of 15 feet per second to convert. The distance she has skied is equal to the product of her speed and the time in seconds: $d = 15k$. The equation $h = 525 - 0.16d$ becomes $h = 525 - 0.16(15k) = 525 - 2.4k$. (*The Heart of Algebra*)

10. **A.** If $f(x) = 2 - 3x - x^2$, then $f(-1) = 2 - 3(-1) - (-1)^2 = 2 + 3 - 1 = 4$. (*Passport to Advanced Math*)

11. **B.** To simplify $\dfrac{a}{b}\left(ab - \dfrac{b^2 c}{a} \right)$, multiply using the distributive property: $\dfrac{a}{b}\left(ab - \dfrac{b^2 c}{a} \right) = \dfrac{a}{b} \cdot ab - \dfrac{a}{b} \cdot \dfrac{b^2 c}{a}$.

Cancel wherever possible: $\dfrac{a}{\cancel{b}} \cdot \dfrac{a\cancel{b}}{1} - \dfrac{\cancel{a}}{\cancel{b}} \cdot \dfrac{\cancel{b^2}^{\,b} c}{\cancel{a}}$. Multiply what remains: $a \cdot a - bc = a^2 - bc$. (*Passport to Advanced Math*)

12. **C.** First, simplify the polynomial by removing parentheses and collecting like terms:

$$p(x) = 2\left(x^2 - 5x + 3\right) - 2(k + x)$$
$$= 2x^2 - 10x + 6 - 2k - 2x$$
$$= 2x^2 - 12x + (6 - 2k)$$

The first two terms, $2x^2$ and $-12x$, are both divisible by $2x$, but $6 - 2k$ is not. This signals that the value of k must result in a constant term of zero. If $6 - 2k = 0$, then $2k = 6$, and $k = 3$. (*Passport to Advanced Math*)

13. **D.** If $y = x^2 - bx + c$ passes through the point (3, 2), then you can replace x with 3 and y with 2 in the equation. Substitute and simplify $2 = 3^2 - b \cdot 3 + c$ to get $2 = 9 - 3b + c$. Subtract 9 from both sides to get $-7 = -3b + c$. Then add $3b$ to both sides: $3b - 7 = c$. (*Passport to Advanced Math*)

14. **36** To solve $7 - \dfrac{z}{3} = -5$, subtract 7 from both sides to get $-\dfrac{z}{3} = -12$, and multiply both sides by -3.

$-3\left(-\dfrac{z}{3} \right) = -3(-12)$ yields z = 36. (*The Heart of Algebra*)

15. $\frac{1}{3}$ Begin by removing parentheses and combining like terms. Be careful of signs when distributing the –3:

$$6(2-x)-3(2x+1)=5$$
$$12-6x-6x-3=5$$
$$9-12x=5$$

Subtract 9 from both sides to get $-12x = -4$. Then carefully divide both sides by –12: $x = \frac{-4}{-12} = \frac{1}{3}$. *(The Heart of Algebra)*

16. $\frac{1}{2}$ To simplify $\frac{(3a)^2 b^2}{18(ab)^2}$, first clear parentheses: $\frac{(3a)^2 b^2}{18(ab)^2} = \frac{(3a)(3a)b^2}{18(ab)(ab)} = \frac{3^2 \cdot a^2 \cdot b^2}{18 \cdot a^2 \cdot b^2}$. Then cancel:

$\frac{3^2 \cdot \cancel{a^2} \cdot \cancel{b^2}}{18 \cdot \cancel{a^2} \cdot \cancel{b^2}} = \frac{9}{18} = \frac{1}{2}$. *(Passport to Advanced Math)*

17. **1** If $x - 3$ is a factor of $x^2 + kx - 12k$, then $x = 3$ is a zero. Therefore, $3^2 + k \cdot 3 - 12k = 0$. Simplify and solve:

$$9+3k-12k=0$$
$$9-9k=0$$
$$9=9k$$
$$k=1$$

(Passport to Advanced Math)

Section 4: Math Test – Calculator

1. **C.** The $5 membership fee is a one-time expense and the $10 fee is paid every month. The amount paid in monthly fees for x months is $10x$, to which the one-time fee is added, for a total of $T = 10x + 5$. *(The Heart of Algebra)*

2. **A.** The 34 multi-packs that were sold each contained 4 cupcakes, so the total number of cupcakes sold is $80 + 34(4)$. Divide that by 12 to find the number of dozens: $\frac{80+34(4)}{12}$. *(The Heart of Algebra)*

3. **C.** The change from Monday to Tuesday is $|400 - 250| = 150$. From Tuesday to Wednesday, the change is $|250 - 450| = 200$, and from Wednesday to Thursday, $|450 - 200| = 250$. The change from Thursday to Friday is only $|200 - 100| = 100$. Therefore, the largest change is Wednesday to Thursday. *(Problem Solving and Data Analysis)*

4. **C.** Multiply both sides by 2, and then divide by b, and $A = \frac{1}{2}bh$ becomes $2A = bh$ and then $\frac{2A}{b} = h$.

(Passport to Advanced Math)

5. **B.** You could test each point, but plugging those numbers into both equations would be time-consuming, even with a calculator. Instead, you can solve the system algebraically. To start, multiply the top equation by 2:

$$3x - y = -10$$
$$2(3x - y) = 2(-10)$$
$$6x - 2y = -20$$

Now, you can add the equations:

$$6x - 2y = -20$$
$$\underline{x + 2y = 13}$$
$$7x = -7$$
$$x = -1$$

You can substitute −1 for x to confirm that $y = 7$. See the Appendix for information on how to solve a system on your graphing calculator. (*The Heart of Algebra*)

6. **C.** 5 gallons = 5(4) = 20 quarts, and 20 quarts = 20(32) = 640 ounces. Divide 640 ounces by 2 ounces per container. They can fill 320 single serving containers. (*Problem Solving and Data Analysis*)

7. **B.** If Whitney used 11 gallons of gas, she traveled approximately 11(30) = 330 miles. She traveled at 60 miles per hour, so divide 330 by 60 to get 5.5 hours of driving. (*Problem Solving and Data Analysis*)

8. **B.** 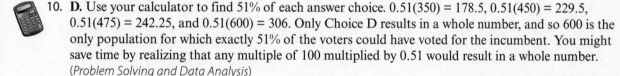 $m = \dfrac{y_2 - y_1}{x_2 - x_1} = \dfrac{\frac{1}{k} - \frac{1}{3}}{\frac{1}{2} - \frac{1}{4}} = \dfrac{\frac{3-k}{3k}}{\frac{1}{4}} = \dfrac{4}{1} \cdot \dfrac{3-k}{3k} = \dfrac{12-4k}{3k} = \dfrac{2}{3}$. Cross-multiply: $36 - 12k = 6k$. Solve for

k: $36 = 18k$ and $k = 2$. (*The Heart of Algebra*)

9. **A.** The outlier, the point standing most clearly away from the line of best fit, is the point at approximately (20, 30). This would be interpreted as 20% of the residents have a college education, and 30% earn less than the national median income. (*Problem Solving and Data Analysis*)

10. **D.** Use your calculator to find 51% of each answer choice. 0.51(350) = 178.5, 0.51(450) = 229.5, 0.51(475) = 242.25, and 0.51(600) = 306. Only Choice D results in a whole number, and so 600 is the only population for which exactly 51% of the voters could have voted for the incumbent. You might save time by realizing that any multiple of 100 multiplied by 0.51 would result in a whole number. (*Problem Solving and Data Analysis*)

11. **B.** x is the number of days the examinations have been going on and y is the number of students yet to be examined. The point (7, 136) indicates that after 7 days, 136 students have yet to be examined. (*The Heart of Algebra*)

12. **C.** Scatterplot A is a negative association; as x increases, y decreases. Plot B is not completely linear, and plot D appears to be quadratic. Plot C is linear and positive because y increases as x increases. (*Problem Solving and Data Analysis*)

13. **A.** The distribution of values is symmetric, and in a symmetric distribution, the mean and median will fall close together at the center of the distribution. If you need to calculate, remember the median is the middle value, and you should be able to estimate that the median will be 7. The height of the columns are the frequency with which the value occurs, and those for 2 through 6 ($2 + 6 + 7 + 11 + 13 = 39$) roughly balance those for 8 through 12 ($15 + 12 + 9 + 5 + 3 = 44$). Calculating the mean also uses the frequencies. Find the sum of $2(2) + 3(6) + 4(7) + 5(11) + 6(13) + 7(17) + 8(15) + 9(12) + 10(9) + 11(5) + 12(3) = 4 + 18 + 28 + 55 + 78 + 119 + 120 + 108 + 90 + 55 + 36 = 711$. Dividing by 100 gives a mean of 7.11. (*Problem Solving and Data Analysis*)

14. **B.** There are 397 women with a college degree out of the 900 subjects: $\frac{397}{900} = 0.44\overline{1} \approx 44\%$. (*Problem Solving and Data Analysis*)

15. **A.** In the survey of 900, there were 130 men without college degrees, or $\frac{130}{900} = 0.14\overline{4}$. Multiply and round to the nearest whole number: $0.14\overline{4}(40,141,741) = 5,798,251.478 \approx 5,798,251$. (*Problem Solving and Data Analysis*)

16. **D.** The probability that a person chosen at random is a woman who has a college degree is

$\frac{397}{900} = 0.44\overline{1} \approx 44\%$, and the probability that a random person is a man who has a college degree is

$\frac{212}{900} = 0.23\overline{5} \approx 24\%$. To find the number of times more likely it is that the person chosen will be a woman with a college degree than a man with a college degree, divide

$\frac{397}{900} \div \frac{212}{900} = \frac{397}{900} \cdot \frac{900}{212} = \frac{397}{212} \approx 1.873$. Round to the nearest hundredth to get 1.87. (*Problem Solving and Data Analysis*)

17. **B.** Divide each price by the number of servings to find the price per serving. Brand A: $\$1.70 \div 4 \approx \$0.43$; Brand B: $\$2.70 \div 7 \approx \$0.39$; Brand C: $\$7.70 \div 9 \approx \$0.86$; and Brand E: $\$5.80 \div 12 \approx \$0.48$. The lowest price per serving is $\$0.39$, Brand B. (*Problem Solving and Data Analysis*)

18. **B.** The original area of the triangle is $\frac{1}{2}(AC)(BD)$. If $\overline{AC}$ is halved and $\overline{BD}$ is doubled, the area

becomes $\frac{1}{2}\left(\frac{1}{2}AC\right)(2BD) = \frac{2}{4}(AC)(BD) = \frac{1}{2}(AC)(BD)$. The area of $\triangle ABC$ is unchanged. (*Problem Solving and Data Analysis*)

19. **C.** In her first year, Celine produced $400 + 150 = 550$ dresses. In year two, she will produce an additional $0.75(400) = 300$ day dresses and an additional $0.20(150) = 30$ evening dresses. That will increase her total production by 330 dresses, for a total of $550 + 330 = 880$ dresses. An increase of 330

compared to the original 550 is $\frac{330}{550} = \frac{3}{5} = 0.6$ or 60%. (*Problem Solving and Data Analysis*)

20. **C.** Your calculator will be helpful here. Multiply each value by its frequency and find the total. $1(9) + 2(4) + 3(6) + 4(6) + 5(2) + 6(2) + 7(3) + 8(4) + 9(3) + 10(11) = 9 + 8 + 18 + 24 + 10 + 12 + 21 + 32 + 27 + 110 = 271$. There are 50 numbers, so divide $271 ÷ 50 = 5.42$. (*Problem Solving and Data Analysis*)

21. **D.** Looking only from $x = -2$ to $x = 2$, the lowest point occurs when $x = -1$. The minimum value of the function is the y-value. The y-value of the function when $x = -1$ is $y = 1$. (*Passport to Advanced Math*)

22. **C.** The distance from Neptune to Pluto is approximately 10 AU. 1 AU = 150 million kilometers, so 10 AU = 1,500 million kilometers = 1,500,000,000 kilometers = 1.5 billion kilometers. (*Problem Solving and Data Analysis*)

23. **A.** Those data points that fall above the horizontal line representing an orbital velocity of 20 kilometers per second are the four points representing Mercury, Venus, Earth, and Mars. These four planets all fall between 0 and 2 AU from the sun. (*Problem Solving and Data Analysis*)

24. **C.** Assuming the relationship described by the equation is valid at a distance of 50 AU, then in the equation $V = 29.731d^{-0.5}$, replace d with 50 and evaluate:

$$V = 29.731(50)^{-0.5} = 29.731(0.141213562) ≈ 4.2045 ≈ 4.20$$

(*The Heart of Algebra*)

25. **A.** Let w represent the width of the garden and let the length $l = 2w + 1$. The area is $A = lw = w(2w + 1)$, and that area is to be 78 square feet. Solve to find w:

$$w(2w+1) = 78$$
$$2w^2 + w - 78 = 0$$
$$(2w+13)(w-6) = 0$$

$$2w + 13 = 0 \qquad\qquad w - 6 = 0$$
$$2w = -13 \qquad\qquad w = 6$$
$$w = -6.5$$

A negative width is not possible, so the garden is 6 feet wide and $2(6) + 1 = 13$ feet long. Fencing 3 sides, 2 widths and 1 length, will require $2(6) + 13 = 25$ feet of fencing. (*Passport to Advanced Math*)

26. **D.** It is helpful to make a sketch.

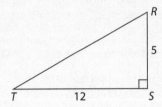

Use the Pythagorean theorem to find the length of the hypotenuse.

$$c^2 = a^2 + b^2 = 5^2 + 12^2 = 25 + 144 = 169$$

$$c = \sqrt{169} = 13$$

The question primarily tests your knowledge of the trigonometric ratios: $\sin(\angle R) = \dfrac{TS}{RT} = \dfrac{12}{13}$,

$\cos(\angle R) = \dfrac{RS}{RT} = \dfrac{5}{13}$, and $\tan(\angle R) = \dfrac{TS}{RS} = \dfrac{12}{5}$. Only Choice D is correct. (*Additional Topics in Math*)

27. **B.** You can check the lines graphed to see that they are accurate and to determine which line corresponds to each inequality. Checking intercepts can help in that process. The purpose of the question is to determine the direction of the shading. You could choose a point in each section to test in the two inequalities, but that will be time-consuming. Instead, in each inequality, isolate y. $3x - y \geq 5$ becomes $-y \geq 5 - 3x$ or $y \leq 3x - 5$. Don't forget that the direction of the inequality reverses when you divide by a negative number. The shading for this inequality will fall below the line. That puts it in region B and/or C. $2x + 3y \geq 18$ becomes $y \geq \dfrac{18 - 2x}{3}$ and the shading will be above the line, in region A or B. Only region B satisfies both inequalities. (*The Heart of Algebra*)

28. **1** There is enough information to determine the equation of the parabola, but it is not necessary to do so. The parabola is symmetric about its axis of symmetry, an imaginary vertical line through the vertex. The point $(0, 1)$ is on the parabola, so its mirror image across that axis of symmetry is the point $(6, 1)$, so $r = 6$ and $t = 1$.

If you don't spot that shortcut, you'll need to use the three known points on the parabola to find its equation. Start with $y = ax^2 + bx + c$. Replace x with 0 and y with 1, and you'll find $c = 1$. Then take $y = ax^2 + bx + 1$, substitute $x = 3$ and $y = -3.5$, and simplify to get $-3.5 = a(3)^2 + b(3) + 1$ or $9a + 3b = -4.5$. Repeat with the point $(8, 9)$ to get $9 = a(8)^2 + b(8) + 1$ or $64a + 8b = 8$ or $8a + b = 1$. Solve the system to find a and b.

Multiply the second equation in the system by 3 so you can subtract and solve for a:

$$
\begin{aligned}
9a + 3b = -4.5 &\rightarrow & 9a + 3b &= -4.5 \\
8a + b = 1 &\rightarrow & \underline{-24a - 3b} &= \underline{-3} \\
& & -15a &= -7.5 \\
& & a &= \frac{1}{2}
\end{aligned}
$$

Now substitute $\frac{1}{2}$ for a in the second equation and solve for b:

$$
8\left(\frac{1}{2}\right) + b = 1
$$
$$
b = -3
$$

The equation of the parabola is $y = \frac{1}{2}x^2 - 3x + 1$. Find the equation of the line using the points $(0, 7)$ and $(3, 4)$. The slope is $\frac{7 - 4}{0 - 3} = -1$ and the y-intercept is 7. The equation of the line is $y = 7 - x$. To find the point of intersection, solve $7 - x = \frac{1}{2}x^2 - 3x + 1$.

$$
7 - x = \frac{1}{2}x^2 - 3x + 1
$$
$$
\frac{1}{2}x^2 - 2x - 6 = 0
$$
$$
x^2 - 4x - 12 = 0
$$
$$
(x - 6)(x + 2) = 0
$$

$$
\begin{array}{ll}
x - 6 = 0 & \qquad\qquad x + 2 = 0 \\
x = 6 & \qquad\qquad x = -2
\end{array}
$$

It is safe to assume $r = 6$, not -2, and use the line to determine that $t = 1$. (*Passport to Advanced Math*)

29. **3** A group of 60 students can be divided into four groups of seven and four groups of eight, a total of eight groups. There are 11 adults, so three groups can have a second adult. (*The Heart of Algebra*)

30. **84** If the area of the ellipse is 21π, the product $ab = 21$, $a = 7$, and $b = 3$. The length of the major axis is 14 and the length of the minor axis is 6. The major axis is the length of the rectangle and the minor axis is the width. The area of the rectangle is $A = (14)(6) = 84$ square units. (*Passport to Advanced Math*)

31. **2** A circle of radius 4 has area $A = \pi(4^2) = 16\pi$. An ellipse with major axis of 8 and minor axis of 4 has $a = \dfrac{8}{2} = 4$ and $b = \dfrac{4}{2} = 2$. The area of the ellipse is $A = \pi ab = \pi(4)(2) = 8\pi$. The ratio of the area of the circle to the area of the ellipse is $\dfrac{16\pi}{8\pi} = 2$. (*Passport to Advanced Math*)

Scoring the Full-Length Practice Test

To calculate your score on the full-length Practice Test, add up the total number of questions you answered correctly for each section of the test:

The Reading Test	Number correct: _____
The Writing and Language Test	Number correct: _____
The Math Tests (total number correct on both math sections)	Number correct: _____

For your Reading and Writing score, look up the raw score for each section and find the converted score. Add the two converted scores (Reading Test + Writing and Language Test). Then, multiply that number times 10. That is your Reading and Writing score.

For your Math score, using the total number correct on Section 3 and Section 4, look up the raw score, and find the converted score. That is your Math score.

Raw Score (# of correct answers)	Converted Reading Test Score	Converted Writing and Language Test Score	Converted Math Test Score
48	38		760
47	38		760
46	37		750
45	37		750
44	36	38	740
43	36	38	740
42	36	37	730
41	35	37	730
40	35	36	720
39	35	36	710
38	34	35	690
37	34	34	680
36	33	33	670
35	32	32	650
34	31	31	640

33	30	31	630
32	30	30	620
31	29	30	610
30	28	29	600
29	28	29	590
28	27	28	580
27	27	28	580
26	26	27	570
25	26	27	550
24	25	26	540
23	25	26	530
22	24	25	520
21	23	25	510
20	23	24	500
19	22	23	490
18	22	22	480
17	21	22	470
16	20	21	460
15	20	20	440
14	19	19	430
13	18	18	420
12	18	17	400
11	17	17	390
10	17	16	370
9	16	15	360
8	16	15	340
7	15	14	320
6	14	13	290
5	13	13	270
4	12	12	240
3	11	11	220
2	10	10	210
1	9	9	190
0	8	8	160

Appendix: Using a Graphing Calculator

The graphing calculator is more and more commonly used in math classes, so you may have some experience with one before you take the PSAT. The use of calculators is permitted on one section of the PSAT, and you may notice that many of the questions in that section can be answered without a calculator, but a calculator is helpful. Although no question on the PSAT requires the use of a *graphing* calculator, it can also be helpful on the section where calculators are permitted. That doesn't mean you should run out to buy a graphing calculator if you don't already own one. You never want to go into the PSAT with a calculator that's new to you. Better to bring the scientific calculator you've used for years than waste test time trying to figure out how some new graphing calculator works.

Even with a familiar calculator, don't automatically assume the calculator is the best method for solving the problem. It will take time to type in the correct key sequence. Can you solve the problem more quickly without the calculator? Does the calculator really offer an advantage? It may, so be prepared to take that advantage, but don't unthinkingly grab the calculator every time. There are some questions for which the calculator, although permitted, is the more difficult method, and of course, a whole section in which the calculator is not permitted.

If you choose to bring a graphing calculator to the PSAT, spend some time before the test making sure you know the key sequences for common tasks. Different makes and models of calculators operate in different ways, and there isn't room in this book to explain all of them. This appendix will cover a few graphing calculator techniques that may help you solve several common types of problems. The examples here illustrate the commonly used graphing calculators in the TI-84 series. Before you take the PSAT, spend some time looking through these pages, making adjustments if your calculator is different.

A. Evaluate a Numerical Expression

You could do problems like this without a calculator, or with even the simplest of calculators. What the graphing calculator offers is the ability to type in the entire expression, as you see it.

1. Evaluate $[2(3 - 4 \cdot 2) - 7(-2)] \div 8$.

   A. 1.25
   B. 0.5
   C. 2
   D. −3

Calculator solution:

Although the problem uses square brackets as well as parentheses, you'll use parentheses for both on the calculator.

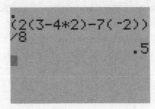

Correct answer: B

> TIP: Most calculators have a subtraction key and a negative number key. You want the subtraction before the 4 and before the 7, but the negative number key on the last 2.

2. The volume of a cylinder can be found using the formula $V = \pi r^2 h$, where r is the radius of the circular base and h is the height of the cylinder. Find the volume, in cubic centimeters, of a cylinder with a radius of 3 centimeters and a height of 8 centimeters.

   A. 24π
   B. 48π
   C. 72π
   D. 192π

Calculator solution:

Note that all your answer choices are in the form of an integer multiple of pi, so don't include your calculator's pi key in your calculation. $V = \pi r^2 h = \pi \cdot 3^2 \cdot 8$, but you just need to do $3^2 \cdot 8$ and tack on the pi. You can follow the 3 with the squaring key, usually labeled $\boxed{x^2}$, or you can type 3^2, or simply 3*3.

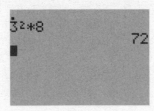

Correct answer: C

3. A function f is defined by $f(x) = 6 - 3x - 2x^2$. Find $f(-2)$.

   A. $f(-2) = -8$
   B. $f(-2) = 16$
   C. $f(-2) = 28$
   D. $f(-2) = 4$

Calculator solution:

Evaluating $f(-2)$ simply means replacing all the x's with -2 and simplifying. The question really is asking about order of operations, and your calculator knows the rules. To find $f(-2) = 6 - 3(-2) - 2(-2)^2$, enter $6 - 3(-2) - 2(-2)\text{^}2$. Note the use of the subtraction minus sign outside the parentheses and the negative number minus sign on the negative 2s inside the parentheses.

$$6-3(-2)-2(-2)\text{^}2$$
$$4$$

Correct answer: D

B. Evaluate Trigonometric Ratios and Functions

Once upon a time, values of trigonometric ratios like sine, cosine, and tangent had to be looked up in books of tables. Now there are keys on scientific calculators and graphing calculators to give you those values.

4. In right triangle $\triangle RST$, side $\overline{RS}$ measures 8 inches and $\angle RTS$ measures 30°. Find the length of hypotenuse $\overline{RT}$ in inches.

   A.   4
   B. $4\sqrt{2}$
   C. $4\sqrt{3}$
   D.   16

Calculator solution:

If you know the special right triangle relationships, this question doesn't need a calculator at all, but if you're tackling it with just a basic knowledge of right triangle trig, your calculator can help. Again, a scientific calculator would do the job, but the graphing calculator gives you the ability to type in the calculation all at once. Sketch the triangle, set up the basic relationship, and isolate your variable.

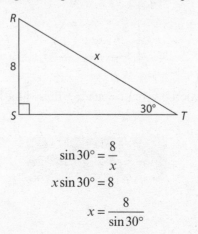

$$\sin 30° = \frac{8}{x}$$
$$x \sin 30° = 8$$
$$x = \frac{8}{\sin 30°}$$

Then you can use your calculator to find your solution.

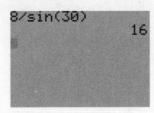

Correct answer: D

5. In right triangle $\triangle ABC$, leg $\overline{AB}$ is 18 centimeters and leg $\overline{BC}$ is 10 centimeters. To the nearest degree, what is the measure of $\angle C$?

   A. 29°
   B. 32°
   C. 57°
   D. 61°

Calculator solution:
Draw and label a sketch and set up the basic relationship: $\tan \angle C = \dfrac{18}{10}$. You need to find the measurement of the angle whose tangent is 1.8.

You can use the inverse tangent function on your calculator. Press $\boxed{\text{2nd}}$, $\boxed{\text{tan}}$, 18 $\boxed{\div}$ 10, $\boxed{)}$, $\boxed{\text{ENTER}}$. Round to 61°.

tan⁻¹(18/10)
          60.9453959

Correct answer: D

6. If $f(x) = \cos(x)$, where x is measured in degrees, what is the value of x when $f(x) = \dfrac{\sqrt{2}}{2}$?

   A. 30°
   B. 45°
   C. 60°
   D. 90°

Calculator solution:

This question is asking you to solve $\cos(x) = \dfrac{\sqrt{2}}{2}$. Here again you can use the inverse trig function. Press [2nd], [cos], $\sqrt{(}$ 2) [÷] 2, [)], [ENTER].

Correct answer: B

> **TIP:** When entering the division of $\sqrt{2}$ by 2, be sure to close the parentheses before the division sign. If your calculator gives you a box under the radical to type in, make sure you move out of that box before you type the division sign. If not, you'll get $\sqrt{2/2}$ or $\sqrt{\dfrac{2}{2}}$, which is 1.

C. Perform Arithmetic with Complex Numbers

Complex numbers are built from the imaginary unit, which is defined to be $i = \sqrt{-1}$. Depending on what math courses you've taken before the PSAT, you may or may not be comfortable working with complex numbers. Even if all you know is that $i = \sqrt{-1}$, you could make that substitution and then work your way through the question, but that will take time. Examine the keyboard of your calculator carefully and you should find, probably as a second function above a key, an i, which will help you get through any complex-number questions. On the TI-84, it's [2nd][.] and you can use it like any number or variable.

7. Find the simplest form of $i + i^2 + i^3 + i^4$.

   A. $i + 1$
   B. 1
   C. −1
   D. 0

Calculator solution:

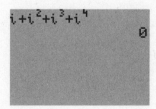

Correct answer: D

8. Which of the following products is a real number?

    A. $(2 + 3i)(3 - i)$

    B. $(2 + 3i)(4 - 6i)$

    C. $(2 - 6i)(4 - 3i)$

    D. $(2 + 3i)(3 - 2i)$

Calculator solution:

If you looked at the answer choices and pretended that i was a variable, you'd probably figure out that you need to use the FOIL method, but the "real number" part of the question points to the fact that, although i is an imaginary number, $i^2 = -1$, which makes it a real number. You're looking for the product in which the i disappears. The calculator can help.

```
(2+3i)(3-i)
                9+7i
(2+3i)(4-6i)
                  26
(2-6i)(4-3i)
             -10-30i
(2+3i)(3-2i)
              12+5i
```

Correct answer: B

9. $\dfrac{4 + 6i}{1 - i} =$

    A. $-1 + 5i$

    B. $-3 + 2i$

    C. -1

    D. 5

Calculator solution:

Dividing complex numbers is really about rationalizing the denominator, but the calculator will do the work whether you know that or not.

```
(4+6i)/(1-i)
               -1+5i
```

Correct answer: A

> **TIP:** When entering a division in which the numerator or denominator (or both) have more than one term, make certain both the numerator and denominator are enclosed in parentheses. In the question above, omitting parentheses would change the calculation to $4 + 6i /1 - i$, or simply $4 + 6i - i = 4 + 5i$.

D. Solve an Equation Using Zeros (*x*-intercepts)

There are several ways you can solve an equation using a graphing calculator. One is to move all the terms of the equation to one side, equal to zero. Enter the non-zero side of the equation in a Y= slot as an equation to graph. The solution of the equation, the value that makes the left side equal zero, is the *x*-intercept of the graph. It's important that you set an appropriate window to let you see where the *x*-intercept is.

10. What is the value of t in the equation $\dfrac{t}{5} - \dfrac{t}{3} = 2 + \dfrac{t}{15}$?

    A. $t = -\dfrac{2}{3}$

    B. $t = -10$

    C. $t = -1$

    D. $t = \dfrac{60}{13}$

<u>Calculator solution:</u>
Move all terms to one side.

$$\frac{t}{5} - \frac{t}{3} = 2 + \frac{t}{15}$$

$$\frac{t}{5} - \frac{t}{3} - 2 - \frac{t}{15} = 0$$

Enter the non-zero side of the equation in a Y= slot as an equation to graph. You will probably have to use *x* as your variable rather than *t*, but that won't affect the solution.

The solution of the equation, the value that makes the left side equal zero, is the *x*-intercept of the graph. It's important that you set an appropriate window to let you see where the *x*-intercept is. Use your answer choices to help you set a reasonable window. Based on the answer choices, you'll need to see the *x*-axis down to at least –10 and up to about 5.

```
WINDOW
 Xmin=-15
 Xmax=5
 Xscl=1
 Ymin=-1
 Ymax=1
 Yscl=1
↓Xres=1
```

Your answer choices will also help you decide if you can judge that intercept by sight or need to use the intercept tool on the calculator. For this question, it would seem safe to just eyeball it, but if you needed more help, here's the typical sequence on a TI calculator.

1. Press [2nd], then [TRACE] and choose 2: ZERO from the menu.

2. Move your cursor to the left of the intercept and press [ENTER]. A small arrow will appear to mark the spot.

3. Move the cursor to the right of the intercept and press $\boxed{\text{ENTER}}$. Another arrow will appear.

4. You'll be asked to guess, by moving your cursor closer to the intercept, and then hit $\boxed{\text{ENTER}}$. The coordinates of the intercept will appear at the bottom of the screen.

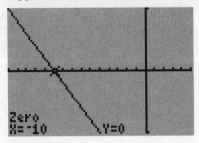

Correct answer: B

11. If $f(x) = 3 - \sqrt{x+4}$, for what value of a does $f(a) = 0$?

    A. 3
    B. 5
    C. 7
    D. 9

<u>**Calculator solution:**</u>
The real zeros of a function are the x-intercepts of its graph, the values of the variable that make the function equal zero. Graph $Y1 = 3 - \sqrt{X+4}$ and find the x-intercept.

Press $\boxed{\text{2nd}}$, then $\boxed{\text{TRACE}}$, and choose 2: ZERO. Move the cursor to the left of the intercept and press $\boxed{\text{ENTER}}$. Move the cursor to the right of the intercept and press $\boxed{\text{ENTER}}$. Guess, then press $\boxed{\text{ENTER}}$.

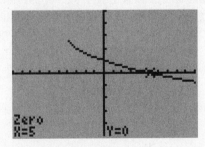

Correct answer: B

12. Find the real zeros of the function $g(x) = 4 - x^2$.

    A. 4
    B. 4 and –4
    C. 2
    D. 2 and –2

<u>Calculator solution:</u>

A function may have more than one real zero, as this one does. In this case, the symmetry of the graph tells you the two intercepts are opposites, but if that's not the case, just repeat the steps for each intercept.

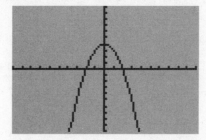

Correct answer: D

TIP: It's also possible for a function to have no real zeros, in which case you wouldn't find any x-intercepts. Before you draw that conclusion, check that you're looking at the graph in an appropriate window. If your window isn't set correctly, you might not see the x-intercept(s) because they're outside the viewing window.

E. Solve an Equation or Inequality Using Intersecting Graphs

Another method of solving an equation is to graph $y =$ the left side and $y =$ the right side, and find the point(s) where their graphs cross. The x-coordinate of the point at which the two graphs intersect is the value that makes the left side equal to the right side, the value that solves the equation, and the y-coordinate is what each side equals.

13. Find the value of x for which the square root of x is four less than half of x.

    A.   4
    B.   9
    C.   16
    D.   25

<u>Calculator solution:</u>

This question requires solving $\sqrt{x} = \dfrac{x}{2} - 4$. If you don't want to square both sides, try this calculator method instead: Graph the left side of the equation as Y1 and the right side as Y2.

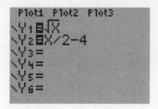

Use the answer choices to help you set a window, in this case, positive numbers up to 25 on the *x*-axis. Experience with the square root function suggests positive *y*-values up to 5.

You may be able to eyeball the point of intersection, but to verify it, take the following steps:

Press $\boxed{\text{2nd}}$, then $\boxed{\text{TRACE}}$, and choose 5: INTERSECT. The cursor appears on one graph. Press $\boxed{\text{ENTER}}$. The cursor jumps to the other graph. Press $\boxed{\text{ENTER}}$. When asked for a guess, move your cursor closer to the point and press $\boxed{\text{ENTER}}$. The coordinates appear at the bottom of the screen.

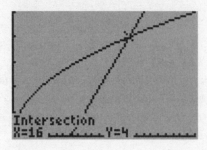

Correct answer: C

14. A certain type of bacteria grows in such a way that the population of the colony doubles every 3 hours. If you begin a culture with four bacteria, after how many hours will the population be 128?

    A. 5
    B. 10
    C. 15
    D. 20

<u>Calculator solution:</u>

The equation $P = 4\left(2^{\frac{x}{3}}\right)$ models the population *P* of the colony of bacteria after *x* hours. Solving $128 = 4\left(2^{\frac{x}{3}}\right)$ algebraically may not be your favorite method, but any of these calculator methods will work. Just set your window carefully.

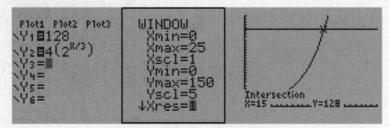

Correct answer: C

You can use a graph to solve an inequality as well as an equation, if you make small adjustments.

15. For which of the following is $|x - 3| \leq 4$?

   A. $x \geq 7$
   B. $x \leq -1$
   C. $-1 \leq x \leq 7$
   D. $x \leq -1$ or $x \geq 7$

Calculator solution:

The absolute value symbol doesn't appear on the keyboard. Press $\boxed{\text{Math}}$, cursor to NUMBER, and the first function, abs(, is the absolute value function. Graph each side of the inequality, and look not just for the point(s) of intersection, where the two sides are equal, but also for where $|x - 3|$ is less than 4.

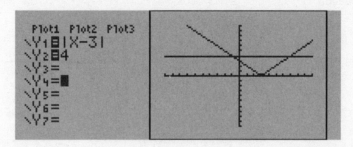

You can use the intersect feature, once for the intersection on the left of the y-axis and again for the one on the right, and you'll find they are $x = -1$ and $x = 7$. The graph of $|x - 3|$ is below the line $y = 4$ when x is between -1 and 7.

Correct answer: C

F. Solve a System of Equations Using Intersecting Graphs

You can use the intersecting graphs to solve a system of equations if you graph each equation in the system.

16. The sum of two numbers is 12.7 and their difference is 3.5. Find the numbers.

   A. -1.1 and 4.6
   B. 8.1 and 4.6
   C. -8.1 and 11.6
   D. -8.1 and 4.6

Calculator solution:
This question asks you to solve the following system:

$$x + y = 12.7$$
$$x - y = 3.5$$

Rearrange each equation to isolate y. Enter one of the equations as Y1 and one as Y2, and find a comfortable window.

Press $\boxed{\text{2nd}}$, then $\boxed{\text{TRACE}}$, and choose 5: INTERSECT. The cursor appears on one graph. Press $\boxed{\text{ENTER}}$. The cursor jumps to the other graph. Press $\boxed{\text{ENTER}}$. Guess, then press $\boxed{\text{ENTER}}$. The coordinates appear at the bottom of the screen.

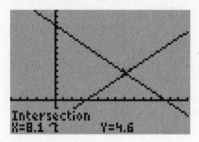

Correct answer: B

17. Find the solution of the following system:

$$3x - 7y = -13$$
$$2x + 5y = 1$$

    A. $x = -2, y = 1$
    B. $x = 2, y = -1$
    C. $x = -1, y = 2$
    D. $x = 1, y = -2$

Calculator solution:
The calculator doesn't care if your equation is tidy or not, so when you solve for y, simplify if you can conveniently do so, but don't spend a lot of time on that. You probably chose to use the calculator to save time; don't spend time on things you don't need to do. $3x - 7y = -13$ becomes $y = \dfrac{-13 - 3x}{-7}$ and $2x + 5y = 1$ becomes $y = \dfrac{1 - 2x}{5}$. Enter one equation as Y1 and the other as Y2.

Press $\boxed{\text{2nd}}$, then $\boxed{\text{TRACE}}$, and choose 5: INTERSECT. The cursor appears on one graph. Press $\boxed{\text{ENTER}}$. The cursor jumps to the other graph. Press $\boxed{\text{ENTER}}$. Guess, then press $\boxed{\text{ENTER}}$. The coordinates appear at the bottom of the screen.

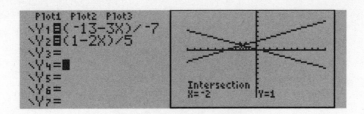

Correct answer: A

G. Find Statistical Measures of Center

The graphing calculator gives you the ability to do many statistical calculations, and for many of them, it provides more than one way to get that information. The quickest, simplest method produces many different statistics at once.

18. For the data set shown below, find the difference of the median and the mean.

$$12, 15, 17, 18, 18$$

- **A.** 1
- **B.** 2
- **C.** 3
- **D.** 4

Calculator solution:

To begin, you need to enter your data into a list. Press 2nd + to get to the Memory menu, and choose 4: ClrAllLists. Press ENTER until you see the word DONE on the screen.

Press STAT, choose 1: EDIT, press ENTER, and move your cursor to the first empty slot under L1.

Type the numbers in the data set, one on each line, under L1. Press ENTER to move to the next line. When you are done, press 2nd, then MODE to return to the main screen.

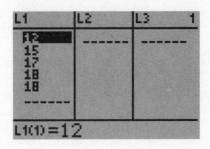

Press $\boxed{\text{STAT}}$, move the cursor to CALC, and choose 1: 1-VAR STATS.

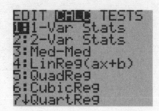

Press $\boxed{\text{ENTER}}$ until a list of statistics appears.

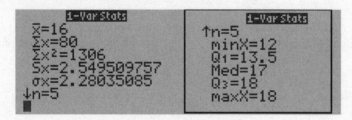

The arrow at the beginning of the line ↓ $n = 5$ means that you can move the cursor down to see more. When you do, you'll see the screen on the right above. Notice that the arrow changes to an up arrow.

That's a long list, and you don't need all of those statistics. Here are the values you might want: $\bar{x}$, the mean; minX, the smallest data value; Q1, the first quartile; Med, the median; Q3, the third quartile; and maxX, the largest data value.

For this data set, the median is 17 and the mean is 16, so the difference is 1.

Correct answer: A

TIP: If you just hit $\boxed{\text{ENTER}}$ immediately after 1-Var Stats, the calculator will assume your data is in L1. If you put your data in a different list, like L2, type $\boxed{\text{2nd}}\boxed{2}$ (or whatever number), then press $\boxed{\text{ENTER}}$.

H. Create a Plot of Data Points and Find an Equation to Fit Them

If you put data points into a list, the graphing calculator can create a scatterplot and find the line of best fit for you.

19. Each time Karen goes for a run, she records the distance she ran (in miles), her time for the run (in minutes), and her heart rate (in beats per minute) at the end of the run. Her record for five recent runs is shown in the table below. Which equation best describes the relationship between her times and her heart rate?

Distance (miles)	1	1.5	2	2	1.5
Time (minutes)	9	13	17	16.5	12.5
Heart Rate (beats/minute)	97	109	121	120	108

A.   heart rate = 24(minutes) + 73

B.   heart rate = $\dfrac{1}{3}$(minutes) − 23

C.   heart rate = 3(minutes) + 70

D.   heart rate = 0.13(minutes) − 0.14

Calculator solution:

Read the question carefully to see which variables your equation should include. In this case, you want to relate heart rate to the time spent running.

Press 2nd + to get to the Memory menu and choose 4: ClrAllLists. Press ENTER until you see the word DONE on the screen.

Press STAT, choose 1: EDIT, press ENTER, and move your cursor to the first empty slot under L1.

Type the times, one on each line, under L1. Press ENTER to move to the next line. When you are done, move the cursor to the first empty line under L2. Enter the heart rates under L2, one on each line. Make sure that the entries in L1 and those in L2 are in the same order, so that they form matched pairs. When you are finished, press 2nd, MODE to return to the main screen.

Press 2nd Y= to get to the Plot menu. Choose a plot and press ENTER to begin editing it.

With your cursor on the word ON, press ENTER, then move the cursor down to the next line. For TYPE, choose the first image and press ENTER. Move the cursor to Xlist and if L1 does not already appear, type 2nd 1 ENTER. Move the cursor to Ylist and type 2nd 2 ENTER. Choose whichever mark you like

323

and press ENTER. Press ZOOM and choose 9: ZoomStat, which will set a reasonable window. The scatterplot will display.

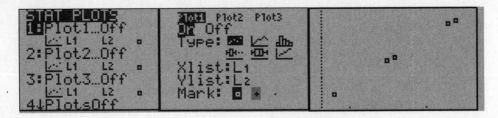

To find the linear equation that best fits this data, press STAT, move the cursor to CALC, and choose 4: LinReg(ax+b).

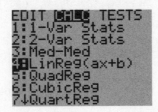

Press 2nd 1 to enter L1 as your Xlist and press 2nd 2 to enter L2 as your Ylist. Skip over FreqList and for StoreRegEq, press VARS, move the cursor to Y-VARS, and choose 1: Function. Press ENTER. Choose 1: Y1. Press ENTER. Move the cursor to CALCULATE and press ENTER.

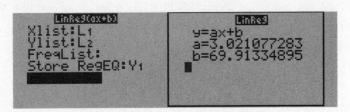

The values of a, the slope, and b, the y-intercept, are displayed and the equation is entered into Y1. Press GRAPH to see the line. If you round to the nearest whole number, the equation of the line is approximately $y = 3x + 70$.

Correct answer: C